*The*
*Garland*
*Library*
*of*
*the*
*History*
*of*
*Western*
*Music*

*One hundred*
*eighty-five*
*articles in*
*fourteen volumes*

*General Editor*
*Ellen Rosand*
*Rutgers University*

*Contents*
*of*
*the*
*Set*

*Volume Ten*

*Twentieth-Century*
*Music*

*Garland Publishing, Inc.*
*New York & London*
*1985*

*Library of Congress Cataloging-in-Publication Data*
Main entry under title:
Twentieth–century music.

   (The Garland library of the history of western music ; v. 10)
   Reprint of articles and essays originally published 1949–1981.
   1. Music—20th century—Addresses, essays, lectures.
I. Title: 20th-century music.   II. Title.
ML97.T95   1985    780'.904    85-16145
ISBN 0-8240-7459-9

The volumes in this series have been printed on acid-free,
250-year-life paper.

Printed in the United States of America

# Contents

# Acknowledgments

Babbitt, Milton. "Some Aspects of Twelve-Tone Composition," *The Score and I.M.A. Magazine*, No. 12 (June 1955), 53–61. Copyright © 1955 by *The Score*, reprinted by permission of Kraus-Thomson Ltd.

Berg, Alban. "Why Is Schönberg's Music So Hard to Understand?," trans. Anton Swarowsky and Joseph H. Lederer, *The Music Review*, XIII (1952), 187–96. Copyright © 1952 by *The Music Review*, reprinted by permission

Berger, Arthur. "Problems of Pitch Organization in Stravinsky," *Perspectives of New Music*, II/1 (Fall–Winter 1963), 11–42. Copyright © 1963 by *Perspectives of New Music*, reprinted by permission

Boulez, Pierre. "Schönberg Est Mort," in *Relevés d'apprenti*, ed. Paule Thévenin (Paris: Éditions du Seuil, 1966), pp. 265–72. Copyright © 1966 by Editions du Seuil, reprinted by permission

Boulez, Pierre. "Stravinsky Demeure," in *Relevés d'apprenti*, ed. Paule Thévenin (Paris: Éditions du Seuil, 1966), pp. 75–145. Copyright © 1966 by Editions du Seuil, reprinted by permission

Cage, John. "Forerunners of Modern Music," *The Tiger's Eye*, I/7 (March 1949), 52–56. Repr. in Cage, *Silence* (Middletown, Conn.: Wesleyan University Press, 1961; repr. 1967), pp. 62–66. Copyright © 1949 by John Cage, reprinted from *Silence* by permission of Wesleyan University Press

Cone, Edward T. "Sound and Syntax: An Introduction to Schoenberg's Harmony," *Perspectives of New Music*, XIII/1 (Fall–Winter 1974), 21–40. Copyright © 1974 by *Perspectives of New Music*, reprinted by permission

Cone, Edward T. "Stravinsky: The Progress of a Method," *Perspectives of New Music*, I/1 (Fall 1962), 18–26. Copyright © 1962 by *Perspectives of New Music*, reprinted by permission

Craft, Robert, and William Harkins. "Stravinsky's Svadebka (Les Noces)," *New York Review of Books*, XIX/10 (14 December 1972),

# *Preface*

*The Garland Library of the History of Western Music*, in fourteen volumes, is a collection of outstanding articles in musicology that have been reprinted from a variety of sources: periodicals, *Festschriften*, and other collections of essays. The articles were selected from a list provided by a panel of eminent musicologists, named below, who represent the full range of the discipline.

Originally conceived in general terms as a collection of outstanding articles whose reprinting would serve the needs of students of musicology at the graduate and advanced undergraduate level, the series took clearer shape during the process of selecting articles for inclusion. While volumes covering the conventional chronological divisions of music history had been projected from the very beginning, several other kinds of volumes cutting across those traditional divisions and representing the interests of large numbers of scholars eventually suggested themselves: the volumes on opera, source studies, criticism, and analysis.

Indeed, although the general objective of excellence remained standard for the entire series, the specific criteria for selection varied somewhat according to the focus of the individual volumes. In the two on opera, for example, chronological coverage of the history of the genre was of primary importance; in those on source studies, criticism, and analysis the chief aim was the representation of different points of view; and in the volumes devoted to chronological periods selection was guided by an effort to cover the various geographical centers, genres, and individual composers essential to the understanding of a historical era.

The articles themselves were written over a period spanning more than a half century of modern musicological scholarship. Some are "classic" statements by scholars of the past or early formulations by scholars still active today, in which musicological method, intellectual vision, or significance for their time rather than any specific factual information is most worthy of appreciation. Others represent the most recent research, by younger scholars as well as more established ones. No general attempt has been made to bring the articles up to date, although some authors have included addenda and misprints have been corrected where possible.

Since no single reader could be fully satisfied by the selection of articles in his own field, the aims of this collection, by necessity, have had to be considerably broader: to provide not only a wide range of articles on a large number of topics by a variety of authors but to offer the student some sense of the history and development of individual fields of study as well as of the discipline as a whole. The value of these volumes derives from the material they contain as well as from the overview they provide of the field of musicology; but the series will fulfill its function only if it leads the student back into the library, to immerse himself in all the materials necessary to a fuller understanding of any single topic.

Ellen Rosand

# Panel of Advisors

Richard J. Agee, The Colorado College

James R. Anthony, University of Arizona

William W. Austin, Cornell University

Lawrence F. Bernstein, University of Pennsylvania

Bathia Churgin, Bar-Ilan University

Edward T. Cone, Princeton University

John Deathridge, King's College, Cambridge

Walter Frisch, Columbia University

Sarah Ann Fuller, SUNY at Stony Brook

James Haar, University of North Carolina at Chapel Hill

Ellen Harris, University of Chicago

D. Kern Holoman, University of California at Davis

Robert Holzer, University of Pennsylvania

Philip Gossett, University of Chicago

Douglas Johnson, Rutgers University

Jeffrey Kallberg, University of Pennsylvania

Janet Levy, New York, New York

Kenneth Levy, Princeton University

Lowell Lindgren, Massachusetts Institute of Technology

Robert Marshall, Brandeis University

Leonard B. Meyer, University of Pennsylvania

Robert P. Morgan, University of Chicago

John Nádas, University of North Carolina at Chapel Hill

Jessie Ann Owens, Brandeis University

Roger Parker, Cornell University

Martin Picker, Rutgers University

Alejandro Planchart, University of California at Santa Barbara

Harold Powers, Princeton University

Joshua Rifkin, Cambridge, Massachusetts

John Roberts, University of Pennsylvania

Stanley Sadie, Editor, *The New Grove Dictionary of Music and Musicians*

Norman E. Smith, University of Pennsylvania

Howard E. Smither, University of North Carolina at Chapel Hill

Ruth Solie, Smith College

Maynard Solomon, New York, New York

Ruth Steiner, The Catholic University of America

Gary Tomlinson, University of Pennsylvania

Leo Treitler, SUNY at Stony Brook

James Webster, Cornell University

Piero Weiss, Peabody Conservatory

Eugene K. Wolf, University of Pennsylvania

# Some Aspects of Twelve-Tone Composition

## MILTON BABBITT

To disdain an alliance with those journalist critics, official composers, and custodians of musical patronage who regard the mere presence of "twelve tones" as sufficient evidence of a fall from musical grace, or, on the other hand, with that smaller group—created, perhaps, by understandable reaction—which regards the same phenomenon as a necessary and sufficient condition for the presence of profound musical virtues, is to deny oneself the possibility of making any convenient summary of American twelve-tone music. For American twelve-tone composers, in word and musical deed, display a diversity of "idioms," "styles," compositional attitudes and accomplishments that almost seems calculated to resist that segregation by identification which many of their enemies, and some of their friends, would impose upon them. If this extreme diversity is, to some degree, a reflection of that multiformity which characterizes all aspects of American cultural life, it is also symptomatic of the relative isolation in which each composer pursues his own work and determines his own direction. The interaction of ideas and influences that probably would be produced by a wide knowledge and intimate understanding of each other's work can scarcely exist when this body of music goes largely unpublished, unrecorded, and unperformed by the larger orchestras or by the widely known and travelled chamber music groups. In this respect, it must be added, twelve-tone music suffers only slightly more than other "difficult," "advanced" music—to the extent that the label itself supplies a basis for automatic rejection; for the American "music lover's" conservatism, a conservatism of ignorance rather than of considered choice, is nurtured and fostered by performers, concert managers, and Boards of Directors, for their own comfort, convenience, and profit.

Finding oneself a member of a minority within a minority may pro-

FROM *The Score*, no. 12 (June, 1955), 53–61. Reprinted by permission of the American Society of Music Arrangers.

vide solace for but few composers; observing "unintelligible" music from abroad being treated with respect and awe while comparable American music produces only anger and resentment may result in nothing more substantial than righteous indignation, while the realization that, if one's own music is performed infrequently if at all, the last three works of Webern are yet to be heard in New York, provides chilly comfort. Nevertheless, the number of twelve-tone composers here, as elsewhere, continues to increase.

The strategic date in the pre-war development of twelve-tone composition in the United States was that on which Schoenberg arrived here in 1933. Prior to that time, only the compositions of Adolph Weiss—Schoenberg's first official American student in Germany—and the *Dichotomy* of Wallingford Riegger had directed any attention to the American manifestations of twelve-tone composition, and Weiss soon became less associated with composition and more with performance, while *Dichotomy* remained a relatively singular work in Riegger's output until about 1943, when he became more closely identified with twelve-tone music.

Schoenberg's residence in the United States affected the musical climate not only because of his mere physical presence, or his activity as a teacher, but also, and primarily, because of the increased interest in, and performance of his music that resulted. The arrival of Ernst Krenek, five years later, added another figure who, through his writing and teaching as well as his music, directed attention to twelve-tone composition. Before the outbreak of the war, a number of young American composers—including George Perle, Ben Weber, and the present writer—were identified with the "twelve-tone school."

Since the war, the music of such composers as Erich Itor Kahn, Kurt List, Jacques Monod, Julius Schloss, and Edward Steuermann—whose careers had begun in Europe—have been relatively widely heard, while among the "natives," Robert Erickson, Richard Maxfield, Dika Newlin, George Rochberg, and Keith Robinson are but a few of those whose music is evidence of the creative interest in twelve-tone composition among the younger composers.

In addition, there are those composers—including the most widely known—who have indicated their awareness of and interest in twelve-tone composition, either in an isolated work, or by frequently employing certain techniques that are associated generally with twelve-tone music.

The above list of composers is neither complete nor presumed to be representative or selective. As has been indicated, no one can be in a position to possess adequate enough and accurate enough information to compile a comprehensive list. Very likely there are composers often performed and exerting real musical influence whose music is unknown beyond a specific locality.

For this, and other obvious reasons, the present article, rather than

360

including the customary descriptive catalogue—consisting of the names of composers whose music is of necessity scarcely known to the readers of the article, attached to adjectival paragraphs and four-bar musical quotations that possess meaning only to the extent that they are misleading—will concern itself with a brief presentation of the sources and nature of one significant phase of twelve-tone activity in the United States that should be of particular interest to non-American readers for its obvious relation—in intent, if not in inception and method—to a widespread and more highly publicized development on the Continent.

The first explicit steps in the direction of a "totally organized" twelve-tone music were taken here some fifteen years ago, motivated positively by the desire for a completely autonomous conception of the twelve-tone system, and for works in which all components, in all dimensions, would be determined by the relations and operations of the system. Negatively, there was the motivation by reaction against the transference to twelve-tone composition of criteria belonging to triadic music.[1] The specific bases, discussed below, for achieving a total twelve-tone work, were arrived at by the end of the war, and when, a short time later, there were reports of a group of young French, Italian and German composers who apparently shared like aims, their work was eagerly awaited. However, their music and technical writings eventually revealed so very different an attitude toward the means, and even so very different means, that the apparent agreement with regard to ends lost its entire significance. The most striking points of divergence can be summarized in terms of the following apparent attributes of the music and the theory associated with it. Mathematics—or, more correctly, arithmetic—is used, not as a means of characterizing or discovering general systematic, pre-compositional relationships [see addendum 1, page 369], but as a compositional device, resulting in the most liberal sort of "programme music," whose course is determined by a numerical, rather than by a narrative or descriptive, "programme." The alleged "total organization" is achieved by applying dissimilar, essentially unrelated criteria of organization to each of the components, criteria often derived from outside the system, so that—for example—the rhythm is independent

[1] e.g., that of consonance and dissonance, carried over from a domain where the structure of the triad is the criterion of intervallic stability to a domain where the triad has no such prior function, and where—thus—criteria of consonance and dissonance, if the terms have any meaning whatsoever, must be determined by principles relevant to twelve-tone phenomena. The same applies to the transference of the external "forms" of triadic music to twelve-tone contexts, resulting in a divorce of these "forms" from their essential tonal motivations; this, at best, leads to a merely thematic formalism, and if one is seeking mere formalisms, there are certainly more ingenious ones than "sonata-form," "rondo-form," etc., for all that they might not possess this purely verbal identification with the hallowed past.

of and thus separable from the pitch structure; this is described and justified as a "polyphony" of components, though polyphony is customarily understood to involve, among many other things, a principle of organized simultaneity, while here the mere fact of simultaneity is termed "polyphony." The most crucial problems of twelve-tone music are resolved by being defined out of existence; harmonic structure in all dimensions is proclaimed to be irrelevant, unnecessary, and perhaps, undesirable in any event; so, a principle, or non-principle, of harmony by fortuity reigns. Finally, the music of the past—and virtually all of that of the present, as well—is repudiated for what it is not, rather than examined—if not celebrated—for what it is; admittedly, this is a convenient method for evading confrontation by a multitude of challenging possibles, including—perhaps—even a few necessaries. This latter represents a particularly significant point of divergence from the development to be considered here, which has its specific origins in the investigation of the implications of techniques of the "classics" of twelve-tone music. Indeed, it is a principle that underlies the bulk of Schoenberg's work (namely, combinatoriality),[2] and another, superficially unrelated, principle occupying a similar position in the music of Webern (derivation), that have each been generalized and extended far beyond their immediate functions, finally to the point where, in their most generalized form, they are found to be profoundly interrelated, and in these interrelationships new properties and potentialities of the individual principles are revealed.[3]

Quite naturally, it was the "early American" works of Schoenberg that were the most influential. As an example of a typically suggestive, but by no means unusual, passage, consider the opening measures of the third movement of the *Fourth Quartet*. Even a cursory examination reveals a number of significant techniques of local continuity and association: the exploitation of ordered adjacencies (the repeated adjacencies C-B of bar 619 and G♭-F of bar 617 cross-associate with the opening two notes of the movement and the G♭-F of the first violin in bar 621 to effect the closure of a structural unit [see addendum 2, page 369]: the three-note adjacency C-B-G of 619 also registrationally duplicates the first three notes of the movement), delinearization (the dyads of the first violin line of 620–1 are distributed among the three instruments that immediately follow [see addendum 3, page 369]), intervallic preparation and association (the simultaneously stated fourths of 619, 620 and 621 prepare the predefined fourth of the cello and viola in 623; the repeated C-B states with regard to the G in 619 the intervallic succession continued by the relation of the D♯-E to the B in the same measure), mo-

---

[2]See footnote 6.

[3]Much of the remainder of this article is a highly condensed version of certain sections from the author's *The Function of Set Structure in the Twelve-Tone System* (1946).

tivic progression (the joining of forms of the set in 618 gives rise to the motive stated in the prime set itself by the last three notes, and the third, fourth, and fifth notes; the distribution of the elements of the inverted set between second violin and viola in 623 results in a three-note motive in the second violin which is the retrograde inversion of notes five, six, and seven of the simultaneously stated prime, at precisely the same total pitch level, and at the same time, the resultant viola line reveals two 16th-note groups of four notes each which symmetrically permute the minor second and major third), functional "orchestration" (the six-note unit of the first violin in 620-1 combines with the six-note unit of 622-3 to form a set), etc. But of far greater systematic significance, and far more susceptible to extension, is the familiar Schoenbergian principle of constructing a set in which linear continuity can be effected between sets related by the operation of retrograde inversion, by equating the total, unordered[4] content of corresponding hexachords [see addendum 4, page 369] at a specific transpositional level [see addendum 5, pages 369-370]. Such a set created by this ordering of hexachords supplies the basis of progressions in bars 616 to 619, and, in general, such "secondary set" construction supplies a basis of progression beyond mere set succession [see addendum 6, page 370]. A necessary corollary of this structural characteristic is that corresponding hexachords of inversionally related forms of the set, at the specific transpositional interval, possess no notes in common, and therefore span the total chromatic, thus creating an "aggregate."[5] In bar 623, successive aggregates are formed by the simultaneous statements of the prime form in the cello and the inverted form in the viola and second violin.

In almost all of his twelve-tone works (indeed, in all of his twelve-tone works of this period) Schoenberg employed a "semi-combinatorial set"[6] of the type just described; in his later works, his increased pre-

___

[4]i.e., the total pitch content, without considering the order.

[5]"Secondary set" and "aggregate" are necessary terms to define elements that arise compositionally, but are not pre-defined systematically. A secondary set (for example, that defined by the second hexachord of the prime set and the first hexachord of the inversion at the required transposition) is, indeed, in the strictest sense, a set, since it states a total ordering of the twelve tones (see addendum 7, page 370); however, it is not necessarily equivalent to a derived set (see addendum 8, page 370), nor is it ever one of the fundamental forms of the set. Of course, it can be thought of as a linear juxtaposition of parts of primary forms of the set (see addendum 9, page 370). An aggregate can be thought of as a simultaneous statement of such parts (see addendum 10, page 370), but in essence it is very different, since it is not a set, inasmuch as it is not totally ordered, because only the elements within the component parts are ordered, but not the relationship between or among the parts themselves (see addendum 11, page 370).

[6]"Semi-combinatoriality" indicates the property of creating such secondary sets, or aggregates, between a specific pair of forms (in the case of hexachordal semi-combinatoriality); "all-combinatoriality" denotes the possibility of constructing such secon-

occupation with the hexachord as an independent unit led to his using it often without regard to fixed ordering, but merely with regard to total content. Strangely, he never used the other two types of semi-combinatorial sets: that which gives rise to secondary set relationships between inversionally related forms of the set [see addendum 13, page 370], and thus, aggregates between retrograde inversionally related forms, or that which gives rise to secondary set relationships between retrograde related forms, and thus aggregates between prime related forms. (Obviously, any set creates aggregates between retrograde related forms, and secondary sets between prime related forms.)

The structural significance of such sets suggests a generalization to the construction of sets in which secondary set and, thus, aggregate structures obtain between any two forms of the set. There are six such "all-combinatorial" source sets, here indicated arbitrarily as beginning on the note C, for purposes of easy comparison:

(1)  C-C♯-D-D♯-E-F / F♯-G-G♯-A-A♯-B
(2)  C-D-D♯-E-F-G / F♯-G♯-A-A♯-B-C♯
(3)  C-D-E-F-G-A / F♯-G♯-A♯-B-C♯-D♯
(4)  C-C♯-D-F♯-G-G♯ / D♯-E-F-A-A♯-B
(5)  C-C♯-E-F-G♯-A / D-D♯-F♯-G-A♯-B
(6)  C-D-E-F♯-G♯-A♯ / C♯-D♯-F-G-A-B

It must be emphasized that these are "source sets,"[7] and that any ordering, to effect a specific compositional set, may be imposed on either hexachord without affecting the combinatorial properties. Among these six source sets, beyond many other secondary bases of similarity and dissimilarity, the first three sets possess the common property of creating combinatorial relationships at one and only one transpositional interval; they are thus termed "first order" sets [see addendum 14, page 370]. Set (4) possesses two such interval levels, and is termed "second order"; set (5), of "third order," possesses three such levels; set (6), of "fourth order," possesses six such levels. There is an inverse relationship between the multiplicity of these functional transpositions and the intervallic content within the hexachord. Thus, first order sets exclude one interval, second order sets exclude two, third order sets exclude three, and fourth order sets exclude six [see addendum 15, page 371]. As a re-

---

dary sets or aggregates among any pairs of forms of the sets, at one or more transpositional levels. "Combinatoriality" is the generic term including both the others (see addendum 12, page 370).

[7]"Source set" denotes a set considered only in terms of the content of its hexachords, and whose combinatorial characteristics are independent of the ordering imposed on this content.

sult, all-interval sets, for example, can be constructed only from first order sets; even so, there is basically only one independent all-interval set that can be constructed from each first order source set. (This excludes such sets as that of the first movement of Berg's *Lyric Suite*, which uses the elements of set (3), though not combinatorially. This set is a derived set, as defined below, since the two hexachords are related by retrogression.)

It is of interest to note that Schoenberg employed set (5) in his *Suite*, op. 29, but only as if it were merely semi-combinatorial; however, in his last, unfinished work, *The First Psalm*, he used the same source set, but the "set table" indicates his awareness of the total combinatorial resources of the set.

In addition to the value of such sets in effecting an interrelation of the "vertical" and "horizontal" far beyond mere identity, in generating fixed units of harmonic progression within which the components can in turn generate associative and variable relationships, and in determining transpositional levels, there is a far more fundamental aspect, in that a hierarchy of relationships exists among these sets as determinants of regions, an hierarchical domain closely analogous to the "circle of fifths," and defined similarly by considering the minimum number and the nature of the pitch alterations necessary to reproduce source sets at various transpositional levels. For example, in set (1), the transposition of note C by a tritone—the excluded interval—or the similar transposition of the symmetrically related note F, reproduces the set structure a half step lower in the latter case, or a half step higher in the former case, with maximum association of content to the original set. Thus, any degree of motion away from the pitch norm is measurable. Also, the motion from the region whose structure is defined by one such source set to that defined by another source set is achieved and measured in precisely the same manner. For example, the transposition of the note C♯ in set (1) by a tritone results in set (2); likewise, the symmetrically related E, when so transposed, results in set (2). These properties suggest that whether the source sets are used as specific compositional sets or not, they possess properties of so general a nature as to warrant their presence as implicit structural entities.

An investigation of the six all-combinatorial source tetrachords reveals a hierarchical universe analogous to that of the hexachord. There are four such tetrachords of first order, one of second, and one of third order [see addendum 16, page 371]. An understanding of their implications, and of those of the analogous trichordal units, together with the interrelationships among all types of combinatoriality, though fruitful enough in itself, leads one inevitably to a consideration of the technique of derivation.

Although this technique has often been used independently, it is

7

only when considered in relation to combinatoriality that its extraordinary properties are fully revealed. Consider the set, so characteristic of Webern, that is used in his *Concerto for Nine Instruments*. It is presented in four three-note units: B-Bb-D, Eb-G-F♯, G♯-E-F, C-C♯-A; the first "prime" three-note unit is followed by its retrograde inversion, its retrograde, and its inversion. Though Webern uses this set as his total set, it is obviously possible to apply this technique to a three-note unit of any set, and thus—by the operations applied to the total set—generate a derived set.[8] Any three-note unit—with the exception of the "diminished triad"—can generate such a set,[9] and, in terms of the total content of hexachords, three independent sets can be generated. Of these, at least one is all-combinatorial. Of the twelve permutationally independent three-note units that exist, two generate one all-combinatorial set each, seven generate two, and two generate three (indeed, one of these latter two can generate four, though obviously not within the trichordal permutation of a single derived set). For example, the set of the Webern Concerto, though not so utilized,[10] is a representation of source set (5); by interchanging the second and fourth units, we have a representation of source set (1). The eleven three-note units are individually unique with regard to the combinatoriality of the source sets represented by their derived sets, so that a given three-note unit of a set is a unique means of effecting change of both functional and structural areas. Consider a set constructed from source set (1), with the following initial hexachord: C-Eb-D-E-C♯-F. The first three notes can generate derived sets of combinatoriality defined by source sets (1) and (2). Considering the first possibility, if we choose as the transpositional level for the three-note unit that defined by its pitch level in the original set, we derive the following initial hexachord: C-Eb-D-Db-Bb-B, which is a transposition of the original combinatorial structure; on the other hand, the original three-note unit, if transposed to D-F-E, could have generated a hexachord at the same pitch level as that of the original set; this, in turn, establishes a new transpositional level for the original hexachord, beginning on D. The original three-note unit also can generate the hexachord: C-Eb-D-G-E-F, and thereby establish the combinatorial region defined by source set (2).

In this manner, the functional and structural implications of a compositional set can be determined by the derivational interrelationships

8

---

[8] A derived set is *not* a new set in the composition. It can be thought of, also, as resulting from the juxtaposition of segments from the fundamental forms.

[9] For example, the triad C E G, A F D, C♯ A♯ F♯, G♯ B D♯. (Observe that this is also an all-combinatorial set.)

[10] Webern does not exploit the combinatorial properties of this set; he does not create progression through secondary sets or aggregates, nor does he determine his transpositions in terms of such properties.

of such units, in relation to the original set, and to each other, as defined hierarchically by the total domain of source sets.

As there are combinatorial trichords, tetrachords, and hexachords, so are there three-note generators, four-note generators, and six-note generators;[11] the extraordinary interrelationships that exist within and among the domains so defined emphasize the essential significance of the inherent structure of the set, and the unique compositional stage represented by the fact of the set, as the element with regard to which the generalized operations of the system achieve meaning, and from which the progressive levels of the composition, from detail to totality, can derive.

The twelve-tone structuralization of non-pitch components can be understood only in terms of a rigorously correct definition of the nature of the operations associated with the system. In characterizing the prime set, it is necessary to associate with each note the ordered number couple—order number, pitch number, measured from the first note as origin—required to define it completely with regard to the set [see addendum 17, page 371]. Then, as transposition is revealed to be mere addition of a constant to the pitch number, inversion—in the twelve-tone sense—is revealed to be complementation mod. 12 of the pitch number. (In other words, pitch number 4 becomes pitch number 8, etc.; naturally, interval numbers are also complemented.) Likewise, retrogression is complementation of the order number, and retrograde inversion is complementation of both order and pitch numbers. Any set of durations—whether the durations be defined in terms of attack, pitch, timbre, dynamics, or register—can be, like the pitch set, uniquely permuted by the operations of addition and complementation, with the modulus most logically determined by a factor or a multiple of the metric unit.[12] Thus, the rhythmic component, for example, can be structured in precisely the same way, by the identical operations, as the pitch component; rhythmic inversion, retrogression, and retrograde inversion are uniquely defined, and combinatoriality, derivation, and related properties are analogously applicable to the durational set. The result can be a structuring of all the durational and other non-pitch components,[13] determined by the opera-

[11]i.e., 3, 4 or 6-note units which serve to generate derived sets.

[12]"Set of durations" means specifically a "set" in the sense of twelve-tone set. By durations defined in terms of attack, is meant the time that elapses between actual attacks, measured in terms of a fixed unit of durational reference. Likewise, timbral duration is defined by the duration of a certain timbre or, conceivably, of related timbres. The same with registrational durations.

[13]The question of structuralizing non-pitch elements is certainly a very complicated one. If, for example, a rhythmic set is constructed with combinatorial characteristics, then secondary set structure, aggregate structure, derived set structure can all be arrived at in precisely the same manner as with pitches. The specific use of these means would depend upon the pitch structure of the composition.

The "form" would arise out of the specific implications of the set itself, in terms

tions of the system and uniquely analogous to the specific structuring of the pitch components of the individual work, and thus, utterly non-separable.

Even this extremely incomplete presentation should indicate the possibility of twelve-tone music, organized linearly, harmonically in the small and in the large, rhythmically—indeed, in all dimensions—in terms of the essential assumptions of the system.

Certainly, the resources indicated here do not constitute a guarantee of musical coherence, but they should guarantee the possibility of coherence. Above all, it is hoped that they serve to give at least some indication of the extraordinary breadth and depth of the twelve-tone system.

---

of its total content, the content of the derived sets which its generators give rise to, the transpositional levels to which the derived sets lead, etc.

Naturally, this does not mean to say that a given set uniquely implies a given composition, but rather that a given set defines, in these terms, certain general possibilities which are uniquely associated with this set.

10

1. "Pre-compositional relationships" are not relationships calculated by the composer before beginning to compose but are instead relationships resulting from operations within whatever musical system is being employed. For example, in twelve-tone music there will be for each set (twelve-tone row) a specific transpositional level of its inversion which exchanges the order position of any two pitch classes of the prime form of any set. (E.g., if the prime form began C,D,A, the inversion on D would maintain the first two pitch classes as adjacencies but reverse their order positions, D,C,F.) Precompositional relationships exist within the twelve-tone system (and in any musical system) whether a composer elects to display them consciously or not.

2. In the prime form of the set (see addendum 18 for terminology) that Schoenberg used for the *Fourth Quartet* (C,B,G,A♭,E♭,D♭,D,B♭,G♭, F,E,A), C and B (and later in the set also G♭ and F) appear as adjacencies. In RI$_8$ (A♭,D♭,*C,B,*G,D♯,*E,D,A,B♭,G♭,F)* those same dyads again appear as adjacencies, although in different order positions. This precompositional relationship is prominently displayed in the first eight measures of the piece.

3. In measure 620 and 621 the first violin presents the last six notes of RI$_8$ (E,D,A,B♭,G♭,F). A transposition of the retrograde (R$_9$) immediately follows, the first hexachord of which contains those *same* notes, this time broken up into dyads and presented simultaneously (viola, E,D; 2nd violin, A,B♭; 'cello, F,G♭). For further discussion of the *Fourth Quartet* see Babbitt's "Set Structure as a Compositional Determinant" in the *Journal of Music Theory*, 5, no. 2 (April, 1961) 72-94.

4. A hexachord is a collection of six notes or pitch classes. The term is usually used in reference to the first or last six pitch classes in a set (i.e., the first hexachord and the second hexachord).

5. By "linear continuity" is meant the formation of secondary sets. In the *Fourth Quartet,* when P$_0$ is followed by RI$_8$ (the pitches are given in Addendum 2) the second hexachord of P$_0$ and the first hexachord of RI$_8$ (in measures 616 to 619), having no pitch classes in common, thus together form a complete twelve-tone set. This set is not, however, the basic set of the piece on which operations (e.g., R,I, RI) are effected, hence the term "secondary" set. It follows, of course, that the first hexa-

chords of both these forms ($P_0$ and $RI_8$ ) have exactly the same pitch content irrespective of ordering, as do also the second hexachords.

6. For example, relationships of the type displayed in Addenda 2 and 3 or larger-scale relationships such as those between nonadjacent notes.

7. This is easiest to see if one thinks of the sets stated linearly, first the prime form and then the inversion. The secondary set is therefore a result of the juncture of those two sets.

8. See footnote 8 on page 366.

9. If $P_0$ is followed immediately by another $P_0$ then the last hexachord of the first set and the first hexachord of the second set form a secondary set. This is, of course, a trivial example of secondary set formation.

10. If, as in Addendum 7, the prime and the inversion are capable of forming secondary set structures, then their simultaneous statements would result in corresponding hexachords having the same pitch class content (irrespective of the ordering within each of these hexachords). However, if the *retrograde* inversion were used in place of the inversion, the corresponding hexachords would display all twelve pitch classes. These are aggregates: vertical-type constructions, whereas secondary sets are of a linear type.

11. For instance, the intervals created *between* the notes in the corresponding order positions of the two sets.

12. It is perhaps helpful to consider the general shape of the hexachords when trying to get a mental picture of the properties of combinatoriality. A hexachord containing the notes C-C♯-D-D♯-E-F♯ is a solid chromatic cluster broken only by the whole-step interval between E and F♯ (F is missing between E and F♯). Obviously, the shape of a hexachord utilizing the remainder of the chromatic pitches would be exactly the same as the first hexachord except upside-down (the half-step vacancy appearing at the other end). A set made up of two hexachords of the types just mentioned is semi-combinatorial and displays RI combinatoriality in the formation of aggregates. In addition, a hexachord whose pattern is symmetrical within itself, such as C-D-D♯-E-F-G, is obviously more flexible in that it can display a combinatorial relationship with more forms of the set. An all-combinatorial set must display this intervalic symmetry. Note the shapes of the six all-combinatorial source hexachords given in the following paragraph of the text.

13. That is, between the *prime* and one or more inversional form of the set.

14. For example, if source set #1 were ordered D♯-C-E-F-D-C♯/B-A-F♯-A♯-G♯-G, then a secondary set could be formed with the retro-

grade inversion *only* at RI₁, and, correspondingly, the inversional level for aggregates could only be I₅. A secondary set with the inversion could *only* be at I₁₁, and thus the retrograde inversion aggregate level could *only* be RI₇.

15. This is taking into consideration every interval between every note within the hexachord.

16. First order (1) C-C♯-D-D♯, (2) C-D-D♯-F, (3) C-D-F-G, (4) C-C♯-D-F♯; second order (5) C-C♯-F♯-G; third order (6) C-C♯-F♯-A.

17. The Schoenberg set given in Addendum 2 would be represented 0,0; 1,11;2,7;3,8;4,3; etc.

18. Additional Terminology.

A *pitch class* is a collection of pitches in which the fundamental frequency of each pitch is a whole number multiple of every other pitch within the class. In other words, the pitch class C would be made up of all C's. This is a useful concept generally, and, indeed, a necessary one in twelve-tone music in that the notes of the basic set and its transformations do not designate the register in which the notes are to appear. The ordering of the twelve pitch classes most basic to a piece of twelve-tone music is known as the *prime* form of the *set* (twelve-tone row) abbreviated P. The standard transformations are inversion (I), retrograde (R), and retrograde inversion (RI). A numerical subscript indicates the beginning note. The first note of the prime is always zero no matter what pitch class it is. Zero is used instead of 1 for the sake of the correspondence between the order number and the pitch number in the representation of the set (and its transformations) as a series of ordered number pairs. (See Addendum 17 and the corresponding section of the text.) P₁₁ means the prime form of the set eleven half steps above whatever zero represents. Note that R₀ means the retrograde beginning on whatever note P₀ begins on; it is not just P₀ backwards. For a more exhaustive treatment of this aspect of twelve-tone music see Babbitt's "Twelve-Tone Invariants as Compositional Determinants" in *The Musical Quarterly*, 46, no. 2 (April, 1960), 246–259.

# Bibliography

Some of the bibliography relating to twelve-tone music has already been mentioned in the bibliography following "Post-Romanticism: Impressionism and Expressionism" (see page 341). A bibliography of twelve-tone music has been prepared by Ann Phillips Basart, *Serial Music: A Classified Bibliography of Writings on Twelve-tone and Electronic Music*

(Berkeley, Calif., University of California Press, 1961). This lists every major article and book on the subject written prior to 1960 but is of course now considerably out of date. It can be updated by a study of the articles and reviews printed in issues of *Perspectives of New Music, Journal of Music Theory,* and *The Score* that have appeared since then. The issues of *Perspectives* are especially valuable. George Perle's *Serial Composition and Atonality* (Berkeley, Calif., University of California Press, 1962) remains one of the most lucid introductions to twelve-tone music and treats the subject from Schönberg to Babbitt.

A listing of even the major composers using serial techniques is impossible here. Some are mentioned in the above selection; other names are given in the entry on "Serial Music" in the *Harvard Dictionary of Music,* 2d ed. (1969). Many of the works of Schönberg, Berg, and Webern are published in Vienna by Universal Edition. Publishers vary for other composers.

14

# Why is Schönberg's music so hard to understand?

BY

ALBAN BERG

TRANSLATED BY ANTON SWAROWSKY AND JOSEPH H. LEDERER

IN answering this question one might be inclined to ferret out the ideas
behind Schönberg's music, to examine the music in terms of intellectual
content: to do, in other words, what is done so frequently: approach music
with philosophic, literary, and other considerations.   This is not my intention!
I am concerned only with what takes place musically in Schönberg's work,
with the compositional means of expression.   This, like the specific language
of any work of art (one presupposes its acceptance as such) is the only meaningful one.   Generally speaking, to understand this language in its entirety and
details means recognizing the entrance, duration, and end of all melodies,
hearing the simultaneous sounding (*Zusammenklang*) of the voices not as

random occurrences, but as harmonies, and experiencing the small and large concatenations and contrasts as such. It means following a piece of music as a person with full command of the language follows the wording of a piece of poetry. For one who is able to think musically, this is equivalent to understanding the work itself. Therefore, the question at the head of our investigation seems already answered if we can only succeed in examining Schönberg's musical ways of expression for their intelligibility, and in determining the extent of their lucidity.

Knowing how much can be accomplished through detailed examination, I want to do this on the basis of a single example chosen at random, there being few passages in Schönberg's music which would not serve equally well.

It may be that today, ten years after their composition, the ten measures of Ex. 1 (the first of the D minor Quartet) are not considered unintelligible or even difficult. Still, one who wishes to recognize only the main voice and follow it, on first hearing, to the end of these ten measures will encounter difficulties as early as the third bar, especially if he would like to experience the main voice as a single melody, which, since it is precisely that, should be as singable as the beginning of one of Beethoven's quartets. Accustomed to a melodic structure the main feature of which is the symmetry of its periods, and a thematic structure limited to even numbered measure groups (rules governing all music of the last 150 years with few exceptions), an ear so restrictively pre-conditioned begins to doubt the correctness of the first bars of the melody, which, contrary to expectations, consists of two and a half bar phrases.

Avoidance of thematic structure built on two or four measures is, after all, nothing new. On the contrary, Bussler[1] says quite correctly that "the greatest masters of form (he means Mozart and Beethoven) cherish free and bold constructions and rebel against being squeezed into the confines of even numbered measure groups". But how seldom does one find such a thing in the classics or among classical composers (with the possible exception of Schubert). And how is it that this faculty, so natural to the eighteenth century and before, got lost in the period of romantic music (Brahms' folk melodies excepted), the music of Wagner, and the whole New German school that ensued! Even the theme of Strauss' *Heldenleben*, which once seemed so audacious, is conspicuous for being built entirely on two to four bar phrases leading to a repetition of the first after the usual sixteen measures. In the music of Mahler and—to mention a master of a completely different style—Debussy, we find melodic structures with even numbers of bars almost exclusively. And when Reger (the only post-romantic exception besides Schönberg) prefers rather free constructions, reminiscent of prose, as he

[1] Ludwig Bussler, 1839-1900, German writer and theoretician.

himself says,[2] then this is the reason for the relative formidability of his music. I would go so far as to say the only reason—since none of its other qualities: the motivic development of the multi-toned phrases, the harmonic structure, certainly not the contrapuntal mode of writing, would render his musical language incomprehensible.

Understandably, when free and asymmetrical construction of themes is considered to be just as natural as the two, four, and eight bar kind—and that is perhaps the most important element in Schönberg's way of writing—such music is likely to be followed with difficulty or, as in his later works, not at all.

During its rapid growth and surging restlessness, the theme, in our example, utilizes the right of variation in the second repetition of this rhythmically almost incomprehensible phrase. If, then, such a theme should receive the following shortened form

the listener loses the thread before the first melodic climax is reached two measures later:

the sixteenth note motive of this climax may strike the listener as having dropped out of thin air, though, again, it is only the natural continuation of the principal theme secured also through variation. Indeed, just this succession of chromatic jumps of a seventh, as may be observed even today at performances of the Quartet, presents an insuperable obstacle for one who is used to a gradual unfolding of the theme, or possibly only one development, through sequences and unvaried repetitions. Moreover, the listener is generally unable to fit the motive of the sixteenth note figures into a harmonic scheme. It is present, of course; but the notes speed by too quickly. Thus he loses the last means of orientation to appreciate this portion for its cadential value, let alone experience it as a *caesura* or climax. He hears it rather as an arbitrary grouping of "cacophonies" produced by the zigzag of the first violin part, which seems senseless to him. Of course he loses the continuity and with it, the new, though connected theme constructions which contain the richest motivic detail, and lead, nineteen measures later, to a repetition of the principal theme in E flat.

How much easier for the listener if the beginning of the Quartet—forgive my irreverence—were to take the following form, deliberately avoiding the rich rhythmic construction, motivic variation, and thematic detail, and retaining only the number of measures and the organic melodic invention.

---

[2] An expression used by Schönberg, independently of Reger, to refer to the language of his own music.

Ex.5

Here the asymmetry of the original is actually made to disappear, being replaced by a two bar construction capable of pleasing even the most obdurate listener. The motivic and rhythmic growth unfolds slowly, eschewing every possibility of variation; an *alla breve* of sixteenth notes, over which a listener might stumble, is completely avoided, and with it, the final obstacle: the difficulty of hearing as melody these chromatic jumps of a seventh, accomplished by continuing harmonization on the half bar and by not speeding up beyond the value of an eighth note. Should a theme, so mutilated, still stand in danger of not being understood, then an exact repetition in the principal key entering immediately after the first statement is finished will guarantee a general understandability, verging on popularity.

How different with Schönberg! "To penetrate into the psychology of his creative process, the sketchbooks, used exclusively in the epoch of this Quartet, are of supreme importance. No one who has skimmed through them could brand his music as contrived, cerebral, or any of the other catchwords used by those who want to protect themselves from Schönberg's over-rich imagination". Also, "each thematic idea is invented along with its countersubject".[3]

And all this needs to be heard! One might receive a general impression of the beginning of the Quartet, and still miss the persuasive melody of the middle voice. This voice, an exception, is built on one or two bar phrases, set contrapuntally against the first five measure groups of the violin theme.

Ex.6   *mp*

If the listener misses the expressive singing of the bass part, likely because of its dissolution into two—now three bar phrases, then he cannot grasp correctly even the principal theme.

Ex.7

[3] *Arnold Schönberg* by Egon Wellesz.

One who does not react spontaneously to the beauty of such themes (and this type of music in general) requires at least the ability to keep separate such characteristically distinct voices. He must also be able to recognize melodic segments of varied lengths, continually beginning and ending anew at different points in these first six bars. This means following their various paths, in addition to coming sympathetically to rest when they sound simultaneously, as well as coping with Schönberg's infinitely varied and differentiated rhythms—all of which constitutes a formidable task.

In the face of the aforementioned, consider the above quoted cello part in which a hopping, syncopated eighth note scale develops out of the long drawn *legato* phrases[4] as early as in the seventh measure. Two bars later a seven-tone theme of weighty quarter notes, rushing upward, alternately in fourths and thirds (E flat, A flat, C, F) is added in contrast, thus revealing two integral motivic parts of the Quartet. Observe how these rhythmic figures are made to relate contrapuntally to the other parts, whose note value-relations develop along entirely different lines.

When music contains rhythms in such abundance and in so concentrated a form, vertically as well as horizontally, one really has to be completely deaf or malicious to call it "arhythmical"! Of course if this word is made to mean all note and metric combinations not directly derivable from mechanical movement (*e.g.* millwheel and railway) or body movement (march, dance, *etc.*) I cannot object to its application to Schönberg's music. But then I must insist on the same treatment for the music of Mozart and the other classical masters, where they have not sought to produce regular, and hence easily understandable rhythms (as in scherzo and rondo movements, or others borrowed from the old dance forms).

Or is it possible that this word "arhythmical" is not really a musical term at all, but—like "ethos", "cosmos", "dynamics", "mentality" and other catchwords of our time—a word which applies where there is any motion at all, whether it be in art or sport, philosophy or industry, world history or finance! Such a term, stemming as it does from other than the motion of music, is not exclusively definable in the context of music. Rather, it is vague, permitting one to talk of the rhythm of music in the same tone of voice one might use to mention a drop in the stock market. Such looseness of nomenclature is out of the question for anyone who can discern the rhythmic occurrences in a piece of music, where they originate from musical detail and expand over the whole work. Unfortunately, the blame for this adulteration of terms lies where, for professional reasons, we might least expect it: that is, with a good many composers themselves. This only proves how hard it is to understand a music which demands critical judgment in terms of its own art—not some extraneous "point of view".

Thus we return to the domain of our investigation: why it is so hard to understand Schönberg's music. As we have seen, its riches—the thematic,

---

[4] If the sixth measure is recognized as a variation of the third, and the seventh as nothing else but a variation of the preceding one, then the feeling of musical coherence (without which music would be meaningless) is immediately achieved.

contrapuntal, and rhythmic beauties—have created these very difficulties. There remains only to discuss the harmonic richness, the unending supply of chords and chord combinations, which, after all, are nothing but the result of a polyphony quite unique in contemporary music: a juxtaposition of voices, the melodic lines of which possess a flexibility heretofore unknown. Their superabundance of harmony was, therefore, just as misunderstood as everything else, and with as little justification.

This strict chorale-like four part writing is by no means the nucleus of an *adagio*, extending in a wide sweep, as one might easily imagine. It is the harmonic skeleton of the beginning of this much discussed Quartet.

Incredible that anything so simple could ever have missed being understood, that, moreover, audiences, in search of sensation, regarded it as an orgy of dissonances. With striking logic, various and sundry chords are here assembled in the confines of ten rapidly moving *alla breve* bars. This alone can explain why a listener accustomed to the poverty of harmonic degrees in other contemporary composers, is not equal to the task of comprehending fifty or more chords in a few seconds. He therefore charges "decadence" (another deadly *cliché*) where only wealth and abundance reign. The structure of the chords and their different combinations cannot be the reason why this music is so hard to understand. The last example was meant to demonstrate this. Not even in the least accented sixteenth note of these ten measures can one find a harmonic sound that might give pause to an ear conditioned by the harmonic conventions of the last century. Nor will the two whole tone chords at *, with their harmonic preparation and resolution, be the cause of moral indignation in anyone who prefers not to appear ridiculous in the eyes of the whole musical world.

One can see from this how inappropriate it is, and always was, to say that "modern" voice leading lacked consideration for the resulting vertical sounds, since everything I have shown in these ten bars could be proven for any part of this work. Even the boldest harmonic developments are far from a confluence of accidental sounds. Neither here nor anywhere else does anything happen by accident. Anyone who, in spite of all this, cannot follow the music should consider it his own fault and, without embarrassment, trust the ear of a master who conceives all these seemingly difficult matters as easily as he dashes off the most complicated counterpoint exercises for his students, and who, when asked if a particularly difficult passage of his had ever been realized, replied jocularly and profoundly, "Yes, when I composed it".

A mode of composing that results from such unerring musicianship embraces all compositional possibilities and is, therefore, never totally comprehensible. This analysis, complete though I have tried to make it, has by no means exhausted the possibilities of these few measures. One could say, for instance, that the voices, initially invented in double counterpoint—thus polyphonic in this respect also—permit a many-sidedness, which, of course, appears in the various recapitulations of the principal theme. Even in this early work of Schönberg he lets the violin and cello change places, avoiding all mechanical repetitions. Illustrating it graphically, what stands (in the first measures of the Quartet) in vertical order

| | | |
|---|---|---|
| 1 | | 3 (in octaves) |
| 2 | is now brought into the sequence of | 2 |
| 3 | | 1 |

At the third appearance (p. 8) the secondary voices, while retaining the same melodic tones, are radically varied. The sequence is then

2 (variant in sixteenths)
1 (in octaves)
3 (embellished by eighth note triplets)

Finally, the principal and secondary parts—not to mention their combinations with other themes—appear in the last exposition of the last principal section (p. 53) in the sequence of

3 (variant in eighth note triplets, but different from the preceding one)
1 (in octaves)
3 (inversion in eighths with diminution).

But these opening ten measures and their varied repetitions constitute a very small fraction of this work which lasts nearly an hour, and can only give an idea of the profusion of polyphonic and harmonic detail released in thousands of measures and unknown since Bach. It may be said without exaggeration that the minutest part—each accompanying figure—is important for the development and changing rhythm of these four voices, that it is, in other words, thematic. And all this in one big symphonic movement, the colossal architecture of which we cannot even begin to discuss in the framework of this article. It is hardly surprising that with such things going on, an ear accustomed to the music of the last century cannot take it all in. The music of that period is homophonic almost throughout: the themes are built on two or four measure phrases, the growth and development of which would be unthinkable without sequences, copious repetitions—mostly of the mechanical type—and the relative simplicity of harmonic and rhythmic events thereby conditioned. Imbued with such things for decades, the listener of today is incapable of understanding music of a different kind. Deviation from even one of these familiar musical features—though the rules may well permit it—is irritating to him. How much more so when, as in Schönberg's music, there exists a simultaneous combination of all these qualities, usually regarded as attributes of good music, but generally found isolated and diffused throughout various epochs.

Think of the polyphony of Bach, of the theme structure of the classics and their antecedents, often quite free in rhythm and construction, exhibiting a mastery of the variation form; of the Romantics with their juxtaposition of keys, only distantly related, bold, even today; of Wagner's new chord structures, achieved through chromatic alteration and enharmonic change, and his effortless way of incorporating them into the tonality; finally of Brahms' thematic and motivic work, often encompassing the finest detail of art. Obviously, music that combines all the possibilities handed down to it by the classics must differ from a contemporary music, which—as I will show—is not a synthesis of this kind. It is in spite of these qualities, recognizable as attributes of every good music, and in spite of the richness with which they are employed in all musical fields—or actually because of them— that Schönberg's music seems as recondite as it does.

I shall be reproached for having proved something that did not need proving: the difficulty of the D minor Quartet, a tonal piece which long ago ceased to be a problem and has even been generally accepted and understood! This may be somewhat exaggerated, and I admit that the question at the head of this article would appear answered only if everything here, based on a few measures in the minor mode, had been shown on the basis of at least one example of the so-called "atonal" music. But, after all, this article does not deal exclusively with the question of difficulty, but also with the proof that every event in this music is completely above-board and fashioned only along the lines of highest art. Of course this was easier to show using an example still based on major and minor tonality. But it is nonetheless appropriate for our study, since in earlier times it prompted as much agitation as his "atonal" music today. Now, however, when I view them both as accomplished facts—which they surely are—I need only apply everything I have said about these ten measures to any passage of his later or very latest works. This is possible not only because of the creativeness of Schönberg, the "father of atonal thought", as he is generally called, but also because of the music's acceptance by a large part of the musical world. This would appear to have solved the riddle of our title and established that both kinds of music encompass the same high standards of art—and therefore employ legitimate means of expression. Thus it will be clear that the music's abstruseness lies not so much in its so-called "atonality", which by now is the means of expression for so many contemporaries, but in that structure of

Schönberg's earlier music, the inexhaustible artistic techniques—applied also in this later harmonic style—the use of all compositional possibilities of the music of centuries: in short, its boundless opulence. Here we find the same variety of harmonic treatment, with various degrees of cadence; also melodies suitable to such harmonic treatment, making boldest use of the possibilities of the twelve tones; the unsymmetrical, free thematic construction of themes, with its motivic work never ebbing; the art of variation, projecting itself thematically as well as in the harmonization, contrapuntally as well as in the rhythm; also the polyphony that expands over the whole work and the unequalled technique of contrapuntal part-writing; and finally the variety of rhythms, subject both to their own laws and those of variation, so that in this respect also, Schönberg aims at an art of construction entirely remote from the "dissolved rhythm" so foolishly attributed to him.

Viewed from such a universal standpoint, how different in every respect is the position of other contemporary composers, even if in their harmonic language they have broken with the predominance of the triad. In their music, too, we can find the artistic techniques just enumerated, but never—as with Schönberg—combined in the work of a single personality. Rather, they are always distributed among various groups, schools, years, nations and their respective representatives. One type likes the polyphonic way of writing which reduces thematic development and the art of variation to a bare minimum. The other prefers bold harmonic structure which does not shrink from any chord, though its melodic construction scarcely goes beyond homophony and may even be characterized by the use of only two and four measure phrases. The "atonality" of the one consists in putting wrong basses to primitively harmonized periods; others simultaneously provide two or more (respectively major and minor) keys, whereby the other musical features of each attest to a frightful poverty of invention. A music characterized by frequently changing melody and free thematic constructions suffers from an inertia of harmony, as shown by its dearth of harmonic degrees, sustained chords, endless pedal points and continually recurring chord clusters. I would almost go so far as to assert that a music so constructed cannot exist without mechanical repetitions and the most primitive sequences. This is shown especially in the rhythm, which reaches the very limit of monotony, often only simulating a richness of form, through changing time signatures and rhythmic displacement, where everything else is poverty. More often than one would think, this rhythm—sometimes rigid, sometimes hammering, sometimes dancelike and similarly animated—is the only thing keeping such otherwise unsubstantial music from falling apart. The practitioners of this technique of composition are the ones sure to be called "strong rhythmic talents".

The orientation toward these more or less rigid principles, often degenerating into one-sidedness—this satisfaction with being (as the beautiful saying goes) "modern, but not extreme"—helps such "atonal" or "progressively orientated" music to be understood and moderately liked. After all, it may confront the listener with one or more difficult problems, but in all other respects it does not deviate from the usual, often not even from the deliberately primitive.

23

Thanks to these negative qualities it can also please the ears of the musically less gifted: in other words, it makes "easy listening". Even more so, since composers of such music can conform to style by being aware only of their special brand of modernity, without also accepting responsibility for a combination of all these possibilities. That inescapable necessity of accepting even the most extended consequences of musical universality is found only once: namely in the music of Schönberg. Having said this I believe the last and perhaps strongest reason for its abstruseness has been stated. However, the fact that this noble compulsion is being fulfilled with a sovereignty bestowed, I would say, only upon a genius, allows for the assumption, or, rather, the assertion, that when the "classics of our time" belong to the past, Schönberg will be among the very few remembered as a classic for all time. For not only has he, as Adolf Weissmann so aptly says, "drawn the last bold conclusions from musical culture",[5] but he has also progressed further than those who, lacking definite direction, looked for new paths, and—consciously or unconsciously—negated the art of this musical culture. Thus, without being a prophet one can say even today on Schönberg's fiftieth birthday that the work he has already given the world seems to have secured not only the pre-eminence of his personal art, but, more important, that of German music for the next fifty years.

24

From the special issue of the *Musikblatter des Ambruch* honouring Schönberg on his fiftieth birthday, 13th September, 1924

---

[5] *Music in World Crisis* by Adolf Weissmann.

# PROBLEMS OF PITCH ORGANIZATION
# IN STRAVINSKY

ARTHUR BERGER

ANYONE WHO undertakes an investigation of the essential relationships of tones in the works of Stravinsky may find himself somewhat at a disadvantage as a result of the fact that no significant body of theoretical writing has emerged to deal with the nature of twentieth-century music that is centric (i.e. organized in terms of tone center) but not tonally functional.[1] There are, to be sure, a number of labels in circulation for referring to this music: pantonality, pandiatonicism, antitonality, modality, tonicality—even "atonality" has been stretched to embrace it. But their function is largely identification, and where any one of them presumes to represent a theory, this is more likely to be descriptive of surface detail than in the nature of an interpretation of internal relations or structural significance. Moreover, instead of searching for the differentia of the music they designate by ascertaining, for example, its own unifying principles, the tendency has been to rely rather too heavily on the established rules of formation.

A worthwhile objective is certainly an approach that would no longer use tonality as a crutch, a new branch of theory, as it were, starting from what this music itself is, rather than dwelling upon its deviation from what music was previously. (Granted we might still be ultimately obliged to come to terms with traditional schemata, since it is untenable to claim for the music in question anything like the degree of cleavage with tonality that characterized twelve-tone composition.) But until such a theory is crystallized and implemented with a vocabulary of sufficient currency to make it reliable as a means of communication, we cannot legitimately be expected to more than simply attempt to gravitate in the general

[1]Tonality, according to the restricted sense in which it is construed here, is defined by those functional relations postulated by the structure of the major scale. A consequence of the fulfillment of such functional relations is, directly or indirectly, the assertion of the priority of one pitch class over the others within a given context—it being understood that context may be interpreted either locally or with respect to the totality, so that a hierarchy is thus established, determined in each case by what is taken as the context in terms of which priority is assessed. It is important to bear in mind, however, that there are other means besides functional ones for asserting pitch-class priority; from which it follows that pitch-class priority per se: 1) is not a sufficient condition of that music which is tonal, and 2) is compatible with music that is not tonally functional.

· 11 ·

direction of the self-contained approach the new theory may someday provide. That the attempt might indeed be rewarding was one of my main thoughts as I undertook this discussion of Stravinsky's "pre-twelve-tone" works, prompted by a desire to assemble some observations that seemed to me interesting enough to share. In organizing the observations I found it convenient to group them into four sections: I) diatonic writing in which "tone center" is not functional "tonic";[2] II) a symmetrical scale used in such a way as to emphasize tritone relation; III) the same scale with minor-third emphasis; IV) interaction between diatonic elements of I and the symmetrical scale of II and III. The prognosis for self-contained treatment seemed encouraging to me in the ground covered in I and II, but III is a turning point—a concern with the traditional minor third itself, perhaps, being symptomatic. In IV the synthesis produces a curious alchemy that brings tonal functionality in its wake. Yet this conclusion does not, I trust, invalidate the initial intention; since it is better for tonal functionality to insinuate itself gradually, than for it to confine all discussion at the outset to the level of established theory.[3]

# I

A suitable point of departure from which to approach one of the main problems of concern to us is the familiar *Danse Russe* (in the 1911 version),[4] where the "white notes"—which I take to conveniently represent the total content of any of the so-called "diatonic" scales—may be said to comprise the referential collection of pitch classes inferable from the main theme of the rondo and/or the codetta at No. 44. The referential order of intervals, on the other hand, varying independently of the referential collec-

[2] For purposes of non-tonal centric music it might be a good idea to have the term "tone center" refer to the more general class of which "tonics" (or tone centers in tonal contexts) could be regarded as a sub-class (see note 1).

[3] Any attempt at a statement of what I assume tonal functionality to be would, I fear, result in a disquisition—consigning the Stravinsky discussion to a postscript. This article could not have been written without the author's relying on the reader to supply the precariously evasive first principles and to take it on faith that thought has been given to the much needed revaluation of tonality that is now taking place. Indeed, as a gesture to this revaluation I have taken what may, perhaps, be the needless precaution of borrowing the latest terms (e.g. "simultaneity" where "chord" might have been perfectly adequate); but having done so, I feel I should say a few words, however informal, regarding them. In the first place, those who are in close touch with the rethinking responsible for the new nomenclature and who tend to forget its limited currency, are the ones whose obligation it is to define and justify it, which thus is not my intention here. To avoid the linguistic battle over what constitutes a "chord," I shall simply add to what I have already remarked about "simultaneity" that its attraction for me has something to do with its being a fair substitute for the German *Zusammenklang*. "Pitch class" (or "p.c.," in the folksy abbreviation used by a young contributor elsewhere in this issue) is useful to distinguish an observation about a pitch, say C, that may occur in any octave from an observation about a given C (such as middle C). Finally, notwithstanding the suggestion in note 2 regarding "tone center" vis-à-vis "tonic," for that future time when a new theory is evolved, I feel uneasy about present usage which equates them: hence the precautionary "priority," a more noncommittal term than "tone center." By virtue of its freedom from conventional

tion, is defined by the pitch class to which priority is assigned, and this, in turn, is decided on the basis of contextual evidence. In Ex. 1, G priority is indicated by the simultaneities in the strings on the first beats of the odd-numbered measures (where G is emphasized by doubling and its "low" registral position); and at its first return (No. 38) it is confirmed by a G tremolo. (The melodic line itself gives inadequate information for this priority.)[5] The referential ordering of intervals that may be inferred from G as 0 yields the following scale (in semitonal measurement): 0, 2, 4, 5, 7, 9, 10.

Ex. 1

---

associations it even lends itself to being applied below to a tone that is hierarchically at the head of a three-tone group in the "*Petrouchka* chord" without necessarily being a tone center as it is here understood. But normally "C priority" will mean "C is the tone center." It may be idle to add that the borrowing of these terms (as also the semitonal numbering, 0–11) is no more to be taken as evidence that the writer shares the total philosophy that gave rise to them than the use of the terminology of logic by some of my most esteemed colleagues is to be taken as a proof of the logical consistency of their arguments.

[4] Use of this version (except in one instance where the new orchestration is more practical for quotation) should avoid the objection that what are cited below as similarities between Stravinsky's early and recent practices are not altogether reliable simply because the new version of *Petrouchka* may embody some of his recent attitudes.

[5] The argument for G priority is supported by Stravinsky's own interpretation of this passage in the 1947 revision. Thus, among other things, the G is further emphasized by virtue of the fact that it is doubled by the basses not only, as in the old version, in its first appearance but in each subsequent appearance as well. Considerable "interference" qualifies G: e.g. an A pedal point (potentialized in the A priority of the subsidiary themes at Nos. 34 and 41) and a doubling of the tritone, to both of which I shall return later (see p. 22 below). In Exx. 1 and 2, the alternation of the triads B-D-F and C-E-G produces the whole step of the opening tremolo of the work (D-E or A-G)—a relationship that is made explicit when the opening section returns in its D-major metamorphosis at the beginning of the fourth tableau. Such are some of the large structural issues that are, of course, also relevant in different ways to other musical examples given here, insofar as complete data in terms of the totality of relations is to be sought. But especially since music is heard in time, local events may also, I believe, be considered as having independent validity, since they are more than a *tabula rasa* to be inscribed by total structure.

The codetta affirms the familiar referential ordering of the C major scale, for which the main evidence is the cadence, and especially the final simultaneity (Ex. 2b), which gradually materializes over a G pedal after No. 44 (*x* in Ex. 2a) and then persists to the end.

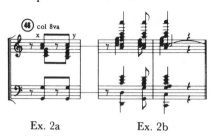

Ex. 2a          Ex. 2b

It may be wondered why we should be burdened with two referential categories: the collection and the ordering of intervals, since theme and codetta could both be referred to the C major scale, in terms of which the G-emphasis could be regarded simply as a prolonged functional "dominant seventh"; or the theme could be referred to one interval-ordered pitch-class collection, and the codetta to another. Now, the first alternative leads to the proverbial historical search for correspondences which we should like to avoid if possible; while the second alternative, although it allows the independence of a G priority among white notes—and is to this extent preferable—ignores common pitch-class content. To retain both categories, therefore, seems desirable.

Since the major scale and tonality are strongly inter-identified, however, it may be insisted that the functioning of the referential collection tonally when the referential ordering is that of the major scale, but not tonally when the same referential collection has the referential ordering of the other available white-note scales, engenders an interaction between tonal and non-tonal procedures—such interaction being implicit in the very existence of common pitch-class content. It would therefore seem to follow from this that what to some may appear to be unjustifiable tonal bias is not only legitimate but necessary for dealing rationally with this music. A self-contained theory, in order to refute this argument, would ultimately have to demonstrate that, though elements of the major scale provide the conditions for tonal functionality, Stravinsky does not significantly realize these conditions.

This is something I am not prepared to demonstrate now. However, it is not insignificant in the present regard that in *Agon* (a transitional work between the "neoclassic" and the "twelve-tone" periods), relations similar to those in *Petrouchka* appear four decades later, with C priority (i.e. as distinguished from a tonal functional "C major") still treated as just one referential ordering among all the others obtainable within the white-note collection. The *Pas-de-Quatre* from *Agon* and the *Danse Russe* differ mark-edly from one another on every conceivable level, so that apprehension of any similarity requires a high degree of abstraction. For example, the pitch class C is prominent from the outset of the former, while in the latter it is not. But if we discount the support this C gets in *Agon* from repetition and instrumentation, the B-C in the first simultaneity (Ex. 3a) may be said to have its counterpart in *Danse Russe* (*y* in Ex. 2a), though its appearance in the *Petrouchka* movement is, of course, delayed until almost the end. Furthermore, the measures with the triplet figure (Ex. 3b) carry in dis-tilled form the G implications of the *Danse Russe* theme, return in like rondo fashion (MM. 21 and 36, though the last time with a problematic B♭), and stand in analogous relation to the C-dominated simultaneity at the movement's end (Ex. 3c).

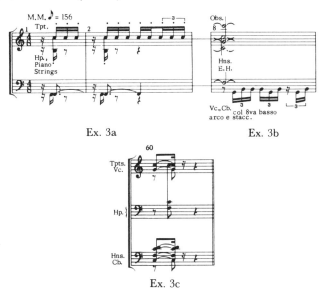

Ex. 3a          Ex. 3b

Ex. 3c

Having taken due cognizance of the parallelism, however, let us pause over this last simultaneity.

G gives C the acoustical support of the fifth—the assumption of the possibility of such acoustical support being indispensable to this entire discussion. At the same time, G's association with D, and even, to a certain extent, with F, forms a sub-complex of the simultaneity relating directly to the referential order that governed the measures with triplet figure. There are other ramifications, since F serves a double purpose, being also associated timbrally (in the harp) with C, in such a way as to allude to F's role on a secondary level of importance—as lowest tone both in the open-ing simultaneity and in the one in winds in Ex. 3b. As such, the F may be compared to the A in the final simultaneity of *Danse Russe,* except that this A is not only an allusion to earlier events in the movement, but also a simple continuation of an insistent element of the immediately preceding measures. The main point, however, is that the G supporting C in the final simultaneity of *Danse Russe* does not, unlike the G at the end of *Pas-de-Quatre,* directly relate back—by virtue of special contextual associations—to the G priority that accounts for so large a part of the *Petrouchka* movement as to make the absence of such a relationship quite perceptible.[6]

Another example of what I have in mind—less complex than the one from *Agon* because the movement has less complex relationships—is provided by *Dumbarton Oaks* Concerto, where the referential white-note collection is that of "E♭ major." Extra doubling and the neighbor-note motion around G at the opening of the finale substantiate the triad G-B♭-D (Ex. 4a), defining a referential ordering of the scale: 0, 1, 3, 5, 7, 8, 10, whose normal abstract representation (always reading upwards), incidentally, indicates an ordering of intervals retrograde-inversionally related to the ordering of the major scale, similarly represented. The last eleven measures of the movement do not deviate from the pitch content of E♭ major, but E♭ priority has only begun to gradually infiltrate the original G priority since about No. 74, and even now, in the final simultaneities, retains from the G priority a G (as lowest voice), and a D (Ex. 4b).

Ex. 4a

Ex. 4b

[6] The abruptness of the ending may well be a theatrical allusion to the character of a peasant dance. Thus, something of the same nature occurs on another dimension when the long continued motion ceases at this same cadence without warning.

Despite its triadic elements, the ending, like that of *Pas-de-Quatre,* is far from a "resolution" in the harmony-book fashion, yet in an empirical sense, the basic structural issues are all resolved.

It may have occurred to some readers that this discussion could benefit from the paraphernalia of "modality," which would seem so very appropriate for the identification of the different interval-orderings within the white-note collection. But quite apart from the multifarious confusions with which this notion is laden, it does not really apply here. To claim that the finale of *Dumbarton Oaks* is "Phrygian" discloses nothing of the peculiar symbiotic relationship between scales with common referential collection but different interval orderings. It is quite frankly only on the most trivial level that "modality" can be helpful, i.e. by freeing us from dependence on the concept of "major" scale for identifying the referential collection. "D-mode," "E-mode," etc. rid modern modal nomenclature of extraneous historical implications; and by simple substitution of "scale" for "mode" (e.g. "D-scale") we, in turn, may derive a nomenclature that analogously circumvents the implications of "modality," both modern and archaic. According to such a convention, each letter-name can define a different ordering of the white-note collection (including C), the same letter-name being retained for transpositions, so that *Dumbarton Oaks* may be said to open in the E-scale on G and to close in the C-scale on E♭. <sup>31</sup>

Before dispensing with "modality," it is tempting to make a special case for the *Hymne* of *Sérénade en la,* which has an opening section in the E-scale on A (with few deviations from the referential collection up to m. 19), closes with a transitory allusion to it (m. 77), and has about a third of the movement (mm. 52-76) dominated, despite "black" patches, by a transposition of the E-scale to the form referable directly (i.e. without transposition) to the white-note collection. The symbiotic relation between referential order and referential collection seems unimportant here, until attention is drawn to the inside pun of the opening measures, at which point the modal interpretation collapses. In these measures, the referential ordering of the C-scale (transposed to F), which played such important a part in *Danse Russe* and *Dumbarton Oaks,* covertly intrudes by way of the elements of the triad F-A-C which, in a narrow grammatical sense, account for most of the simultaneities through the third beat of m. 5. But any realization of their potency for the assertion of F priority is studiously avoided owing to their employment in such a way as to firmly assert A by virtue of various kinds of articulation: repetition, doubling, registration (A in outer voices and the more exposed inner ones), and accentuation (both quantitative and qualitative).

This by now classic example of the extent to which pitch-class priority may be stipulated by compositional procedures, serves as an appropriate transition from contexts referable to the white-note collection to contexts referable to a more complex collection. In the latter, all possible modes of articulation become more necessary than ever for the assertion of pitch-class priority—so much so, in fact, that the absence of such articulation, as it soon will be seen, may place the music in those interstitial realms between the centric and noncentric.

## II

Without criteria for selection of certain pitches over others, the passage from *Les Noces* (Ex. 5) cannot be referred to the white-note collection, though an observer with strong tonal bias might claim that, except for what may be regarded as a "closely related" E, all the tones are accommodated by B♭ "harmonic minor"—and thus (so the argument would go) what results is simply another "diatonic" scale of the white-note class.

Ex. 5

Now I do not wish to tangle here with questions of the "hybrid" minor formations, except to stress that they do not fulfill the conditions of the white-note collection of being capable of having its elements arranged in an uninterrupted series, the first and last tritone-related and the adjacencies separated by the identical interval—the only such possible interval being, within the white-note collection, the fifth. But even if the interpretation of the "hybrid" minor scales was acceptable in its tonal functional sense, it would be hard to prove that the F♯ (G♭) is treated *functionally*, so that if it is to be said that there is any correlation at all with B♭ minor it would seem to be more statistical than anything else.

Should this, too, be considered insufficient grounds for rejecting the "B♭ minor" interpretation, there would still remain the more serious objection that may be levelled against the low hierarchical position assigned in this scheme to the E♭—namely as appoggiatura to D♭. Thus the dyad formed by the linear expression of E♭-D♭ associates with D-C of the preceding section (No. 27ff.), where D may be interpreted as the pitch class of priority, as well as with the E-D at the opening of the work, where the insistence on the soprano's E$_5$ leaves no doubt at all as to the priority of E. The position of E♭ is, then, hierarchically of a higher order than that of appoggiatura to D♭, though there is insufficient evidence to establish its priority as *the* tone center; therefore, when the mezzo-soprano line at No. 35 is heard in transpositions on C (No. 38) and on A (No. 39) these tones by analogy also have a certain potentiality for assertion of priority, each tone in its turn.[7] If an assessment is made of the relative weight of these transpositions, it is observed that A priority receives most substantiation: 1) from the A's on each quarter beat of the pianos' ostinato at Nos. 35-40; 2) from the significant reinforcement just before No. 39 by the octave doubling and by the new $A_4$ on the offbeats; 3) from the bass voice's entrance (6 measures after No. 36 and 3 measures after No. 37) with what starts on A as another transposition, but continues as a variant that will be prominent at No. 40.

These bits of evidence, while not particularly effective in asserting A in this section of *Noces,* are significant in the light of the A priority ultimately realized in the modified return of the material at Nos. 82-87:

Ex. 6

[7] In the two transpositions, the original undergoes the following slight modifications: in both of them, m. 6 is truncated and the (B♭) grace-note omitted; where the transposition on C has the contour A-C-E, identical interval order calls for A-C♯-E, which is restored when this transposition recurs at No. 85.

where the E tremolo acoustically supports A₃ of the pianos, and the A priority operative since No. 78 predisposes the ear toward the continued acceptance of this priority as asserted by the A's of long duration at No. 82.

But the question remains: why, given reasonable evidence to verify it, is A priority still in a certain doubt at Nos. 35-40? A search for the answer may lead one to contemplate the curious consistence that pervades forty-five measures at Nos. 35-40, and the same number of measures (of slightly longer duration because of some 3/4 meter) at Nos. 82-87, as a result of which everything, both linear successions and simultaneities, fits together like well-meshed gears, so that it is not surprising to discover, from a tabulation of the total pitch content, that a single referential collection of eight pitch classes accounts for it all—with a few exceptions so marginal as scarcely to require mention (some dozen tones, mainly ornamental, and most of them at Nos. 35-40). If it is granted that the pitch class A is the most likely element to determine the referential order within the collection, the scale drawn from the collection may be represented as follows:

|  | i | ii | iii | iv | v | vi | vii | viii | (i) |
|---|---|---|---|---|---|---|---|---|---|
|  | a | B♭ | c | D♭ | e♭ | E | f♯ | G | (a) |
| pitch numbers: | 0 | 1 | 3 | 4 | 6 | 7 | 9 | 10 | (1) |
| intervals: |  | 1 | 2 | 1 | 2 | 1 | 2 | 1 | (2) |

A formal approach to this scale (hereafter referred to as "octatonic") would calculate the structure and enumerate the properties at once.[8] Here the approach will be inductive, so that only such properties will be considered as are demonstrated by the musical examples discussed. Thus, the passage from *Noces* makes us aware of the high degree of similitude that the scale generates to the end that it yields identical interval content for the reproduction of the linear configuration at 0, 3, and 6 (hence the lower-case letters in the scale representation above). Substantial preservation of pitch content from one transposition to another is also available. The form on A, for example, requires no pitch classes not present at the original statement on E♭—provided the piano's A is counted. Naturally, what holds true for 0, 3, and 6 will hold true for 9, and indeed a transposition on this element is ultimately suggested between Nos. 83 and 84, where we are again reminded of the common pitch content, since it is

[8] Messiaen classifies this scale among "modes of limited transposition" in *Technique de mon langage musical* (Paris: Leduc, 1944, pp. 52f.). Its limitation to three transpositions becomes evident when the twelve pitch classes are arranged into the three available diminished-seventh chords: combination of any two yields the scale's total pitch content, and only three such combinations are, of course, possible. Also, between any two collections of scale content there will be one of these chords in common. (If the chords are designated X, Y, and Z, they yield XY, YZ, and XZ.) Taking his cue from Messiaen, Roman Vlad draws attention to Stravinsky's use of the scale (*Stravinsky*, London: Oxford University Press, 1960, pp. 7f.), without, however, exploring the special properties that will presently be seen to arise out of the ordering in which there is a semitone between first and second degrees.

34

produced as a result of the transposition at 0 crossing over to the one at 6.

Since each trichordal partition defines the interval order: 1, 2, it is easy to see what accounts for the symmetry. In combination, the four partitions produce a scale of whole and half steps. The fifth scale degree, at the interval of 6 semitones from A, is an axis around which the two halves of the octave are symmetrical; and at the interval of 3 or 9 there is another axis around which two quarters of the octave (halves of the tritone) are analogously symmetrical.

When we had only the simpler relations of the white-note collection to cope with (in Part I), the following condition prevailed: within any given white-note collection, for each pitch class there was only one possible referential interval ordering in which it could have priority. Within any given octatonic collection, by contrast, the first element of any of the partitions of the octave at 0, 3, 6, and 9 has the potentiality of being the pitch class of priority in an identical ordering referable to the same given octatonic collection, and this also holds true, analogously, for 1, 4, 7, and 10, with respect to a different ordering, of which more will be said later. That is to say, not only is each of the partitions a "transposition" of the other, in a sense, but the interval ordering of the total collection defined in relation to the first element of each partition is also identical; hence, each of the four possible orderings is also a different "transposition" of the octatonic scale. (Strictly speaking, this is really "rotation," since the collection has only three transpositions—see footnote 8.) Therefore, in the interval ordering of the scale as represented above, there are, loosely speaking, four potential "tone centers" of equal weight and independence.

In *Noces*, the two-part partition of the octave concerned us more and seemed more prevalent than the four-part partition. If the octave is assumed—as I have already assumed the fifth—then a hierarchy is thus established, contingent on the octave as a fundamental construct within the semitonal system. This attaches special importance to the fact that A-Eb and its complement Eb-A are intervals each adding up to 6 semitones, while A-C, which is 3 semitones, has a complement of 9. For if the octave takes precedence the symmetrical position of 3 within the tritone is of less consequence than the relation of 3 to the octave, thus placing it on a different, or "lesser," hierarchical plane with regard to its potentiality for symmetry than the relation of 6 to the octave, but on a higher plane with regard to its potentiality for differentiation.

The, so to speak, equality (i.e. numerically) between the interval of a tritone and its complement is, if not the final verification, then at least highly symptomatic of the identity relation between these "two" intervals, or between their elements, or, specifically in *Noces*, between A and Eb. In addition, each tritone-related element has the potentiality, within the octatonic scale, to stand in an identical relation to any available interval ordering (this order and relation being parallel rather than symmetrical)

—i.e. to be an element of a transposition with identical interval ordering and/or identical interval content. Therefore, given any two tritone-related pitch classes within the octatonic scale, to establish the priority of one over the other within the scale's limits, this identity between the configurations of which they are respectively the members must be eliminated. One of the ways in which this can be brought about is demonstrated by the section of *Noces* between Nos. 82 and 87, where the high degree of similitude observed earlier at approximately No. 39, between the elements gravitating around A and those gravitating around E♭, is now scarcely present at all, as a result, on the one hand, of the continuing fifth (the E tremolo)—the E♭'s fifth being transitory—and on the other, of the sustained A's, all of which leaves no doubt as to the pitch class of priority, even though the transposition at 6 lingers on after No. 86 in very nearly its original form.

Since each scale degree of the octatonic scale is tritone-related, the noticeable presence of this interval is stipulated for any context referable to the collection of this scale; and any part of *Noces* where it is used will be more or less associated with the basic simultaneity at No. 1, where E is in the voice and B♭ is in the piano. (Thus, the mezzo-soprano's E♭ and the piano's A at No. 35 actually reverse the opening roles of the "black" and "white" notes.) Similarly, in *Petrouchka* it is clearly evident to the ear that the scale emerges directly out of the frequent expression of the tritone as a dyad (usually linear) in the first tableau: B♭-E at Nos. 7, 9, 17, 22; F-B at Nos. 8, 11, 23; both forms alternately between Nos. 24 and 27, and, the form of most immediate concern here, C-F♯ in the interlude between the first and second tableaux. (In the total structure, the limited associations of identical pitch-class content also lend significance to F-B in the main simultaneities of *Danse Russe* (Ex. 1 above) as a verticalization of the linear dyads at Nos. 8, etc. According to this interpretation, G priority is a prolongation of the fourth degree of the basic D-scale of the first tableau, indeed, of the whole work; and the A pedal is an allusion to the supporting fifth of this D priority, an allusion clearly pointed up by the return of the tritonal dyads of No. 8 in the section of *Danse Russe* following No. 42.)[9]

To regard C-F♯ of the interlude as a foreshadowing of the "*Petrouchka* chord" is to admit some evidence for the standard interpretation of this configuration as a confluence of two sub-complexes "based" on these two pitch classes, rather than as a unitary sonic event. So Stravinsky considered it, and, to judge from one of his most recent published remarks, probably still does: "I had conceived of the music in two keys in the second tableau as Petrouchka's insult to the public. . . ."[10] However, since the entire configuration may now be subsumed under a single collection with a single referential order, i.e. the octatonic scale, the dubious concept of

[9] See note 5.    [10] *Expositions and Developments*, New York: Doubleday & Co., 1962, p. 156.

"polytonality" need no longer be invoked; nor does such an interpretation make it impossible to acknowledge a certain compound nature of the configuration, since this can be done entirely within the referential collection of the octatonic scale, by means of the partitions.

To evaluate the pitch-class priority, if any, of the "*Petrouchka* chord," it is well to determine beforehand toward what priority the ear may be disposed at its entrance, especially since the eight measures that precede this entrance deploy the octatonic scale from which the "chord" is drawn. The brief introduction to the second tableau involves, to begin with, the placing in the clearest relief a prolongation of G as the supporting fifth of the C which is carried over from the final simultaneity of the first tableau (Ex. 2b above) by a kind of liaison—the liaison, namely, of the C of the linear tritone in the interlude between tableaux. Example 7 shows how the piano both articulates the C-G and segregates, from the intervening stepwise semitonal activity (mm. 3-6), the following six elements of the octatonic scale: c, D♮, e♭, E, f♯, G. (Since all the essential features are preserved in the more concise 1947 orchestration, this version is quoted here. No. 93 of the new version corresponds to No. 48 of the original.)

Ex. 7

· 23 ·

37

The simultaneity in the woodwinds in the third and fourth measures dissociates itself from the prolonged "neighbor-note" motion of the intervening elements by virtue of its duration, so that its content, all of it referable to the octatonic collection, may be applied to the higher level on which the scale is deployed—especially the A, which is not supplied by the piano. Whether the A♯ at No. 94 is similarly qualified to be applied to that level is very dubious, despite the octave doubling, accent, and exposed position at the beginning of a phrase. The understatement of this A♯ is far more striking—viz. the descent from G of m. 1, in Ex. 7, via flutes and violins, to G of m. 6, which deviates from stepwise semitonal motion only to avoid it, with the result that "in the place" of A♯ there is an extra B.

A♯ is a crucial element in more than one way; kept in reserve, essentially, for the first dyad of the "*Petrouchka* chord" (Ex. 8), it provides special conditions for a relationship which strongly counterpoises the tritone-related triads of the standard interpretation. Thus, if we assume that the horizontalized C triad of the first clarinet preserves the registration of the same pitch classes just as they occurred in the piano left hand at No. 93, the A♯, which can belong to an identically ordered triadic complex in relation to F♯, is precisely the element that avoids the identity by initiating a registral distribution for the F♯ triad (i.e. a first inversion) that is different from the registration of the C triad. Furthermore, the interval of 2 semitones formed by the simultaneity of this A♯ with C becomes a principal defining agency of the total configuration. (Notice how it is stressed by the registral extremities of the contour at *x* in Ex. 8.)[11]

Ex. 8

The other vertical dyads in Ex. 8, if less prominent than that just indicated, should also be weighed against the tritone-related triads, since these dyads, along with the A♯-C, describe the interval content of the conjunct trichordal partitions of the octatonic scale: 2, 3, 1, in that order.

When, however, during the vertical statement at No. 51 (to return to the 1911 version), there is a concurrent linearization from which the F♯ triad is filtered out, isolating the C triad (cornets and trumpets), the interpretation of the chord as two triadic sub-complexes is strengthened, as is also the priority of C. Then, in the continuation of the linear statement, when the sub-complexes intersect, the balance shifts to the unified

[11] A♯-C verticalizes the important unifying whole step, i.e. the opening D-E (see footnote 5). The interval's prominence as a linear dyad in *Noces* will also be recalled.

interpretation, substantiated by an arrangement of the elements (Ex. 9b) in what corresponds to "stepwise" representation of an incomplete octatonic scale "gapped" at two parallel positions (namely, where the interval of 3 occurs):

Ex. 9a            Ex. 9b

A♯ is first element in the above representation not because of priority, but on contextual grounds (the registration of the tremolo in piano and strings as in Ex. 9a); for in so symmetrical an arrangement even C priority, with all its backing (among other things, the support of the fifth) is not conclusive. Surely, an eventuality of this order must be what Stravinsky had in mind when he spoke of "polarity" in *Poétique Musicale,* and though he now cautions us that the book was one of those "written through other people,"[12] I take the liberty of quoting him on that concept:

> What preoccupies us, then, is less tonality, properly so called, than what might be described as the polarity of a sound, of an interval, or even of a sonic complex [*complexe sonore*].[13]

While the meaning is perfectly clear, it is tempting to speculate on whether Stravinsky's choice of "polarity," a word which cannot accurately be applied (as he applies it) to one thing without its opposite, either had implications that escaped the intermediary who transcribed his thoughts, or—which seems more likely—reflected an awareness, if only on a subverbal level where it was difficult to articulate, of the special properties of the tritone which make it possible for pitches at 0 and 6 (capable of graphic representation as "poles" in a circle of fifths, whether or not one accepts the assumption on which this circle is predicated), by virtue of similitude or equal and thus independent weight, to remain in equilibrium or—to the end that a tone center is asserted by neither—to stand in a certain opposition. This speculation might easily take flight in a direction which would establish, as a necessary condition of "polarity," the denial of priority to a single pitch class precisely for the purpose of not deflecting from the priority of a whole *complexe sonore*. And from here, it would be a simple step to the conclusion that short of twelve-tone and so-called "atonal" procedures, nothing provides this condition better than the

39

[12] *Op. cit.,* p. 153.

[13] *Poétique Musicale,* Cambridge, Mass., Harvard University Press, 1942, p. 26 (translation mine). Later statements of the pre-twelve-tone Stravinsky take a more positive attitude toward tonality. Only a decade ago, speaking of his Cantata, he declared, "tonality is my discipline" (New York *Herald Tribune,* December 21, 1952; sec. 4, p. 5).

octatonic scale. It is not the intention, however, to make exalted claims for this scale, but rather, to observe its behavior in such concrete manifestations as the "*Petrouchka* chord," to which, after this digression, we had better promptly return.

From the vantage point of the "gapped" scale, the C and F♯ can figure just as prominently as they do in the familiar interpretation, with the important distinction that they now function as basic elements not so much in terms of two triads, but primarily, in terms either of two trichords, each with the interval order of 2, 1 (the notes with stems down in Ex. 9b), or of two tetrachords, each with the order of 2, 1, 3 (the notes with stems up)—in the latter case, the result of a partitioning of the octave to produce two conjunct segments. And the reason C and F♯ rather than, say, A♯ and E, are hierarchically higher terms for defining the relationship, is that since C has a certain priority, F♯, which stands in an identical relation to its two adjacencies, will also have analogically a certain priority within its own trichord (though one priority may be more strongly asserted than the other)—which brings us back to the statement made above as to the scale's potentiality for more than one tone center.

The inexhaustible "*Petrouchka* chord," needless to say, is far from accounted for by this brief treatment, the ramifications of which the reader will have to infer for himself. Yet, before leaving it, two small points should be resolved. First, there is the A♯, whose important function would seem to render it worthy of consideration for priority. Such priority, however, would yield the interval order 2, 1, for the conjunct trichords of the complete octatonic scale, instead of 1, 2, which—for reasons that will later become more apparent—has been posited as the fundamental form for Stravinsky. If nowithstanding this, A♯ priority is still considered, it might be well to keep in mind that it makes for conditions distantly akin to those determined by the "B♭ minor" interpretation in *Noces*. But, as the reader must be aware, though evidence has been given for C priority of the chord, no firm commitment has been made here with regard to this or any other priority at all. Which brings us to the second point: namely, the "polytonality" of the chord. Though I realize the disadvantages of making such a statement without a disquisition on one's theory of tonality, a "polytonal" interpretation, insofar as it may have any validity at all, is even more problematic than the determination of single priority. For the "gapped" scale affords far too little information for the delineation of "keys" of any kind.

## III

Let us make a fresh start, at a place in no way remote from this discussion up to here, but somewhat closer to the generally accepted analytical approaches. For it is untenable to pass from the tritone-related elements to those relations defined by the interval of 3 semitones without acknowledging Stravinsky's acceptance, until very recently, of the triad and its related chordal complexes, the permutations of which, often metamorphosing but never completely disguising the "basic" interval content (by such means as doubling, vertical spacing, inversion, etc.), have produced results admittedly very far indeed from the concept "triad" called to mind by the textbook representation. That this acknowledgement of preassumed interval complexes will not involve relinquishing the notion that certain compositional procedures arise directly out of the independent choice of intervals should soon become evident. Meanwhile, it will be necessary to resort to chordal nomenclature—though often purely denotationally.

To say that *Jeu de rapt* is a veritable primer of the ways in which the octatonic scale may be arranged into four major triads or seventh chords is not to deny its abundance of detail. In considering the six measures at Nos. 42-43 of *Sacre* (two representative measures of which are given in partial reduction in Ex. 10), I shall ignore most of this detail (articulation, etc.) and concentrate upon the chordal regimentation of the elements

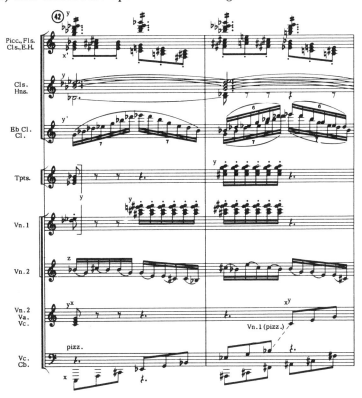

Ex. 10

· 27 ·

41

ushered in by the return of the first simultaneity (that at No. 37) as a kind of signal for the filtering out, at this point, of all pitch content not referable to the octatonic scale. In triadic terms, these are the discernible configurations: 1) major triads on C, E♭, F♯, and A (horizontal at, for example, $x$; vertical at $x'$—the latter being double-reed timbre rather than simultaneities as such); 2) dominant sevenths in first inversion (horizontal at $y'$, but mostly vertical, $y$); 3) a brief vertical statement of the C triad at $y^x$ (part of the simultaneity of No. 37); 4) a linear expression of the diminished-seventh chord ($z$).

Configuration $z$ places directly in evidence a determining factor of similitude: it partitions the octave at different positions from those at which the four roots drawing the pitch-class content of their triads and dominant sevenths from it partition the octave; at the same time, $z$ has an interval content identical with that of the only possible configuration (another diminished seventh) that can be formed by these chord roots; and the two semitone-related diminished sevenths (or any two diminished sevenths with no "common tones" at all) will, of course, always contain the total collection of an octatonic scale (see *Sacre*, Nos. 30 and 70, where these parallel diminished sevenths, horizontalized, are articulated to show their "whole-step" relation). The identity is stressed by the order in which the vertical configurations enter: $y^x$(C) and $y$ on E♭ (the latter being the second element by virtue of duration), then $y$ on F♯, and finally, $y$ on A—piling up a simultaneity of three sub-complexes in m. 2 (note the weak articulation of G in the dominant on E♭). The "pyramided" entrances of $y$ on E♭, F♯, and A are twice repeated; but the C triad (which took the form $y^x$ at No. 42) does not recur in its original vertical form, though it is significant that among the linear triads ($x$) the one on C is timed to replace $y^x$ (in Ex. 10, $x^y$ is the beginning of one of these). Each tritone-related pair (either $y$ on E♭ and A, or the combination of $y^x$ with $y$ on F♯) inevitably contains the same interval content as the "*Petrouchka*" chord," but note in the combination of $y^x$ with $y$ on F♯ the similar interval order as well. (Pitch-class content, incidentally, is identical, too.)[14] It should also be noted that the tritone-related triads and/or dominant sevenths, such as are contained in the "*Petrouchka*" chord," are not very different from those complexes that are related by the interval of 3 and/or 9. For by simply exchanging, in the "*Petrouchka*" chord," the

42

[14] This is a mild form of a phenomenon that may be observed again and again in much more noticeable fashion in Stravinsky, as will become apparent from a comparison of the musical examples presented in the course of this discussion: namely, the association of given chordal relations with fixed pitch classes. In this sense, as in many others, Stravinsky is like the old masters who, as has often been remarked, for each key had their special way of writing. Thus Mozart, for example, had his "E-flat" manner or style, and this was different from his "C-major" style, etc.

F♯ for an E♭, we derive a configuration whose sub-complexes are the dominant sevenths on C and E♭—all of which is nothing but a function of the diminished seventh that is the common pitch-class source for the chord roots that define the other diminished seventh encompassed by the octatonic scale.

If, from Ex. 10, the interval content of any two transpositions with adjacent roots (i.e. related by the interval of 3 semitones) is extracted out of the four available ones, the tritone-related triads are no longer present, but it follows from what has been just said, that there will still remain a substantial degree of interval content in common with the *"Petrouchka chord"*; and if, moreover, the amount of timbral differentiation that was present in the passage from *Sacre* is reduced to a minimum in the articulation of these two triads as sub-complexes in a larger configuration, common interval content will then be supplemented by another common factor: the special timbral consistence of the famous "chord." From all this, a family resemblance should result—as may be observed in the configuration of brief duration in *Dumbarton Oaks*:

Ex. 11

43

where, when the elements are apprehended as a whole, the typical Stravinskyan "accordion"-effect, much retarded, but belonging to the same general class as the *"Petrouchka* chord," will be recognized by anyone who does not take the analogy too literally. With sufficient confidence, therefore, it may be said that what passes for one of the most peculiarly Stravinskyan "sounds," rises out of the octatonic scale.

Detailed analysis of this excerpt, to be sure, reveals the subtleties of differentiation to which the referential relationships lend themselves, and it becomes apparent that, in compensation for absence of marked timbral differentiation, the longer durations on the alternate beats dwell separately on each dominant seventh: first, the one on A♭, then the one on F. This phenomenon, of course, is simply a product of the different intersections of the stationary element (A♭-A-C) and the vertical dyads in the flute and clarinet lines; and in this process, according to conventional interpretation, A♭ and A each assume the opposite roles of "chord tone" and "non-chord tone"—roles that they reverse when the intersection changes.

· 29 ·

Whereas *Jeu de rapt* delineated two diminished sevenths—one formed by the dominant-seventh roots and the other formed by the common pitch-class content source of the dominant sevenths—only the second type is evident here, demarcated by the octave-doubled C in terms of which the elements of the diminished seventh are clearly apprehended as agents of the four-part partition. But the diminished seventh seems to me, in significance, to be secondary to the trichordal stationary element which is capable of providing a modest exemplification of a useful compositional procedure, the preserved consistencies of which it would be profitable for us to follow within contexts referable to the octatonic scale.

The nature of these manifestations becomes apparent from a correlation of the stationary trichord ab-A-C with a trichord formed from elements of the combined dyads: Eb-f-Gb. In each trichord the common intervals (the semitone and 3 semitones) are in a different arrangement. Or if it is assumed that the somehow "disembodied" intervals constitute a "basic cell," then they may be said to have undergone "transformation." Now, since each conjunct partition of the octatonic scale contains the intervals of 1 and 3, the scale is singularly adapted to transformation involving these two intervals. Hence when the above-mentioned trichords are conjoined, other transformations will result: f-Gb-ab; f-ab-A; Gb-ab-A.

At the same time, it would be injudicious to ignore the conventional interpretation of "non-chord tone" and "major-minor" when the interval of 3 or 4 is taken as a "fixed" quantity and the semitone as a "movable" one, so that the latter is—to pursue the metaphor of the "disembodied" intervals—like something capable of being "attached" at any of the four possible positions "inside" or "outside" either form of the third (which is sometimes said, as a result, to be "bracketed"). But if somewhere in the background the procedure of transformation exerts any effect at all as an operation in which essentially no single interval has any priority, chances are very good that the implications of such a procedure will insinuate themselves into a context that is either tonal or otherwise centric, with the result that the choice or assertion of the "fixed" interval may be insidiously placed in doubt; and it is thus that there arises in Stravinsky's music another occasion for the pun, different in detail from that of the *Sérénade*, but not altogether dissimilar in intent.

In this regard, the theme with variations from the *Octuor* (Ex. 12) is singularly apropos:

Ex. 12

for here, permutations of four pitches, to which the main linear aspect of
the theme is entirely confined through the B♭ of m. 7, horizontalize such
transformations as those just discussed. The representation of the scale of
*Noces* (p. 20) could serve here, too, and though it cannot be claimed that
relations between one work and another are compositionally valid, a
study of both contexts enables us to check one against the other to substantiate the A priority. The *Octuor*, to be sure, shares this priority only insofar
as the position of A within the linear statement of the melody is concerned,
since the simultaneities on the offbeats assert D. The A may thus be said
to have "second-order" priority, for, as the dominant segment of D, it
both supports and is subservient to D. At No. 39, the second-order is
replaced by first-order priority, since the context also asserts A.

The pun this passage was chosen to illustrate involves both A and B♭.
Thus, whereas A offers acoustical support to the D minor of the simultaneities, the collection to which the linear statement that gravitates around
A is referable has no D at all! Furthermore, the pitch succession of the
linear statement is to D minor something like what the passage in Ex. 5
from *Noces* is to B♭ minor—namely, to a certain extent the affinity is
purely statistical: as witness, the "irregular" progression of C. The very
foundations of A-C♯ as the "fixed interval" are thereby shaken—hence,
the irony of B♭, which carries with it implications of the statistical B♭
minor that was rejected in *Noces* but that becomes more compelling here,
owing to 1) the fact that the "foreign" E and irregular F♯ are not heard
until m. 7; 2) the separate timbral plane of the melody (so that the ear
may hear it as something unaffected by the D minor harmony), and 3) a
degree of B♭-orientation among the simultaneities. From the viewpoint of
a basic cell, B♭-C♯ could be the "fixed" element onto which C and A are
variously "attached."

Into the larger context of the D minor, B♭ introduces a doubt, and the
doubt is an irresistible excuse for the pun which assumes the form of a
susceptibility to the accidental suggestion only to make it immediately
apparent that within the octatonic collection it is the A, rather, that has
priority. What fleetingly takes place is like that familiar optical illusion,
which makes us see checks of a linoleum, alternately with white in relief on
black, and black in relief on white. To equate this with "keyshift," "polytonality," and such, is to miss the point, for it is rather, as may be seen
below, merely a function of the affinity between the minor and the octatonic scales (Roman numerals denote scale degrees; the sixth degrees of
both minor forms are included):

|          | i   | ii  | iii | iv  | v   | vi  | vii | viii |
|----------|-----|-----|-----|-----|-----|-----|-----|------|
|          | a   | B♭  | c   | D♭  | e♭  | E   | f♯  | G    |
| B♭ minor | VII | I   | II  | III | IV  |     | VI  | VI   |
| D minor  | V   | VI  | VII | VII |     | II  |     | IV   |

· 31 ·

Other ambiguities interpretable mainly in terms of basic cell and/or major-minor are observable in the relation between the melody and chordal accompaniment. For example, D-f-F♯, formed by the indirect relation of the simultaneities of mm. 1-2 with those of m. 3, results from the infiltration of the linear A-c-C♯, or its retrograde inversion, a-B♭-C♯, into the rest of the context.

From the frequency with which this interval complex (i.e., 1 and 3) occurs in the *Octuor* it is obvious that the most important determinants of both motivic and structural relationships in Stravinsky's "neoclassic" music were already crystallized in 1923—such determinants, for example, as those that were to invest *Orpheus* twenty-five years later with a special imprint, and in their most familiar form, dominate the *Symphony of Psalms.*

IV

"[T]wo minor thirds joined by a major third":[15] such is the way Stravinsky recently characterized the "double" version of the basic cell as manifested in *Psalms,* from which it is evident that both major-minor and the semitone-related dyads defined the relation in his mind. The arrangement of the four pitch elements is the same as in the *Octuor;* and here once again we encounter the pun, but on a higher structural level, where the "optical illusion" is exploited in such a way that, to pursue the image, both white checks and black checks are alternately validated, each for a substantial period of time. Equating "fixed" with "priority," in the first movement of the *Psalms,* the lower third of the pair may be said to be the "fixed" element (*x* in Ex. 13a); whereas in the C-minor fugue, the relationship is reversed (*y* in Ex. 13b). The motive on B, the supporting fifth (*y* in Ex. 13a) which has second-order priority, anticipates the relationship as it is found in the fugue subject.

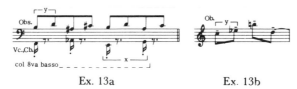

Ex. 13a          Ex. 13b

The four-element configuration receives mostly simple motivic treatment in the first movement. Versions of the basic cell like those in mm. 2-3 (e.g. at *x* in Ex. 14), articulated by the extremities of the contours and their directional changes, are rare here. Transformation is much more likely to be found in the last movement, but details of that movement are beyond the scope of the present discussion.

[15] PERSPECTIVES OF NEW MUSIC, Fall, 1962, p. 16.

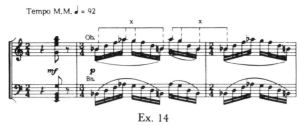

Ex. 14

The broad structural plan, unifying the main pivots of all three movements, also reveals the influence of the configuration, *qua* basic cell. Taking the main pitch classes of priority, without regard to temporal ordering, they could almost have outlined the motive if E-G-e♭ were followed by G♭. That the tritone-related C, instead, is the other term in this relationship, not only places the whole plan in the category of transformation but has provocative implications as to the significance of the octatonic scale for compositional structure. Among these implications, the presence of supporting fifth is a significant one to which I shall return, but right now let us contemplate the symmetry (absent from the parallel dyads of the motive) created by the two intersecting retrograde-inversionally related trichords:

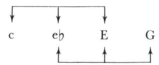

47

While the basic cell provides the means to circumvent triadic interpretation, it is very doubtful indeed that such interpretation, along with its tonal implications, can be ignored here, especially in view of the fugal statements. Even the first movement, which least calls for such an interpretation, since of all three it is the one where the octatonic scale plays the largest role, cannot readily escape it altogether, dominated as it is by an E-minor triad. True, the celebrated *"Psalms* chord" is like no E-minor triad that was ever known before, but if its uniqueness should be considered by anyone to free it from tonal association, its implications do not; for it is implicated indirectly with the fate of C minor through that special registration that exposes the octave doublings of G in the quasi-mirror arrangement of intervals. Whenever the *"Psalms* chord" punctuates the movement, it not only asserts E priority but prefigures the alternate G priority which will eventually serve as dominant of C minor.

Thus, the *"Psalms* chord" is involved, either directly or indirectly, with all three of the principal structural issues of pitch-class priority with which the first movement is concerned. (E♭ priority does not become an issue until later.) As to these issues themselves in terms of the broad plan of the present discussion, they are particularly significant inasmuch as they return us by a circuitous route to the white-note scales that occupied us in Part I. The E-, G-, and C-scales, it will be recalled, were precisely those that Stravinsky favored among the orderings available in the white-note collection.

In dealing with these three priorities, let us take them in order by first observing (Ex. 15) the simple expression of those tones that may be referred to the interval ordering that E defines within the white-note collection:

Ex. 15

The white-note collection stated at No. 2 without deviation provides the basis for bringing the G- and C-scales into direct contact with the E-scale in what was described above as a symbiotic relation. Whereas formerly such a symbiotic relation was achieved with either the E- or G-scale vis-à-vis the C-scale, now for the first time we have all three scales at our disposal at once—which should provide optimum conditions for the diatonic exchange. That this result does not obtain, derives from the fact that both the number and character of the terms involved in the symbiotic relation have now been expanded to encompass the octatonic scale, which acts as a catalyst upon the others.

Examination of this symbiotic relation not only reveals more clearly the nature of different referential interval orderings and Stravinsky's reasons for bringing some rather than others into contact with the octatonic scale, but in addition—as another aspect of the same thing—it illuminates the structure defined by the order of intervals in the octatonic scale itself. Further, it even answers questions that may have been bothering the reader in regard to it—such as, in particular, why is the form with the semitone between first and second degrees fundamental?

To this end it will be useful to set up the octatonic scale as a norm against which to measure degrees and types of similitude and differentiation of each ordering, along the lines of what was done above to collate the minor and octatonic scales. Let us imagine the octatonic scale acting as a filter through which only the intersecting elements will pass. Now, as may be seen from comparison of Tables A and B, the results are very different, according to whether the intersecting white-note scales start on odd or even degrees of the octatonic scale.

· 34 ·

## TABLE A*

|   | i | ii | iii | iv | v | vi | vii | viii |
|---|---|----|-----|----|----|----|-----|------|
|   | e | F | g | A♭ | b♭ | B | c♯ | D |
|   | 0 | 1 | 3 | 4 | 6 | 7 | 9 | 10 |
| C | I |   |     | III |    | V | VI |      |
| D | I |   | III |    |    | V | VI | VII |
| E | I | II | III |    |    | V |    | VII |
| F | I |   |     | III | IV | V | VI |      |
| G | I |   |     | III |    | V | VI | VII |
| A | I |   | III |    |    | V |    | VII |
| B | I | II | III |    | V |   |    | VII |

## TABLE B

|   | i | ii | iii | iv | v | vi | vii | viii |
|---|---|----|-----|----|----|----|-----|------|
| C | VII | I | II |    | IV |    |    | VI |
| D |   | I | II | III | IV |    |    | VI |
| E |   | I |    | III | IV |    | VI |    |
| F | VII | I | II |    |    | IV |    | VI |
| G |   | I | II |    | IV |    |    | VI |
| A |   | I | II | III | IV |    | VI |    |
| B |   | I |    | III | IV | V | VI |    |

## TABLE C

|   | i | ii | iii | iv | v | vi | vii | viii |
|---|---|----|-----|----|----|----|-----|------|
| C |   | III | IV | V |    | VIII |    | II |
| D |   | II | III | IV |    | VI |    | I |
| G |   | VI | VII | I |    | III |    | V |
| E (on G) |   |   | VII | I | II | III |    | V |
| "A" (on C) |   |   | IV | V | VI | VII |    | II |

* (Large Roman numerals refer to white-note scale degrees.)

The results of rotation, inferable from comparison of Tables A and B, concern us mainly where they reveal a reversal of the entries under columns v and vi, so that while the lower tetrachords remain more intact in Table B, the perfect fifths above the pitch classes of priority are "filtered out"—a critical loss in terms of the assertion of nonfunctional tone center, assumed as fundamental to the organizing principle of the music being considered here. In this sense, the scales represented by the intersecting elements in Table B stand hierarchically lower than those in Table A in their relationship to the octatonic scale. Certain qualifications of this statement, however, are in order: (1) the B-scale, by its nature, cannot fulfill (because the diminished fifth is its normal fifth degree) what is here assumed to be Stravinsky's requirements; and since he treats it generally as the usual stepchild that it has long been taken to be, it may be eliminated altogether; (2) the C- and A-scales, with but four intersecting members in Table A, are at a disadvantage, not only numerically, but because their so-called "pentatonic" arrangement does not fulfill the conditions of the white-note collection with regard to the tritone and the series of fifths mentioned above (p. 18), so that, depending on what is assumed to be their "filtered-out" elements, the C-scale could equally be the F- or G-scale, and the A-scale could be the D or E; and even where this is rectified, in Table B, the absent third of the C-scale leaves room for the possibility of "minor," while the fourth degree of the A-scale is particularly "weighted" by the presence of its associated triad (i.e., Bb-Db-F).

Since the special value placed on the presence of the fifth in support of the first degree is due to the fact that we are dealing with a system based on pitch-class priority, it follows that every other means for defining this first degree is of primary importance. In this regard, it is immediately striking that the E-scale, under the conditions of intersection of Table A, is the only scale (i.e. satisfying the requirements of supporting fifth) that retains both elements that stand in relation of adjacencies to its first degree. On the other hand, it could be argued that the tetrachords remaining intact in Table B provide significant means for identity, precisely in the environment of any potential tone center. The tetrachord with interval order 2, 1, 2, it could be pointed out, is one that proliferates in manifold folktune-derived motives and melodic fragments throughout Stravinsky's "Russian" period, especially in the compound form that yields the D-scale (cf. *Petrouchka*, Nos. 5, 8, 20, 42, 103, etc., etc.). What could be more natural than a merger of two predilections—the other being his well-known one for the tritone—out of which would issue a new scale: D, e, F, g ; G♯, a♯, B, c♯, two tritone-related tetrachords thus bringing the D-scale into the orbit of the octatonic scale? The answer to this question is fundamental: if such were the case the octatonic scale would suffer a severe loss of identity. Thus, in terms of the important first degree (or of each "accented" element of the disjunct dyads in the normal representation of the scale), the succession of consecutive scale degrees would yield nothing different from any referential ordering of intervals in the familiar white-note vocabulary until the fifth degree were reached—and even this, in terms of Classical practice, could be a so-called "tendency tone." It is the new "rhythm," in the ordering of intervals, that defines the uniqueness of the relations Stravinsky employed: namely, an ordering that gives up its secret, not at the fifth, but at the *fourth* degree, defining a tetrachord whose first and fourth elements are related by the interval of 4 semitones.

We may now, after this digression, return to *Psalms* and the "minor thirds joined by a major third, the root idea of the whole symphony"; and by the same token, the "root idea" of the octatonic scale, of which this work is an epitome, since in its motive and/or basic cell, as expressed at No. 7 (Ex. 13a), on both B and E, in terms of E priority, there is clear

50

delineation of the scale's total interval content. The minor thirds define the conjunct symmetrical equal partitions of the octave; and the "major third" defines the tetrachord. And the motive, along with its transposition at the tritone (starting on B in the second and fourth oboes in diminution), yields the scale's total pitch content. The similitude between the octatonic scale and the E-scale, moreover, is such that any statement to the effect that the first movement is in the E-scale, is immediately subject to qualification, since it is almost equally in the octatonic scale.

That this movement is less tonally oriented than the others, is a function of this E priority, whether in the form referable to the white-note collection or not. An important symptom of this function is the absence of the "subdominant," A, from the intersection of the E-scale with the octatonic, subdominant having no structural function here. Stravinsky does, however, make a minimal concession to tonal treatment of E in m. 8, where A, the first deviation from the octatonic collection, brings F♯ in its wake, with the significant effect that nowhere else but here is the "*Psalms* chord" attacked without caesura—thus giving a sense of "E minor cadence," "justified" ostensibly by the liaison, or vice versa. (Compare F♯ followed by F♮ before No. 12, and also m. 10 of the *Concerto per due pianoforti soli.*)

Pursuing the image of the symbiotic relation, let us consider further the E, G, C (priorities) and the octatonic scale's effect on them. Both the E and G priorities will come into contact with C priority, but the relationship will not be established through common pitch-class content, such as we observed much earlier in *Danse Russe*, for example, since the C priority reached will be not that of C major, but that of C minor (of the fugal exposition). Moreover, since the pitch class C is not referable to the collection of the octatonic scale deployed here, that scale will be prevented from being placed in a direct relation with any C priority. (It is also quite significant that E♭, too, is absent from this octatonic collection.) If E priority has potentiality for relating to C minor, such potentiality is a product of the octatonic influence on G priority.

As intermediary, G priority assumes the various characteristics of all the others. For example, just before No. 2, in the piano, there is a linear statement of the E-scale on G (*x* in Ex. 16) in anticipation of the first "pure white" statement of the E-scale.

Ex. 16

· 37 ·

A certain symmetry between E and G here flows out of those by now familiar properties of the octatonic scale, as a result of which G can define the octave partitioning on 3 in terms of E as 0, each one capable of relating to identical interval order and/or content. At the same time, it should be noticed that the present characteristics of G-priority may also be interpreted in relation to C minor, as a linear expression of the pitch content of the A-scale on C (what is called "natural" minor)—compare *E (on G)* and *A (on C)* in Table C.

The chameleon-like behavior imposed in the compositional process on the tones surrounding G whenever it comes into prominence, is adumbrated in the first three measures, where allusion is immediately made to the three main structural pitch classes. (I shall not discuss the usual claims as to the anticipations of E♭ major.) I cannot even begin to defend this statement in available space, but I should like to draw attention to these conditions favoring G: (1) the "*Psalms* chord" predisposing us to it; (2) the change of contour where G follows Ab; (3) G-B in the "chord," returning —this time as a familiar element— after B♭-A♭.

If all this is so interpreted because of the later contextual amplification of the G-relation, it is nonetheless significant that the elements are here already present: e.g. the intersections of the E-scale on G and of the G-scale itself, respectively, with the octatonic scale—see Tables A and C. And the other set of elements that should be mentioned here is the similar intersection of the E-scale itself. (In each of these cases, there are the five intersecting scale degrees observable in the Tables.) While there are other intersections as well, these are the ones concerning us, because in this movement they will be the predominant issues. It will be noted that according to this interpretation, the "harmonic" minor of C results from the further intersection, on a "lower" level, between the E-scale on G and the G-scale.

Though a resemblance to the relationship that obtained among the three dominant sevenths in *Jeu de rapt* (on E♭, F♯, and A) may still be observed, it is obvious that there is less identical interval content here, with E as root of a minor triad, G as root of a dominant seventh in first inversion, and B♭ as root of a dominant seventh in root position. The dominant seventh on E, in woodwinds (*y* in Ex. 16), could, of course, if used at the opening, have restored some of the parallelism. But the composer of *Psalms* avoids such parallelism, much more than the composer of *Sacre*. Thus, a comparison of what are, broadly speaking, the same relations, in four different works—two earlier examples (Ex. 17a and b) with two more recent ones (Ex. 17c and d)—reveals, in the last two, the establishment of the relationship in mm. 1-2 of *Psalms* as a kind of norm—the relative emphasis varying considerably from one work to the other. The

different degrees of—to borrow Edward Cone's concept[16]—"stratification" (that is, the merging of "strata," their intersection, coexistence,
separation, etc.) would make a fruitful study in which the comparison,
not simply of one work to another, but rather—and far more significantly
—of the various parts of the *Psalms* itself, would yield manifold relational
fluctuations of such a kind that these degrees could be virtually represented on a graph.

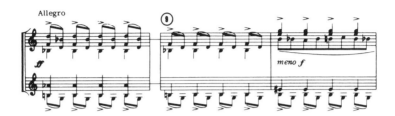

Ex. 17a, "Danse du diable," *Histoire du Soldat*

Ex. 17b, *Symphonies of Wind Instruments*

53

[16] "Stravinsky: The Progress of a Method," PERSPECTIVES OF NEW MUSIC, Fall, 1962, pp. 18-
26. Though, as it should be obvious by now, my "harmonic" analysis would be somewhat
different from Cone's, I find that the "stratification" approach has possibilities for further
development in, so to speak, a "stratification of strata." The various dimensions could be stratified—priority itself, for example—both in themselves and in relationship one to another. It is
significant that Cone places Nos. 4-6 on a single stratum, which is appropriate in view of the
perseverance of the octatonic scale. A stratification within this stratum or on another level
could draw attention to the shift from a stratum for E priority to a stratum for G priority.

Ex. 17c, Symphony in Three Movements

54

Ex. 17d, *The Rake's Progress,* Act II, Sc. 3

Note that in the earlier examples (17a and b) the entrance of the E (F♭ in the *Symphonies*), which is the first element in *Psalms,* is delayed; while in Ex. 17d it is near at hand but still the last of the elements to be heard. Ex. 17c, the only one of the three in which the relations are transposed (the A corresponds to E of *Psalms*) is otherwise closest to *Psalms* in the temporal order in which the three chords are presented, and in their disposition.

The elements of mm. 1-2 of *Psalms* are encountered again in prolongation at Nos. 4-6, where the octatonic scale perseveres for eleven measures (Exx. 18a and b), which is longer than anywhere else in the work. (There is a notable deviation in the tenors at No. 5—the A, which again tries to upset the octatonic hegemony.)

Ex. 18a            Ex. 18b

Assertion of E priority at No. 4 is followed by a shift to G priority at No. 5, articulated timbrally and by increased density and loudness, though within the ostinato context of pervasive eighth-notes suffused in double-reed sonority, the differentiation is not serious. The implications, by contrast, are very serious, indeed, since this is as close as the music will ever come to the outlining of tones of a dominant of C, such as that at the movement's end. If the fugato had started at No. 6 as the result of a ruthless cut, the approach to it, loosely speaking, would be similar to what it actually is.

Though the movement of F to D (sopranos at Nos. 5-6) does not favor tonal functional interpretation, the vertical B-D-F at No. 6 (Ex. 19) invests this section—retroactively, as it were—with dominant seventh association:

**Ex. 19**

In this reciprocal relation the simultaneity at No. 6 has the function of a continuation of whatever degree of dominant seventh is, indeed, associated with Nos. 5-6, establishing the conditions for one of Stravinsky's most striking ironies: here, ostensibly within easy reach, is the goal not only of the movement, but of the entire work. Yet, we shall not achieve it now, as long as the "incomplete" dominant seventh is not "resolved." Since, moreover, the "key" implied is that of the referential ordering defined by C within the white-note collection, it may be said, pursuing further this anthropomorphic description of tonal behavior, that the referential ordering defined by E within the white-note collection, "wants to"—insofar as its influence is indirectly exerted here—go to "C major." But C is not referable to the octatonic collection, which repeatedly in the course of the movement exerts its influence against the assertion of the pitch class C.

Confronted with broadly tonal issues such as these, the critical question is, again, where to draw the line between an intervallic, incipiently serial, "non-tonal" interpretation of this music and the tonal bias that obviously governed its conception. To be sure, since there is no "resolution," there is no yielding here to the imperatives of tonal functionality. Furthermore, it is significant that what tonal implications do present themselves are distinctly parenthetical—part of the irony being that the most important issue of the whole composition is tossed off in a little woodwind aside, well-nigh frivolous in this reverent atmosphere. It is also true that the context is typically "neoclassic,"—more precisely,—"neo-Baroque"; so that the transitory tonal investiture could conceivably be regarded as merely a form of parody, *à la manière de* . . . , of a kind not to be expected from the "Russian" works. But then all at once one may think of the F at No. 46 in *Sacre* which, despite the intervening measures, is similarly related to the octatonic collection at No. 42 as a pitch class not subsumed within the collection—the C-major triad operative since the beginning of *Jeu de rapt* having prepared all along for this goal.

If an adequate theory is to be developed to deal with such relationships as have just been discussed, what attitude should be adopted toward them? Are they actually tonal functional relations or are they "semblances,"[17] and if the latter, in what sense? Surely it is illuminating to approach Stravinsky's music from the angle of the octatonic scale and the basic cell. But Stravinsky, for all his genuine independence and original musical outlook, was born into a generation that had, in a manner of speaking, a "congenital" orientation toward those concepts of "traditional harmony" that are now being questioned.

Consequently, even though an attempt was made here to avoid tonal theory as a norm from which to depart, we found ourselves eventually obliged to confront it as a result of certain potentially tonal interpretations which arose out of what I believe to be the essential nature and significance of the music. The validity of these interpretations, their relation to tonal functionality or, conceivably, their relevance to a functionality of a new order—these are problems that ought to be seriously explored, preferably in a concerted effort. Our ultimate desideratum in doing so should be an approach from the vantage point of contemporary concepts. But it need not follow from this that because music is written today without reference to the postulates of tonality these should not be taken into account when they illuminate structural meaning in such works as those composed by Stravinsky before he undertook the discipline of twelve-tone composition. (That they should be applied to the music he wrote since undertaking that discipline, I am not, however, convinced.) Thus, any residuum or—if such is the case—"semblance" of tonality must be dealt with accordingly, both in the light of our total theoretical knowledge and in the light of interval relationships, whether of the basic cell, independent pitch-class formations, or the diatonic and symmetrical scales. I leave these considerations as a query in the hope that a new branch of theory may someday provide an answer.

---

[17] I choose this word instead of "resemblance" for the reason that somewhere in back of my mind I have the archaic sense, according to OED, of "an appearance or outward seeming of (something which is not actually there or of which the reality is different from its appearance)."

# SCHÖNBERG EST MORT

Prendre position quant à Schönberg?

C'est certainement une nécessité des plus urgentes; c'est, néanmoins, un problème fuyant, qui rebute la sagacité; c'est, peut-être, une recherche sans issue satisfaisante.

Il serait vain de le nier : le « cas » Schönberg est, avant tout, irritant, par ce qu'il comporte de flagrantes incompatibilités.

Paradoxalement, l'expérience essentielle que constitue son œuvre est prématurée dans le sens même où elle manque d'ambition. On pourrait volontiers renverser cette proposition et dire que se manifeste l'ambition la plus exigeante où apparaissent les indices les plus périmés. Il est à croire que dans cette ambiguïté majeure réside un malentendu plein de malaise à l'origine des réticences plus ou moins conscientes, plus ou moins violentes, ressenties face à une œuvre dont on perçoit malgré tout la nécessité.

Car nous assistons avec Schönberg à un des bouleversements les plus importants que le langage musical ait été appelé à subir. Certes, le matériau proprement dit ne change pas : les douze demi-tons; mais la structure organisant ce matériau est mise en cause : de l'organisation tonale nous passons à l'organisation sérielle. Comment cette notion de série est-elle venue à jour? A quel moment de l'œuvre de Schönberg se situe-t-elle? De quelles déductions est-elle le résultat? En suivant cette genèse, il semble que nous serons bien près de déceler certaines divergences irréductibles.

Disons, avant tout, que les découvertes de Schönberg sont essentiellement morphologiques. Cette progression évolutive part du vocabulaire post-wagnérien pour arriver à une « suspension » du langage tonal. Bien que dans *Verklärte Nacht*, dans le premier *Quatuor*, opus 7, dans la *Symphonie de chambre*, on puisse voir indiquées des tendances très nettes, ce n'est qu'avec certaines pages du *Scherzo* et du *Finale* du *Quatuor*, opus 10, que l'on assiste à un véritable essai de décollage. Toutes les œuvres que nous venons de citer sont donc, en quelque sorte, des préparations; il est à croire que nous pouvons nous permettre de les regarder aujourd'hui surtout d'un point de vue documentaire.

La suspension du système tonal se produit efficacement dans les *Trois Pièces pour piano* qui constituent l'opus 11. Puis les recherches prennent une acuité de plus en plus pénétrante et aboutissent au retentissant *Pierrot lunaire*. Nous observons dans l'écriture de ces partitions trois phénomènes remarquables : le principe de la variation constamment efficace, soit la non-répétition; la prépondérance des intervalles « anarchiques » — présentant la plus grande tension relativement au monde tonal — et l'élimination progressive du monde tonal par excellence : l'octave; un souci manifeste de construire contrapunctiquement.

Il y a déjà divergence — sinon contradiction — dans ces trois caractéristiques. Le principe de variation s'accommode mal, en effet, d'une écriture contrapunctique rigoureuse, voire scolastique. Dans les canons exacts, en particulier, où le conséquent reproduit textuellement l'antécédent — les figures sonores comme les figures rythmiques —, on observe une grande contradiction interne. Si, d'autre part, ces canons se produisent à l'octave, on conçoit l'extrême antagonisme d'une suite d'éléments horizontaux régis par un principe d'abstention tonale, alors que le contrôle vertical met en relief la plus forte composante tonale.

Néanmoins, une discipline se dessine, qui va être féconde dans ses conséquences; retenons plus particulièrement la possibilité, tout embryonnaire encore, d'un passage d'une suite d'intervalles de l'horizontal au vertical et réciproquement; la séparation des notes données d'une cellule thématique de la figure rythmique qui lui a donné naissance, cette cellule devenant ainsi une suite d'intervalles absolus (si l'on emploie ce terme dans son acception mathématique).

Revenons sur l'emploi des intervalles que nous avons appelés « anarchiques ». Nous retrouvons très souvent dans les œuvres de cette période des quartes suivies de quintes diminuées, des

tierces majeures prolongées de sixtes majeures et tous les renversements ou interpolations que l'on peut faire subir à ces deux figures.
Nous y observons la prépondérance d'intervalles — si le déroulement est horizontal — ou d'accords — si l'on coagule verticalement — qui sont le moins réductibles à la classique harmonie
de tierces superposées. D'autre part, nous notons la grande abon-
dance de dispositifs disjoints d'où il résulte un étirement du registre,
et ainsi une importance donnée à la hauteur absolue d'un son, qui
n'avait guère été soupçonnée jusqu'alors.

Un tel emploi du matériau sonore a suscité un certain nombre
d'explications esthétisantes dont on s'est servi comme réquisitoire
ou au mieux comme plaidoyer bienveillant excluant cependant
toute idée de généralisation. Schönberg lui-même s'en est ouvert à
ce sujet d'une façon qui autorise à parler d'expressionnisme : « Dans
mes premières œuvres du nouveau style, ce sont surtout de très
fortes licences expressives qui m'ont guidé en particulier et en
général dans l'élaboration formelle, mais aussi, et non pas en
dernier lieu, un sens pour la forme et la logique hérité de la tradition
et bien éduqué par l'application et la conscience. »

Cette citation dispense de toute inutile glose et l'on ne peut
qu'acquiescer à cette trajectoire première, où le mode de penser
musical manifeste une interdépendance d'équilibre par rapport
aux recherches considérées du seul point de vue formel. En somme,
esthétique, poétique et technique sont en phase — si l'on nous
permet de nouveau une comparaison mathématique —, quelque
faille que l'on puisse déceler dans chacun de ces domaines. (Nous
nous abstenons délibérément de toute considération sur la valeur
intrinsèque de l'expressionnisme post-wagnérien.)

Il semble bien que dans la suite de ses créations qui commence
avec la *Sérénade*, opus 24, Schönberg se trouve dépassé par sa propre
découverte, le *no man's land* de rigueur pouvant se situer en les
*Cinq Pièces pour piano* de l'opus 23.

Point limite de l'équilibre, cet opus 23 est l'inaugural manifeste
de l'écriture sérielle à laquelle nous initie la cinquième pièce —
une Valse : il est loisible à chacun de méditer sur cette très « expres-

sionniste » rencontre de la première composition dodécaphonique avec un produit-type du romantisme allemand (« S'y préparer par les immobilités sérieuses », aurait pu dire Satie).

Nous voilà donc en présence d'une nouvelle organisation du monde sonore. Organisation encore rudimentaire qui se codifiera surtout à partir de la *Suite pour piano*, opus 25, et du *Quintette à vent*, opus 26, pour arriver à une schématisation consciente dans les *Variations pour orchestre*, opus 31.

Cette exploration du domaine dodécaphonique, nous la pouvons amèrement reprocher à Schönberg, car elle a été menée avec une telle persistance dans le contresens, qu'il se rencontre difficilement dans l'histoire de la musique une optique aussi erronée.

Nous n'affirmons pas cela gratuitement. Pourquoi?

Nous n'oublions pas que l'instauration de la série provient, chez Schönberg, d'une ultrathématisation où, ainsi que nous l'avons dit plus haut, les intervalles du thème peuvent être considérés comme des intervalles absolus, déliés de toute obligation rythmique ou expressive. (La troisième pièce de l'opus 23, se développant sur une suite de cinq notes, est particulièrement significative à cet égard.)

Force nous est d'avouer que cette ultrathématisation reste sous-jacente dans l'idée de *série* qui n'en est que l'aboutissant épuré. Du reste, la confusion, dans les œuvres sérielles de Schönberg, entre le thème et la série est suffisamment explicite de son impuissance à entrevoir l'univers sonore qu'appelle la série. Le dodécaphonisme ne consiste alors qu'en une loi rigoureuse pour contrôler l'écriture chromatique; à ne jouer que le rôle d'un instrument régulateur, le phénomène sériel est, pour ainsi dire, passé inaperçu de Schönberg.

Quelle était donc, avant tout, son ambition, une fois la synthèse chromatique établie par la série — en d'autres termes, ce coefficient de sécurité adopté? Eriger des œuvres de même essence que celles de l'univers sonore à peine quitté, où la technique nouvelle d'écriture « ferait ses preuves ». Mais pouvait-elle donner des résultats probants, cette technique nouvelle, si on ne prenait la peine de rechercher le domaine spécifiquement sériel des structures? Et nous entendons bien le mot structure depuis la génération des éléments composants jusqu'à l'architecture globale d'une œuvre. Somme toute, une logique d'engendrement entre les formes sérielles proprement dites et les structures dérivées a été en général absente des préoccupations de Schönberg.

Voilà ce qui crée, semble-t-il, la caducité de la majeure partie de son œuvre sérielle. Les formes préclassiques ou classiques qui régissent la plupart de ses architectures n'étant, historiquement, aucunement liées à la découverte dodécaphonique, il se produit un hiatus inadmissible entre des infrastructures rattachées au phénomène tonal et un langage dont on perçoit encore sommairement les lois d'organisation. Non seulement le projet que l'on se proposait échoue : c'est-à-dire qu'un tel langage n'est pas consolidé par ces architectures; mais on observe l'événement contraire : ces architectures annihilent les possibilités d'organisation incluses en ce nouveau langage. Deux mondes sont incompatibles : et l'on a essayé de les justifier l'un par l'autre.

On ne saurait qualifier cette démarche de valable; aussi a-t-elle donné les résultats que l'on pouvait en escompter : le pire malentendu. Un « romantico-classicisme » déjeté où la bonne volonté n'est pas ce qu'il y a de moins rebutant. On n'accordait certes pas un grand crédit à l'organisation sérielle en ne lui laissant point ses propres modes de développement pour lui en substituer d'autres apparemment plus sûrs. Attitude réactionnaire qui laissait la porte ouverte à toutes les survivances plus ou moins honteuses. Nous n'allons pas manquer de les trouver.

La persistance, par exemple, de la mélodie accompagnée; d'un contrepoint basé sur une partie principale et des parties secondaires (*Hauptstimme* et *Nebenstimme*). Nous dirions volontiers que nous nous trouvons en présence d'une hérédité des moins heureuses due aux scléroses difficilement défendables d'un certain langage bâtard adopté par le romantisme. Ce n'est pas seulement dans ces conceptions périmées mais bien également dans l'écriture elle-même que nous percevons les réminiscences d'un monde aboli. Sous la plume de Schönberg abondent, en effet, — non sans créer l'agacement —, les clichés d'écriture redoutablement stéréotypés, représentatifs, là aussi, du romantisme le plus ostentatoire et le plus désuet. Nous voulons parler de ces constantes anticipations avec appui expressif sur la note réelle; nous voulons signaler ces fausses appoggiatures; encore, ces formules d'arpèges, de batteries, de

61

269

répétitions, qui sonnent terriblement creux et sont tout à fait dignes de leur appellation de « parties secondaires ». Signalons enfin l'emploi morose et maussade d'une rythmique dérisoirement pauvre, voire laide, où certaines ruses de variation à l'égard de la rythmique classique sont déconcertantes de bonhomie et d'inefficacité.

Comment pourrions-nous alors nous attacher sans défaillance à une œuvre qui manifeste de telles contradictions, de tels non-sens? Encore les manifesterait-elle à l'intérieur d'une technique rigoureuse, seule sauvegarde! Mais que penser de la période américaine de Schönberg où apparaissent le plus grand désarroi, la plus déplorable démagnétisation? Comment pourrons-nous juger, sinon comme un indice supplémentaire — et superflu — de ce manque de compréhension et de cohésion, cette revalorisation de fonctions polarisantes et même de fonctions tonales? La rigueur dans l'écriture est pour lors abandonnée. Nous voyons resurgir les intervalles d'octave, les fausses cadences, les canons exacts à l'octave. Une attitude telle atteint une incohérence maxima qui n'est, du reste, que le paroxysme, jusqu'à l'absurde, des incompatibilités de Schönberg. N'aurait-on abouti à une nouvelle méthodologie du langage musical que pour essayer de recomposer l'ancienne? Une déviation aussi monstrueuse d'incompréhension nous laisse perplexe : il y a dans le « cas » de Schönberg une « catastrophe » déroutante, qui restera sans doute exemplaire.

En pouvait-il être autrement? Il serait d'une naïve arrogance de répondre maintenant par la négative. Néanmoins, il est possible de discerner pourquoi la musique sérielle de Schönberg était vouée à un échec. Tout d'abord, l'exploration du domaine sériel a été menée unilatéralement : il y manque le plan rythmique, et même le plan sonore proprement dit : les intensités et les attaques. De cela, qui songeait sans ridicule à lui faire grief? Relevons, en revanche, une préoccupation très remarquable dans les timbres, avec la *Klangfarbenmelodie* qui, par généralisation, peut conduire à la série de timbres. Mais la cause essentielle de l'échec réside dans la méconnaissance profonde des FONCTIONS sérielles proprement dites, engendrées par le principe même de la série — sinon elles s'y devinent à un état plus embryonnaire qu'efficace. Nous voulons dire ainsi que la série intervient chez Schönberg comme un plus petit commun dénominateur pour assurer l'unité sémantique de l'œuvre; mais que les éléments du langage ainsi obtenus sont organisés par une rhétorique préexistante, non sérielle. C'est là, nous pensons pouvoir l'affirmer, que se manifeste l'INÉVIDENCE provocante d'une œuvre sans unité intrinsèque.

Cette inévidence du domaine sériel chez Schönberg a suscité suffisamment de désaffections ou de prudentes fuites pour qu'une mise au point soit nécessaire.

Nous prétendons ne pas faire preuve d'un démonisme hilare, mais bien manifester le bon sens le plus banal en déclarant que, après la découverte des Viennois, tout compositeur est *inutile* en dehors des recherches sérielles. L'on ne pourra guère nous répondre au nom d'une prétendue liberté (ce qui ne veut pas pour autant dire que tout compositeur sera utile dans le cas contraire) car cette liberté a un étrange spectre de survivante servitude. Si l'échec Schönberg existe, ce n'est pas en l'escamotant que l'on entreprendra de trouver une solution valable au problème posé par l'épiphanie d'un langage contemporain.

Il faudrait peut-être tout d'abord dissocier le phénomène sériel de l'œuvre de Schönberg. On a confondu l'un et l'autre avec un plaisir visible, une mauvaise foi souvent peu dissimulée. On oublie aisément qu'a travaillé également un certain Webern; il est vrai que l'on n'en a guère encore entendu parler (si épais sont les écrans de médiocrité!). Peut-être pourrait-on se dire que la série est une conséquence logiquement historique — ou historiquement logique, au gré de chacun. Peut-être pourrait-on rechercher, ainsi que ce certain Webern, l'ÉVIDENCE sonore en s'essayant à un engendrement de la structure à partir du matériau. Peut-être pourrait-on élargir le domaine sériel à des intervalles autres que le demi-ton : microdistances, intervalles irréguliers, sons complexes. Peut-être pourrait-on généraliser le principe de la série aux quatre composantes sonores : hauteur, durée, intensité et attaque, timbre. Peut-être... Peut-être... pourrait-on réclamer d'un compositeur quelque imagination, une certaine dose d'ascétisme, un peu d'intelligence aussi, une sensibilité, enfin, qui ne s'effondre pas au moindre courant d'air.

Gardons-nous de considérer Schönberg comme une sorte de Moïse qui meurt face à la Terre Promise, après avoir rapporté

les Tables de la Loi d'un Sinaï que d'aucuns voudraient obstinément confondre avec le Walhalla. (Pendant ce temps, la danse
pour le Veau d'Or bat son plein). Nous lui devons vraisembla-
blement *Pierrot lunaire*...; et quelques autres œuvres beaucoup
plus qu'enviables. N'en déplaise à la médiocrité environnante qui,
très spécieusement, voudrait limiter les dégâts à l'« Europe Centrale ».

Il devient indispensable pourtant que s'abolisse un malentendu
plein d'ambiguïté et de contradiction; il est temps que l'échec
soit neutralisé. Une forfanterie gratuite, pas davantage une benoîte
fatuité ne prennent part à cette mise au point, mais une rigueur
qui s'exempte de faiblesse ou de compromission. Aussi n'hésiterons-
nous pas à l'écrire, sans aucune volonté de scandale stupide, mais
sans hypocrisie pudique comme sans inutile mélancolie :

SCHÖNBERG EST MORT.

# STRAVINSKY DEMEURE

Essayer de porter un jugement sur l'œuvre de Stravinsky est une tentative déconcertante et vaine. Il apparaît de plus en plus évident que, en dépit de « renouvellements » constants, poursuivis avec moins de bonheur que de désenchantement, il n'est pas d'auteur dont le nom soit plus étroitement attaché à une seule œuvre, disons à une seule série d'œuvres. Stravinsky c'est d'abord *le Sacre; Petrouchka, Renard, Noces* et *Chant du Rossignol* forment une constellation dont l'importance n'est pas niée, mais dont le pôle attractif reste toujours ce *Sacre,* hier scandaleux, aujourd'hui prétexte à quels dessins animés ! Il est curieux de constater que, des deux grands « scandales » de la musique contemporaine, c'est-à-dire *le Sacre* et *Pierrot lunaire,* le sort est sensiblement parallèle : de même que *le Sacre* reste, aux yeux du grand nombre, LE phénomène Stravinsky, *Pierrot lunaire* reste également LE phénomène Schönberg. Nous pourrions grosso modo ratifier cette opinion car, dans l'un comme dans l'autre cas, il n'y eut pas, en effet, coalescence plus grande entre les ressources du langage et la force poétique, entre les moyens d'expression et la volonté d'expression.

En ce qui concerne plus spécialement Stravinsky, ses admirateurs et ses détracteurs ont tiré chacun à soi cette œuvre-clef et ont voulu y voir soit l'origine de toutes ses glorieuses épopées de rajeunissement, soit, très intrinsèquement, le point de départ de toutes ses turpitudes. On a écrit les mots imprudents de chef-d'œuvre à peine concevable pour l'esprit humain et d'expression précoce chez un jeune auteur manquant de maturité. On a parlé de lyre en fer forgé et de barde russe. Bref, un certain nombre de sottises de part et d'autre.

On serait enclin à penser que cette œuvre vaut mieux que tous les éloges dont on l'a accablée; quant à ceux qui y décèlent les incapacités de Stravinsky, qu'on leur décerne le bon point de la prophétie rétroactive.

Ne serait-il pas plus sérieux de s'occuper du *Sacre* en tant que production musicale, et de constater dans quel domaine nous pouvons nous livrer à une exploration fructueuse après avoir jeté par-dessus bord un certain vocabulaire exclamatif, sentimental et périlleusement pythique auquel ne paraît pas devoir renoncer l'exégèse musicale?

D'une audition de cette partition, il ressort de façon assez immédiate que, à part l'*Introduction, le Sacre* est écrit gros, je veux dire qu'il utilise essentiellement des plans très contrastés, une écriture globale. Cette impression n'est pas inexacte. Justifiée, en effet, par toutes les structures tonales de l'œuvre, elle se dément paradoxalement par les constructions rythmiques. Ce qui frappe le plus l'auditeur du *Sacre,* c'est la massivité de ces accords répétés, de ces cellules mélodiques à peine variées, et c'est pourtant là que se manifeste au plus haut degré l'invention de Stravinsky, difficile à imaginer en 1913, et inégalée pendant environ les vingt-cinq ou trente années qui suivirent. On se contenta d'imiter l'écriture, l'irrégularité et le nombre des changements de mesure, sans se préoccuper d'une réalité quelconque de leur emploi. Aussi ne faut-il pas s'étonner de voir que *le Sacre* n'a pas eu de portée véritable, sauf une tendance au dionysiaque et à la musique « méchante », comme on l'a dit, et qu'œuvre la plus connue du domaine contemporain, c'est aussi l'œuvre sans descendance. A tel point que le jazz a pu passer pour apporter à la musique un considérable renouvellement rythmique, avec sa pauvre et unique syncope et son inséparable mesure à quatre temps. (Stravinsky n'a-t-il point donné le change lui-même avec ses *Rag-Time?*) Pourquoi, depuis si longtemps, cette inexplicable carence? Peut-être, dirons-nous, la rencontre de la complexité du vocabulaire et de la syntaxe rythmique de Stravinsky ne pouvait se prêter à des déductions valables qu'avec un vocabulaire morphologiquement

**76**

et syntaxiquement aussi complexe, tel qu'il devait être mis au point par Webern [1].

\*\*\*

Il est à remarquer dès maintenant que, loin d'être, en effet, une libération au point de vue tonal, le langage de Stravinsky consiste en des attractions puissantes créées autour de certains pôles, ces pôles étant les plus classiques qui soient, à savoir la tonique, la dominante, la sous-dominante. Une tension plus ou moins grande s'obtient grâce aux appogiatures non résolues, aux accords de passage, à la superposition de plusieurs modalités sur une même note attractive, à la disposition des différentes formes d'accords en étagements compartimentés. Mais, d'une façon générale, les grands thèmes de l'œuvre sont diatoniques, et très primitivement diatoniques; on constatera même que quelques-uns de ces thèmes sont sur des modes défectifs à cinq sons. De thèmes à tendances chromatiques, il y en a notamment peu, et, à part un jeu très fréquent sur le majeur-mineur, le chromatisme ne revêt que des aspects sans caractère destructeur à l'égard des notes attractives, ou ne peut même avoir pour but que d'assurer une dissymétrie sonore dans les enchaînements un peu usés (je pense en particulier à la série de tierces parallèles que l'on trouve dans le *Jeu du Rapt* et dans les *Jeux des Cités rivales,* accompagnées d'un égal parallélisme en tierces ou en sixtes dont tantôt la note inférieure tantôt la note supérieure est haussée d'un demi-ton). Encore faudrait-il opposer dans toute la partition un certain diatonisme horizontal et un chromatisme vertical, sans exclure la disposition contraire. A tout le vocabulaire sonore, Stravinsky donne solution par des complexités greffées sur l'ancienne organisation; c'est pourquoi cette attitude peut prendre un aspect de timidité ou de déroute, maintenant que l'on connaît les expériences faites à Vienne à la même époque.

Il est indéniable, également, que Stravinsky possède, à un moindre degré, le sens du développement, c'est-à-dire du phénomène

1. Notons toutefois l'emploi chez Berg d'une structure rythmique organisée par ce qu'il a appelé le « Monoritmica » ou le « Hauptrhythmus ».

sonore en constant renouvellement. Peut-être estimera-t-on ceci faiblesse — et en effet ce l'est; me permettra-t-on de penser que c'est là un des principaux points de départ de cette force rythmique qu'il allait être obligé de déployer pour faire front à la difficulté d'écrire? Je ne crois pas être très paradoxal en affirmant que, ces coagulations horizontales ou verticales étant matériaux simples et aisément maniables, l'on pouvait tenter une expérience rythmique de façon beaucoup plus aiguë. A l'inverse, du reste, de ce qui s'est passé à Vienne, où l'écriture était en train de subir une transformation radicale à l'intérieur d'une organisation rythmique à peine plus que traditionnelle, où les complexités s'étayaient sur l'inébranlable principe du mètre régulier.

Nous aurons maintes fois l'occasion, au cours de l'analyse qui va suivre, de vérifier cette antinomie rythme-son, pour qu'il soit suffisant maintenant de l'avoir signalée.

*
* *

Nous n'allons pas suivre la partition page par page et en découvrir un à un les moyens d'expression; il serait plus profitable, je crois, de procéder par ordre croissant de complexité, en allant de la structure d'une simple phrase jusqu'à la « polystructure » des superpositions d'un développement. Peut-être pourra-t-on plus aisément, à partir de cette démarche, aborder les conclusions qui s'imposent à la fin de cette investigation prolongée dans le domaine stravinskyen.

Prenons donc comme premier exemple une phrase des plus simples, en *si* majeur-mineur, dont les cinq notes constitutives sont : *si do♯ mi fa♯*, le *ré♯* ne se faisant entendre que sur la conclusion suspensive. C'est par elle que débutent les *Cercles mystérieux des Adolescentes* (au chiffre 91 de la partition d'orchestre).

Exemple I.

Nous avons placé l'un au-dessous de l'autre les cinq membres de phrases, c'est-à-dire les deux antécédents, les deux conséquents et la conclusion. En dessous, nous avons placé la pédale rythmique constituée par les quatres notes de ce thème : *si do♯ mi fa♯,* qui sont disposées en agrandissement de registres, la seconde majeure *mi fa♯* devenant septième mineure, la seconde *do♯ si* devenant neuvième majeure.

Exemple I bis.

Nous voyons que l'antécédent I est bâti sur un rythme de quatre noires + deux noires :

les trois premières notes en valeur globale — en valeurs séparées, noire pointée, croche, noire — étant formées par une broderie de la dominante *fa♯*; l'antécédent II est construit de la même façon, mais entre les deux dernières noires se place un *fa♯*, échappée, dont la valeur est l'unité, c'est-à-dire la noire, ce qui donne donc quatre noires + trois noires. Le conséquent I est basé sur la condensation de l'antécédent I par la suppression de la broderie initiale et le transfert de la dominante *fa♯* à la tonique *si,* ceci nous donne deux noires + deux noires; le conséquent II, parallèle à l'antécédent II, utilise le même procédé par rapport au conséquent I, soit l'adjonction d'un *fa♯,* mais cette note se situe cette fois avant les deux dernières noires et se trouve ainsi transformée en appogiature de la sous-dominante *mi;* en valeurs, nous obtenons deux noires + trois noires. La conclusion occupe trois noires + trois noires. Nous avons donc quatre membres de phrases d'une durée inégale 6, 7, 4, 5, et une conclusion dont la durée rejoint celle du premier antécédent, mais avec cette différence de la division interne en 4 + 2 et 3 + 3. Sous cette structure mobile, nous avons une structure fixe de quatre croches qui vient harmoniquement et rythmiquement interférer avec la première. En effet, le départ des deux antécédents corrobore le départ de la pédale rythmique en se plaçant sur son temps fort, *mi fa♯,* tandis que le départ des deux conséquents est en contradiction avec cette même pédale rythmique en coïncidant avec son temps faible *do♯ si;* la conclusion revenant au temps fort et joignant ses propres deux fois trois noires aux trois fois deux noires de la pédale rythmique.

Cette subtilité de construction rythmique se reflète dans la conception harmonique de ce passage. Sous les *fa♯* brodés des deux antécédents et sous le *fa♯* échappée de l'antécédent II et le *fa♯* appogiature du conséquent II, il y a un accord majeur-mineur appogiaturé, composé d'un accord de *si* mineur à l'octave supérieure, et, à l'octave inférieure, d'un accord de *si* variable formé

80

par la tierce ou la tonique haussée d'un demi-ton; trois solutions se présentent donc : accord 1 : *si ré# fa#* (tierce haussée), accord 2 : *si# ré♮ fa#* (tonique haussée), accord 3 : *si# ré# fa#* (tierce et tonique haussées). L'antécédent I utilise les accords 1 et 2. L'antécédent II utilise les accords 3 et 1 pour la dominante brodée, l'accord 3 pour l'échappée. Le conséquent II utilise l'accord 2 pour l'appogiature. Démontrons clairement le jeu de ces symétries : l'antécédent II utilise l'accord 3 non encore utilisé et se termine par lui symétriquement par rapport à l'accord 1; cet accord 1 est placé sur le *fa#* après la broderie symétriquement par rapport à l'antécédent I, où il se trouve sur le *fa#* avant la broderie; enfin dans le conséquent II, le *fa#* appogiature utilise l'accord 2, puisque l'antécédent II a utilisé l'accord 3. Ce qui fait que l'ordre de seconde audition des accords 3 et 2 est renversé par rapport à leur premier passage 2 et 3, l'accord 1 se plaçant en tête à chaque fois et tirant une plus grande importance du fait de sa position à chaque extrémité de la broderie du *fa#* dominante, les accords 2 et 3 étant une fois sur le *fa#* dominante, une autre fois sur le *fa#* appogiature ou échappée, note de moindre importance tonale.

D'autre part, le *si* échappée, deuxième croche, commun à tous les groupes, est harmonisé avec un accord de sous-dominante mineure, tandis que le *si*, note réelle, qui commence les deux conséquents, est harmonisé avec un accord de tonique avec sixième degré majeur.

Les deux dernières noires *mi do#*, également communes à chaque groupe, sont harmonisées avec des accords dont les trois notes supérieures sont identiques, mais dont les notes inférieures varient de la façon suivante : le premier a le mouvement de basse *do# mi* avec *do# - mi - sol♮* au premier accord et *mi-sol♮* au deuxième; le second a la basse *do#* immobile mais le mouvement de voix intérieure *mi sol♮* avec *do# - mi♮, do# - sol♮* ; le troisième a le mouvement de basse *la# do#* avec *la# - do# - sol♮* et *do# - sol♮* ; le quatrième a le mouvement de basse inverse *do# la#* avec *do# - mi - sol♮* et *la# - do#*. Dans ce dernier accord, le *la#* de l'octave supérieure est supprimé pour faire valoir la septième *la# - la♮*. Les mouvements de basses sont donc toujours différents, mais toujours d'une tierce mineure; de plus, l'accord sur *mi* est le même dans l'antécédent I et le conséquent II, l'accord sur *do#* le même dans l'antécédent II et le conséquent I, si bien que l'ordre de deuxième audition de ces accords est rétrograde par rapport à leur ordre de première audition.

Pour la conclusion, la mélodie fait entendre le *ré♯* jamais placé auparavant, alors que la basse l'accompagne d'un accord de quarte sensible sur *la♮* jamais entendu auparavant en tant que basse.

Enfin, sur le conséquent I, il y a déroulement régulier des quatres notes *si do♯ mi fa♯* en noires, auxquelles sous le conséquent I s'ajoute *ré♮*, avant la cadence sur l'accord où *ré♯* joue le rôle de sensible.

Prenons maintenant des exemples où il y ait non seulement des divisions rationnelles de l'unité, mais aussi des divisions irrationnelles, je veux dire des quintolets, des triolets et toutes valeurs ainsi déduites. Soit cette phrase, devenue fameuse, qui commence l'œuvre :

Exemple II.

Je ne pense pas qu'elle soit devenue fameuse seulement à cause de son exposition dans la tessiture aiguë du basson avec attaque si tendue sur ce *do♮*. Je ne crois pas qu'elle le doive non plus à sa consonance modale défective, sans *fa♮*, somme toute très traditionnelle — les notes de tension, la dominante *mi* et la sous-dominante *ré* sont à distance de quarte de part et d'autre de la tonique et les repos ont lieu tous hiérarchiquement sur la médiante et la tonique *la* —, consonance modale contrariée d'ailleurs par une cadence avec *do♯* comme médiante, avec déjà l'antinomie du majeur-mineur, et contrariée ensuite, de façon plus énergique, par cette même cadence sur *do♯* avec une broderie chromatique amplifiée de la première broderie simple, les notes cadentielles étant redoublées à la quarte inférieure. Je crois que la réputation très justifiée de cette phrase vient également de son propre développement rythmique très remarquable à beaucoup d'égards.

Cette phrase peut se diviser en quatre fragments d'inégales longueurs : I, III, II, IV dans l'ordre décroissant. D'autre part, les deux premières sections contiennent des triolets, les deux dernières n'en ont aucun, la deuxième ayant donné naissance sur le *sol♭* à un motif adjacent qui n'utilisera, au cours du développement de l'*Introduction,* que des triolets.

Analysons le fragment I : il est formé de quatre cellules; la première est composée de deux valeurs globales égales : noire et noire, la première restant unité, la deuxième divisée en quatre doubles croches; la deuxième cellule est également composée de deux valeurs globales égales : noire et noire, divisées également toutes les deux en triolets de croches; la troisième cellule se compose de trois valeurs unitaires avec division en deux croches : elle est donc l'expression exactement contraire de la seconde, de plus, elle lui est symétrique en tension puisqu'elle monte sur la cinquième note au *ré*, sous-dominante, alors que la cinquième note de la deuxième cellule descendait au *mi* dominante; enfin la quatrième cellule comprend quatre valeurs unitaires, la première étant divisée en un quintolet de doubles croches, la seconde et la troisième étant liées, la quatrième étant écourtée par une anticipation de la cellule suivante. On a donc le schéma suivant :

Valeurs
unitaires:

Divisions:

Ce qui nous permet de déduire que la cellule $a4$ est symétrique rétrograde — dans le temps sonore donc — de la cellule $a1$, avec toutefois la précipitation rythmique dans $a4$ qui les différencie, ainsi que le nombre de valeurs unitaires. D'autre part, les cellules $a2$ et $a3$ sont inverses dans le temps sonore et symétriques dans l'espace sonore. Remarquons le nombre croissant de valeurs unitaires qui corrobore ces symétries et parallélismes de construction. De plus, aucune valeur ou division de valeur se trouvant dans une cellule ne se trouve reproduite dans une autre. Enfin, l'attaque du $do\natural$, par quoi débute chacune des cellules — que j'ai indiquée par des flèches — se produit en $a1$ sur temps fort, en $a2$ sur partie faible du triolet, en $a3$ sur partie faible de la valeur unitaire, en $a4$ de nouveau sur temps fort. Constatons encore que la cadence sur $do\sharp$ se produit sur $a1$ et sur $a4$, et que la broderie de cette cadence se produit en $a3$ avec un triolet, rappelant ainsi le rythme de $a2$.

Le fragment II, nous l'avons dit, développe l'élément triolet et module puisque nous trouvons $si\flat$ et $sol\flat$, notes étrangères au mode initial. Il se compose de quatre valeurs unitaires allongées d'une anticipation (une croche) dans la précédente cellule. Il développe même l'élément triolet à l'intérieur du triolet :

Le fragment III est une reprise légèrement variée du fragment I, la cellule $a6$ étant la reprise de $a1$, précédée d'une anticipation (une croche de triolet), qui rappelle celle du fragment II et lui est inégale. La cellule $a7$ est la reprise textuelle du fragment $a3$, la cellule $a8$ est la reprise abrégée de $a4$ avec deux valeurs unitaires au lieu de quatre. Nous ne comptons pas dans cette cellule les

84

trois *la*, blanches liées, puisqu'ils sont un simple prolongement de son sur un nouveau motif qui aura également un rôle très important au cours de l'*Introduction*. Les triolets sont donc exclus de cette variation, après le fragment II qui leur était consacré. On observe ainsi les lois de symétrie du fragment I, mais simplifiées et dans les groupes extrêmes.

Le fragment IV est une reprise élidée $a9$ du fragment $a3$ — avec une seule valeur unitaire mais avec la tension à la sous-dominante qui constitue le phénomène propre à ce fragment — suivie d'une reprise $a10$ du fragment $a8$. Le fragment IV est la désinence exacte des fragments I et III. On a donc comme structure générale : équilibre des valeurs (fragment I), éclatement par dissociation des valeurs (fragments II et III), désinence par répétition élidée (fragment IV).

Un exemple nous donnera encore une idée de la grande diversité rythmique déployée dans toute cette *Introduction* par Stravinsky. Il se situe au chiffre 9 de la partition (ex. III).

Le fragment que nous citons est basé sur les quatre notes *fa si♭ do mi♭*, redoublées à l'octave supérieure.

La phrase que nous avons appelée *a* se compose de deux fragments ; le fragment I est divisé en quatre cellules répétées deux à deux d'une façon légèrement variée.

La cellule $a1$ part sur le *fa* commun aux deux phrases *a* et *b* ; elle se compose de deux croches et d'un quintolet de doubles croches, soit deux valeurs unitaires ; la cellule $a2$ part sur le *do* à la quarte grave et se compose d'une noire et d'un sextolet de doubles croches, soit également deux valeurs, ce qui représente une variation de la cellule $a1$ ; la cellule $a3$ est une oscillation sur la première noire, en triolet, avec précipitation rythmique sur le *fa♮* soit deux valeurs unitaires également, la deuxième étant une noire ; la cellule $a4$ est la cellule $a3$ avec élision de la deuxième noire. On a donc une oscillation du *fa* au *do♮*, puis retour au *fa* ; ce sont les deux notes-pivots de ce fragment ; d'autre part, la cellule $a3$ est disposée symétriquement par rapport aux cellules $a1$ et $a2$ quant à la division de ses valeurs unitaires.

Le fragment II est une variation très légère du premier en ce sens que $a5$ étant identique à $a1$, $a6$ présente cette différence avec $a2$ : la première valeur unitaire est divisée en quintolets comme la

Exemple III.

deuxième de *a*1 et de *a*5. La valeur unitaire non divisée de *a*3 se trouve supprimée et remplacée par un trille dans *a*7, elle comporte de plus un aboutissant sur *fa*♮ qui la prolonge d'une valeur unitaire, d'où la suppression de *a*4 à la reprise.

La phrase que nous avons appelée *b* est composée de deux fragments. Le départ de I est semblable au départ de *a*1, par une quarte, mais cette quarte monte au *si*♭; on a ensuite un accent sur *mi*♭, puis une désinence précipitée avec un quintolet de triples croches, qui retourne au *fa*♮. Le fragment II présente l'allongement par une noire de ce *mi*♭ et la désinence allongée par le fait de la transformation du quintolet de triples croches en quatre triples croches avec aboutissement sur *fa* noire. L'accent est donc mis ici sur *si*♭ et *mi*♭.

**86**

Les phrases *c* et *d* viennent se greffer sur la noire ajoutée du fragment *b*II et unir les deux registres caractéristiques de *a* et de *b*. Elles viennent également présenter en raccourci toutes les divisions employées dans les deux phrases principales : divisions binaires (triples croches), ternaires (sextolets de triples croches), irrationnelles (quintolets de triples croches). Enfin elles corroborent les notes-pivots *do*♮ et *si*♭ qui forment l'ambiguïté de cette superposition.

Si je me suis étendu longuement et de façon aussi détaillée sur l'analyse de ces quelques passages de l'*Introduction*, c'est qu'une telle expérience est exceptionnelle, même chez Stravinsky, et qu'un aussi grand raffinement dans l'asymétrie et la symétrie des périodes, qu'une variation aussi renouvelée du phénomène rythmique par l'emploi des valeurs irrationnelles ne se retrouvent à peu près plus dans son œuvre, à part certains passages du *Rossignol*. Sa technique principale, nous le verrons tout au long du *Sacre*, consistant en la division rationnelle (2, 4, 8) ou la multiplication rationnelle d'une valeur unitaire. Mais nous aurons encore à revenir sur cette *Introduction*, remarquable quant aux développements individuellement superposés, à la structure complexe qui en résulte et au phénomène de « tuilage » de la composition, c'est-à-dire de recouvrement des développements les uns par les autres.

Jusqu'à présent nous ne nous sommes occupé que des thèmes qui se construisent mélodiquement, en une seule dimension. Nous allons aborder, avec l'exemple suivant (ex. IV), l'étude d'un thème dont la structure peut se doubler d'éléments contrapunctiques, éléments qui, encore que très simples, modifient cependant son aspect extérieur de façon suffisante à le pouvoir différencier des précédents. Cet exemple est emprunté à un passage de la *Danse sacrale*, au chiffre 151 de la partition. Nous y trouvons une sensibilité chromatique qui se manifeste curieusement dans un très bref raccourci.

Ce thème, dont la cellule génératrice est extrêmement courte, fait trois apparitions au cours de ce développement et les trois fois avec des dissymétries assez notoires pour être remarquées avec profit.

Cette cellule génératrice à proprement parler se compose de trois notes en descente chromatique dans un quintolet de doubles

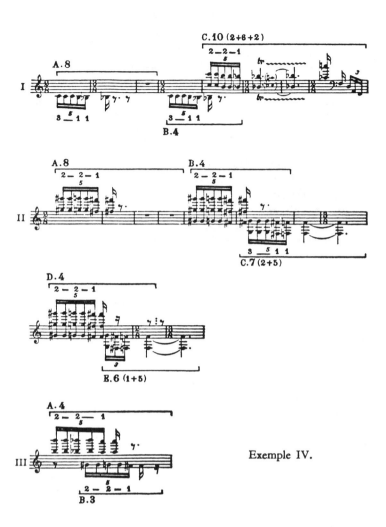

Exemple IV.

78

crouches. Dans sa première apparition, la première note du quintolet est répétée trois fois, les deux autres une seule fois. L'aboutissement a lieu sur la troisième note avec une longueur variable qui, pour cette première apparition, est très brève : une double croche suivie d'un silence qui complète sa valeur réelle de six croches.

88

Ce qui donne, pour cette cellule initiale, une durée globale de huit croches. Appelons-la fragment A.

Le fragment B qui la suit par juxtaposition est une répétition de cette même cellule avec la valeur d'aboutissement écourtée de quatre croches, ce qui nous donne une valeur totale de quatre croches. La répartition à l'intérieur du quintolet reste la même : *do* trois fois, *si♮* une fois, *si♭* une fois.

Le fragment C se superpose contrapunctiquement au fragment B en entrant sur la valeur d'aboutissement de ce dernier, il est de dix croches et voici comment il se décompose : premier groupe : le quintolet *do si♮ si♭* avec *do* répété deux fois, *si* répété deux fois, *si♭* une fois; la valeur d'aboutissement est de six croches (une blanche pointée, trillée), aboutissant par glissando à un troisième groupe commençant par l'accord *la♭ fa la♮*, c'est-à-dire le joint entre le chromatisme précédent et l'arpège qui va suivre. Cet arpège est la transformation en intervalles disjoints du quintolet chromatique; la différence rythmique est que les cinq notes, conséquent du quintolet antécédent, s'y divisent en deux doubles croches et un triolet de doubles croches, expression d'un ralentissement et d'une précipitation rythmiques par rapport à ce quintolet, les doubles croches et le triolet de doubles croches formant l'encadrement exact des valeurs de cinq. Notons avant d'en terminer avec cette période I, que le fragment A est exposé en sons simples dans le médium; que le canon entre B et C se fait à l'octave supérieure et à distance de deux croches, que cette réponse est en octaves, et que la disposition des quintolets se fait dans l'ordre

suivant : $\underbrace{\overset{3\ 1\ 1}{\frown}}_{5}\quad \underbrace{\overset{3\ 1\ 1}{\frown}}_{5}\quad \underbrace{\overset{2\ 2\ 1}{\frown}}_{5}$

La période II est le renversement de la première, avec un quatrième fragment ajouté.

Le fragment A est à l'image exacte du fragment A de la période I, c'est-à-dire qu'il dure huit croches, et se compose d'un quintolet de doubles croches et d'une valeur de six croches. Toutefois, ce quintolet a la disposition $\underbrace{\overset{2\ 2\ 1}{\frown}}_{5}$.

Le fragment B est également à l'image exacte du fragment B de la période I, durée quatre croches, avec cette même différence

89

que le quintolet a la disposition $\underset{5}{\overset{2\ 2\ 1}{\frown}}$. Il suit également le fragment A par juxtaposition.

Le fragment C se superpose, contrapunctiquement, également à la noire, mais la valeur d'aboutissement est écourtée, ne durant que cinq croches, et ne comporte pas le troisième groupe conclusif symétrique que possédait le fragment C de la période I. Notons de plus que l'exposition du fragment A se fait dans l'aigu en octaves, puis en doubles octaves, et que la réponse est au médium en octaves (avec l'octave supérieure), d'où croisement des registres, alors que dans la période I les registres étaient distincts. La disposition des quintolets s'est donc faite dans l'ordre inverse de la première fois : $\underset{\smile}{2\ 2\ 1}$ $\underset{\smile}{2\ 2\ 1}$ $\underset{\smile}{3\ 1\ 1}$.

Les fragments B et C sont suivis, par juxtaposition de nouveau, de la répétition de leur canon, avec élision de la réponse; le fragment D étant identique au fragment B, le fragment E présente à la place du quintolet un triolet de doubles croches sans répétition, la valeur d'aboutissement étant la même qu'en C, de cinq croches; la valeur globale de ce groupe est par conséquent de six croches.

Enfin, la période III se compose de la cellule A — valeur quatre croches, le quintolet étant divisé en *si* deux fois répété, *si♭* deux fois également, et *la* une seule fois énoncé — et de la cellule B — réponse en canon à la tierce mineure inférieure avec même division du quintolet, la valeur d'aboutissement étant écourtée d'une croche; le canon a lieu pour la première fois, à la distance d'une croche, c'est-à-dire à l'intérieur du quintolet qui lui sert d'antécédent.

Aucune des trois périodes de ce thème, en apparence pourtant si sommaire, n'a donc la même physionomie, et chacune d'elles se fonde sur une sensibilité chromatique extrêmement aiguë, dont il est possible de relever un autre exemple dans cette même œuvre. Il s'agit (ex. V) du thème qui unit les *Jeux des Cités rivales* au *Cortège du Sage*.

Nous notons à partir du chiffre 64 de la partition jusqu'au chiffre 69. Nous avons une broderie inférieure de *sol♯*, tantôt à distance de seconde mineure sur *sol♮*, tantôt à distance de seconde majeure sur *fa♯*, l'une redoublée, quand l'autre est simple, et réciproquement. Les cellules varient de la façon suivante :

90

Exemple V.

1) 5 mesures, c'est-à-dire 4 + 1 mesures; broderies :
   2 fois *sol*♮, 1 fois *fa*♯;
2) 4 mesures : broderies : 1 fois *sol*♮, 2 fois *fa*♯;
3) 2 mesures, par élision d'une des broderies et de la répétition
   de l'autre : 1 fois *fa*♯;
4) 3 mesures, par élision de la répétition d'une broderie :
   1 fois *fa*♯, 1 fois *sol*♮.

Dans le *Cortège du Sage* :

5) 4 mesures : 2 fois *sol*♮, 1 fois *fa*♯;
6) 4 mesures : 1 fois *sol*♮, 2 fois *fa*♯.

A partir de là, le thème, vu les superpositions rythmiques, se
fige dans la physionomie de cette cellule jusqu'à la fin du développement. Nous pouvons constater le parallélisme des cellules 5
et 6 et l'élision contrastante des deux cellules centrales. Ce qui
différencie également ce thème lors de son exposition dans les
*Jeux des Cités rivales,* c'est la durée constamment inégale des cellules,
qui décroît jusqu'à deux et croît pour retrouver la valeur composante stable : quatre, lors du *Cortège du Sage.* Notons enfin que
l'ordre des broderies est toujours *sol*♮ *fa*♯, il est modifié seulement
dans les cellules 3 et 4 pour prendre auditivement l'ordre contraire :
deux fois *fa*♯, une fois *sol*♮.

82

Exemple VI.

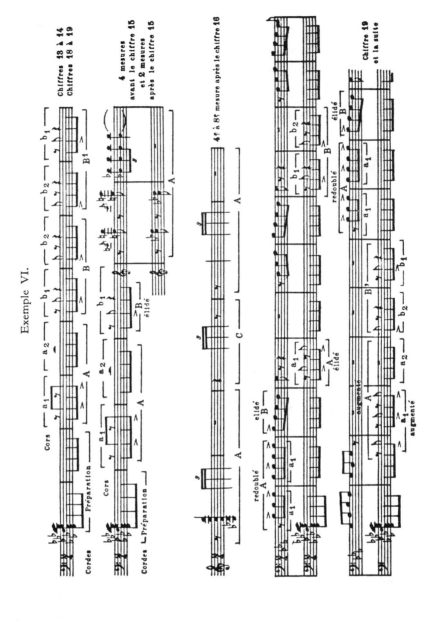

On voit ainsi que la construction de ce thème est basée sur un balancement extrêmement équilibré où nous retrouvons la même sensibilité chromatique que dans le thème, analysé plus haut, de la *Danse sacrale,* sensibilité dont l'expression exacte se trouve dans le jeu des symétries rythmiques.

Le phénomène le plus important, à mon avis, dans le domaine thématique du *Sacre* est l'apparition d'un thème rythmique à proprement parler, doué de sa propre existence à l'intérieur d'une verticalisation sonore immobile.

Le premier exemple dont nous prendrons connaissance se trouve dans *les Augures printaniers,* au chiffre 13 de la partition (ex. VI).

Le thème rythmique se trouve formé par des accentuations sur un déroulement régulier de croches. La première apparition de ces accords répétés dure huit mesures et se développe de deux en deux mesures. Nous avons d'abord une préparation sans accent de deux mesures. Puis, une cellule A se subdivise en un accent sur chaque partie faible de temps (*a*1) dans la première mesure, et un silence dans la seconde (*a*2). La cellule B se subdivise en un accent sur la partie faible du temps fort de la première mesure (*b*1) et un accent sur le temps fort de la seconde mesure (*b*2). La seconde cellule B' est dans l'ordre rétrograde de la première : *b*2 *b*1 avec les mêmes caractéristiques.

Ce thème d'accentuation revient sous une forme élidée de quatre mesures avant 15 jusqu'au chiffre 15. La préparation sans accent est d'une mesure, diminuée de moitié sur la première. La cellule A revient identique à elle-même. Enfin la cellule B, qui était redoublée, est ici élidée d'une de ses composantes et ne comporte que *b*1.

Le thème d'accentuation s'osmose ensuite dans le thème mélodique qui se développe à partir de 15 et lui donne le départ au moyen de la cellule A.

Il reparaît lors du développement médian dans les accords de quintes superposées qui se trouvent à partir de la quatrième mesure après 16. Il y a d'abord la cellule A, puis une nouvelle

93

cellule C, dont c'est la seule apparition, qui consiste en l'accentuation du temps faible, jamais encore entendue, enfin la reprise de A. Cette cellule C est, du reste, un des principes du développement de cette partie médiane, puisqu'on le retrouve en pédale rythmique sur une tenue de *do*.

A la reprise du premier développement, nous avons, du chiffre 18 au chiffre 19, une répétition exacte du thème rythmique dans son exposition du chiffre 13 au chiffre 14.

A partir du chiffre 14, le thème rythmique passe tantôt du thème mélodique aux accords répétés d'accompagnement. Et nous avons dans l'ordre analysé sur l'exemple : mélodiquement, A (*a1 a1*) modifié par redoublement, B (*b2*) élidé ; harmoniquement, A (*a1*) élidé; trois mesures de transition sans accent; harmoniquement, B normal (*b1 b2*); trois mesures et demie de transition sans accent; harmoniquement, A augmenté par adjonction d'une accentuation sur partie faible du deuxième temps, B' rétrograde de B (*b2 b1*); mélodiquement, A transformé par redoublement (*a1 a1*), B élidé (*b2*). A partir de là, il n'y aura plus aucune accentuation jusqu'à la fin de ce développement.

La disposition de ce thème rythmique appelle quelques remarques sur sa structure générale, où nous découvrirons encore des effets d'asymétriques correspondances.

Dans la première partie de ce thème — jusqu'au changement harmonique — nous avons la structure :

ABB' AB élidé A, de deux cellules qui se répondent en effets contrariants; le disposition ABB' n'étant pas symétrique, la disposition ABA l'étant, d'autre part B paraissant élidé dans la deuxième disposition.

La cellule médiane est symétrique ACA.

Dans la reprise, la structure apparaît : ABB' — *A redoublé B élidé* A élidé — B — A augmenté B' *A redoublé B élidé,* soit quatre cellules divisées en une et trois : la première cellule ABB' — asymétrique, la deuxième et la quatrième présentant une symétrie dans leurs composantes extrêmes par rapport à la troisième formant centre. Remarquons, pour notre curiosité personnelle, que le déroulement des éléments non symétriques de la deuxième et de la quatrième cellules (AAB') sont dans une asymétrie inverse au déroulement de la première cellule (ABB'); mais peut-être est-ce là pousser bien loin les conséquences d'une telle organisation.

Enfin, nous pouvons encore remarquer que, dans son ensemble, cette organisation présente deux structures parallèles placées de part et d'autre d'une organisation symétrique, et que les périodes non accentuées que nous avons signalées pendant l'analyse sont en ordre croissant à partir du chiffre 19, la première étant de six noires, la deuxième de sept noires, la dernière de quatorze noires, c'est-à-dire un peu plus que la somme des deux autres.

Si nous avons pris d'abord pour exemple ce thème d'accentuation, c'est qu'il est relativement assez simple et qu'il a la particularité de se greffer tantôt sur un rythme tantôt sur un thème mélodique. Mais nous allons analyser maintenant un thème uniquement rythmique sans accentuation, où les périodes s'organisent sur un seul accord. C'est le premier couplet de la *Danse sacrale* qui nous le fournira, du chiffre 149 de la partition au chiffre 154 (ex. VII). Nous avons mis l'accord en face de l'analyse rythmique.

Nous voyons tout d'abord que les cellules composantes sont de même famille deux à deux, $b_4$ $c_4$ valeurs paires (quatre croches) $a_3$ $a_5$ valeurs impaires (trois et cinq croches), $c_4$ étant de nature neutre puisqu'il ne peut pas se rétrograder, $b_4$ et $a_3$ étant rétrogradables, $a_5$ pouvant tantôt être neutre, tantôt se rétrograder, conjuguant ainsi les trois autres cellules. Nous établissons le schéma :

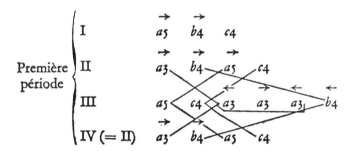

Nous remarquons que la période II est la permutation des cellules $a_5$ et $b_4$ de I, $a_5$ devenant neutre — avec adjonction de $a_3$.

95

86

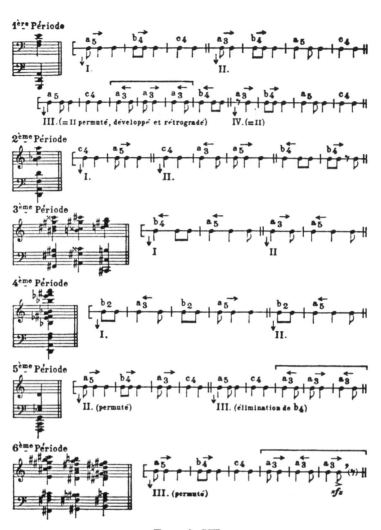

Exemple VII.

Le fragment III est une permutation de II (en diagonale) avec $\overrightarrow{a_3}$ agrandi de part et d'autre par sa rétrogradation. Enfin le fragment IV est un retour à la disposition du fragment II.

Nous constatons maintenant que toutes les périodes qui suivent, et qui sont indiquées chaque fois par un changement d'accord, sont toutes dérivées de la première par un travail extrêmement habile.

La deuxième période (chiffre 154 à 157), toujours bâtie sur un seul accord, cet accord étant toutefois brodé, se compose de :

$$
\begin{array}{ccc}
 & \overleftarrow{\phantom{a}} & \\
c_4 & a_5 & = \text{I} \\
c_4 & a_3 & a_5 = \text{II} \\
\overleftarrow{b_4} & \overrightarrow{b_4} &
\end{array}
$$

c'est-à-dire qu'elle reproduit les fragments I (en rétrograde) et II (en rétrograde avec permutation de $a_5$ et $a_3$) en rejetant les deux cellules $b_4$ à la fin, qui forment un troisième fragment.

La troisième période, modulante — sur trois accords — est une période d'élimination; elle comprend :

$$
\begin{array}{cc}
\overleftarrow{b_4} & \overleftarrow{a_5} = \text{I} \\
\overrightarrow{a_3} & \overleftarrow{a_5} = \text{II}
\end{array}
$$

Le premier fragment reproduit le fragment I de la première période avec élimination de $c_4$, le deuxième fragment reproduit également le fragment II de la première période mais avec élimination, cette fois, de $b_4$ et de $c_4$.

La quatrième période, basée de nouveau sur un accord, identique à celui de la deuxième période, et identiquement brodé, est également une période d'élimination et de réduction; elle comporte :

$$
\begin{array}{cccc}
 & \overleftarrow{a_3} & & \overleftarrow{a_5} \\
b_2 & a_3 & b_2 & a_5 = \text{II} \\
 & \overleftarrow{a_5} & & \\
b_2 & a_5 & & = \text{I}
\end{array}
$$

**97**

87

Le premier fragment est le fragment II de la première période avec les cellules $b_4$ et $c_4$ transformées; $b_2$ peut, en effet, être indifféremment la diminution de $c_4$ et l'élision de $b_4$; elle devient ainsi une cellule neutre. Le deuxième fragment est le fragment I de la première période avec compression de $b_4$ et de $c_4$ transformés en $b_2$.

Suit une élimination régulière de sept croches successives amenant une seconde partie dans le développement rythmique. Cette seconde partie comprend seulement deux périodes; elle commence après une anacrouse d'un demi-soupir.

La cinquième, basée sur un accord non brodé, se compose ainsi :
$\overrightarrow{a_5} \quad \overrightarrow{b_4} \quad \overrightarrow{a_3} \quad c_4$, le premier fragment, qui est le fragment II avec permutation de $a_3$ et de $a_5$; $a_5 \quad c_4 \quad \overleftarrow{a_3} \quad \overrightarrow{a_3} \quad \overleftarrow{a_3}$, le deuxième fragment, qui est le fragment III de la première période avec l'élimination de $b_4$.

La sixième, sur un accord brodé, comprend : $\overrightarrow{a_5} \quad \overrightarrow{b_4} \quad c_4 \quad \overrightarrow{a_3} \quad \overleftarrow{a_3} \quad \overrightarrow{a_3}$, qui est le fragment III de la première période avec permutation de $b_4$.

Notons quelques particularités sur cette cellule $a_5$ qui peut être neutre où rétrogradable. Dans la première période d'exposition, elle est d'abord dans le sens droit, puis trois fois neutre.

Quant aux périodes de développement de la première partie : dans la deuxième, la cellule est deux fois dans le sens droit; dans la troisième, deux fois dans le sens rétrograde; dans la quatrième, une fois dans chaque sens. Un équilibre s'établit ainsi entre les cellules droites et les cellules rétrogrades. Dans les périodes de la seconde partie, on revient à la prédominance des cellules droites et neutres.

On peut voir à quelle richesse de variation rythmique, sans aucun changement dans les valeurs de ces cellules, on peut arriver par leur simple permutation et l'application d'un procédé aussi simple que celui de la rétrogradation.

Ayant fait un tour d'horizon assez complet des procédés rythmiques linéaires chez Stravinsky, il faudrait essayer de voir comment

98

ces procédés peuvent fournir une structure de développement, car c'est là qu'ils recevront leur entière justification.

En général, le développement rythmique le plus simple chez Stravinsky, à part le procédé linéaire étendu à tout l'orchestre, est celui de l'apparition de deux forces rythmiques. Cet antagonisme peut mettre en jeu deux rythmes simples, ou bien un rythme simple et une structure rythmique, ou encore deux structures rythmiques.

Notre premier exemple portera sur l'antagonisme d'un rythme simple et d'une structure rythmique (ex. VIII — *Jeu du Rapt,* chiffre 46).

Le rythme simple que nous appellerons B est d'abord d'une valeur de trois croches (B3) et se répète deux fois; puis il diminue, devient d'une valeur de deux croches (B2) et se répète six fois; il augmente jusqu'à six croches (B6) et se répète deux fois; diminue jusqu'à quatre croches (B4) et se répète deux fois. Les apparitions de même valeur ont donc lieu deux par deux. Il est exprimé par une basse ou un accord.

La structure rythmique et mélodique qui lui est opposée est composée de cinq séquences.

La première, AI, se compose de deux fragments égaux de cinq croches, *a* et *b* (anacrouse et accent).

La seconde, AII, comprend le fragment *a* (anacrouse) élidé d'une croche, le fragment *b* (accent), le fragment *b* augmenté d'une croche (répétition de l'accent), et le fragment *c* de cinq croches (désinence).

La troisième, AIII, est une variation et une condensation de A; elle se compose de quatre fragments dont la teneur mélodique est identique, la valeur de six croches divisées inégalement en deux fois trois, trois fois deux, trois fois deux, deux fois trois, c'est donc une cellule symétrique.

La quatrième, AIV, est formée de deux cellules égales, toujours de six croches, divisées en deux fois trois.

La cinquième, AV, est aussi formée de deux cellules égales de six croches, divisées en trois fois deux.

AIV et AV ne sont que la séparation par rythme semblable de AIII. A partir de AIII, la physionomie du groupe A est donc immobile.

99

90

Exemple VIII.

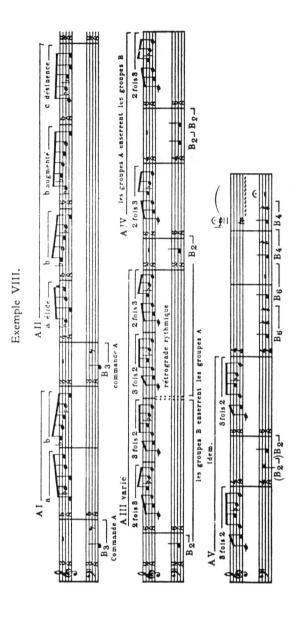

Comment s'organise le développement, l'une par rapport à l'autre, de ces deux structures? Remarquons qu'elles sont imbriquées l'une dans l'autre mais par juxtaposition. C'est-à-dire que leurs périodes dépendent réciproquement l'une de l'autre.

Tout d'abord les rythmes B3 commandent les périodes AI et AII. Puis les groupes B2 enserrent le groupe AIII, formant ainsi une symétrie. Le groupe AIV enserre deux groupes B2, le groupe AV enserre de la même façon deux groupes B2, formant également deux autres symétries. Ce groupe central est donc entièrement de structure symétrique. Enfin le groupe A est éliminé, il ne reste plus que le groupe B.

Nous constatons donc que dans la

première partie : le groupe A est mobile, B immobile et que la disposition est asymétrique;

deuxième partie : les groupes A et B sont immobiles et symétriques;

troisième partie : le groupe B est mobile.


Il y a donc chassé-croisé de la mobilité d'un rythme à son immobilité dans les deux groupes, chacun suivant la démarche inverse de l'autre.

Passons à l'étude de la superposition d'un rythme se développant et d'une structure rythmique fixe. C'est le cas qui se produit au chiffre 86 de la partition (ex. IX).

Nous avons deux éléments constructifs dans cette structure : un groupe broderie conjoint sur la dominante *si♭*; un groupe contrepointant cette broderie conjointe, formant broderie également, disjointe cette fois-ci, et oscillant dans le sens dominante — tonique — dominante. Dans la cellule A, nous trouvons ces deux éléments avec l'appui d'un rythme non rétrogradable pour la broderie conjointe se produisant tantôt sur le demi-ton, tantôt sur un ton; rythme non rétrogradable, c'est-à-dire symétrique par rapport à son centre

pour AI : ♩· ♩ ♩ ♩·     ou pour AII : ♩· ♩ ♩ ♩ ♩·

101

Exemple IX.

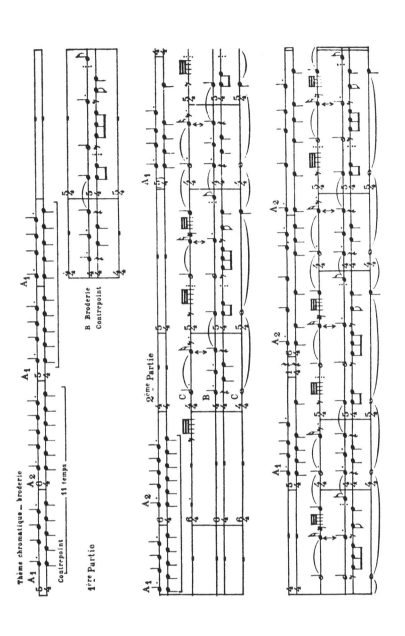

avec l'appui d'un déroulement régulier de noires pour la broderie disjointe qui ne descend du *si♭* que jusqu'à ce qu'on pourrait appeler le deuxième degré sensible (*fa♭*) du mode employé dans tout ce passage. Cette superposition donnée aura son propre développement rythmique.

Dans la cellule B, nous avons l'élément broderie conjointe de *si♭* qui devient une broderie — toujours à distance d'un ton entier — de l'accord de dominante appogiaturé placé sur *si♭*. Le rythme en est ordonné par une disposition symétrique des valeurs autour d'une noire liée à une autre noire,

valeurs impaires d'un côté (3 et 3), valeurs paires de l'autre (4 et 4). Cet ordre de valeurs est déplacé par des accents en un parallélisme symétrique.

En effet, la dernière blanche d'une cellule perd une croche par anticipation de la cellule suivante, croche qui se joint donc à la première noire pointée de cette deuxième cellule. Le groupe broderie disjointe en contrepoint a un aspect rythmique différent de la broderie conjointe, déjà par le fait qu'au lieu de se répartir en 4 + 5 noires, il va utiliser la division contraire 5 + 4, division rendue apparente par la répétition des silences :

On voit que ces silences sont au nombre de deux dans chaque mesure, les deux seconds étant diminués de moitié par rapport aux deux premiers. Dans cette broderie disjointe, enfin, l'oscillation va toujours jusqu'à la tonique, qu'évitait la cellule A, nous l'avons vu. Cette cellule B organise donc les mêmes éléments que A, mais elle restera en pédale rythmique.

Enfin, l'antinomie broderie note réelle, que nous avons vu s'établir sous différentes formes dans les deux cellules A et B, mais toujours sous forme oscillante, va s'établir sous une forme immobile avec deux accords, l'accord réel en tenue ininterrompue chaque fois que cette identique broderie est attaquée dans la cellule B. Toutefois, cet accord-broderie en tenues interrompues participe par ses accentuations à la broderie disjointe. Il continue ainsi les deux divisions rythmiques de la cellule B.

Nous avons ainsi, à l'intérieur d'une vaste broderie de la dominante *si♭*, et donc d'une immense disposition statique, la hiérarchie suivante :

Groupe A : Rythmiquement mobile    : Oscillation de la note réelle à la broderie ;

Groupe B : Rythmiquement immobile : Oscillation de l'accord ou de la note réelle à l'accord broderie ou à la broderie ;

Groupe C : Rythmiquement immobile : Fixité dans la superposition de l'accord réel et de l'accord broderie.

Nous allons voir maintenant comment ces groupes réagissent les uns sur les autres par leurs caractéristiques rythmiques. On peut distinguer deux parties de développement dans le fragment que nous étudions, la première étant à prépondérance rythmique du groupe A, la deuxième établissant la suprématie des groupes B et C.

Dans la première partie, le groupe A se module rythmiquement de la façon suivante :

| 11 temps | 10 temps | 5 temps | 11 temps |
|---|---|---|---|
| A1 A2 | A1 A1 | Silence égal à A1 | A1 A2 |

On retrouve là encore le grand souci de Stravinsky d'établir des interférences à l'intérieur des symétries de disposition. Point n'est besoin de les expliquer, tellement, de par leur définition numérique et musicale (son, silence), elles sont évidentes.

Le groupe B est embryonnaire et n'a pas encore pris sa physionomie réelle, il est exposé une seule fois en préfiguration et se place de façon à se terminer en même temps que le silence du groupe A, dont la durée égale A1, pour laisser la réexposition A1 A2 à découvert. Les quatre premiers temps de son exposition coïncident donc avec les quatre derniers du groupe A1, les quatre derniers se déroulant à découvert. Enfin le groupe C est absent.

Dans la deuxième partie, le groupe B est exposé une fois à découvert, puis se renouvelle trois fois en superposition avec A. Le groupe C est cette fois-ci exposé et se poursuit parallèlement au groupe B. Quant au groupe A, il fait une première apparition (A1) sur le début du deuxième groupe B. Le troisième groupe B commande une seconde apparition de A1. L'intervalle de silence entre ces deux A1 est donc de quatre noires, silence dont la durée est commandée par le groupe B, à l'inverse de ce qui se produisait dans la première partie. A partir de ce moment, les deux groupes se superposent en apparente indépendance. En réalité, il reste treize temps à remplir si l'on veut coïncider avec la fin d'un autre groupe B. Les solutions se présentent donc de la façon suivante : comment trouver une équivalence aux deux groupes A1 (dix temps — son) et à un silence de quatre noires, avec une durée globale de treize noires. Stravinsky a choisi la solution la plus équilibrée dans le sens contraire avec deux groupes A2 (douze temps — son) et un silence d'une noire. De plus, il a choisi de placer les silences de façon dissymétrique, le silence inclus entre les deux groupes A1 se trouvant inclus sous sa nouvelle forme entre les deux groupes A1 et les deux groupes A2. Il en résulte la juxtaposition des deux A2, et dans cette seconde partie, l'ordre décroissant des silences du groupe A (neuf, quatre, un, zéro).

Il est évident que nous n'avons pas voulu faire là une analyse du processus créateur tel qu'il s'est produit réellement; nous avons simplement tenté une analyse *a posteriori* des faits musicaux procédant de la création.

Pour compléter l'analyse de ce passage et y ajouter un élément de curiosité (parfois de coïncidence, peut-être) nous pouvons regarder d'assez près comment apparaît le thème de la broderie conjointe un peu avant d'avoir sa propre structure. Au chiffre 83 de la partition, nous le voyons se dérouler à la basse où il prend donc une valeur exceptionnelle en tant que soutien harmonique :

Exemple IX bis.

Il est, du reste, mis en relief par la particularité suivante : l'aigu se compose d'accords de quatre sons se déroulant régulièrement en croches. La disposition sonore est donc serrée dans l'aigu et le haut-médium, avec valeurs courtes, espacée dans le grave avec valeurs longues. La double broderie (à distance de un demi-ton, puis à distance de ton) est alors présentée sous la forme contrapunctique renversée de la figure qu'elle présentera dans son développement et autour de la note *la*, un demi-ton au-dessous du futur *si♭*. Elle se produit dans l'ordre rythmique :

d'où symétrie des valeurs impaires par rapport aux valeurs paires, symétrie que nous retrouvons plus loin sous la forme

ou encore sous la forme

Je ne pense pas qu'il y ait là simplement coïncidence, mais bien une volonté d'opposer les valeurs paires aux valeurs impaires, ou, si l'on veut parler de façon plus « solfège », les valeurs normales aux valeurs pointées.

Le mouvement des croches (valeurs courtes) passe ensuite dans le grave et le bas-médium pour précéder la seconde préfiguration de la cellule A1 qui se présente cette fois sous sa forme réelle : hauteur, durée et timbre. De nouveau, une coupure où le mou-

97

vement des croches occupe tout le registre du grave à l'aigu avec retour au grave. Cette dernière interruption dure onze temps, c'est-à-dire l'exacte durée des deux cellules A1 et A2 conjuguées dans la première présentation complète du groupe A. Il n'y a peut-être ici qu'un hasard, félicitons-nous qu'il soit aussi heureux. Car il conviendrait de faire remarquer, à mesure que nous avançons dans cette étude, que les rapports arithmétiques, somme toute fort simples, dont nous découvrons l'existence plus ou moins consciente, nous ne voulons pas les faire remarquer en tant que seuls rapports arithmétiques, ce serait d'une politique à courte vue ; mais comme la manière la plus préhensible d'apercevoir l'équilibre des structures mises à jour. Cette mise au point réalisée, nous entreprendrons d'aller à la recherche de structures plus complexes, et surtout d'apercevoir de quelles façons elles peuvent régir l'architecture d'un ensemble musical.

*<br>**

Nous allons procéder ainsi : nous nous attacherons tour à tour, par ordre de complexité croissante, à la *Glorification de l'Élue*, la *Danse de la Terre*, la *Danse sacrale*, enfin à l'*Introduction*, pièce la plus extraordinaire de toute cette œuvre, défiant toute analyse par les interférences multipliées avec lesquelles joue son développement.

La forme de la *Glorification de l'Élue* pourrait être sommairement qualifiée de forme ternaire : une exposition, un milieu, une réexposition, ce que, dans le jargon de composition, on appelle la forme lied. C'est en effet une forme ternaire où les différenciations sont cependant d'un ordre tout autre que dans son habituel emploi. Voici pourquoi :

La première partie utilise la combinaison presque contrapunctique de trois cellules rythmiques mobiles. Je dis : presque contrapunctique, car elles ne font que mordre l'une sur l'autre, et il n'y a pas, à proprement parler, de superposition contrapunctique. Toutefois, cette architecture rythmique a lieu sur des plans horizontaux, en dépit des aspects verticaux qu'elle peut prendre à l'audition.

La deuxième partie est basée sur le cloisonnement vertical et antagoniste de deux répartitions (sonore et rythmique) avec prépondérance de l'une ou de l'autre dans la durée. J'insiste sur l'idée de juxtaposition et de cloisonnement *vertical* qui sont donc la caractéristique essentielle de l'opposition entre la première et la deuxième partie, les cellules étant également mobiles dans les deux cas.

Dans la troisième partie, enfin, on utilise seulement une cellule rythmique, la première des deux autres étant supprimée, la deuxième servant d'introduction et n'étant plus reprise. La divergence : horizontal-vertical, est donc abolie.

Ce qui établit le schéma d'organisation rythmique : horizontal, contrepointé, trois cellules; vertical, juxtaposé, deux cellules; horizontal-vertical, une cellule. Le phénomène du rythme impose donc une architecture à cette *Glorification de l'Élue* autant et plus que la disposition sonore qui, malgré des répartitions diverses, reste statique dans tous les cas.

Il me reste à justifier ces conclusions par l'analyse du texte musical lui-même.

La première partie se compose de trois organisations sonores-rythmiques que nous appellerons *a, b, c* (ex. X).

La cellule *a* ou *a'* est fixe et comporte en principe cinq croches, la croche étant sa valeur unitaire, la différenciant ainsi de *b* et de *c* qui ont pour valeur unitaire la noire. Cette cellule *a*, nous l'appellerons donc *a*5. La combinaison *aa'* est de sept croches. Elle peut être précédée d'une anacrouse *x* de durée variable, à base ternaire (6, 9) alors que *a* est impair. Nous trouverons également la cellule *a* en diminution sous une forme élidée, de forme *a*2. Néanmoins, sous cette forme, elle ne joue aucun rôle constructif à proprement parler, car elle est toujours l'aboutissement du groupe *b*.

Le groupe *b* est composé : 1. d'une montée chromatique sur un accord avec vitesse croissante par l'utilisation alternée des groupes irrationnels et des groupes rationnels (triolet de croches, quatre doubles croches, quintolet puis sextolet de doubles croches, enfin triples croches) aboutissant sur la valeur unitaire avec attaque brève (double croche, demi-soupir pointé); 2. d'une montée par intervalles disjoints (les deux appuis se trouvant sur deux sauts de septième majeure) en valeurs irrationnelles répétées (triolets de croches). Le groupe *b* original se compose de cinq noires, nous l'appellerons *b*5. Le groupe se transforme par élision en *b*4,

100

Exemple X.

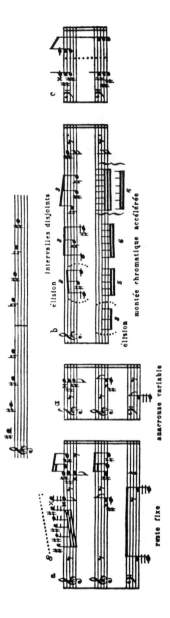

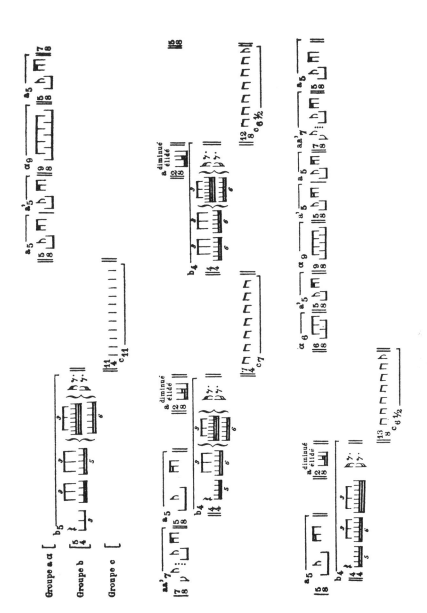

101

chacun de ces groupes $b_4$ différant par l'élision dissemblable de ses composantes.

Le groupe $c$ se constitue d'un accord répété. Cet accord peut être plaqué ou divisé en deux frappés (deux croches), mais toujours de valeur unitaire : la noire. Ce groupe est en constante diminution, il vaut d'abord onze noires ($c_{11}$) en accords plaqués, puis sept noires en accords divisés ($c_7$), enfin par élision six noires et une croche ($c6\frac{1}{2}$).

Du point de vue dynamique sonore, on peut constater que le groupe $a\alpha$ est à la fois statique (anacrouses répétées $\alpha$) et dynamique (accent désinence, $a$); que le groupe $b$ est purement dynamique, montée chromatique et disjointe sur un accent; quant au groupe $c$, il est uniquement statique. Pour établir l'équilibre de ces différentes caractéristiques, nous avons vu que, pratiquement, l'on ne peut dissocier les groupes $b$ et $c$ et qu'ils forment un bloc antagoniste de $a$, le statique $a$ étant toujours immédiatement enchaîné au dynamique $b$.

Cette première partie comporte en somme trois étapes dans son développement. La première consiste à exposer $bca$ les uns à la suite des autres. La composition étant : $b_5 \mid c_{11} \mid a_5\ a'_5\ \alpha_9\ a_5\ aa'_7\ a_5$.

Ce dernier $a_5$ donne sur sa deuxième croche le départ de la seconde étape qui donnera la prédominance aux groupes $b$ et $c$; on a en effet : $b_4\ c_7$ enchaînant sur $b_4\ c6\frac{1}{2}$, puis de nouveau, comme une répétition élidée, $a_5$ lié à $b_4\ c6\frac{1}{2}$. Il y a donc alternance constructive dans le contrepoint de ces structures rythmiques entre le groupe $a$, d'une part, les groupes $b$ et $c$ d'autre part. Enfin n'oublions pas l'élision de $a$ diminuée ($a_2$) qui vient se placer à la fin de chaque groupe $b$.

Alors que la deuxième étape s'enchaîne à la première, la troisième vient par juxtaposition et consiste en le seul développement du groupe $a$ qui se fait de la façon suivante : $\alpha_6\ a'_5\ \alpha_9\ a'_5\ \underline{a_5\ aa'_7}$

$a_5$. On voit que, par rapport au groupe de la première étape, il ne présente que d'infimes modifications qui sont le transfert d'une valeur $a_5$ du début au milieu de l'ensemble et par un groupe d'anacrouse $\alpha_6$, inemployé jusque-là; enfin, les groupes d'anacrouse $\alpha_6$ et $\alpha_9$ sont tous les deux des groupes appogiaturés.

Plus n'est besoin, je pense, de faire remarquer encore une fois ces symétries dans l'asymétrie ou ces asymétries dans la symétrie qui, dans la construction rythmique du *Sacre,* sont un des phénomènes essentiels. Aussi bien passerons-nous à la deuxième partie de la *Glorification de l'Élue,* qui commence au chiffre 111 de la partition et marque, avons-nous dit, le cloisonnement alternatif de deux structures verticales. Ces deux structures en présence, appelons-les A et B.

Exemple XI.

Elles ont en commun une pédale brodée de *fa♮,* à distance de demi-ton de part et d'autre de ce *fa♮* (*sol♭, mi♮*), avec la différence toutefois — du moins au début de A — que cette double broderie se fait en sens contraire (*fa mi sol♭* pour A, *fa sol♭ mi* pour B) et qu'il y a un certain renversement dans la figure résultant des intervalles employés soit en septième majeure, soit en demi-ton. Ce que l'on peut appeler leur composante mélodique est, en revanche, dirigée, *grosso modo,* en sens contraire : descendant, *si♭ la♭ sol♭* pour A (le *do* étant soit broderie, soit échappée, on me permettra de ne point l'inscrire comme note réelle); montant *si♭ do ré♭* pour B. Cette double symétrie des groupes autour de *fa* dominante et de *si♭* tonique installe donc le ton de *si♭* mineur, la première et la troisième partie s'appuyant principalement sur une sous-dominante altérée de *do♯* mineur.

La structure A se décompose en une anacrouse fixe de trois croches — qui n'apparaîtra que trois fois — n'utilisant pour ses divisions de la valeur unitaire que des valeurs irrationnelles (triolet de croches, sextolet et septolet de doubles croches), et en un groupe mobile de valeur unitaire la noire, dont l'essentiel du rythme est fourni par des triolets. La pédale de *fa* est exprimée

113

en noires. La structure B se compose d'accords en accentuation sur la partie faible des temps (appelons-les contretemps rationnels, alors que nous appellerions les contretemps de A irrationnels), elle a également pour valeur unitaire la noire. La pédale de *fa* est exprimée en croches.

Cette deuxième partie de la *Glorification de l'Élue* se décompose, à l'égal de la première, en trois phases :

Première phase : le groupe A s'exprime seul avec une préfiguration de B ; il est en constante augmentation. Si nous donnons à A comme indice le nombre de valeurs unitaires qu'il comporte, sans tenir compte de l'anacrouse fixe dont nous avons parlé, nous obtenons le schéma suivant :

$$\underbrace{A_3 \; A_4 \; A_6}_{\substack{\text{avec} \\ \text{anacrouse}}} \; | \; B_5 \; | \; \underbrace{A_9}_{\substack{\text{sans} \\ \text{anacrouse}}}$$

Cette phrase se termine par l'élision de A à caractère cadentiel suspensif : $A_2$. Remarquons de plus que c'est très logiquement l'intrusion du groupe B qui fait supprimer l'anacrouse de A.

Deuxième phase : le groupe B s'exprime seul par une oscillation constante de valeur sur une pédale rythmique fixe. Ce qui nous donne $B_5 \; B_6 \; B_5 \; B_6 \; B_5$.

Troisième phase : les groupes A et B vont s'alterner par cloisonnement, le groupe A ayant toujours le caractère cadentiel suspensif. Nous obtenons quant à l'analyse de cette phase : $B_5 \; | \; A_3 \; | \; B_6 \; | \; A_2 \; | \; B_3 \; | \; A_4$ ; enfin une cadence agrandie termine toute cette seconde partie. Le seul élément de jonction dans ce cloisonnement est la continuité de la pédale rythmique de quatre croches sur broderie de *fa* pendant l'alternance des deux groupes. Nous ferons remarquer enfin que le groupe B augmente puis diminue ($5 \nearrow 6 \searrow 3$) alors que le groupe A observe la démarche contraire ($3 \searrow 2 \nearrow 4$).

La troisième partie revient à la première partie, harmoniquement et rythmiquement. Nous avons déjà dit qu'elle introduisait la suppression totale de *c* et la suppression de *b* qui ne figure qu'à titre de transition entre la deuxième et la troisième partie. Il reste donc seulement le schéma de *a* en une seule construction à double versant puisque la reprise est textuelle : $a_5 \; a'_5 \; \alpha_9 \; a_5 \; aa'_7 \; a_5 \; | \; \alpha_6 \; a'_5 \; \alpha_9 \; a'_5 \; a'_5 \; aa'_7 \; a'_5$. Les particularités de ce schéma ont déjà été étudiées.

Je pense que nous avons démontré par cet exemple que la
« forme » était constituée au moins autant par des caractères
structurels rythmiques d'une assez grande complexité, que par
des relations harmoniques, fort simples.

La *Danse de la Terre* est infiniment plus complexe, sinon dans
l'architecture globale, du moins dans les structures rythmiques
périodiques. Certaines structures, nous aurons l'occasion de le
constater, font penser, avec leurs semi-fixités et leurs alternances
rapides, aux structures rythmiques des batteries d'Afrique noire.
Dans cet ordre d'idées, je crois même que la *Danse de la Terre* est
une des pièces les plus remarquables de toute la partition.

Harmoniquement elle s'établit — comme à peu près toujours
chez Stravinsky — sur une distribution par gros plans ; ici, autour
d'une tonique : *do*.

Premier plan, continu : gamme par tons entiers partant de la
quarte augmentée pour finir à la tierce ;
Deuxième plan, interrompu : accord parfait de *do* majeur avec
adjonction de l'appogiature *fa♯*, également sa
broderie à distance de ton : l'accord parfait de *ré*
majeur ;
Troisième plan, continu : accord de quartes dont la polarité
attractive est *do* (*mi♭ si♭ fa do*), cette polarité se
révélant au fur et à mesure du développement.

L'architecture de cette pièce est binaire, et voici sur quelles
oppositions elle joue. La première partie repose sur une pédale
rythmique fixe, elle n'utilise aucune superposition de structure —
si ce n'est une préfiguration sporadique de la cellule rythmique
principale de la deuxième partie — mais des éléments développés
par cloisonnement avec interdépendance des composantes. Dans
la seconde partie, la pédale grave rythmique est agrandie et acquiert
ses propres fluctuations périodiques ; la cellule rythmique, en
préfiguration dans la première partie, organise deux structures
parallèles, totalement indépendantes entre elles et indépendantes
également de la pédale rythmique transformée ; à la fin se superpose,

105

en rappel, l'idée directrice de la première partie. On saisit immédiatement les rapports qui s'établissent : la fixité devient mobile, les structures verticales interdépendantes deviennent des structures horizontales indépendantes ; même intrusion de part et d'autre de l'élément opposé à celui qui organise leur composition. La seule caractéristique commune aux deux parties — rythmiquement, j'entends bien — est la même « polydivision » de l'unité (en croches, doubles croches, et triolet de croches).

La première partie est constituée par la pédale fixe que nous appellerons P3 ; elle s'exprime donc dans une mesure ternaire qui donnera son apparence à toute la pièce, les rythmes réels étant autres, comme nous allons le voir immédiatement.

106

Exemple XII.

Sur cette pédale rythmique se développent, par cloisonnement, trois éléments que nous avons différenciés ; l'élément A, qui est l'accord parfait de *do* majeur avec l'appogiature *fa♯* ; l'élément B, qui est un arpège en septolet et sextolet de doubles croches, précédé ou suivi de silences — où, en s'éliminant, ne peuvent rester que les silences ; l'élément A', qui est la broderie de l'accord d'*ut* sous la forme d'un accord de quarte sensible, lui-même brodé. D'une façon globale, le plan de cette première partie s'établit ainsi : préparation, qui comprend l'élément B ; premier schéma A ; premier schéma A' et B ; deuxième schéma A ; deuxième schéma A' et B ; troisième schéma A.

Occupons-nous d'abord des schémas A. Ils sont construits sur un rythme de 2/4 qui contraste donc avec la pédale rythmique (3/4).

Le premier schéma A est ainsi composé :

les valeurs sont comptées en croches et ne tiennent pas compte de la durée plus ou moins brève de l'attaque; le premier schéma se produit sous la forme :

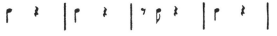

Le deuxième schéma A :

Enfin le troisième schéma A :

↑ Appogiature rythmique

Il est indispensable de faire quelques remarques au sujet de ces schémas. Le premier a la valeur 4 comme valeur de début et comme valeur de conclusion; ces deux valeurs 4 sont donc symétriques par rapport à la dissymétrie centrale 5 3. Le deuxième schéma est l'ordre rétrograde du premier avec la suppression de la dernière valeur 4 de conclusion. Le troisième schéma est la réunion des deux premiers, avec une appogiature rythmique de 2 sur la valeur de 4 initiale, et l'adjonction de cette cellule appogiaturée dans son ordre rétrograde, ce qui donne la symétrie semblable à celle que nous avons observée dans le premier schéma. (Remarquons que le premier schéma étant en sens droit, le deuxième étant rétrograde, le troisième est la réunion neutre des deux; car on peut dire premier schéma droit puis deuxième schéma droit, ou bien deuxième schéma rétrograde; ceci étant une conséquence naturelle des rétrogradations.)

Les schémas A′ et B sont un peu plus complexes. Définissons les broderies A′ par le chiffre de leur valeur unitaire, dans l'ordre où elles se produisent pour la première fois (ex. XII).

Nous définissons en revanche globalement l'arpège B et son silence par l'addition des valeurs unitaires. On établit ainsi :

| le premier schéma | A′ | B | A′ | B | A′ | B | A′ | B |
|---|---|---|---|---|---|---|---|---|
| | 1 2 3 4 5 | 2 | 1 | 2 | 2 3 | 1 | 1 | 1 |
| | | arpège et silence | | arpège et silence | | silence | | silence |

| le second schéma | A′ | B | A′ | B | A′ | B | A′ | B |
|---|---|---|---|---|---|---|---|---|
| | 1 2 3 | 1 | 2 4 (= 4 5 | 1 | 2 4 | 4 | 2 4 | 3 |
| | | silence | rythmiquement) | silence | | arpège et silence | | arpège et silence |

Il est facile de voir par quelles propriétés ces deux schémas sont tirés l'un de l'autre. Les groupes A′ ont une même valeur globale et s'éliminent de façon contraire dans le premier et le second schéma. Dans le premier, on a l'exposition 1 2 3 4 5, puis les deux éliminations : 1 2 3, 1 ; ce sont donc les dernières broderies qui sont éliminées, en deux fois deux.

Dans le second schéma, on a une exposition variée : 1 2 3 2 4 (où, rythmiquement, ce dernier 2 4 équivaut à 4 5 du premier schéma) ; puis les deux éliminations 2 4, 2 4. Ce sont donc les trois premiers groupes qui sont éliminés, en une seule fois trois.

Les groupes B, que l'on appellera groupes d'interruption, se suivent d'abord dans l'ordre : B2 B2, B1 B1, puis dans l'ordre : B1 B1, B4 B3. Cet ordre est donc asymétrique par rapport aux valeurs B1 égales, les valeurs B4 et B3 étant irrégulières par rapport à B2 B2. (Cette irrégularité vient simplement de la pédale rythmique P3 qui impose sa période à A′ et B.) De plus, ces interruptions B se produisent de façon dissemblable dans le premier et le second schéma ; on s'en rend compte aisément dans les schémas tels que je les ai donnés, par l'adjonction de doubles barres et de flèches, qui facilitent la compréhension des groupes. Il en résulte des décalages structurels extrêmement simples mais extrêmement efficaces; nous nous sommes longuement attardé sur d'autres cas semblables pour qu'il ne soit maintenant plus besoin d'y revenir.

Il conviendrait néanmoins de faire encore une remarque sur l'emplacement de ces deux schémas l'un par rapport à l'autre, et sur la réalisation de leur équilibre. Le premier et le second schéma A équivalent en valeur architecturale au troisième schéma A, et ils équivalent en durée au premier schéma A' B (premier schéma A : trois mesures, deuxième schéma A : deux mesures; premier schéma A'B : cinq mesures). Le premier schéma A'B équivaut en valeur architecturale au deuxième schéma A'B, ce dernier équivalant en durée au troisième schéma A (six mesures dans les deux cas).

Ainsi les valeurs architecturales de ces groupes et les durées s'équilibrent dans des tensions contraires d'égale force, avec des dispositions dissymétriquement variées qui font de ce début de la *Danse de la Terre* un modèle exceptionnel que nous retiendrons sous la forme :

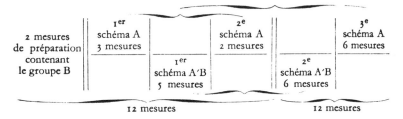

Sur la dernière valeur du deuxième schéma A se greffe un élément en triolets qui va être prépondérant dans la deuxième partie, que nous appellerons élément *b*; nous lui donnerons son contexte dans l'étude de cette deuxième partie. Définissons-le maintenant comme un saut de quarte descendante suivie de la répétition de la note d'arrivée; il utilise la division en triolets de croches; appliquons-lui comme coefficient le nombre de valeurs unitaires, c'est-à-dire de noires, qu'il emploie (ex. XIII).

Nous obtenons comme fréquence d'apparition de cette cellule : *b*2; silence de 12; *b*2; silence de 7; *b*1; *silence de* 1; *b*2, *b*1; silence de 6; *b*1 *b*1; *silence de* 1; *b*1; silence de 1. Les groupes *b* augmentent tandis que les silences intermédiaires diminuent. Sauf cette progres-

sion, il n'y a pas de particularité remarquable dans cette préfiguration, si ce n'est la présence de *b1* au début de chaque groupe *b*,
présence que l'on pourra remarquer plus tard au début de chaque
période commandée par *b*; si ce n'est encore la symétrie des deux
derniers groupes *b* avec précipitation par élision dans le second.

Mais passons dès maintenant à l'étude des éléments qui compo-
sent la deuxième partie. La pédale de trois sons de la gamme par
tons sur *do* tonique, de fixe devient mobile, avons-nous dit. Elle
devient en effet un développement rythmique en trois grandes
périodes. Convenons que les trois sons *fa♯ sol♯ si♭*, nous les appelons P3; que les six sons *fa♯ sol♯ si♭ do ré mi*, nous les appelons Π6
(ex. XIII); nous avons donc une première période composée de
trois combinaisons différentes : P3 P3 Π6, Π6 Π6, P3 Π6. La
deuxième période est la répétition de la première avec permutation
de ses deux dernières combinaisons, à savoir : P3 P3 Π6, P3 Π6,
Π6 Π6. La troisième période, enfin, est la répétition de ces deux
mêmes combinaisons; P3 Π6, P3 Π6, Π6 Π6, Π6, Π6. Le
développement de cette basse est, comme on le voit, très facile à
saisir, et, d'une certaine façon, assez régulier.

Le deuxième élément, se greffant sur cette gamme par tons, est
cet intervalle de quarte avec répétition sur la note d'aboutissement
(*mi♭ si♭*) que nous avons déjà signalé, il varie de *b1* à *b3*; il est
accompagné de ce que l'on pourrait appeler une cellule-broderie *a*,
dont la valeur est immobile : *a2*. Il fait deux seules apparitions

sous la forme *a3* qui est son allongement par *b*. Puis, comme groupe cadentiel adjoint à *a* et *b*, il y a un groupe neutre *c* : les frappés de ses valeurs unitaires forment le rétrograde des frappés sur ses valeurs de division (notes sur lesquelles j'ai placé des flèches dans l'exemple), rétrograde qui est en parallélisme avec la gamme par tons. Ses périodes sont extrêmement complexes; vouloir essayer de les analyser peut paraître soit une tentative arbitraire, soit même un contresens.

Je distinguerai cependant quatre ordres de groupes :

1. Un groupe cadentiel fixe : *c*;

2. Un groupe de broderie semi-cadentielle fixe : *a2 b1, b1 a2*;

3. Des groupes de broderie variable sans tendance cadentielle, mais à caractère d'accentuation : *a3 b3, a2 b2, a2 b2 a2, a2 a2 b2*, provenant de la jonction d'éléments *a* et *b* d'une même durée;

4. Enfin des groupes variables de répétition, plus exactement de prolongation ou d'attente rythmiques : ce sont les répétitions de *b, b1, b2, b3*.

Étant donné cette classification, que je crois justifiable, nous obtenons pour les périodes *a-b-c* le nombre de 5.

I :      *b1 b3 b2*         *a3 b3*       *a2 b1, a2 b1*
       (4ᵉ ordre)    (3ᵉ ordre)    (2ᵉ ordre)

II :    *b1*     *b3 a3, a2 b2 a2*    *b3 b1 b2*
     (4ᵉ ordre)    (3ᵉ ordre)     (4ᵉ ordre)
    *b2 a2*   *(a2) b1, a2 b1, b1 a2*    *c*
    (3ᵉ ordre)    (2ᵉ ordre)    (1ᵉʳ ordre)

III :   *b1 b3*     *a2 b2 a2*     *b1 a2*      *c*
     (4ᵉ ordre)    (3ᵉ ordre)    (2ᵉ ordre)    (1ᵉʳ ordre)

IV :   *b1 b2*     *b2 a2*     *b1 b2*     *b1 a2*     *c*
     (4ᵉ ordre)    (3ᵉ ordre)    (4ᵉ ordre)    (2ᵉ ordre)    (1ᵉʳ ordre)

V :    *b1 a2*     *b1 b2*     *b1 a2*    *(a2) b2*
     (2ᵉ ordre)    (4ᵉ ordre)    (2ᵉ ordre)    (3ᵉ ordre)
    *b1 b2, b2 b1*     *c*
    (4ᵉ ordre)    (1ᵉʳ ordre)

On s'aperçoit ainsi que les quatre premières périodes observent la même loi qui est de tendre vers la cadence à partir d'une répétition variable (I : 4$^e$; 3$^e$, 2$^e$; II : 4$^e$, 3$^e$; 4$^e$, 3$^e$, 2$^e$, 1$^{er}$; III : 4$^e$, 3$^e$, 2$^e$, 1$^{er}$; IV : 4$^e$, 3$^e$; 4$^e$, 2$^e$, 1$^{er}$). La cinquième période est la seule où s'observe le processus contraire (V : 2$^e$, 4$^e$; 2$^e$, 3$^e$, 4$^e$; 1$^{er}$), c'est-à-dire qu'elle tend d'un ordre semi-cadentiel à un ordre d'attente rythmique pour rejeter isolément, avec d'autant plus de force, le groupe de cadence qui le termine et donne également la conclusion à toutes les autres périodes. On peut encore vérifier de quelle façon, suivant les périodes, varient les groupes d'un même ordre variable. Je me contenterai de signaler qu'ils procèdent tous deux par élimination de $a_3$ et de $b_3$, somme toute, qu'ils procèdent par cellules courtes, avec élimination des cellules plus longues, alors qu'on verra le troisième élément périodique procéder partiellement de façon contraire.

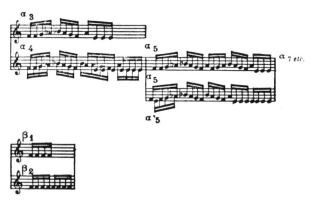

Exemple XIII *(suite)*.

Le troisième élément de la construction que nous analysons est un élément parallèle au deuxième en ce sens qu'il utilise des cellules α et β dont la fonction est la même que celle des précédentes *a* et *b*; α est une cellule-broderie, β est une cellule de notes répétées. Il n'y a pas, dans ce troisième élément, de groupe cadentiel neutre et fixe comparable à *c*. Notons de plus que la cellule α est, en général, plus longue que la cellule *a*, alors qu'au contraire la cellule $\beta$ est plus courte que la cellule $b$, ce qui dissout leur parallélisme. Le troisième élément se greffe sur la deuxième période du deuxième élément, exactement sur son premier groupe de troisième ordre, $b_3 \, a_3$, et revêt la forme similaire : $\beta_3 \, \alpha_3$, pour trouver, après, sa périodicité particulière.

La cellule $\beta$ a trois valeurs $\beta_1 \; \beta_2 \; \beta_3$ qui créeront une discrimination dans l'organisation des groupements $\beta\alpha$. Grâce à cette discrimination, on aperçoit trois périodes :

I : $\beta_3 \, \alpha_3$; $\beta_2 \, \alpha_4$; $\beta_1 \, \alpha_3 - \beta_1 \, \widetilde{\alpha_4 \, \alpha_3}$

II : $\beta_2 \, \alpha_4 \, \alpha_5$; $\beta_1 \, \alpha_5$; $\beta_3 \, \alpha_3 \, \alpha_3 - \beta_1 \, \widetilde{\alpha_7}$

III : $\beta_2 \, \alpha_3$; $\beta_1 \, \alpha_4 \, \alpha_3 \, \alpha'_3 \, \alpha'_7 \, \alpha'_5 \, \alpha_3$

On voit que les deux premières périodes déroulent trois groupes $\beta\alpha$ se différenciant par $\beta_3, \beta_2, \beta_1$, puis un groupe $\beta\alpha$ de conclusion se différenciant par $\beta_1$, ce dernier groupe étant le même dans les deux cas à une légère variante près ($\alpha_7$ au lieu de $\alpha_4 \, \alpha_3$). La troisième période élimine $\beta_3$, mais le groupe de conclusion commençant par $\beta_1$ est ici extrêmement agrandi et forme l'essentiel de cette dernière période. Remarquons donc que, pour sa conclusion, ce troisième élément emploie un procédé d'agrandissement, alors que le deuxième élément, dans sa cinquième période, on s'en souvient, renversait l'ordre hiérarchique au cours de son déroulement, ce qui isolait la conclusion.

Nous avons montré schématiquement dans l'exemple XIV comment se produisait la superposition de ces différentes structures périodiques, en respectant l'écriture de la partition, c'est-à-dire la division en mesures à trois temps. Nous indiquons de plus (ex. XV) comment s'effectuent les cadences lors du déroulement du groupe $c$.

Enfin, pour terminer l'analyse de la *Danse de la Terre*, il nous reste à voir de quelle façon les éléments de la première partie apparaissent à la fin de la deuxième partie et viennent se superposer dans une période conclusive, dérivée, par un procédé très simple, de leur première forme.

Exemple XIV.

114

Exemple XV.

Nous avons en effet, six mesures avant la fin, la reprise des groupes A et B qui nous ont été familiers dans la première partie (voir ex. XII).

Le groupe B est normal, se composant d'un arpège suivi d'un silence, chacun sur une valeur unitaire; il sert d'introduction aux groupes A, de même qu'il l'avait fait au début de la première partie. Suit le groupe A ainsi décomposable :

Ce dernier schéma de A est donc identique, en sa première phase, au premier schéma de la première partie, avec cette différence que les valeurs impaires y sont redoublées, la valeur paire, en revanche, ne prenant place qu'une seule fois. Sa seconde phase est la répétition variée du deuxième schéma de la première partie, les valeurs impaires étant interverties, la dernière valeur, paire, venant à contretemps.

Je pense que l'on a pu ainsi contrôler l'extrême complexité du développement de la *Danse de la Terre*, où pour la première fois, semble-t-il, furent réalisées, au point de vue rythmique, des oppositions de structure, jouant sur des indépendances horizontales et des interdépendances verticales, sur des organisations monorythmiques ou polyrythmiques du matériau sonore. Ces oppositions, on va les retrouver de façon encore plus caractérisée, tout au long de la *Danse sacrale*.

*<br>* *

On s'est toujours borné à dire de la *Danse sacrale* qu'elle était un Rondeau; on n'affirme, ce faisant, que la plus stricte mais la plus sommaire évidence. Peut-être serons-nous plus curieux et tâcherons-nous d'apercevoir les raisons de l'organisation en « Rondeau ». Elles ne se résument pas à de simples questions formelles — du formalisme le plus banal — mais mettent en jeu à peu près tous les schémas rythmiques que l'on a pu apercevoir ici et là dans *le Sacre*, se confrontant ici sous le patronage bien ambigu de cette forme Rondeau (qui, on le sait, avec la forme « Variation », est des plus lâches ou, si l'on veut, des moins rigoureuses). On distingue donc deux refrains, deux couplets et une coda sur le refrain.

Les refrains et la coda sont monorythmiques, c'est-à-dire qu'un seul rythme gouverne ce que l'on ne saurait appeler proprement une polyphonie, mais une verticalisation harmonique. Le premier couplet comporte deux schémas rythmiques, l'un extériorisé verticalement, l'autre horizontalement. Enfin le deuxième couplet est une superposition polyrythmique horizontale.

Le deuxième refrain est, du reste, une reprise textuelle du premier, à un demi-ton inférieur. Le schéma de ces deux refrains est extrêmement simple à établir. Il se compose de trois éléments (ex. XVI).

116

Exemple XVI.

Un élément A qui se constitue d'accords répétés servant de
préparation à l'élément B, formé de l'accent suivi de sa désinence.
Disons que les éléments A et B forment un groupe Γ. Un groupe C
vient, par changement d'accord, équilibrer le groupe Γ; groupe C
qui se compose d'une préparation suivie d'un accent puis se
transforme en préparation accent désinence avec une distribution
fixe de valeurs : doubles croches pour la préparation, croches pour
les accents, doubles croches pour la désinence (voir ex. XXII,
cette succession complète étant analysée dans sa transposition
de la coda). On peut distinguer deux périodes dans le développement de ce rythme (ex. XVII).

**127**

Exemple XVII.

$$
\text{I} \begin{cases}
1. - \underbrace{A_3\ A_5\ B_7}_{\Gamma_{15}}, \underbrace{A_5\ B_7\ A_3}_{\Gamma'_{15}}, \text{ ce qui donne :} \\[4pt]
2. - \underbrace{C_8, A_4\,B_7, C_5, A'_5\ A_4\,B_7\ A_3}_{} : C_8\ \Gamma_{11}\ C_5\ \Gamma_{19}
\end{cases}
$$

$$
\text{II}\ . - \underbrace{A_5\ B_4, A_2\ B_4, A_3\ A_5\ B_4, C_5, C_7}_{\Gamma_9\ \Gamma_6\ \Gamma_{12}\ C_5\ C_7} :
$$

On remarquera que, si A et C varient irrégulièrement, B ne comporte que deux valeurs fixes B7 et B4, la seconde venant comme élision de la première.

Dans la première période, on remarquera la disposition symétrique A3 | A5 B7 d'une part, A5 B7 | A3 d'autre part.

La deuxième période utilise A4, contraction de l'élément A5 apparu dans la première période; et une forme A'5, dérivée de C8.

La troisième période introduit B4, contraction de B7, ainsi que les variantes C5 et C7 : elles serviront plus tard au développement terminal.

Le premier couplet comporte le thème rythmique vertical que nous avons longuement analysé dans l'exemple VII, soutenant une construction thématique horizontale analysée dans l'exemple IV. Nous ne reviendrons donc pas sur ce développement.

Le deuxième couplet se développe en trois étagements qui ont leur période propre et se superposent par entrées successives. Ce deuxième couplet est sectionné en son milieu par un court rappel du refrain ainsi constitué : A3 A5 B7 A2 B4, soit Γ15 Γ6.

Il n'utilise donc pas le groupe C qui, nous le verrons, est l'élément essentiel de la coda.

La première partie ne met en jeu que deux superpositions (ex. XVIII), une pédale variée rythmiquement (P), et un groupe sujet-réponse (S-R) à intervalle de quinte comportant de légères différences chromatiques que voici. En S, les trois notes 1 2 3 sont à distance de ton *do si♭ la♭*. En R (transposé), la note 1 est baissée d'un demi-ton (*do♭*). En S' (transposé également), les notes 2 et 3 sont haussées d'un demi-ton *si♮ la♮*.

Exemple XVIII bis

120

Exemple XVIII.

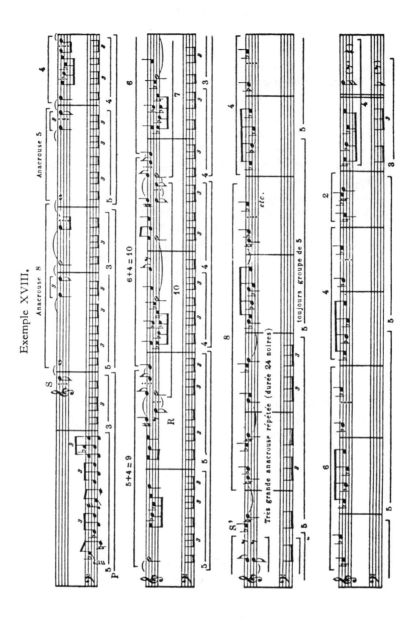

Mais commençons plus logiquement par l'étude rythmique de la pédale. La cellule qui lui donne naissance a une durée de cinq noires. Elle se base sur une alternance de croches, et de triolets de croches dans l'ordre : une fois deux croches, un triolet, une fois deux croches, deux triolets. On peut noter également dans cette cellule une espèce de *Klangfarbenmelodie*, quoique à un état très rudimentaire, incluant même les instruments de percussion comme tam-tam et grosse caisse. Cette cellule de cinq noires peut s'abréger à trois ou à quatre, par élision de sa dernière ou de ses deux dernières valeurs unitaires. Les éléments qui organisent le développement de cette pédale vont deux cellules par deux cellules et voici leur succession dans la première partie : 5 3 5 3 5 4 5 5 4 4 4 3 5 5 5 5 5 3.

Sur la dernière croche du premier élément 5 3, part le sujet S sur une anacrouse répétée deux fois, la première durant huit noires, la seconde cinq. Après cette anacrouse double, se déroule la tête du sujet (quatre noires), puis, par deux fois, le sujet entier (neuf noires et dix noires), enfin, de nouveau, la tête du sujet deux fois également : la première durant six noires, la seconde précédée d'une grande anacrouse de vingt-quatre noires et durant quatre noires. La réponse R se produit à la fin du premier sujet S exposé complet; il ne comporte du reste que la tête d'une réponse entière. Enfin, la variante du sujet S′, à distance d'un demi-ton supérieur, se place à la fin de la réponse, sous l'anacrouse simplifiée qui précède le dernier déroulement du sujet S proprement dit. Il s'élimine irrégulièrement en des périodes dont la durée, en noires, est : 8, 4, 6, 4, 2.

Dans la deuxième partie (ex. XIX), à ces mêmes éléments pédale et couple sujet-réponse, vient s'ajouter un élément harmonique H qui, rythmiquement, se rattache au couple sujet-réponse, lié d'abord au sujet varié S′ ensuite à la réponse R. Vers la fin de cette deuxième partie, la pédale se double d'une réponse P′ ayant sa propre période. Commençons par l'étude de cette pédale et de sa réponse. De la mobilité rythmique elle passe à une cellule fixe de cinq noires répétée neuf fois suivie par une cellule de trois noires. Sur la dernière noire de la sixième répétition, se greffe la réponse P′ de valeur quatre noires, tout d'abord répétée deux fois, puis superposée en canon (toujours de valeur 4, ce qui donne

122

Exemple XIX.

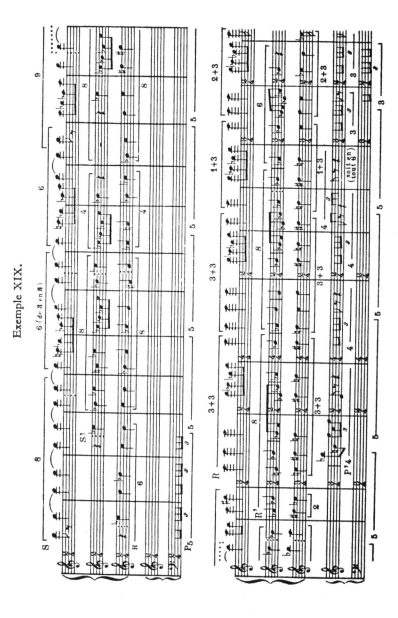

une valeur globale de 6 pour ces deux cellules P′), enfin deux cellules de trois noires. Le groupe S comporte tout d'abord une anacrouse de huit noires, puis deux fois la tête du sujet (six noires), enfin le sujet entier coupé en son milieu par une syncope (durée globale, neuf noires).

Le groupe S′ est d'une durée de huit noires, puis, par élimination des broderies initiales, décroît à la durée moitié : quatre noires, enfin revient à la durée huit noires, éliminant toujours les broderies initiales, mais les remplaçant par des silences équivalents.

Le couple sujet-réponse se développe ensuite en R et R′, R à la quarte supérieure de S, R′ à la quarte inférieure de S′, les périodes de R′ étant respectivement d'une durée de huit noires, huit noires, six noires; les périodes de R étant trois plus trois noires, trois plus plus trois noires, une plus trois noires, deux plus trois noires (la différence ne provient, on le voit, que des répétitions inégales de la note initiale).

Le groupe H, de soutien harmonique, suit, ainsi que je l'ai dit, les périodes de S′ — c'est-à-dire : huit noires, quatre noires, huit noires — précédées, avant l'entrée de S′ lui-même, d'un groupe de six noires. Entre la fin de S′ et le début de R, prend place un intervalle de deux noires définissant une période intermédiaire égale dans H, qui prend alors la périodicité de R (soit : $3 + 3$, $3 + 3$, $1 + 3$, $2 + 3$ noires). En fin de compte, on a les schémas :

$$\begin{cases} S : 8\ 6\ \overset{\frown}{6\ 9}, \\ R : 6\ 6\ \ 4\ \ 5 \end{cases} \qquad \text{6 et 9 ayant une note commune}$$

$$\begin{cases} S' : 8\ 4\ 8 \\ R' : 8\ 8\ 6 \end{cases}$$

$$P' : 4\ 4\ \overset{\frown}{44}\ 3\ 3$$
$$\overset{\smile}{6}$$

Je pense que l'on s'apercevra, sans que je les décrive une fois de plus, des effets d'équilibre dissymétrique organisant ces divers groupes.

133

Le deuxième couplet est suivi de la coda revenant à la monorythmie des refrains. Cette coda est en deux parties. La première est basée sur la prépondérance du groupe Γ (AB), avec deux apparitions du groupe C sous sa première forme, non cadentielle. La deuxième partie est construite sur le seul groupe C cadentiel, comportant des valeurs fixes, que nous avons décrit plus haut (voir ex. XXII). La première partie de la coda comporte le schéma suivant :

I — $A_5 B_4 \mid A_2 B_4$ ; $A_5 B_4 \; A_5 B_4 \mid A_2 B_4$ ; $A_5$

soit : $\Gamma_9 \mid \Gamma_6$ ; $2\,\Gamma_9 \mid \Gamma_6$ ; $\Gamma_5$ élidé ;

II — $A_5 B_4 \mid C_5$ ; $A_5 \mid C_5$

soit : $\Gamma_9 \mid C_5$ ; $\Gamma_5$ élidé $\mid C_5$.
Cette période s'agrandit à l'octave supérieure de la précédente ;

III — $A_5 B_4 \; A_5 B_4 \; A_5 B_4 \mid A_2 B_4$

soit : $3\,\Gamma_9 \mid \Gamma_6$.
Également, cette période s'agrandit à l'octave supérieure de la précédente.

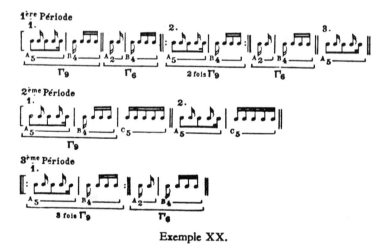

Exemple XX.

On remarquera la place des cellules $C_5$ isolées en plein milieu de cette première partie et préparant le développement de la deuxième partie. On remarquera, de plus, que ce développement est bâti uniquement sur l'alternance de groupes $\Gamma$ à valeur fixe, d'où la tendance cadentielle que va préciser C à l'intérieur de lui-même par la répartition fixe de ses valeurs.

La période I de cette deuxième partie (ex. XXI) est basée sur l'alternance des cellules C et C'; étant composée, par une dissociation, des seuls accords graves de C. On peut distinguer trois petites subdivisions dans cette période I :

1. Alternance de C et de C'. . . . . . . . . . . $C_5$ $C'_5$ $C6$
2. Unicité de C'. . . . . . . . . . . . . . . . . . . . . . $C'_5$ $C'_5$ $C'6$ $C'_5$ $C'8$
3. Alternance de C et de C'. . . . . . . . . . . $C_5$ $C'6$

Exemple XXI.

On observe donc la fixité des durées de cinq et six doubles croches et la seule apparition d'une valeur de huit doubles croches, à la fin de la deuxième subdivision, préfigurant la période II.

Exemple XXII.

Cette période II est consacrée à l'agrandissement rythmique de C, avec suppression de C'. Là encore distinguons trois subdivisions, suivant les valeurs des agrandissements.

1. — $C_5$ $C_6$ $C_7$ $C_8$ | $C_5$ $C_8$
   (C croît progressivement du minimum 5 au maximum 8, puis saute sans intermédiaire du minimum au maximum.)
2. — $C_{14}$ $C_{14}$
   (C se fixe sur une alternance 6 — 8.)
3. — qui comporte les quatre dernières mesures du *Sacre* : les valeurs fixes de C sont abolies; de plus, l'agrandissement n'a pas seulement lieu dans le rythme, mais dans la figure mélodique qui constitue le groupe C.

Signalons qu'avec le groupe $C_8$ était survenue l'indépendance rythmique de la basse, devenant un groupe de deux croches répétées, indépendance préfigurée également dans le tout premier $C'_8$.

Ainsi, cette coda tend d'abord vers la cadence, pour n'être ensuite qu'un grand groupe cadentiel. Je me permets d'insister sur le fait très important, à mon avis, de cette répartition fixe des valeurs à l'intérieur du groupe C, phénomène rythmique qui donne son aspect essentiel à la fin de cette coda : un mouvement apparent dialectiquement lié à une immobilité sous-entendue.

Il nous reste à parler de l'*Introduction,* au mécanisme le plus aisément démontable, mais pourtant le plus secret. Outre cette extraordinaire diversité rythmique dans la variation, outre cet emploi tout à fait exceptionnel des oppositions entre valeurs rationnelles et valeurs irrationnelles et l'imbrication étroite des valeurs longues et des valeurs très courtes (ce dernier procédé déjà familier à Debussy), outre cette perfection dans les structures rythmiques qui l'organisent, toutes choses dont nous avons déjà démontré l'importance au cours de cette étude, je crois que l'*Introduction* du *Sacre* montre un phénomène d'architecture des plus intéressants : une sorte de développement par recouvrement progressif qu'il est donc très difficile, pour ne pas dire impossible, d'analyser en une succession de plans plus ou moins contrastés comme tous les autres développements du *Sacre*. Mais je généralise déjà prématurément, car on ne peut pas ne pas s'apercevoir d'une telle préoccupation à la dimension de l'œuvre entière, et ce sont bien là, me semble-t-il, les raisons qui peuvent expliquer le souci constant de diverses liaisons thématiques, qui, pour ainsi dire, n'ont pas un rapport de structure interne avec le développement en cours. (Signalons un tel besoin chez Berg, par exemple dans la *Suite lyrique*, exprimé de façon certainement plus habile, du moins en général.)

Je n'ai pas pour but d'analyser ici cette *Introduction* en détail; il me faudrait citer alors tout le texte musical, et dans sa version orchestrale, tant la complexité est grande. Ce serait fausser absolument une telle entreprise que de la réaliser sommairement. Je me contenterai donc d'une description aussi précise que possible de l'architecture de cette *Introduction*.

Je crois que l'on peut, sans contestation, voir quatre phases dans ce développement.

*Première phase :* (du début de la partition jusqu'à la mesure venant après le chiffre 3) : une phase d'introduction où l'on peut repérer les deux éléments principaux organisateurs de la deuxième phase.

*Deuxième phase :* 1. Développement du premier motif conducteur une mesure après le chiffre 3, jusqu'au chiffre 4; 2. Développement du deuxième motif conducteur (chiffre 4 au chiffre 6); 3. Reprise du premier motif conducteur suivi d'une cadence selon le deuxième (chiffre 6 au chiffre 7); 4. Les deux motifs sont alternés (chiffre 7 au chiffre 8); 5. On perçoit principalement le deuxième motif conducteur, le premier étant transformé par changement de registres (chiffre 8 au chiffre 9).

*Troisième phase* : 1. Apparition d'un troisième motif conducteur (chiffre 9 au chiffre 10); 2. Superposition de ces motifs principaux et des motifs secondaires (chiffre 10 au chiffre 12).

*Quatrième phase* : Reprise de la première phase simplifiée, tous les motifs secondaires et principaux étant répétés, suivie d'une demi-cadence et d'une préparation de la pièce suivante (chiffre 12 au chiffre 13).

Si l'on veut se rendre compte des véritables caractéristiques de cette *Introduction*, on doit noter la façon dont s'enchaînent et se différencient toutes ces subdivisions. Nous avons montré dans l'exemple II comment la première phrase du basson donnait naissance au second motif conducteur — en triolets — et de quelle façon ce motif, détaché d'elle, régissait ses structures suivantes par la suppression de tout élément de triolet. Il faudrait généraliser ce point de vue et montrer comment un motif ou plusieurs motifs secondaires peuvent, une fois exposés, prendre leur période propre, se détacher du motif principal qui les a engendrés et former la liaison entre deux subdivisions d'une structure. Par exemple, la deuxième phase et la troisième phase ne sont pas simplement juxtaposées, mais les relie un motif qui étale son propre développement pendant la dernière subdivision de la deuxième phase et la première subdivision de la troisième phase; ce motif ne marquera aucune césure pendant le passage de la deuxième phase à la troisième (ex. XXIII). Il prenait naissance dans la troisième subdivision de la deuxième phase et servait en quelque sorte de contrepoint à ce que nous avons appelé le premier motif conducteur (chiffre 6 de la partition). Dans la quatrième subdivision, il se manifestait à l'octave grave (et passait de la flûte au basson — 4ᵉ, 6ᵉ et 7ᵉ mesures après le chiffre 7). Dans la cinquième subdivision, il prend une indépendance totale à l'égard du premier motif conducteur et prend une très grande importance vu ses nombreuses variations rythmiques, importance qu'il garde sous l'exposition du troisième motif conducteur (chiffre 8 puis chiffre 9 de la partition) et pendant toute cette exposition. Son rôle de transition entre la deuxième et la troisième phase étant accompli, ce motif ne paraît plus dans la deuxième subdivision de la troisième phase qui

Exemple XXIII.

est, comme nous l'avons dit, la superposition des trois motifs conducteurs. Remarquons que Stravinsky a signalé lui-même, dans sa partition, l'importance croissante du motif secondaire dont nous avons parlé quand il apparaît dans la deuxième phase. En effet, dans notre troisième subdivision, c'est le premier motif conducteur qui est mis en relief par : « en dehors » (chiffre 6 de la partition). Dans notre quatrième subdivision, lors du changement de registre et d'instrument, c'est le motif secondaire que l'on fait marquer par : « très en dehors ».

Je pense que ce seul exemple aura suffisamment montré les caractéristiques de l'architecture que nous étudions : c'est-à-dire que, sous une structure délimitée en plans précis par des motifs principaux, s'inscrivent des motifs secondaires qui assouplissent et estompent cette structure par un renouvellement constant et leurs façons diversement variées de se superposer aux motifs principaux. C'est ce double plan de développement, double tant par sa fonction que par ses modalités, que nous pouvons estimer comme un enseignement des plus profitables à retenir de cette *Introduction* du *Sacre ;* sans oublier l'individualité de l'instrumentation, manifestation de l'esprit qui anime cette architecture.

**139**

*<br>
* *

Ainsi pensons-nous avoir tenté un travail de mise à jour assez complet, du moins en ce qui concerne le rythme. J'ai noté, en passant, les caractéristiques harmoniques et mélodiques et l'on a pu se rendre compte que si certaines tendaient à un écartèlement du langage tonal, elles sont vraiment l'exception. La plupart des caractéristiques se rattachent, bien au contraire, à des attractions extrêmement fortes sur la tonique, la dominante ou la sous-dominante, ainsi que le prouvent, entre autres, la *Danse sacrale* et la *Danse de la Terre*. S'il y a des essais contrapunctiques, ils sont même franchement faibles, et nous nous reportons au deuxième couplet de cette même *Danse sacrale* (ex. XIX) où le couple sujet-réponse, à part l'anomalie chromatique que nous avons signalée, apparaît des plus sommaires. S'il y a des superpositions de motifs, ils se font de façon extrêmement rigide, chaque motif se déroulant obstinément sur les mêmes intervalles. En somme, il n'y a pas à proprement parler développement, mais répétition variée, non pas réaction chimique mais mélange physique; l'on nous permettra de voir dans cette différence une grande baisse de niveau.

Parlerai-je de la polytonalité que l'on a tant remarquée dans *le Sacre,* au point que l'on n'a plus vu qu'elle? Ce serait anachronique, tant il est vrai que la polytonalité est maintenant placée dans le musée des accessoires inutiles, des masques déconfits. Fort heureusement, *le Sacre* est absent de ces absurdités. Tout au plus signalera-t-on une polymodalité à partir des mêmes notes de polarité. Nous avons déjà cité la *Danse de la Terre* où, sur une tonique de *do* se greffent la gamme par tons entiers et une attraction modale suivant les quartes descendantes (*mi♭ si♭ fa do*); nous avons signalé (ex. VIII) la fixité d'un accord sous l'accord broderie. Nous pouvons encore remarquer, dans l'*Introduction* de la deuxième partie, une modalité unique sur tonique de *ré*, qui joue sur l'ambiguïté suivante : la séparation des notes attractives et des autres notes qui prennent ainsi un caractère d'altération et de passage. C'est précisément à cette hiérarchie qui s'organise à partir des notes attractives que *le Sacre* doit sa physionomie harmonique. Nous sommes on ne peut plus loin de la gratuité polytonale.

Dois-je parler également de ce que l'on a appelé l'absence de mélodie chez Stravinsky? Sans même prendre une attitude polémique, mais étant donné une tradition mélodique héritée d'Italie et d'Allemagne (et j'entends bien parler des Italiens du XVIIe et du XVIIIe, ainsi que des Allemands du XVIIIe et du XIXe), on a constaté que Stravinsky n'avait pas le « don mélodique ». Il reste à savoir si Stravinsky n'a pas plutôt amplifié et divulgué une construction mélodique dérivée d'une certaine forme de chant populaire. Et c'est peut-être en ce point précis que se place le malentendu sur ses thèmes « folkloriques » (un peu de malveillance ne messied point à ce qualificatif ainsi employé pour plagiat et pour manque d'invention). La tendance de Stravinsky à la fixité verticale du matériau sonore, nous la retrouvons en effet sous une forme horizontale. En ce sens que les notes d'un mode étant initialement déterminées à une hauteur donnée, les notes de toute la structure mélodique ne sortiront pas de l'échelle ainsi établie. Comme souvent on n'utilise pas toutes les notes du mode, ou comme, dans le cas contraire, les points d'appui ont la place prépondérante, on saisit immédiatement l'aspect statique que revêt une telle mélodie du point de vue sonore, et c'est, je crois, cet aspect statique de l'échelle qui fait dénoncer une prétendue « absence de mélodie ». On décèle également le rapport avec les mélodies sur les modes défectifs des musiques d'Indochine, du Thibet, par exemple, ou d'Afrique noire et, plus près de Stravinsky, de certaines mélodies populaires dont le reflet sonore nous était déjà familier avec Borodine et Moussorgsky principalement. Il ne s'agit donc pas d'une absence de mélodie, mais d'un certain aspect de la mélodie — à tendance archaïsante du point de vue tonal — ce qui ne fait que corroborer le sursaut de Stravinsky en faveur d'un langage tonal archaïsant à force de se grouper autour d'attractions primairement polarisantes. Nous pouvons énoncer : « archaïsant » sans trop de crainte car le langage du *Sacre* — encore plus, celui de *Noces* ou de *Renard* — a créé, par rapport à l'évolution du langage avec Wagner et après lui, ce que l'on peut appeler géographiquement un phénomène de barre, et cet archaïsme a sans doute permis, comme nous l'avons fait remarquer, des recherches plus audacieuses sur les structures rythmiques.

141

*
* *

J'en arrive à penser, en fin de compte, que cette œuvre a, en dépit de et grâce à ses lacunes, une aussi grande utilité dans l'évolution musicale que *Pierrot lunaire*, par exemple. Car, si l'on ne peut rien retenir des moyens d'écriture du *Sacre* — pas plus que de *Noces* — qui sont une survivance, l'écriture rythmique, en revanche, reste encore à peu près inexplorée, du moins en ses conséquences internes ; il ne fait de doute pour personne que certains procédés plus ou moins mécanisés d'une façon toute contreplaquée ont passé dans le langage contemporain sous forme de coloriage rythmique, de même que l'on s'est appliqué à un coloriage sommaire des tonalités avec quelques intervalles à tendance anarchique. Remarquons qu'il est peu d'œuvres au cours de l'histoire musicale à pouvoir se targuer d'un tel privilège : n'avoir pas, quarante ans après, son potentiel de nouveauté épuisé. Disons qu'ici cette nouveauté est sur un plan unique, celui du rythme ; mais même avec cette restriction, cela représente une somme d'invention et une qualité dans la découverte fort enviables.

Peut-être, au fur et à mesure des conclusions que j'ai tirées à la suite des différentes analyses, m'aura-t-on trouvé une certaine tendance à exagérer les rapports arithmétiques, à ne pas tenir compte de l'inconscient. Dois-je répéter ici que je n'ai pas prétendu découvrir un processus créateur, mais me rendre compte du résultat, les rapports arithmétiques étant les seuls tangibles ? Si j'ai pu remarquer toutes ces caractéristiques structurelles, c'est qu'elles s'y trouvent, et peu m'importe alors si elles ont été mises en œuvre consciemment ou inconsciemment, et avec quel degré d'acuité dans l'intelligence de la conception, ou encore avec quelles interférences entre le travail et le « génie ». Établir une telle genèse du *Sacre* serait d'un grand intérêt spéculatif, s'écartant toutefois du seul but musical auquel j'ai voulu me limiter.

Cependant, il est impossible de ne pas s'interroger avec une certaine angoisse sur le cas Stravinsky. Comment expliquer, après *Noces,* cet épuisement accéléré qui se manifeste par une sclérose dans tous les domaines : harmonique et mélodique, où l'on aboutit à un académisme truqué, rythmique même, où l'on voit se produire une pénible atrophie? Pourra-t-on alors parler de réaction de l'un des domaines sur l'autre? En effet, on peut constater, au début du xxᵉ siècle, une curieuse dissociation entre l'évolution du rythme et l'évolution du matériau sonore : d'une part, Schönberg, Berg, Webern, point de départ d'une morphologie et d'une syntaxe nouvelles mais rattachés à une survivance rythmique (ceci étant une vue très sommaire de l'École de Vienne, car il y a entre eux des différences irréductibles); d'autre part, Stravinsky. A mi-chemin, le seul Bartok, dont les recherches sonores ne tombent jamais dans les ornières de Stravinsky, mais sont fort loin d'atteindre le niveau des Viennois; dont les recherches rythmiques n'égalant pas, de fort loin, celles de Stravinsky, sont encore, grâce à des arrière-plans folkloriques, supérieures en général à celles des Viennois.

Si, donc, nous considérons le cas Stravinsky, ses lacunes d'écriture ont pris le pas sur ses découvertes rythmiques, les ont empêché d'aboutir. Lacunes d'écriture de tous ordres, aussi bien dans le domaine du langage que dans celui du développement. Logiquement, Stravinsky ne pouvait se contenter d'un système sommaire colmaté avec des formules composites et anarchisantes. Retrouver une hiérarchie déjà éprouvée, coloriée avec éclectisme, tel fut le soulagement immédiat par l'hypnose.

Peu nous importent, du reste, ces renversements de prestidigitation — où l'objet escamote le manipulateur — puisqu'il existait auparavant un véritable domaine Stravinsky. Aussi, de cette période où l'on a pris diversement conscience d'un monde nouveau — d'une façon plus ou moins épisodique, plus ou moins rationnelle — faut-il retenir le nom de Stravinsky au tout premier plan; même et surtout lorsque l'expansion tardive de Schönberg, Berg et Webern a mis cruellement en lumière ses erreurs et l'a descendu de son piédestal de mage unique. Que ce soit celle de Stravinsky ou celle de Schönberg, d'ailleurs, les déifications prématurées ne sont pas notre fait. Qui songerait à se plaindre, sinon des sectateurs frénétiquement thuriféraires, de revenir à une optique moins affective?

*P. S.* — L'on pourrait nous blâmer d'une attitude aussi unilatérale à l'égard du rythme, ou au moins s'étonner de l'importance hypertrophiée que nous lui attribuons. En vérité, il nous paraît que le problème même du langage est beaucoup plus près d'une solution avec l'adoption — de plus en plus répandue — de la technique sérielle; dès lors, il s'agit essentiellement de rétablir un équilibre. A côté de toutes les disciplines musicales, en effet, le rythme ne bénéficie que des notions très sommaires que chacun peut trouver dans les solfèges usuels. Faut-il y voir seulement une déficience didactique? On peut plus valablement penser que, depuis la fin de la Renaissance, le rythme n'a pas été considéré à l'égal des autres composantes musicales, et qu'on a fait la part trop belle à l'intuition et au bon goût.

Si l'on veut trouver l'attitude la plus rationnelle à l'égard du rythme dans notre musique occidentale, il faut faire appel à Philippe de Vitry, Guillaume de Machault et Guillaume Dufay. Leurs motets isorythmiques sont un témoignage décisif sur la valeur constructive des structures rythmiques par rapport aux différentes séquences impliquées par les cadences. Quel meilleur précédent invoquer aux recherches contemporaines que celui de cette époque où la musique n'était pas seulement considérée comme un art, mais aussi comme une science : ce qui évitait toutes sortes de commodes malentendus (malgré la permanence d'une non moins commode scolastique).

« L'isorythmie, dit Guillaume de Van dans sa préface au œuvres de Dufay, fut l'expression la plus raffinée de l'idéal musical du XIV$^e$ siècle, l'essence que seul le petit nombre pouvait pénétrer et qui constituait le suprême témoignage de l'habileté du compositeur... Les restrictions imposées par les dimensions rigides d'un plan qui déterminait par avance les plus petits détails de la structure rythmique ne limitaient aucunement l'inspiration du Cambrésien, car ses motets donnent l'impression de compositions libres, spontanées, tandis qu'en fait le canon isorythmique est strictement observé. C'est l'harmonieux équilibre entre la mélodie et la structure rythmique qui distingue les œuvres de Dufay de tout le répertoire du XIV$^e$ siècle (Machault excepté). »

L'on voit donc, chose qui peut sembler impensable à beaucoup d'auditeurs et même à beaucoup de compositeurs contemporains, que la structure rythmique de ces motets *précédait* l'écriture. Non seulement il y a un phénomène de dissociation, mais bien une démarche contraire à celle que nous observons dans l'évolution de l'histoire de la musique occidentale, à partir du XVIIᵉ siècle.

Après cette efflorescence brillante, bien inconnue de nos jours sous cet aspect réservé encore aux seuls spécialistes, on peut voir un essai de contrôle sur le rythme dans les pièces « mesurées à l'antique » de Claude Le Jeune et de Mauduit. La préface d'une édition de cette époque met l'accent sur l'importance que doit revêtir la structure rythmique par rapport au contexte « harmonique ». « Les anciens qui ont traité de la musique, y est-il dit, l'ont divisée en deux parties : harmonique et rythmique... La rythmique a été mise par eux en telle perfection, qu'ils en ont fait des effets merveilleux... Depuis, cette rythmique a été tellement négligée qu'elle s'est perdue du tout... Personne ne s'est trouvé pour y apporter remède, jusques à Claudin Le Jeune, qui s'est, le premier, enhardi de retirer cette pauvre rythmique du tombeau où elle avait été de longtemps gisante pour l'aparier à l'harmonique. »

Il n'est pas question de discuter le bien-fondé de cette descendance gréco-latine, mais de constater plutôt que, avant la solution simpliste de la barre de mesure, on s'était préoccupé de coordonner d'une façon cohérente les données rythmiques de la musique, composantes au même titre que les données harmoniques et contrapunctiques.

Aussi serait-il temps d'adhérer à une telle logique, indispensable si l'on a le souci de remédier au manque de cohésion que nous avons remarqué, au cours de cette étude, entre l'évolution de la polyphonie elle-même et la découverte rythmique. Et nous ne croyons pas nous contredire, ni jouer sur le paradoxe, en avançant qu'il faut d'abord délier le rythme du côté « spontané » qu'on lui a généreusement attribué pendant trop longtemps; c'est-à-dire délier le rythme d'une expression proprement dite de la polyphonie, le promouvoir au rang de facteur principal de la structure en reconnaissant qu'il peut préexister à la polyphonie; ce qui n'a pour autre but que de lier plus étroitement encore, mais combien plus subtilement, la polyphonie au rythme.

135

145

*This article first appeared in the March 1949 issue of* The Tiger's Eye, *a journal edited by Ruth and John Stephan from Bleecker Street in New York. It was translated into French by Frederick Goldbeck, who changed the title to* Raison d'être de la musique moderne. *This was published in* Contrepoints *(Paris) later in the same year.*

# FORERUNNERS OF MODERN MUSIC

136

### *The purpose of music*

Music is edifying, for from time to time it sets the soul in operation. The soul is the gatherer-together of the disparate elements (Meister Eckhart), and its work fills one with peace and love.

### *Definitions*

Structure in music is its divisibility into successive parts from phrases to long sections. Form is content, the continuity. Method is the means of controlling the continuity from note to note. The material of music is sound and silence. Integrating these is composing.

### *Strategy*

Structure is properly mind-controlled. Both delight in precision, clarity, and the observance of rules. Whereas form wants only freedom to be. It belongs to the heart; and the law it observes, if indeed it submits to any, has never been and never will be written.[1] Method may be planned or improvised (it makes no difference: in one case, the emphasis shifts towards thinking, in the other towards feeling; a piece for radios as instruments would give up the matter of method to accident). Likewise, material may be controlled or not, as one chooses. Normally the choice of sounds is determined by what is pleasing and attractive to the ear: delight in the giving or receiving of pain being an indication of sickness.

[1] Any attempt to exclude the "irrational" is irrational. Any composing strategy which is wholly "rational" is irrational in the extreme.

## Refrain

Activity involving in a single process the many, turning them, even though some seem to be opposites, towards oneness, contributes to a good way of life.

## The plot thickens

*When asked why, God being good, there was evil in the world, Sri Ramakrishna said: To thicken the plot.*

The aspect of composition that can properly be discussed with the end in view of general agreement is structure, for it is devoid of mystery. Analysis is at home here.

Schools teach the making of structures by means of classical harmony. Outside school, however (*e.g.*, Satie and Webern), a different and correct [2] structural means reappears: one based on lengths of time.[3, 4]

In the Orient, harmonic structure is traditionally unknown, and unknown with us in our pre-Renaissance culture. Harmonic structure is a recent Occidental phenomenon, for the past century in a process of disintegration.[5]

## Atonality [6] has happened

137

The disintegration of harmonic structure is commonly known as atonality. All that is meant is that two necessary elements in harmonic structure—the cadence, and modulating means—have lost their edge. Increasingly, they have become ambiguous, whereas their very existence as structural elements demands clarity (singleness of reference). Atonality is simply the maintenance of an ambiguous tonal state of affairs. It is the denial of harmony as a structural means. The problem of a composer in a musical world in this state is to supply another structural means,[7]

[2] Sound has four characteristics: pitch, timbre, loudness, and duration. The opposite and necessary coexistent of sound is silence. Of the four characteristics of sound, only duration involves both sound and silence. Therefore, a structure based on durations (rhythmic: phrase, time lengths) is correct (corresponds with the nature of the material), whereas harmonic structure is incorrect (derived from pitch, which has no being in silence).

[3] This never disappeared from jazz and folk music. On the other hand, it never developed in them, for they are not cultivated species, growing best when left wild.

[4] Tala is based on pulsation, Western rhythmic structure on phraseology.

[5] For an interesting, detailed proof of this, see Casella's book on the cadence.

[6] The term "atonality" makes no sense. Schoenberg substitutes "pantonality," Lou Harrison (to my mind and experience the preferable term) "proto-tonality." This last term suggests what is actually the case: present even in a random multiplicity of tones (or, better, sounds [so as to include noises]), is a gravity, original and natural, "proto," to that particular situation. Elementary composition consists in discovering the ground of the sounds employed, and then letting life take place both on land and in the air.

[7] Neither Schoenberg nor Stravinsky did this. The twelve-tone row does not offer a structural means; it is a method, a control, not of the parts, large and small, of a composition, but only of the minute, note-to-note procedure. It usurps the place of counterpoint, which, as Carl Ruggles, Lou Harrison, and Merton Brown have shown, is perfectly capable of functioning in a chromatic situation. Neo-classicism, in reverting to the past, avoids, by refusing to recognize, the contemporary need for another structure, gives a new look to structural harmony. This automatically deprives it of the sense of adventure, essential to creative action.

just as in a bombed-out city the opportunity to build again exists.[8] This way one finds courage and a sense of necessity.

## Interlude (Meister Eckhart)

"But one must achieve this unselfconsciousness by means of transformed knowledge. This ignorance does not come from lack of knowledge but rather it is from knowledge that one may achieve this ignorance. Then we shall be informed by the divine unconsciousness and in that our ignorance will be ennobled and adorned with supernatural knowledge. It is by reason of this fact that we are made perfect by what happens to us rather than by what we do."

## At random

Music means nothing as a thing.

A finished work is exactly that, requires resurrection.

The responsibility of the artist consists in perfecting his work so that it may become attractively disinteresting.

138

It is better to make a piece of music than to perform one, better to perform one than to listen to one, better to listen to one than to misuse it as a means of distraction, entertainment, or acquisition of "culture."

Use any means to keep from being a genius, all means to become one.

Is counterpoint good? "The soul itself is so simple that it cannot have more than one idea at a time of anything. . . . A person cannot be more than single in attention." (Eckhart)

Freed from structural responsibility, harmony becomes a formal element (serves expression).

Imitating either oneself or others, care should be taken to imitate structure, not form (also structural materials and structural methods, not formal materials and formal methods), disciplines, not dreams; thus one remains "innocent and free to receive anew with each Now-moment a heavenly gift." (Eckhart)

If the mind is disciplined, the heart turns quickly from fear towards love.

## Before making a structure by means of rhythm, it is necessary to decide what rhythm is.

This could be a difficult decision to make if the concern were formal (expressive) or to do with method (point to point procedure); but since the concern is structural (to do with divisibility of a composition into parts large and small), the decision is easily reached: rhythm in the structural instance is relationships of lengths of time.[9] Such matters, then, as accents on or off the beat, regularly recurring or not, pulsation with or without accent, steady or unsteady, durations motivically conceived (either static or to be varied), are matters for formal

---

[8] The twelve-tone row offers bricks but no plan. The neo-classicists advise building it the way it was before, but surfaced fashionably.

[9] Measure is literally measure—nothing more, for example, than the inch of a ruler—thus permitting the existence of any durations, any amplitude relations (meter, accent), any silences.

(expressive) use, or, if thought about, to be considered as material (in its "textural" aspect) or as serving method. In the case of a year, rhythmic structure is a matter of seasons, months, weeks, and days. Other time lengths such as that taken by a fire or the playing of a piece of music occur accidentally or freely without explicit recognition of an all-embracing order, but nevertheless, necessarily within that order. Coincidences of free events with structural time points have a special luminous character, because the paradoxical nature of truth is at such moments made apparent. Caesurae on the other hand are expressive of the independence (accidental or willed) of freedom from law, law from freedom.

*Claim*

Any sounds of any qualities and pitches (known or unknown, definite or indefinite), any contexts of these, simple or multiple, are natural and conceivable within a rhythmic structure which equally embraces silence. Such a claim is remarkably like the claims to be found in patent specifications for and articles about technological musical means (see early issues of *Modern Music* and the *Journal of the Acoustical Society of America*). From differing beginning points, towards possibly different goals, technologists and artists (seemingly by accident) meet by intersection, becoming aware of the otherwise unknowable (conjunction of the in and the out), imagining brightly a common goal in the world and in the quietness within each human being.

*For instance:*

Just as art as sand painting (art for the now-moment[10] rather than for posterity's museum civilization) becomes a held point of view, adventurous workers in the field of synthetic music (e.g. Norman McLaren) find that for practical and economic reasons work with magnetic wires (any music so made can quickly and easily be erased, rubbed off) is preferable to that with film.[11]

The use of technological means[12] requires the close anonymous collaboration of a number of workers. We are on the point of being in a cultural situation,[13]

[10] This is the very nature of the dance, of the performance of music, or any other art requiring performance (for this reason, the term "sand painting" is used: there is a tendency in painting (permanent pigments), as in poetry (printing, binding), to be secure in the thingness of a work, and thus to overlook, and place nearly insurmountable obstacles in the path of, instantaneous ecstasy).

[11] Twenty-four or *n* frames per second is the "canvas" upon which this music is written; thus, in a very obvious way, the material itself demonstrates the necessity for time (rhythmic) structure. With magnetic means, freedom from the frame of film means exists, but the principle of rhythmic structure should hold over as, in geometry, a more elementary theorem remains as a premise to make possible the obtaining of those more advanced.

[12] "I want to be as though new-born, knowing nothing, absolutely nothing about Europe." (Paul Klee)

[13] Replete with new concert halls: the movie houses (vacated by home television fans, and too numerous for a Hollywood whose only alternative is "seriousness").

139

without having made any special effort to get into one [14] (if one can discount lamentation).

The in-the-heart path of music leads now to self-knowledge through self-denial, and its in-the-world path leads likewise to selflessness.[15] The heights that now are reached by single individuals at special moments may soon be densely populated.

[14] Painting in becoming literally (actually) realistic—(this is the twentieth century) seen from above, the earth, snow-covered, a composition of order superimposed on the "spontaneous" (Cummings) or of the latter letting order be (from above, so together, the opposites, they fuse) (one has only to fly [highways and topography, Milarepa, Henry Ford] to know)—automatically will reach the same point (step by step) the soul leaped to.

[15] The machine fathers mothers heroes saints of the mythological order, works only when it meets with acquiescence (cf. *The King and the Corpse*, by Heinrich Zimmer, edited by Joseph Campbell).

140

. . . . . . . . . . . . . . . . . . . . . . . . . . . . . . . .

Peggy Guggenheim, Santomaso, and I were in a Venetian restaurant. There were only two other people dining in the same room and they were not conversing. I got to expressing my changed views with regard to the French and the Italians. I said that I had years before preferred the French because of their intelligence and had found the Italians playful but intellectually not engaging; that recently, however, I found the French cold in spirit and lacking in freedom of the mind, whereas the Italians seemed warm and surprising. Then it occurred to me that the couple in the room were French. I called across to them and said, "Are you French?" The lady replied. "We are," she said, "but we agree with you completely."

Richard Lippold called up and said, "Would you come to dinner and bring the *I-Ching?*" I said I would. It turned out he'd written a letter to the Metropolitan proposing that he be commissioned for a certain figure to do *The Sun*. This letter withheld nothing about the excellence of his art, and so he hesitated to send it, not wishing to seem presumptuous. Using the coin oracle, we consulted the *I-Ching*. It mentioned a letter. Advice to send it was given. Success was promised, but the need for patience was mentioned. A few weeks later, Richard Lippold called to say that his proposal had been answered but without commitment, and that that should make clear to me as it did to him what to think of the *I-Ching*. A year passed. The Metropolitan Museum finally commissioned *The Sun*. Richard Lippold still does not see eye to eye with me on the subject of chance operations.

The question of leading tones came up in the class in experimental composition that I give at the New School. I said, "You surely aren't talking about ascending half-steps in diatonic music. Is it not true that anything leads to whatever follows?" But the situation is more complex, for things also lead backwards in time. This also does not give a picture that corresponds with reality. For, it is said, the Buddha's enlightenment penetrated in every direction to every point in space and time.

**66/SILENCE**

# SOUND AND SYNTAX:
## AN INTRODUCTION TO SCHOENBERG'S
## HARMONY*

EDWARD T. CONE

By *sound* and *syntax* I mean to distinguish the two aspects of harmony: chordal vocabulary and harmonic progression. Actually, there is also a third aspect to be considered, one lying somewhere between the first two. It is concerned with connections at the most detailed level: the specific chords chosen, the accessory tones decorating them, the voice-leading from one to the next, and the comparative complexity of the sonorities. Let us call this aspect *succession*. Those familiar with Hindemith's theory will find parallels here: his table of chord-groups is an attempt to classify all possible chordal constructions; his "harmonic fluctuation" is one of the effects of what I have called succession, and his "degree-progression" links succession with harmonic progression in the larger sense. True, his method of analysis is probably even less in vogue today than his music; yet it can often be helpfully suggestive if separated from the rigid interpretations and applications that Hindemith himself often supplied.

My own interest in what I have called chordal vocabulary is not so precisely analytical as Hindemith's. For present purposes I am less concerned with the exact categorization of chords than with a determination of the types of sonorities employed by a given style, with the aim of recognizing the characteristic "sound" of that style. And I am less concerned with establishing roots for these chords—an essential for Hindemith's analysis of degree-progression—than with discovering

* This article is the expansion of a lecture given at the University of Leeds on November 13, 1974, in connection with its Schoenberg Centenary celebration.

the relations between the way the chords are constructed and the way they move. How do the sound and the syntax affect each other, and what kinds of permissible chord-succession result?

One of the earmarks of any well-defined style—whether of a person, or of a composer, or of a composition, or sometimes even of a specific passage—is its sheer sound. By this we recognize, instantly and almost, as it were, intuitively, that a work is by Mozart and not by Chopin, that it is the C major Quartet (K. 465) and not the B♭ (K. 458), that it is the Adagio introduction and not the slow movement. We make this judgment spontaneously, without having to follow specific themes or to trace formal patterns. And an important criterion (though by no means the only one, or necessarily the most important) is the specific chordal vocabulary. Or perhaps better, the vocabulary of characteristic sonorities, since it might include a number of simultaneous combinations of tones that would not qualify under some theoretical rubrics as chords. Now, it is true of any music we consider as typically tonal, although not true exclusively of such music, that whatever sonorities its characteristic vocabulary may include, among these will be the major and minor triads—or at the very least, one major or minor triad or diagnostic component thereof. Moreover, triads are compositionally exploited—e.g., by preponderance, by rhythmic importance, by formal articulation—in such a way that they constitute normal sonorities for such music: sonorities with which all others are implicitly compared. Without a final statement of such a sonority no composition can sound complete—indeed, hardly even a phrase. If, then, a normal sonority is one that is normally used as a cadential chord, its definition can be restricted still further: what might be called the normal form of a normal is a triad in root position (or a diagnostic component). And there is a hierarchy of such triads, the one we call the tonic being the normal of normals.

Classical theory, from Rameau on, has tried to show that tonal syntax is based on the relations among normals: that even the most complex progressions, no matter how elaborated by dissonant chords, chromatic alterations, and non-harmonic tones, can be ultimately reduced to one that consists of connected triads in root positions. Schenker, elaborating the more practical and less abstract principles of thoroughbass, has offered a more convincing alternative. Yet it is one that builds tonal syntax even more firmly on normal ground. For Schenker, the background of every tonal composition is the single tonic triad. The fundamental harmonic progression is from tonic to fifth and back—the defining interval of the triad. Elaborations are effected by arpeggiation, by subsidiary fifth-progressions, by neighboring and other apparent chords produced by voice-leading; but these merely disguise the control of the normal tonic.

Even the principles of succession are subject to the control of the normal triad. Just as the composition typically consists of movement away from and back to *the* normal, so the sound of a typical tonal passage depends on motion away from and toward *a* normal. Even a passage—or more rarely an entire composition—that starts abnormally must, in traditional tonal writing, push toward a normal. Indeed, it is the return to a normal—the resolution of dissonance, as it is usually called—that furnishes much of the local motive power of this music. The tension built up by a series of dissonances depends on our expectation that a triad must ultimately follow. Moreover, certain sonorities strongly imply specific syntactic situations. The most obvious example is the primary ("dominant") seventh. Whether natural or applied, we confirm the regularity of its resolution to its tonic by calling all other resolutions deceptive.

Classical tonality (and by classical I mean standard, without reference to historical period) thus displays a consistency of sound, syntax, and succession—a synthesis based on a characteristic vocabulary that included the triad, and on a chord grammar that related all other sonorities to the triad as normal. But as the late Romantic style developed in the nineteenth century, it appeared increasingly to question the assumptions underlying this synthesis. In particular, the triad became less and less characteristic of the sound of this music; yet at the same time it remained the normal to which all successions of dissonances, no matter how protracted, must ultimately resolve. And a stubbornly triadic syntax often underlay passages expressed in the most complex sonorities. Compare, for a moment, the opening of "Fingal's Cave" with that of *Tristan and Isolde*. Mendelssohn relies on a succession of normals, modified by simple dissonances immediately resolved. The clarity of the sound is matched by that of the chordal progression, which, stating successive triads on B, D, and F♯, arpeggiates in harmonic terms the tonic that is melodically arpeggiated by the opening motif (Ex. 1). The Wagner example *sounds* as unlike as can be: a chromatic melodic line supported by a succession of dissonances stretched almost to the breaking-point, achieving a resolution only on a conventionally deceptive triad modified by an appoggiatura. Yet the sequential pattern—although based on a series of sevenths, not triads

143

Ex. 1

—reveals, just as "Fingal's Cave" does, the arpeggiation of a minor triad, E-G-B, each member of which, as a dominant, points to a corresponding element of the unstated triad, A-C-E, implied as the normal of the entire deceptive progression (Ex. 2). Sound and syntax are here in a state of the gravest tension, and an extraordinary genius like Wagner can only just hold them together. Even a great talent like Strauss occasionally fails, as when the high dissonance level of *Electra* is suddenly relaxed for a conventional cadence.

144

Ex. 2

A younger composer like Schoenberg, coming to maturity during this critical period in the development—or the decline—of the style, could hardly hope to master at once the complexities of advanced tonal chromaticism with complete success. Indeed, the system had arrived at the point where such success was hardly possible, for the search for new harmonic resources was pushing beyond the limits of the tonal realm. It was Schoenberg's gradual realization of this situation that made of him a seminal figure in the development of twentieth-century music; and it is their reflection of this gradual realization that makes his early works so fascinating.

One would not expect the music of such a gifted composer to display obvious discrepancies of style: incompatible sonorities, inconsequent chord successions, meaningless progressions. But there are at least three kinds of inconsistency of which the early Schoenberg is guilty: inconsistency between sound and succession, between succession and syntax, and between sound and syntax. His early songs offer examples of all three.

"Schenk mir deinem goldenem Kamm", Op. 2 No. 2, presents an almost classical instance of the first. Why is the perfect cadence in mm. 5–6 almost bathetically saccharine? Not because the final chord is a triad: there have been two in the first measure. Not because it is major: if anything, a minor resolution, affording less contrast, would be even less acceptable. Not because of the descending fifth chordal succession: that is prominent throughout the phrase, which can be heard as a clear, though highly chromatic, elaboration of the opening F♯. No: the cadence fails because even such a short passage has conditioned us to expect each member of a fifth-succession to be adorned with a dissonance, whether chordal seventh, suspension, passing-tone, or neighbor. If, taking a cue from Wagner's handling of a somewhat analogous problem at the first cadence of *Tristan*, we alter the final consonance by the addition of an appoggiatura, all is saved (Ex.3).

Ex. 3

Note that the same objection does not apply to the V⁷-I in G minor of mm. 7–8. Although equally unadorned, the resolution here is protected by the fermata, the rest, and the consequent delay of the new tonic, which enters only as an upbeat of the next phrase. But by the time we return to the original key in m. 19, the old context has been reestablished, and once more the consonance disappoints us.

Was Schoenberg himself a bit uneasy about this letdown? Perhaps that is why his final tonic is as beautifully delayed as any in *Tristan*, again an obvious model. The last functional dominant (m. 36) is separated from the final tonic by six measures; its immediate resolution, although to a consonance, is deceptive. The tonic, when it arrives, is preceded by a seventh—but not of its own dominant, which is elliptically omitted: the bass, in a formula frequently used to end these songs, traverses a tritone. Tonal demands are met, but the flatness of a direct authentic cadence is avoided.

In Op. 3 No. 5, "Geübtes Herz", occurs another case of this kind, one that is perhaps even more striking because it mars an otherwise totally consistent texture. The song carefully avoids sudden changes in harmonic tension. It adorns all triads with appoggiaturas or else gingerly approaches them through relatively mild dissonances until the entrance of the Neapolitan sixth, forte, on a downbeat, after the harshest sonority in the entire composition (mm. 18–19), comes as a rude and inexplicable shock.

Succession and syntax come into conflict in Op. 3 No. 2, "Die Aufgeregten". The introduction, through its combination of rhetorical gesture (a recitative-like declamation supported by powerful chords and rhythmic motifs) and harmonic progression (basically a descending half-step sequence apparently leading to a functional dominant), appears to be preparing for a tonic G minor. But the resolution is deceptive: the body of the song begins in a tentative F minor (Ex. 4).

146

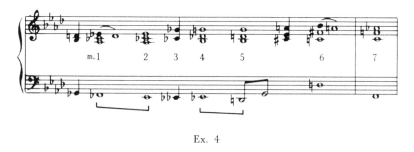

Ex. 4

During its course it returns to the introductory motifs and even frankly to the dominant of G (mm. 13–14), again to resolve deceptively, this time leading to an authentic cadence in G♭ (Ex. 5). When the introduction is recapitulated, almost literally, the acute listener, accepting the clue of the VI-II-V-I progression in G♭, may decide that tonal

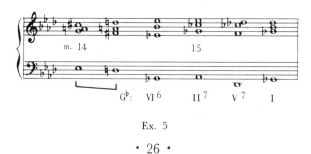

Ex. 5

syntax will after all prevail; the expected tonic on G will arrive to round off the piece. But he would be wrong. What prevails is the rule of succession that dictates a deceptive resolution for the seventh on D. Schoenberg tries to achieve here a tour de force, admirable even in its failure. Presenting yet another deceptive resolution, he uses this as a passing chord to the original F, which closes the song as a normal, if not as a fully established tonic (Ex. 6).

Ex. 6

I have described this song as one displaying unconventional successions that are inconsistent with its traditional syntax, but a more profound analysis would reverse these terms: it would find a general non-tonal syntax at odds with the local preservation of certain conventional chord successions. For even if a final resolution to G were achieved, the structure would still depend on voice-leading rather than on functionality; only now it would be based on the passing chromatic motion F-G♭-G♮ instead of the neighboring F-G♭-F of the actual composition.

It is instructive to compare this song with an earlier one, Op. 2 No. 3, "Erhebung", which is troubled by a similar problem, but in a much less strenuous setting. Its syntax is frankly tonal; yet its ending is no more satisfactory than that of "Die Aufgeregten". This is because strong expectations have been aroused during the approach to the final climax (mm. 17–20), which seems to express an intention to modulate to the dominant, E. But no: a tendency to thwart the tonicization of V has been set up as early as mm. 2–3 and strengthened by the passage leading into the reprise at mm. 11–12, essentially a V of V resolving deceptively to I. And when the same situation recurs in m. 21, the pull of the succession is too strong, despite the altered context. Once again a tonic resolution rejects the demand for a dominant; this time syntax unmistakably gives in to succession.

In contradistinction to the last two examples, Op. 3 No. 3 is successful in its own idiosyncratic terms. The song sounds tonal, but it is actually so only in an inverted sense. The chordal progressions that have traditionally taken on the burden of large-scale structure are now demoted to details of succession; the harmonic motion is assigned to progressions once typically subsidiary or even decorative. For here a tonic, B♮ minor, is established by a series of plagal (descending-fourth) progressions skillfully united by a combination of diatonic and chromatic linear connections. The rare descending-fifth progressions— which never involve the tonic—are only sequential details. (See, for example, mm. 4–7.) Yet they are not obtrusively out of place, for the ambiance is superficially tonal. The song thus demonstrates that one can employ unconventional syntactic structure in a context of apparently conventional tonality. The title, "Warnung", is perhaps more appropriate than the composer realized. For, along with "Die Auf-geregten", this song can indeed be heard as a warning: that henceforth tonal syntax must not be accepted as all-powerful; that the traditional subordination of voice-leading to harmonic progression may be reversed; that a functional dominant is not necessary for the establishment of a normal. The corollary that the normal need not be a tonic in traditional terms may not have occurred to Schoenberg at this point, but it was bound to sooner or later.

Tonal syntax vies with novel sound in Op. 2 No. 1, "Erwartung", which is nevertheless both an effective song and an early step in the direction that the composer was to take later. Its first characteristic dissonance is a chord created by applying half-step neighbors to the tonic (Ex. 7a); but in intervallic content it is very close to another characteristic sonority consisting of an appoggiatura applied to a minor dominant ninth (Ex. 7b). Yet this connection of sounds is misleading:

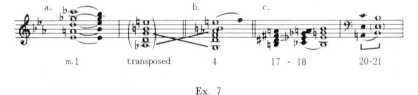

m. 1    transposed    4    17 - 18    20-21

Ex. 7

the progress of the piece is determined, not by the characteristic chords, but by the tonic-dominant syntax of their resolutions. The basic tonal structure is conventional: I-VI-V-I. Only in the approach to the recapitulation does the composer bring sound and syntax into a more intimate connection. By leading into the crucial I$^6_4$ first from an augmented sixth (m. 17) and then from a raised subdominant (m. 20), he surrounds B♮ harmonically by two of the half-step neighbors that characterize the opening dissonance (Ex. 7c). And this chord itself is accorded the status of a true dominant when it succeeds the I$_4^6$ just before the reprise (m. 23). Its retransformation during the next few measures back to its original neighboring status is magical.

Further away from the characteristic tonal sound than any of the songs we have yet examined is Op. 6 No. 4, "Verlassen", which for long stretches forsakes ordinary tonal procedures. Hence its reversion at the climax to a traditional dominant-tonic construction is a striking instance of sound-syntax inconsistency. The ostinato motif of the opening measures, although concealing a normal tonic E♭, certainly gives more emphasis to other sonorities: first to two forms of ninth on E♭, then to two forms of a chord that is to become a great favorite of the composer—the combination of a perfect and an augmented fourth, which for convenience I shall henceforth call an *x*-chord (Ex. 8). The

Ex. 8

149

opening melodic motif of the acompaniment is developed in the first vocal line, which expands it in such a way as to suggest yet another ninth, on D, which includes the second of the *x*-chords (Ex. 9). When

Ex. 9

the harmony at last begins to move, the bass is controlled by this ninth, which is restated as the sonority that leads to the first important harmonic shift. Yet the resolution of the ninth is highly irregular, to a *"Tristan*-chord" whose bass simultaneously completes a chromatic progression derived from the descending component of the opening motifs, and commences a diminution of its ascending component (Ex. 10). This is the complicated context in which the rising climax gradually but ever more insistently asserts a structural dominant. It is prepared by a series of secondary dominant sevenths, all irregularly resolved yet leading clearly to an unmistakable V: Bb (mm. 20–22). Because it is very dissonant and because its resolution to the Eb of the opening motif is disguised and delayed, the specific succession here is appropriate and effective; but that does not alter the basic conventionality of the crucial syntactic structure.

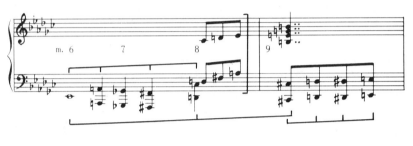

Ex. 10

Another large-scale departure from the tonic soon follows. This one, built on a fundamental D, returns to the tonic by way of the same ninth that originally departed from it—a beautiful example of syntax derived from, rather than opposed to, a characteristic sonority (mm. 42–43). Yet Schoenberg still feels that he must confirm the final cadence with another true dominant—one so simple in form and so directly followed by its tonic that, unlike its climactic predecessor, it introduces what can only be felt as an inappropriate detail of succession. Authentic cadences are comparatively rare in Schoenberg's music, even of this period, for what should by now be obvious reasons. It is too bad that he felt the need of one here.

Before leaving these early, tonally-bound songs, I should like to pay tribute to one of the most beautiful. Superficially adhering to the conventions, ingratiating in sound, Op. 6 No. 1, "Traumleben", might be heard as a regretful, nostalgic farewell to the nineteenth century. But this interpretation would overlook the forward-pointing elements concealed beneath its calm surface. True, it develops a serene, uncontested E major; and although the first phrase begins tentatively, it comes to rest on an authentic cadence. But the dominant of that cadence is anything but typical (Ex. 11). It states simultaneously the boundaries of the first vocal phrase, a minor ninth that is one of the most prominent melodic and harmonic intervals in the song. The melodic reso-

Ex. 11

lution of the dominant is by a diminished fourth (or augmented fifth) already subtly prepared by one in m. 2. What this striking interval (C♮–G♯) does is to call our attention to an association that will be important throughout the song, that of C♮ with the tonic chord of E major. It is the shift from E to a dominant seventh on C that moves into the development (mm. 12–13) and it is the return from this chord, reinterpreted as an augmented sixth, that effects the transformed reprise. Another C, this time as the bass of a first-inversion A♭ (G♯), leads into the tonic of the coda. Most remarkable of all is the way the dominant of the first cadence, in the course of its chromatic elaboration, strikes—at perhaps its moment of greatest tension—a sonority that both sums up the course of the melody so far and forecasts all the tonic cadences to come! For this sonority consists of B, A, E♯ (F♮), and C, the first four tones of the vocal line. B is of course the root of the chord in question; a seventh on A precedes the tonic at the next cadence (mm. 8–9); the cadences involving C have already been discussed—but it should be mentioned that the second of these is introduced by a first inversion F, yielding the bass A-C-E. Lastly, the final cadence of the song involves a root position F (Ex. 12). Thus, despite the unquestioned supremacy of the tonal normal on E, the syntax is based on a characteristic sonority, one that leaves its stamp on both melodic and harmonic progressions throughout. Even in a relatively conservative idiom, Schoenberg is on the verge of the kind of unifica-

151

Ex. 12

tion of simultaneous and successive events that characterizes serial methods.

In the two songs of Op. 14 the role of the triad as normal is seriously questioned. No. 1, "Ich darf nicht dankend", is based on two types of fourth-chord, one the *x*-chord and the other combining two perfect fourths (*y*). Both the sound of these chords and the succession from an *x* to a *y* characterize the highly consistent texture of the song. In proto-serial style, important linear motions as well are governed by these sonorities, as the introductory phrase illustrates: the bass outlines a motion from F♯ to C♯ to B, decorated by neighbors and appoggiaturas (Ex. 13). This phrase shows something else, too: the succession

Ex. 13

*x-y,* after a slight delay, is completed triadically, as the bass of an apparent $^6_4$ moves upward to form a root-position B (minor-major). That, if we are to trust the key-signature and the last chord of the piece, is to be heard as the tonic. But note what a tentative metrical position it occupies, and how it is blurred by an appoggiatura and a moving bass at its reprise in m. 18. And if, as these measures suggest, the syntactic foundation of the song is not functional harmony but the voice-leading implied by the succession *x-y*-triad, then it is interesting that the triad is often either an inversion (as in mm. 11, 16, and 20) or else omitted altogether (as in m. 5). Striking, too, are the sequential chains formed from *x* and *y,* as in mm. 9–10, 13–14, and especially 24–25. The result is to raise the question whether the final chord is really "right". For the first time a triad—the B minor "tonic"—follows *x* instead of *y*. Schoenberg has explained irregularities of this kind in his *Harmonielehre*, where he speaks of harmonic formulas that have become "so unequivocal that the initial chord, once sounded, straightaway and automatically enlists our expectation of the predetermined continuation: the formula leads inevitably to a foregone conclusion. Given such a premise, the intermediate steps can even be omitted, the beginning and the end directly juxtaposed, and the whole progression so to speak 'abbreviated', set down simply as premise and conclusion."[1] Schoenberg adduces in illustration of this principle cadences embodying tritone bass-motion similar to that at the close of Op. 2 No. 2; no doubt he would have argued in the present instance that the same principle would hold despite the unfamiliarity of the idiom. But the more fundamental question would still remain: is the "tonic" chord necessary? Indeed, is the triad a normal for this composition? Could it not—should it not—end with a repetition of the two chords with which it began? In this connection it is perhaps revealing that Op. 14 No. 2, "In diesen Wintertagen", does end with a dissonance derived from its opening measure—although newly redistributed as a triad with added sixth.

*Das Buch der hängenden Gärten*, Op. 15, returns to these problems and begins to provide definitive answers. Look at No. 7. Again, at the outset two dissonances, an augmented triad and an *x*-chord (the tritone at first below, later often above) lead to a consonance, now simply a minor third. This rule of succession is observed more faithfully and completely than that of Op. 14 No. 1, for much of the accompaniment consists of the two chords alternating with chains of parallel thirds. But the rhythmic structure and the dynamic pattern of the first few phrases make it clear that the characteristic dissonances have here become the normals: they are the downbeat resolutions toward which the restless thirds push (e.g., in mm. 3–4). And since this interpretation is confirmed by the rest of the song, it is only proper that the music should end as it began, with the same two characteristic sonorities.

In this respect No. 7 is a microcosm of the entire cycle, all of whose characteristic vocabularies are frankly based on dissonances. Consonant sonorities may of course be included, but they are not specially privileged. Only one, No. 6, can be construed as ending on a consonant triadic normal. In the opening phrase of this song a perfect fifth, Bb-F, comes to rest on what one might suspect to be a more characteristic interval, the tritone Bb-E. In the context, this could well be a "resolution", but during the course of the voice line there are two prominent passages where the original melodic F-E is completed by motion to D (mm. 4–5, 7–10). The second of these is heard in association with two emphatic statements by the piano of the original fifth (mm. 8–9).

153

[1] Arnold Schoenberg, *Harmonielehre,* 3rd ed., Universal, Vienna, 1922, p. 432.

When the vocal line twice more refers to F-E (mm. 10–13) we expect the completion that comes—twice in fact—in the concluding phrases, each time over a B♭ bass (Ex. 14). The song is tonal only insofar as

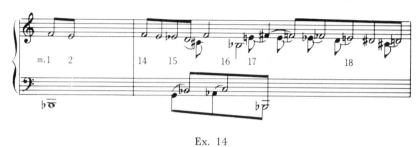

Ex. 14

it as based on a triadic normal. Its principles of succession and syntax come from its own characteristic sounds—notably the association of B♭ with F and E, a grouping that will be immediately recognized as a form of the *x*-chord, a sonority that is almost ubiquitous throughout the cycle.

At least one other song, No. 10, establishes a triadic normal. Even though here, as before, the opening measures state an *x*-chord—both simultaneously and melodically—the tritone D-G♯ is immediately resolved to a perfect fifth. This move, supported by the bass, initiates a progression that can be heard as unfolding a triad on D: major $\frac{6}{3}$ through minor $\frac{6}{4}$ to major $\frac{5}{3}$ (Ex. 15). The rising bass line, with its con-

Ex. 15

cealed arpeggiation, controls the course of the song until the concluding measures. Now the prevailing upward half-step G♯-A is prominently reversed in the bass, leading to G (mm. 28-29). There follows the frankest possible statement of a normal D major as a resolution of the opening motif, but the song is not allowed to end here. The tritone G♯ reappears over the fundamental D and moves to a final resolution

154

—but on A♯, supported by a return to the same dissonant chord on G that immediately preceded the cadence.

Here, then, is another important departure from tonal principles. Schoenberg no longer considers it necessary to end on the normal—even when it is a triad. Not that the step was a revolutionary one: Mozart had taken it in an obvious example, although with parodistic intent. Schumann had been willing to end on an inversion of the tonic; Chopin had added a seventh; Schoenberg himself, as we have seen, had added a sixth (in Op. 14 No. 2). And there are a few curious instances, like Chopin's Second Ballade and Schoenberg's Op. 3 No. 6, "Freihold", which seem to vacillate between two tonics. But the conclusion of "Das schöne Beet" deliberately leads away from its final cadential normal. Why? Whatever expressive reasons might be adduced, the formal one depends on the old problem of consistency of sound, succession, and syntax. Throughout the song, the normal is openly sounded only during the course of a phrase; cadentially it is always side-stepped—until the end. But by then it is too late to introduce a convincingly firm tonic. The tendency of the chord to move on has already been well established, and that is the way it must behave even on its final appearance.

The distinction between normal and non-normal finals must be observed as well when, as in most of Op. 15, the normal is dissonant. Like consonant normals, dissonances may be established at the outset. No. 13, for example, develops by a series of neighboring motions from its opening sonority, to which the last measure of the song returns. But No. 2, which states and then discusses a simpler sonority with clearer tonal implications, moves away after a final return. An arpeggiation of the opening chord, D-F-A-C♯, underlies the entire bass. This moves chromatically from D to F (mm. 1–6), then emphasizes A and F (mm. 7–8). Next, falling chromatically through E (developed in terms of a subsidiary sonority already associated with E in m. 4), it passes beyond D to C♯. But the ensuing resolution back to D, which brings with it a restatement of the opening chord, yields to the prevailing chromatic motion. The bass rises to E♭—a so to speak hyper-dissonant neighbor to an already dissonant normal (see Ex. 16).

More problematic are the dissonant normals that are delayed—established as late goals of harmonic motion, like those delayed tonics of which Brahms was so fond (e.g., that of his Intermezzo Op. 76 No. 4). But whereas one can be certain that Brahms's normal will

155

Ex. 16

be a triad, and can usually predict from the outset just which triad, the range of possibilities open to Schoenberg makes such confidence unwarranted. Still, the main thing is to be able to recognize the normal when it arrives—as I believe one can at the end of No. 5, even though the specific final sonority is unique in the song. Its conclusiveness is due partly to its intervallic make-up: it is framed by a perfect fifth, and in a texture characterized predominantly by tritones it conspicuously contains none; in fact, it is the only sonority on a downbeat that neither contains a tritone nor resolves to one in appoggiatura fashion. More than that, it effects the only cadential point not vitiated by an appoggiatura-like feminine ending. At the same time the sonority is well prepared. The falling D-G of the bass is derived from an early "cadence" (mm. 3–4) that was aborted by an immediate rise in the bass. The piano chords of that cadence return to lead to the close (mm. 15–16), but this time the G remains in place, strengthening the cadential downbeat. A second statement subtly alters the progression, providing a transitional form that enables us to hear the final chords as still another variation of the by now familiar cadence. And although the tritone has been banished from the harmony, the last melodic interval in the vocal line reminds us of its importance.

Despite these examples, it must be confessed that the decision whether a certain ending is normal or non-normal is often problematic when the normal can only be a dissonance, and especially problematic when that dissonance is one not clearly established at the outset. If we heard a traditionally tonal composition end on the dominant seventh, or on a chord neighboring the tonic, we should immediately call that ending non-normal. But it might be very difficult to make such a determination in a more complex situation. In No. 9 is the normal the quasi-dominant that begins and ends the song (except for an evanescent diminuendo)? Or is it the quasi-tonic that twice "resolves" the first sonority (mm. 3 and 9)? Questions of this sort inevitably suggest more general ones. Must the normal always be a chord

· 36 ·

of relative resolution? Must it be among the characteristic sonorities of a composition? Must it always be stated? More drastically, must every composition have a normal?

I shall not try to give general answers—even to the extent of saying that no general answers are possible, for that would be tantamount to answering No in each case. But I believe I can tell what Schoenberg's answer would have been, at least so far as his own music was concerned. Look again at No. 7. You may have wondered why, in my discussion of that song, I avoided stating which of the two opening chords is the normal. Is the first an appoggiatura to the second, or is the second an incomplete neighbor of the first? I see no way to decide the question, nor do I see the necessity for a decision; but that need not mean that the piece lacks a normal. The normal might consist of the succession of the two chords. "Am Strande", a posthumously published song apparently written during the same period as Op. 15, seems to go one step further. The opening consists of an arpeggio succeeded by a chord (*c*), but the arpeggio is soon divided into two components: *a* and *b*—I take the C♮ in the first measure to be a misprint for the B that later consistently replaces it (Ex. 17). During the course

Ex. 17

of the song each of these components is combined with chord *c* (especially in mm. 12–13). The normal, then, might well consist not of one chord but of three, which can be stated not only successively but also in part simultaneously. The conclusion refers only to *a* and *c*, an abbreviation somewhat like the one noted at the end of Op. 14 No. 1.

We thus find Schoenberg, even at this early date (1908–09), already on the verge of serial techniques, although their thoroughgoing adaptation is still years away. For the normal that depends, not on a single chord or tone, but on a succession; the ordered components of a collection that can be stated both successively and simultaneously; the resultant identification of sound and succession: these are basic elements of serialism in general and of the twelve-tone method in particular. One achievement of that method is to be a firmer definition of syntactic principles derived from these premises. Let us therefore con-

· 37 ·

clude this survey of Schoenberg's *Lieder* with a brief look at his three twelve-tone songs Op. 48, to see how each employs its syntax to establish a normal.

No. 2, "Tot", relies on a single form of the row and its retrograde (Ex. 18). Even this distinction, at best a minimal contrast, is often

Ex. 18

blurred. How, then, without inversion or transposition, can one statement be established as normal at the expense of another? The structure of the song is based on the original division of its row into tetrads; the combinations of these three units, progressing from the simpler to the more complex and back, produce an obvious arch-design. The song is over when the original simple disposition returns, with the third tetrad repeatedly stated as a free ostinato beneath the other two. This, then, is the normal: not a chord, not even a succession of chords, but a special way of handling the row.

The syntax of No. 3, "Mädchenlied", is more complex, since it depends on the combination of a prime (with its R) and an inversion (with its RI). The former is shaped, and the latter is chosen, in a manner typical of Schoenberg: the resulting combinations of corresponding half-rows produce twelve-tone aggregates (Ex. 19). Nor are

Ex. 19

such hexadic combinations restricted to the prime against the inversion; the two halves of each form are similarly counterpointed against each other. Again there is a progression from simplicity to complexity and back. At the outset the hexads are divided into triads, regularly and obviously ordered. But as the song develops, dyadic division takes over and the ordering becomes much looser. Even when the triads return they are combined in fresh ways reflecting the freer ordering, and they sometimes overlap one another. The row-forms, once carefully restricted to either voice or piano, now straddle the two. It is through the return of a simple R against RI, with clearly demarked triads, that the piano coda reestablishes a normal.

No. 1, "Sommermüd", employs two transposition-levels of the inversion. As we might expect, the complete pattern is rounded off by a return of the prime, which has been restricted throughout to a single tonal level. But the normal is more specific than that. The song opens with a division of the row into tetrads, of which the third is consistently given to the piano against the other two in the voice. In the piano coda the left hand states each tetrad in turn against a combination of the other two in the right hand. The song is over when the third has taken its turn in the bass. This, then, seems to be the normal: a statement of the prime with the third tetrad harmonically supporting the other two. But what of the larger syntax of the composition? How is the twelve-tone texture related to the choice of the two inversions? Not, as in No. 3, by hexadic combinatoriality. Here, where the primary division of the row is tetradic, the connections from one row-form to the next are established by relations among these segments — and occasionally others, longer or shorter (Ex. 20). The exploited similarities

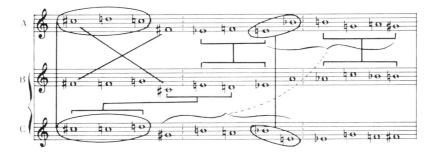

Ex. 20

between the prime $(A)$ and the first inversion $(B)$ adhere to the corresponding segments, whereas some of those involving the second inversion $(C)$ are more abstruse. Hence it is appropriate that this form does come second, and that the main burden of the song rests on the other two.

The above examples suggest the generalization that, for Schoenberg at least, the standard twelve-tone pattern is analogous to the standard tonal pattern: statement of normal, departure from normal, return to normal. If that generalization is valid at all, it must admit numerous exceptions. Just as many tonal compositions diverge from the standard, so do many twelve-tone compositions, including some of Schoenberg's: I need mention only his Violin Phantasy. But whether his composition begins with the normal, or ends with the normal, or both, or neither; whether the normal depends on a certain transposition of the row, or division of the row, or combination of rows—I submit that there is always a normal to be found, and to be heard.

A recent review of a performance of Schoenberg's music compared the composer to "a man who gives up a profitable life as a banker to go exploring at the South Pole." [2] It should be clear why I consider such a view entirely wrong. If we wish to retain the simile of the explorer, let us think of Schoenberg as a mountain climber who, approaching the timberline, realizes that he must give up the protective cover of the forest. But the ground beneath his feet is still the same solid earth.

[2] Donal Henahan in *The New York Times,* Oct. 8, 1974, p. 37.

160

# STRAVINSKY:
# THE PROGRESS OF A METHOD

EDWARD T. CONE

## I

FOR MANY years it was fashionable to accuse Stravinsky, like Picasso, of artistic inconstancy: of embracing a series of manners instead of achieving a personal style. Today it is becoming increasingly clear that Stravinsky, like Picasso, has been remarkably consistent in his stylistic development. Each apparently divergent phase has been the superficial manifestation of an interest that has eventually led to an enlargement and a new consolidation of the artist's technical resources.

This does not mean that all questions concerning Stravinsky's methods are now settled. Some of his most persistent characteristics are still puzzling, and as a result it is hard to explain why some of his greatest successes really work. But they do work, and this essay will try to throw some light on how they work by examining one of these characteristics: the apparent discontinuities that so often interrupt the musical flow.

From *Le Sacre du Printemps* onward, Stravinsky's textures have been subject to sudden breaks affecting almost every musical dimension: instrumental and registral, rhythmic and dynamic, harmonic and modal, linear and motivic. (Almost every one of these can be found, for example, in the first dozen measures of the *Symphonies of Wind Instruments*.) Such shifts would be noticeable in any context, but they are especially so because of other peculiarities of Stravinsky's style. A change of chord after a long-continued static harmony comes as a shock; so does a melodic leap interjected into a predominantly conjunct line; so too a new temporal context after a metrically persistent rhythm.

It could be argued that such points of interruption in scores like *Le Sacre* and *Les Noces* are meant to be analogous to corresponding actions on the stage, and hence that their origin is primarily extramusical and practical. Even so, none of the stage works exhibits so consistent and musically functional use of the device as the "abstract"

*Symphonies*—which would indicate that, whatever its origin, the method was musically important to him. That he has never relinquished it suggests that it is musically necessary.

On examination, the point of interruption proves to be only the most immediately obvious characteristic of a basic Stravinskyan technique comprising three phases, which I call stratification, interlock, and synthesis. By stratification I mean the separation in musical space of ideas—or better, of musical areas—juxtaposed in time; the interruption is the mark of this separation. The resultant layers of sound may be differentiated by glaring contrast, as at rehearsal Nos. 1 and 2 of the *Symphonies*, where changes of instrumentation, register, harmony, and rhythm, reinforce one another. The effect may be much more subtle, as at No. 6, where instrumentation overlaps and there is no change of register. (All references, in this as in other works, are to the revised scores because of their more general availability.) In almost every case, however, there is at least one element of connection between successive levels. In the first example cited the interval of the fourth, F-B♭, is the foundation common to the two areas despite their striking difference in sound.

Since the musical ideas thus presented are usually incomplete and often apparently fragmentary, stratification sets up a tension between successive time segments. When the action in one area is suspended, the listener looks forward to its eventual resumption and completion; meanwhile action in another has begun, which in turn will demand fulfillment after its own suspension. The delayed satisfaction of these expectations occasions the second phase of the technique: the interlock. To take the simplest possible case, consider two ideas presented in alternation: A-1, B-1, A-2, B-2, A-3, B-3. Now one musical line will run through A-1, A-2, A-3; another will correspondingly unite the appearances of B. Although heard in alternation, each line continues to exert its influence even when silent. As a result, the effect is analogous to that of polyphonic strands of melody: the successive time-segments are as it were counterpointed one against the other. The alternation of the first two contrasting areas of the *Symphonies* is an elementary example of this kind, but much more complicated alternations of three or more layers are common. (See fold-out.) (The device is not without precedent, as a glance at the successive partial statements of the ritornello in the first movement of the Fifth Brandenburg Concerto will show. In this connection Stravinsky's own predilection for the Baroque concerto style is illuminating.)

The most interesting phase of the process, the synthesis, is the one most likely to be overlooked. Some sort of unification is the necessary

163

· 19 ·

goal toward which the entire composition points, for without it there is no cogency in the association of the component areas. But it is seldom as explicit as the original stratification, and it almost invariably involves the reduction and transformation of one or more components, and often the assimilation by one of all the others. The diverse elements are brought into closer and closer relation with one another, all ideally being accounted for in the final resolution. But the process is by no means confined to the end of a movement; sometimes it is at work from the beginning. It can take many forms: rhythmic, contrapuntal, harmonic. A small-scale example referring to a limited section begins at No. 46 of the *Symphonies*. The material, first presented on levels separated by register and instrumentation, moves gradually into a *tutti* in which all strata are simultaneously stated.

A description of the technique would be incomplete without mention of two devices the composer uses for mitigating the starkness of the opposition between strata. One is the use of a bridge, such as the two measures just before No. 6 of the *Symphonies*. This motive, linking the preceding statement at No. 3 with the new area of No. 6, effects the gentler stratification previously noted. It is not a transition in the conventional sense, but an area with a life of its own, as its future development shows. Although acting as a bridge in the immediate context, it reaches forward to its next appearance in the interlocking pattern.

The other means at Stravinsky's disposal is what I call divergence: the division of an original single layer into two or more. When the chorale, so long suspended through the course of the *Symphonies*, succeeds in achieving its full expanse, it engenders a divergence (initiated by the horns after No. 66, carried on later at No. 68 by the oboes). A more subtle example is the one introduced by the oboes at No. 3. Here it sounds like a continuation of the first motive, but it proves to be the source of the entire large area beginning at No. 46.

All the examples so far have been taken from the *Symphonies*, the most thoroughgoing of Stravinsky's works in the employment of the technique. Its entire form depends thereon, as I hope the following analysis will make clear. During the years that followed its composition, however, Stravinsky refined his method, as I shall try to show in analyses of the first movements of the Serenade in A and the *Symphony of Psalms*. Finally, a few references to more recent works will attest its continuing importance.

## II

The sketch of the *Symphonies of Wind Instruments* is not meant to serve as a complete linear and harmonic analysis but is rather intended to make clear to the eye the way in which the strata are separated, interlocked, and eventually unified. The thematic material represented by the capital letters is easily identifiable through the corresponding rehearsal numbers in the score; my own notation presents the minimum necessary for following the important lines of connection. These should be read first of all straight across—from the first appearance of A to the second, thence to the third, and so on. If this is done, the continuity of each layer should become immediately clear. When the voice-leading is unusual, or when it has been abbreviated in the sketch, paths are made by unbroken lines, as in the bass of the first appearance of B. Broken lines are used to show connections and transitions between areas, divergences, and elements of unification. The fourth underlying both A and B, for example, is indicated at the outset as a common factor. The transition from A to C at No. 6 is similarly shown, as well as the double connection from C to the following statements of A and B.

One thing the sketch does not show is the contribution of the meter to the differentiation of strata. Taking $\quarternote = 72$ as the common measure, we find the following relationship:

B:      $\quarternote$      $= 72$

A:      $\eighthnote\eighthnote$      $= 72$

C, D, E:   $\eighthnote\eighthnote\eighthnote$   $= 72$    (actually notated:    $\eighthnote\eighthnote = 108$ )

F:      $\eighthnote\eighthnote\eighthnote\eighthnote$   $= 72$    (actually notated:    $\eighthnote\eighthnote = 144$ )

These relationships also contribute to unification. In the first important step toward synthesis, at No. 11, the area referred to as D brings A and C together at a common tonal level against contrapuntal interjections by B. A is assimilated into the faster tempo of C as well, a movement at first resisted but eventually joined by a B transformed for the occasion. Out of this synthesis appears E as a long divergence that shows its close connection by retaining the same tempo. E in turn suffers frequent contrapuntal interjections by D, and after several more serious interruptions it returns to its parent, never to reappear.

The latter half of the piece is largely concerned with the development of the new area F. It has already been suggested that F contains several levels that are unified in the climactic *tutti* at No. 54. The result is an unmistakable emphasis on the fifth A-E as a neighbor to the G-D of the beginning and end. At the same time, another line initiated by the original G-D fifth has descended through F♯-C♯ (No. 9) to E-B (No. 15, and especially after No. 26), and its gradual return to the original level is completed in the final synthesis.

It is thus the role of the late flowering of area B to resolve both of these motions, a role beautifully fulfilled by the last chord. The linear aspects of this synthesis are indicated in the sketch, but even more impressive is the masterly way in which the harmonic progression toward the tonic C is handled. Foreshadowed by the premonitory chords at Nos. 42 and 56, delayed by the long development of section F, clearly approached at No. 65, momentarily circumvented by the divergence within section B, it arrives with inevitability and finality. And although its root is C, the chord is broad enough to contain within itself the triads of G major from the opening and E minor from the long central passage.

This connection of G to E is important for another reason: it demonstrates the influence of the opening motive on the entire course of the piece. Area A is concerned with the contrast of two fifths (or a fifth and a fourth) at the distance of a minor third: G-D and B♭-F. The expression of the same relationship horizontally in the upper voices gives rise to the basic opposition between areas A and B. The progression from G to E and back, again expressed in terms of their fifths, reflects the minor third in the opposite direction. The third thus operates within a single area, by contrast between areas, and through the movement of the whole.

Two recurring transitional passages should be noted: the ones marked X and Y. The former is first used between areas A and C; but later it occurs cadentially attached to A, B, and E—a significant unifying element. Y always functions as a preparation for a longer section: it is used to herald E, F, and the final B.

The most interesting detail of all, however, is the little passage at No. 3. Interpolated as a conclusion to A, it looks forward, both metrically and motivically, to the future F. At the same time it summarizes the two important movements of fifths mentioned above: the neighboring motion from G-D to A-E and back, and the descent from G-D through F♯-C♯ to E-B. And the English horn, its lowest voice, forecasts clearly the tonality of C toward which the entire composition is to move.

· 22 ·

166

## II

The sketch of the *Symphonies of Wind Instruments* is not meant to serve as a complete linear and harmonic analysis but is rather intended to make clear to the eye the way in which the strata are separated, interlocked, and eventually unified. The thematic material represented by the capital letters is easily identifiable through the corresponding rehearsal numbers in the score; my own notation presents the minimum necessary for following the important lines of connection. These should be read first of all straight across—from the first appearance of A to the second, thence to the third, and so on. If this is done, the continuity of each layer should become immediately clear. When the voice-leading is unusual, or when it has been abbreviated in the sketch, paths are made by unbroken lines, as in the bass of the first appearance of B. Broken lines are used to show connections and transitions between areas, divergences, and elements of unification. The fourth underlying both A and B, for example, is indicated at the outset as a common factor. The transition from A to C at No. 6 is similarly shown, as well as the double connection from C to the following statements of A and B.

One thing the sketch does not show is the contribution of the meter to the differentiation of strata. Taking $\quarternote = 72$ as the common measure, we find the following relationship:

B:      $\eighthnote$      $= 72$

A:      $\quarternote$      $= 72$

C, D, E:    $= 72$     (actually notated:    $= 108$)

F:      $= 72$     (actually notated:    $= 144$)

These relationships also contribute to unification. In the first important step toward synthesis, at No. 11, the area referred to as D brings A and C together at a common tonal level against contrapuntal interjections by B. A is assimilated into the faster tempo of C as well, a movement at first resisted but eventually joined by a B transformed for the occasion. Out of this synthesis appears E as a long divergence that shows its close connection by retaining the same tempo. E in turn suffers frequent contrapuntal interjections by D, and after several more serious interruptions it returns to its parent, never to reappear.

The latter half of the piece is largely concerned with the develop-

chord. (Pure but not simple: its unique orchestration and doubling already suggest the important role of G as a future dominant.) B, always easily distinguishable by the predominance of the piano, permits diatonic motion within the static E minor; but C, the vehicle of the vocal lines, contains in its instrumental parts chromatic neighbors that are continually pushing the voices toward C minor or E♭ major. Why?

The answer takes us beyond the confines of this movement. The last appearance of C ends squarely on the dominant of C minor, the key of the second movement. E♭, on which this movement in turn ends, is also prominent in the finale, which resolves its constant struggle between that key and C major in favor of the latter. This completes the circle, so to speak, by its close relation to the opening chord. The following diagram, linking by means of a double line those chords in which the root of one is the third of the other, indicates the progression of the whole symphony:

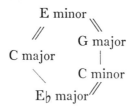

This progression is forecast in the stratum labeled X, which unlike the others does not relate directly to the opening chord. It begins by alternating the dominants of C and E♭ and moves now toward the one key, now toward the other. It is also an important element of unification. Its sixteenth-note motion constantly underlies B; its harmonies are constantly suggested in C, the accompaniment of which is appropriately based on an augmentation of X. But the true resolution of X comes only with the statement of the fugue-subject of the second movement.

Here, then, is the same technique, but used in a highly complex way. B, although divergent from A in rhythm, develops its harmony; although in instrumental and harmonic contrast to X, it utilizes its rhythm. (At one point—during the transition to the first appearance of C—B even embraces the harmony of X.) C, in turn easily distinguished from its neighbors by its orchestration, nevertheless includes and synthesizes the harmony of them all; and the climax at No. 12 combines C with B, and by implication with A. Interesting overlaps occur, as when the piano twice anticipates the entrance of B (once before No. 2 and again before No. 9), or when voices—the property of C—reinforce B's tonic pedal (No. 9). Stratification in one dimension thus proceeds simultaneously with unification in another, and the process embraces not this movement alone but the symphony as a whole.

V

It was suggested at the outset that Stravinsky has never relinquished the method of composition outlined here. A cursory glance at almost any typical piece written before his present twelve-tone period will bear that out. An analysis of the first movement of the *Symphony in Three Movements*, for example, becomes much easier if the principle of stratification is applied. The introduction not only furnishes the basic material of successive divergences forming the important areas of the movement, but also returns at the end to complete its own line and to synthesize the whole. The chief strata of the body of the movement, those beginning at No. 7 and at No. 38, are presented in interlocking pattern; and much that goes on internally within each can be explained by sub-stratifications—such as the contrasting *concertante* areas that comprise the central section.

What is more surprising is to find the same principles at work in the twelve-tone pieces. There is no clearer example of the interlock, for instance, than the recurrent Hebrew letters in contrast to the Latin texts of the "Querimonia" and "Solacium" sections of *Threni*. Each stratum here forms a line unified by melody, harmonic progression, instrumentation, and choice of voices. A more primitive example of the same kind is to be found in the recurring orchestral refrains throughout the *Canticum sacrum*.

It could be argued that these are special cases analogous to stage works, and that only their textual and liturgical demands have elicited a technique characteristic of Stravinsky's earlier period. Yet I believe that a closely related method underlies *Movements*. Here, in a style characterized by wide-ranging, pointillistic melodies, a complete harmonic exploitation of the chromatic scale, and a flexible rhythm free from obvious ostinato patterns, instrumental differentiation becomes the chief source of stratification. This practice is especially obvious in the third and fourth of the *Movements*. In the former, one level is initiated by the piano, one by the oboe and English horn, and one by the harp and trumpets. Only the piano remains unchanged throughout. In the second level, the English horn is replaced first by the clarinet, then by the flutes. In the third, the trumpets are joined by the bass clarinet and are eventually replaced by a clarinet tremolo.

· 25 ·

This element serves as a unifying pedal in a final synthesis of all three layers.

The fourth movement presents one level always opened by flutes and sustained by chords in string harmonics. Each statement of this area is answered by one of the piano, but each phrase of the piano is in turn introduced and interrupted by an orchestral interjection. The interrupting area is always the same: solo cellos or basses. The introductory area constantly changes: from cello harmonics (m. 98) to clarinets (m. 111) to trombones and bass clarinet (m. 125).

These two movements are the most thoroughgoing in their use of the orchestra in this way, but all the sections are influenced by the same approach. It is symbolized by the peculiar layout of the full score—a notational scheme that in fact suggested the one I have used in my own analyses. What is more, the entire work shows evidence of a single plan of orchestral stratification, working its way through all the movements. This can be seen in characteristic idioms of certain instruments: the trumpets, whether playing intervals or lines, constantly emphasize the fifth; until the last movement the trombones are heard only as a group; the clarinet tremolo is carried over from the third to the fifth movement. The succession of the interludes emphasizes first the individual sound of each group in turn—woodwinds, strings, and brass—and then the unification of the three. Prepared as it is by the exceptionally clear differentiation of instrumental areas of No. IV, this interlude comes as a climactic synthesis—the only *tutti* in the entire work. It is typical of Stravinsky's current phase that this is followed by a movement of relative attenuation, decomposing the orchestra once more into stratified layers. It is symptomatic that even the harp tone is here divided as it were in two—into a harp and a celesta component (mm. 183ff.).

Many listeners have noted that *Movements*, for all its references to post-Webern serialism, still sounds unmistakably like Stravinsky. The foregoing account of an enduring feature of his style may suggest one reason why.

170

· 26 ·

# Stravinsky's Svadebka (Les Noces)

### Robert Craft and William Harkins

### I. Avant-Propos

### (R. C.)

*Svadebka*[1] (*Les Noces*) ranks high in the by no means crowded company of indisputable contemporary masterpieces. That it does not immediately come to mind as such is attributable to cultural and linguistic barriers and to the inadequacy, partly from the same cause, of performances. For *Svadebka* can be sung only in Russian, both because the sounds of the words are part of the music, and because their rhythms are inseparable from the musical design. A "translation" that satisfied the quantitative and accentual formulas of the original could retain no approximation of its literal sense. Which is the reason that Stravinsky, who was not rigidly averse to changing sense for sound's sake, abandoned an

tacle, the ordonnance of the text. *Svadebka* is in fact the only theatrical work by him, apart from the much slighter *Renard*, that combines music with a text in his mother tongue, the only work in which ritual, symbol, meaning on every level are part of his direct cultural heredity.

It is also, of all Stravinsky's works, the one that underwent the most extensive metamorphoses; and that not only occupied his mind *during* the longest time but that may have, in aggregate, *taken* the most time. (A later Russia would have awarded him a Stakhanovite medal for his industry alone, if that Russia had recognized *Svadebka*.) The reasons for the long gestation are, first, that Stravinsky several times suspended work to compose other music, which, each time, left him greatly changed. And, second,

how changes in instrumentation have effected changes in musical substance.

### II. Calendar

### (R. C.)

On September 9, 1913, Stravinsky, his wife, three children, and nurse Sofia Dmitrievna left Russia at Alexandrov, the border station, en route from their summer home in Ustilug to their temporary winter one in Clarens. In Warsaw, where he had obtained the necessary exit visas the day before, Stravinsky was joined by his friend and co-librettist of *The Nightingale*, Stepan Mitussov. Having resumed work on the opera after his return to Russia from Paris at the beginning of July, Stravinsky completed the mechanical Nightingale's music on August 1, and, three weeks later, the true Nightingale's aria

pleted the second of the string quartet pieces, in Leysin—and July 24, when he was safely back there working on the final one.[4] Believing that war was imminent—this was a few days after Sarajevo—he went first to Ustilug to salvage some personal possessions, then to Kiev, where he stayed at the home of his father-in-law, 28 Annenskaya Street, and where he acquired a volume of wedding songs published (in 1911) as a supplement to *Pyesni sobrannye P. I. Kireevskim* — "Songs collected by P.[eter] V.[asilievitch] Kireevsky." The songs in this volume served as the main source of the *Svadebka* libretto.[5] (Kireevsky, who died in 1856, was a great Slavophile who compiled some twelve volumes of Russian folk songs, drawing on the work of many other collectors, including Pushkin.)

English version on which he had labored himself in the fall of 1959 and again in December, 1965.

But performances are infrequent as well as inadequate. The four pianos and large number of percussion instruments that comprise the *Svadebka* ensemble are not included in the standard instrumentation of symphony orchestras and other performing units. Then, too, the piece by itself is long enough for only half a program, while the few possible companion works, using many of the same instruments—Varèse's *Ionisation*, Bartók's "Sonata for Two Pianos and Percussion," Antheil's *Ballet Mécanique* (an arrant plagiarism thought to be the apostolic successor at the time)—derive from it as instrumental example.

As a result of the obstacles of language and culture, audiences do not share in the full meaning of the work, hearing it as a piece of "pure" music; which, of course, and as Stravinsky would say, *is* its ultimate meaning. But Stravinsky notwithstanding, *Svadebka* is a dramatic work, composed for the stage, and informed with more meanings on the way to that ultimate one than any other opus by the composer. The drama is his own, moreover, and he is responsible for the choice of the subject, the form of the stage spec-

that he *was* creating something entirely new, both musically—its heterophonic vocal-instrumental style is unique in our music—and in theatrical combination and genre, an amalgam of ballet and dramatic cantata that he was himself unable to describe. "Russian Choreographic Scenes," his subtitle on the final score, does not even mention that the subject is a village wedding and that the scenes or "tableaux" are four: at the Bride's (the ritual plaiting of her tresses); at the Groom's (the ritual curling of his locks); the departure of the Bride for the Church; the wedding feast.

* * *

The aims of the present essay[2] necessarily differ from those of the guidebook the authors are preparing to the facsimile edition of the manuscript scores and sketches from which it has been extracted. The sketches themselves are a study in the processes of growth and refinement that can illuminate not only part of the path of Stravinsky's working mind but also the embryology of the musical mind as a whole. Even with sketches and scores in hand, however, one is limited in the verbal means for this explication to such pedantic tasks as suggesting comparisons between the sketches and the final score, and attempting to explain

which precedes this *japonaiserie*. But another project had been taking shape in his imagination that must also have been discussed during that stopover in Warsaw. For it was Mitussov who, two months earlier, had supplied the manuscript of a song which occurs, virtually as he transcribed it, in the Fourth Tableau of *Svadebka*.

Stravinsky could not have turned his full mind to the new opus until *The Nightingale* was completed six months later. But he was thinking, and even talking, about it: a letter from Prokofiev to Miaskovsky[3] repeats a rumor that plans were afoot to mount it as early as the autumn of 1914. Work on the libretto probably began during May and June. Stravinsky composed no music then—or since the completion of the first of the "Three Pieces for String Quartet" on April 25—and it is unlikely that he was idle creatively for so long, ceaselessly occupied as he was in the far less interesting world of music outside his own head. His notebooks of the time are filled with Russian popular verse, songs and *chastushkas* (folk rhymes), most of it capped with his scansion marks.

The need for additional texts, in any event, was the principal reason for a hurried trip to Ustilug and Kiev between July 2—on which date he com-

Once back in Switzerland, the song cycle *Pribaoutki*—on texts from Afanas'ev,[6] the source, a few years later, of *Histoire du Soldat*—came first. During this time, however, and during a sojourn in Florence with Diaghilev in October, a version of the libretto was pieced together. And by November Stravinsky had drafted some, possibly most, of the music of the First Tableau; or so I deduce from a sketch,

[4] He may have returned to Switzerland (Salvan) as early as July 13. A cable addressed to him there on that date from Diaghilev, in London, expresses the hope that "*Svadebka suit son chemin.*"

[5] The *only* source, actually, apart from three lines in Tereshchenko's *Byt russkago naroda* (vol. 2, p. 332, 1848 edition, used at [93]); and apart from Stravinsky himself, for the author of the unidentified lines, the neologisms, and the many amendments and modifications of the Kireevsky originals can only be the composer. At one time he also planned to borrow a line (at least) from Sakharov's *Pyesni russkago naroda*, so marked by him in his father's bound volumes of the 1838 edition (Song 229, p. 331). His father, who had one of the largest private libraries in Russia, owned a number of Kireevsky's volumes, and Stravinsky was familiar with them when he was young.

[6] See A. Afanas'ev, *Russian Fairy Tales*, translated by Norbert Guterman, commentary by Roman Jakobson (Pantheon Books, 1945).

[1] "Little Wedding," a diminutive form of *svadba*, "wedding."

[2] Read at Emerson Hall, Harvard, August 8, 1972.

[3] *Miaskovsky: Correspondence* (Moscow, 1969).

dated that month, for the section at [21], though the date merely refers to a succession of intervals on the same page that Stravinsky's then seven-year-old elder son had sung (whistled? hummed?), and that his father, with the immemorial pride of the parent in the prodigies of its offspring, had written down. On November 15 Stravinsky composed a *Polka*. Surprisingly remote from *Svadebka*, it was the first of the *Three Easy Pieces* from which the whole of his so-called neoclassicism has been said to stem. But whatever the truth of that, one part of his amazingly compartmented mind—in which *Renard* and *Svadebka* were incubating at the same time with no tangling of stylistic lines—was always several steps ahead.

At the beginning of January, 1915, Stravinsky moved to the Hotel Victoria in Château-d'Oex where, except for brief trips, he remained until March. One night in a funicular near Clarens, he found himself with two deeply inebriated Vaudois for fellow passengers, one of whom sang a tipsy tune while the other interjected an accompaniment of hiccoughs. Stravinsky composed a hocket imitating this debauched duet, perhaps the only *real* hocket ever written though the name has been given to a style of two centuries of European music; and he made capital use of it in the Fourth Tableau of *Svadebka*, increasing the suggestion of drunkenness appropriate to the wedding feast by shifting the music from thesis to arsis. Then, in a powerful unifying stroke, he identified the hocket rhythm with the motive of the Groom, Khvétis Pamfilievitch, which dominates the ending of the work. It hardly needs to be said that what was actually heard in the funicular must have been very different from the constructions it inspired in *Svadebka*. But the incident is typical. Stravinsky was able to hear, and often noted down, the *music* in the rhythms and intervals of machinery, in street noises, in hurdy-gurdies and carousels—and in troubadours, intoxicated or otherwise, such as these Vaudois.

On another excursion (January 28), this time to Geneva, Stravinsky dined with Ernest Ansermet in Maxim's Restaurant, where he happened to hear a cimbalom—which may not have provoked him to say "Eureka" though that is what he thought. *Svadebka*'s original subtitle was "Songs and Dances on Russian Folk Themes, for voices, woodwinds, brass, percussion, plucked and bowed instruments." The plucked instruments were to have included balalaikas, *guzlas*, guitars, but these were replaced in the first scores by a harpsichord—a "plucked" instrument, after all—and a quintet of strings

playing *pizzicato*. The cimbalom, which is not plucked but hammered with wood or padded sticks, nevertheless provided exactly the articulation Stravinsky required as well as a harder and more resonant sound than the jangly balalaika of his native land. It is a large-size dulcimer—the Biblical instrument, pictured on the Ninevah tablets, uncertainly invoked in *Ulysses* ("like no voice of strings or reeds or whatdoyoucallthem dulcimers"), but partly described by Pepys in his diary for May 23, 1662: "Here among the Fidlers I first saw a dulcimore played on, with sticks knocking on the strings, and is very pretty."

That night in Geneva the player[7] favored the composer—not knowing that it *was* the composer—with a demonstration of the instrument, and as a result Stravinsky purchased one for himself and had it sent to Château-d'Oex, where he immediately added it to the orchestra of *Svadebka*. He taught himself to play it, moreover, drawing a chart of its thirty-five strings and notating the instrument's fifty-three pitches on them at the places where they are produced on the actual strings. At first the instrument is indicated in his manuscripts by its Russian name, "tympanon," which is the name employed by its mastermaker and master-player its Stradivarius as well as its Paganini—Pantaléon Hebenstreit, whose patron had been Louis XIV. (Pantaléon's only surviving tympanon, made in 1705, was among the effects of Sacha Votichenko, a descendant of Pantaléon, at the time of his death in 1971 in Scottsdale, Arizona surely one of the odder cultural properties to have turned up in that state since the London Bridge.) In the next five years the cimbalom was never far from Stravinsky's instrumental palette, but he was obliged to abandon it after that because too few players could read and play *his* music. Yet it remained a favorite instrument, and that most genial of his works, *Renard*, cannot be performed without it.

Two weeks later (February 15), Stravinsky was in Rome, playing *The Rite of Spring* (four-hands with Alfredo Casella, in a salon of the Grand Hotel), for a small audience invited by Diaghilev and including Rodin. At this time, *Svadebka* was unveiled privately for Diaghilev (cf. his letter of March 8 to Stravinsky in Château d'Oex), who heard further portions of it in the Hotel Continental, Milan, on April 1, and in Montreux at the end of April. But the only *creative* digression from *Svadebka* between April and the end of the year was the composition of that miniature masterpiece of musical catnip, the *Berceuses du Chat*, the first phrase of which so resembles the first phrase of the soprano in *Svadebka* that the one could have suggested the other and perhaps did, sketches for both being found on the same page. On January 4, 1916, however, in ever

more straitened circumstances because of the war, Stravinsky accepted a commission to compose a chamber opera. This supervention was *Renard*, some of which had been written a year before; it could hardly have been a happier one, but *Svadebka* was shelved for seven more months.

Returning to it after that, Stravinsky was again and almost constantly interrupted: by the excerpting and re-orchestrating of a symphonic poem from *The Nightingale* (completed April 4, 1917); by the composition of several short pieces including the "Etude for Pianola"[8] (completed September 10, 1917); by four changes of residence; by frequent travels (three trips to Spain in 1916 in addition to quite regular visits to Paris, Milan, Rome); by endless questions relating to the performance and publication of his ever more famous works, and by *pourparlers* concerning commissions for future ones. For example, he had been asked, through Léon Bakst, to compose incidental music for Gide's *Cléopatre*.[9] Replying to Bakst, in Paris, from Morges (July 30, 1917), Stravinsky telegraphed that "*Notions du réalisme et synthétisme pour la mise en scène ne m'explique[nt] rien. Attends Gide pour comprendre*"—and the demand for the concrete is so characteristically expressed that the message could have come from any year of Stravinsky's life, 1970 as well as 1917, *mutatis mutandis* in the matter of the authors.

In April, 1917, Stravinsky played virtually the whole of *Svadebka* for Diaghilev in Ouchy and Diaghilev wept by all accounts including Stravinsky's. A month later (May 30) the *New York Herald* quoted the composer as expecting 'to finish *Les Noces Villageoises* this summer." Yet the sketch-score was not completed until October 11, a delay that is in some measure attributable, I believe, to three shocks: the death of his beloved childhood nurse Bertha—"Bilibousch" -Essert (April 28), the death of his younger brother Gury (August 3), and the death of "his" Russia.

For though he hailed the Revolution at the time of its first convulsions—telegraphing to his mother and brother at "Khroukov Canal 6, Petrograd," March 20, 1917: "*Toutes mes pensées avec vous dans ces inoubliables jours de bonheur qui traverse notre chère Russie liberée...*"—he became a Ukrainian revanchist soon after that (even writing to Swiss newspapers on the subject), and then, and more lastingly, an anti-Bolshevik, denouncing "Lénine" (in the same *Herald* interview) as a "fanatic." He quickly foresaw the consequences to himself of the sundering from Russia, in any case, and realized that his voluntary exile was over and the involuntary one had begun. The lament in the epithalamium at the end of *Svadebka* is as much for the loss of Holy Mother Russia as for

the virginity of Nastasia Timofeyevna, Stravinsky's stage bride.

The instrumentation was not yet finished on October 11, however, nor was it to be for another five and a half years. Writing more than a year later (November 19, 1918) to Otto Kling, of the English music publishers J. and W. Chester Ltd., Stravinsky discussed the score as if it *were* complete, but he was trying to negotiate a contract at the time.[10] In a letter of April 6, 1919, to Gustav Gustavovitch Struve, of the temporarily defunct *Editions Russes de Musique*, he refers to *Svadebka* as "a cantato or oratorio, or I do not know what, for four soloists and an instrumental ensemble that I am in too great a hurry to describe." But this ensemble—for which the music is fully scored to the end of the Second Tableau—is described in a letter of July 23, 1919, to Ernest Ansermet:

> I do not know what to do with the *"Noces."* It is ridiculous to stage this *"divertissement"*—for it is not a ballet—without décors, although the décors would not represent anything—being there simply for decoration and *not* to represent anything—with pianola, harmonium, 2 cimbaloms, percussion, singers, and conductor on the stage, together with the dancers. . . .

The percussion was inspired by *Histoire du Soldat*, composed the year before; together with the pianola and cimbaloms, it shows Stravinsky well on the way to the *martellato* ensemble of the final score. He wrote to Kling again on November 23:

> . . . as for the *"Noces"* you must put in the contract that it is to be described on *affiches* and in programs not as a "ballet" but as a *"divertissement."* Here is the complete title of the work: *"Les Noces"* (village scenes): *divertissement* in two parts with soloists and chorus and an ensemble of several instruments.

The contract was signed on December 7. But *Pulcinella*, the *Concertino* for String Quartet, the *Symphonies of Wind Instruments*, *Mavra*, and numerous smaller pieces were composed before Stravinsky could return to and complete the instrumentation. Still another letter to Kling (Paris, May 26, 1921) reveals the composer surrendering to the problem of synchronizing live instrumentalists with the machinery of the pianola:

> As for the *"Noces,"* I am in effect completely reworking the instrumentation for a new ensemble of

[7] Aladar Rácz, whose account of the meeting ("I played a Serbian kolo. . . . Stravinsky wore a monocle, a red tie, a green waistcoat"), and, later, of Stravinsky purchasing a cimbalom (he "prepared the flour-paste, and cleaned the rusty strings himself"), is published in the *Hungarian Book Review* for May-August, 1972, together with some memoirs by Rácz's widow. Both accounts contain chronological and other inaccuracies, however, as shown by a letter to Stravinsky, dated January 29, 1915, from his friend Adrien Bovy.

[8] The instrument was used for rehearsals of the ballet as early as 1912. In the fall of that year Diaghilev proposed that *The Rite of Spring* be "recorded" on it for Nijinsky's rehearsals. An extremely interesting letter from Ansermet to Stravinsky, June 12, 1919, deals with some of the mechanical problems of the *Etude*.

[9] Stravinsky's diary for August, 1917 includes a scheme for this. The project was not closed until December when Ida Rubinstein rejected Stravinsky's conditions.

[10] Stravinsky's contract with Diaghilev for the performances was negotiated for him by Ansermet in London in June, 1919.

winds, percussion, and one or two parts for piano. I think that this new ensemble will suit us as well as the former version which includes mechanical instruments, something that could create all kinds of difficulties for you.

Winds or percussion—"sounding brass or a tinkling cymbal"? But apart from the winds he is nearing the final stage and perhaps the most original "orchestra" in twentieth-century music. The volume of sound is still small, evidently, and in fact the third and fourth pianos were not added, nor the arsenal of percussion instruments expanded to include heavy armaments, until the final score. Thus after beginning with an orchestra that, vast and varied as it was, virtually excluded percussion instruments, he ended with one of percussion only, and in the process arrived at the category of the *actual* orchestra of a Russian peasant wedding; for percussion instruments—pots and pans as well as drums, tambourines, cymbals—were bashed, hammered, clapped together, rattled, and rung throughout the ceremony and celebration in order to drive away evil spirits.

Typesetting the Russian text created new and unforeseen difficulties. Writing to London from Biarritz, August 29, 1921, Stravinsky advised his publisher that

> [Although] the [proof] page that you sent to me is good . . . I ask you to draw the attention of your proof-readers to the Russian text. Literally not a single word is comprehensible. It is an agglomeration of letters with no sense. You must have a proof-reader who knows Russian. Unfortunately I will not have the time to rewrite the whole Russian text in the proofs—and, anyway, it is perfectly clearly written in the manuscript you have. Try to find a Russian proof-reader; so many Russians are without work at the moment.

On October 3, Stravinsky informed a London newspaper that "The Village Wedding" was finished. But he meant the two-hand piano-score, the final proofs of which did not come for another seven months, during which he composed the one-act opera *Mavra*. The full score was finally completed on April 6, 1923, in Monaco, where the ballet—or *divertissement*—was already in rehearsal, and the first performance took place June 13, at the Gaieté Lyrique in Paris, a full decade after the work was conceived.

### III. A Note on the Sketches

**(R. C.)**

Graphic analysis, in the case of *Svadebka*, is helpful as a guide to chronology, for as a rule Stravinsky's Russian script is "printed," rather than cursive, on the more mature and final sketches. (I should add that he drew most of the staves with his own stylus—a roulette, like a tiny, five-furrowed plough, invented and patented by himself though the idea may have come from the Rastral, a five-nib pen used to rule music paper in the eighteenth century. I should add, too, that he used transparent colored inks in some of the *Svadebka* sketches to facilitate reading abbreviated scores; if trumpets and oboes alternate on one line, for example, the music of the former might be "orange," of the latter, "green.") What the sketches reveal, above all, is that in the beginning was the word. In the very act of copying a text, Stravinsky added musical notations, setting a line of verse to a melody or motivic fragment; or giving it unpitched rhythmic values; or designating intervals or chords that had occurred to him in conjunction with it.

In this Stravinsky is at an opposite extreme from, say, Janáček, who, so he confessed, discovered "the musical motives and tempos adopted to demonstrating [the emotions] by declaiming a text aloud and then observing the inflections in my voice." Stravinsky's inspiration in his vocal works came directly from the sounds and rhythms of syllables and words, while structures of poems often suggested musical structures, wordless ones included, such as the imitation of a Russian Alexandrine by Pushkin in *Apollo*.[11] And it is also clear from the sketches that Stravinsky's musical rhythms and stresses are far more commonly suggested by the text than imposed upon it, and that his own claims to the contrary are greatly exaggerated.

In this manner the earliest of the musical notations sprouting directly from texts were used in the Fourth Tableau, which was the last one composed. (The *first* notation for the Fourth Tableau, the song contributed by Stepan Mitussov, occurs at about the halfway point.) But in more than one instance notations found on the same sketch page are widely separated in the final composition. Still, once having found his beginning, Stravinsky seems to have composed from beginning to end, though of course not measure for measure exactly as in the published score. (The chronology can be determined by sketches evincing instrumental improvements from one draft to the next.)

I should add that the sketches oblige all of us who have written about *Svadebka* to eat underdone crow, the largest helping of which is the reward of my own unwisdom. My recantation, moreover, must go all the way back to a statement, published somewhere in my first year of working with Stravinsky, to the effect that music and sound-image were simultaneous and inalterable occurrences in his imagination. This may be true in the case of some of his music—how would anyone know?—but is monumentally *un*true in that of *Svadebka*, in which the sonority is continually and, in the end, totally transformed.

### IV. A Note on Derivations

**(R. C.)**

Stravinsky would never concede that the question of thematic origins was of the slightest importance, and though he was interested in ethnomusicology in his youth, the subject bored him later in life and he would not discuss it. Yet it is no exaggeration to say that all of the melodic material in *Svadebka* is closely related to folk and church music. What I cannot say for certain is how much was actually modeled and how much was "innate"—a combination of memory and of a phenomenal stylistic intuition. Yet I suspect that nearly all of it originated in Stravinsky's imagination. Musicologists have triumphantly traced the phrase at two measures before [3]:

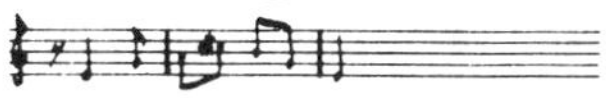

to

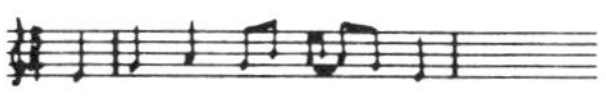

which is from Rimsky-Korsakov's *Polnoe sobranoe sochinenii* (1871). But Stravinsky's sketches reveal that he began with an E minor triad and even further from Rimsky's example than from his own final version.[12]

Béla Bartók observed in 1931 that

> Stravinsky never indicates the source of his themes, no doubt because he wants to imply his indifference to the question. He has claimed the right to use any musical material in his works that he considers useful; and said that, once used, it becomes in some way truly his own. For lack of documents, I am incapable of determining which are the themes he has invented himself, in his "Russian" period, and which he has borrowed from popular songs. But one thing is certain: if among Stravinsky's themes there exist and surely there exist some which are his own invention, they are extremely clever and extremely faithful imitations of popular songs. Moreover, it is remarkable that in his "Russian" period . . . the composer hardly ever uses melodies with closed structures, divided into two or three or more verses, but rather motives of two or three measures, repeating them in *ostinato*. These primitive, brief and often repeated motives are very characteristic of a certain aspect of Russian music. . . . [*La Revue Musicale*, 1955]

In one instance, however, it is possible to follow Stravinsky as he consciously transforms received material. For the music at [50]-[53] is derived entirely (and the music after [53] partly) from the Fifth Tone of the Quamennyi Chant,[13] which is sung at the beginning of the Sunday Dogmatik in the Russian Orthodox Service. Here is a fragment of the Chant:

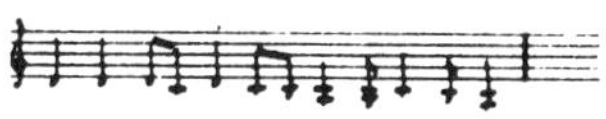

which, after several intermediate stages—including experiments with triplet notation (a symbolism for the Trinity at least as old as Philippe de Vitry)—Stravinsky altered to

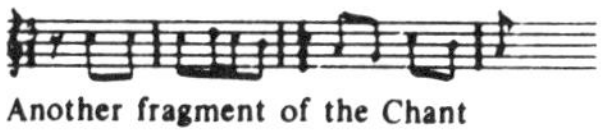

Another fragment of the Chant

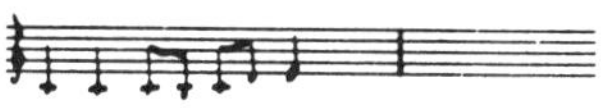

is merely transposed and extended by Stravinsky to

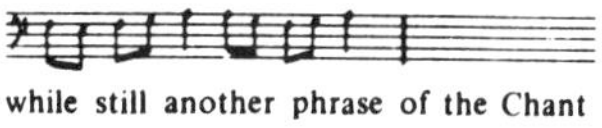

while still another phrase of the Chant

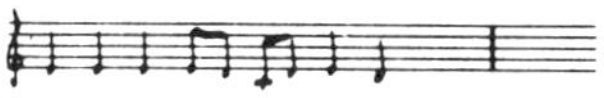

he converts to:

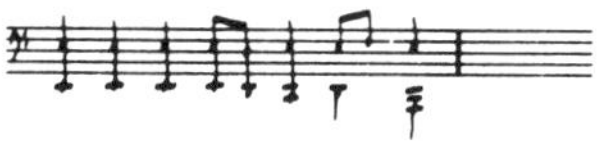

This last became the duet of the two priest-like basses (cf. [50]), which is as close to a representation of the Orthodox service on the stage as Stravinsky ever came,[14] for the singers are unaccompanied, following the Church rule, and are the *only* unaccompanied voices in *Svadebka*. Yet the entire Second Tableau, with, at the end, a *basso ostinato* (A-C-A-C sharp) imitating a great church bell, is "ecclesiastical" music.

* * *

The critical bibliography is slender. The chapter on "Wedding Ceremonials and Chants" in Sokolov's "Russian Folklore" (Macmillan, 1950, for the American Council of Learned Societies, pp. 203-223) is indispensable for the background—but not too *far* back. But the monograph "Igor Stravinsky's '*Les Noces*,' an outline by Victor Belaiev" (Oxford University Press, 1928) is worthless as musical analysis ("the melos of *Les Noces* . . . springs, as it were, from a single melodic germ which is presented in the opening bars") and misleading in most other respects.

The only other essay worth the mention is in *Kniga o Stravinskom*—"Book about Stravinsky" (Triton, Leningrad, 1929, pp. 181-215) by Igor Glebov (pseudonym of Boris Asafiev), English translation by Richard French, 1972. Stravinsky repudiated Glebov's essay in its entirety, and his copy of the book is strewn with question marks, profusely underlined, decorated with marginal rubrics. "What well-thought-out nonsense," he writes at one place. And at others: "What good is all this stupid literature?" and "I am shocked by these pages." When

---

[11] Not that Stravinsky's musical imagination was dependent on words, of course. In November, 1947, after completing the scenario of *The Rake's Progress* with Auden, he immediately composed the string quartet *Prelude to the Graveyard Scene*, being inspired by its subject but not yet having the libretto.

[12] Which is not to deny the many borrowings from the collections of Rimsky and others, including the *Firebird* melodies

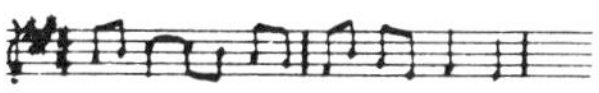

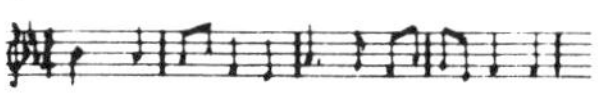

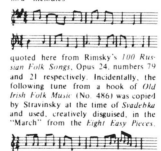

quoted here from Rimsky's *100 Russian Folk Songs*, Opus 24, numbers 79 and 21 respectively. Incidentally, the following tune from a book of *Old Irish Folk Music* (No. 486) was copied by Stravinsky at the time of *Svadebka* and used, creatively disguised, in the "March" from the *Eight Easy Pieces*.

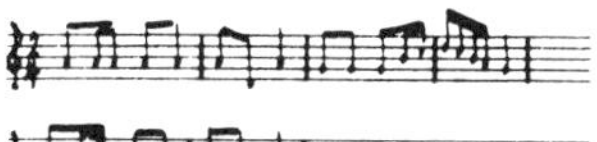

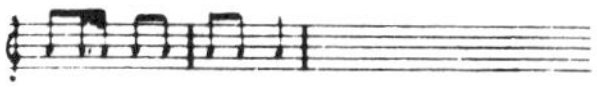

[13] From the *Oktoëchos* or "Book of Eight Tones." Russian ecclesiastical chant, which derives from the Byzantine, is based on a system of eight *echoi*. These are the Byzantine modes as distinguished from *tonoi*, the Greek modes and each of them possesses different melodic formulas. Thus the Sticheron (Psalm tropes), Troparion (hymns sung between the verse of the Psalms), and Irmos (a Byzantine strophic chant) are sung to eight different "Tones" (same sense as in Gregorian Chant), each of which includes three versions for the Sticheron, three for the Troparion, and three for the Irmos. Each, moreover, changes every week at Sunday matins. The Fifth Tone of Sticheron, the one Stravinsky chose, is sung after the matin Psalm, "Lord, I cried unto Thee," and it occurs during the part of the service in which typological parallels are drawn between Old and New Testament prophecies.

[14] He was appalled by a project of Diaghilev to exploit the "theater" of the Church and its gorgeous robes, golden orarions, etc., in a ballet.

Glebov writes that "We must not forget that *Svadebka* is an incarnation of the ancient cult of birth and multiplication," Stravinsky underscores the "We must not forget" and adds: "Better forget, for this has nothing to do with it." At the end, the composer writes: "Dear friend" (he had known Glebov before the Revolution) "this is entirely your own concoction. *Svadebka* is something else than a symphony of Russian songs in a Russian style."

When apprehensible at all, Glebov's analysis of the melodic content in terms of "intonations," and of the rhythmic structure in terms of numbers of measures, is irrelevant. Unfortunately, too, his better insights are substantiated with false arguments; thus, he understands the rhythmic mechanization as style but has obviously never heard of the proportional system on which it is based. He compares *Svadebka* to *The Rite of Spring*—inevitably at that time, when even non-Russians *not* making a case for the superiority of the composer's "Russian" works were raising the specter of Antaeus. (By the mid-Twenties even dug-in Stravinskyans began to fear that without Russia the wells of the composer's inspiration were in danger of drying up.)

But the two pieces can be more fruitfully compared for their differences than for their similarities. *The Rite* is a succession of dance movements, each, to a degree, complete in itself, and each manifesting a classical outline of a first section, middle section, recapitulation. *Svadebka*, on the other hand, is non-stop; its materials are exposed in fragmentary as well as complete form, as a name is evoked by its initials (*pars pro toto*); and it depends on fusings, interweavings, trellises of cross-connection. Hence the unities of the two pieces are of a very different order. And finally, no matter how much new ground is staked out in *The Rite*, its antecedents—in the Russian "Five," in Debussy—are apparent. *Svadebka*, however, is all new.[15]

Yet Glebov's essay is worth reading for the "anthropological background," the rituals and cultural traditions (of exogamous marriage, for one) or, in a word, for everything which Stravinsky took for granted but of which Western audiences are largely unaware. Glebov's emphasis is often wrong; thus he exaggerates the role of the *skomorokh*,[16] and misunderstands both the irony and the religion (greatly overdoing the pagan underground). Nor is he of any help with the text, even failing to mention Kireevsky. His terminology, too—"psalmody," "clausula"—is anachronistic and inapt. Yet he is the only commentator who understands the vital element of lamentation. In addition, his hints—that the *Druzhki*'s music resembles the music of Russian village street criers, that the Matchmaker may be compared to Nekrassov's character of that name—are invaluable for non-Russians.

[15] Glebov's likening it to Vecchi's *Amfiparnasso* (1594)—cf. Casella's little monograph on Stravinsky (1926)—is far-fetched but may have been suggested by Stravinsky himself, who was fond of throwing out false trails of this kind.

[16] An entertainer who performed at country fairs, singing, dancing, clowning, juggling.

And finally, *Svadebka* was new when Glebov wrote, yet he saw its originality and its true stature more clearly than any other critic of his time, *or* of ours. This is doubly remarkable when one remembers that he was writing in a country that had begun to shut down against its greatest composer. In fact the book was banned in the USSR, despite Glebov's patriotic—or, better, telluric—invocation to Stravinsky at the end of this chapter: "Our musical age is the age of Stravinsky; *Svadebka* could have been composed only by a composer of a country in which the elemental power of communion with Nature [has] not yet been lost by the bourgeoisie." The tone, though a little overwrought, is not unlike that of Turgenev's deathbed letter to Tolstoy: "Great writer of the Russian land. . . ."

### V. The Scenario
### (R. C.)

Stravinsky composed the libretto—selected, colligated, and edited it—from

Kireevsky's collection of songs. But the first version was much longer than the final one, for Stravinsky had originally planned to dramatize the complete wedding ritual, and not to begin with the plaiting of the Bride's hair, where the score now starts. His first draft of the scenario is as follows:

#### Svadebka
Fantasy in 3 Acts and 5 Scenes
ACT I
 The Inspection
ACT II
 Scene 1
 The Bargain
  a. At the Bride's
  b. At the Groom's (An Incantation Against Sorcery—see page 49 [in Kireevsky])
 Scene 2
  a. Devichnik (The Bride's Party) [Dyevishnik = Maiden's Day, the day before the wedding]
  b. The Girls Take Her to the Bath
 Scene 3
 In the Bride's House Before the Departure for the Church
ACT III
 The Beautiful Table

I have been unable to determine at what point Stravinsky scrapped this more comprehensive scheme and abandoned the preliminary Matchmaking scenes, the *Devichnik*, and the ritual dunking[17] of the Bride. The final version, in any case, reduced this plan to four scenes: Act II, Scene 1, a and b, Scene 3, and Act III, and it changed the content of Act II, Scene 1, b, abandoning the Incantation in favor of more barbering. The reduction in size was accompanied by a drastic change in genre. Whether or not *Svadebka* was closer to opera in Stravinsky's mind than to the "ballet cantata" it finally became, he appears to have begun with musical characterizations in a conventional operatic way, fitting out the *Druzhka* (Best Man), for instance, with a hunting-horn fanfare—in his secondary role of Master of Ceremonies the *Druzhka* evidently blew a horn—which, transformed beyond recognition except for rhythm, became the music of the bass voice at [53].

[17] His sketches contain a note to the effect that "among the songs collected by Pushkin see pages 54-60 [Kireevsky]"; references are found to "dancing in the bath"; and a reminder to "See 'Customs, Songs, Rituals, etc.' in the Province of Pskov, pages 48-54 [Kireevsky]," which refers to the same thing. I should add that the sketches contain several reminders to look up words in Dal's Dictionary. Professor Harkins remarks, incidentally, that at [52] "Stravinsky has retained the Pskov Dialect use of *ch* for standard Russian *ts* in one word (*chérkov* for *tsérkov*, 'church') but corrects it elsewhere in the same quotation (*potselovát* for Pskov *pochelovát*, 'to kiss'). The apparent inconsistency is probably to be explained by the fact that the nonstandard form *chérkov* is relatively more comprehensible, particularly in combination with *sobor*, 'cathedral,' than is *pochelovát*."

In the final form of the work, roles of this kind do not exist but are replaced simply by voices, none of which is more than loosely identified with the stage characters. Thus the Bride and Groom may seem to be "sung" by, respectively, soprano and tenor; yet no direct identification exists and the same two voices also "speak" for the Bride and her Mother (cf. [21]). Even the Groom's final love song is "impersonated" for him by the bass.

The change in genre led to greater abstraction in the stage movement, too. Thus none of the four final scenes is actually "depicted," "enacted," or even narrated; by this time Stravinsky had renounced the use of narrative, substituting a collage of verse. In effect, *Svadebka* is a verse play for voices speaking out of turn. And as for the stage action, the choreography was conceived as an extension of music: this is to say that gesture and movement were to be stylized according to the rhythmic patterns of the music and not in imitation of popular or ethnographic dances.

As in *The Rite of Spring*, Stravinsky began with stage pictures in mind, even depending on them. But when the music had been completed he began to pare the stage directions away and actually to forget them, until there existed no picture but only music. Many of his stage directions in *Svadebka* are quotations from Kireevsky. The following are some from the sketches, all later than the scenario above, and intended for the four-tableaux final score—though only one of them appears there even in part. The first is a syndiasmic epigraph from Kireevsky than Stravinsky appended to an early draft of the full score:

*Two rivers flow together*
*Two matchmakers come together,*
*They think about the ashblond braid,*
*How will we unplait this ashblond braid?*
*How will we part the braid in two?*

#### First Tableau
The father and mother meet the bride with an icon, when she comes home from the bath. After the blessing, the bridesmaids seat the bride on a bench at the table, and place a dish before her, next to which they place a comb. Each bridesmaid approaches the bride, takes the comb from the table, combs her tresses, replaces the comb on the table and leaves some money in the dish. [Kireevsky, p. 241]

After that the bridesmaids take the bride to the middle of the parlor, and they themselves go up to the father and mother of the bride and make low bows before the icon. The bride, meanwhile, wails to her father and mother. [Kireevsky, p. 240, No. 876]

When the bridesmaids leave, the bride sits on the middle bench by the beautiful window and wails [laments] for her father and mother. Her parents bless her with the icon. The bride goes on wailing. [Kireevsky, p. 241]

The parents go to the bride and stand on both sides of her in turn, hugging and embracing her in turn.

#### Second Tableau
The bridegroom's train enters. The cart is drawn by village women from the opposite side of the stage from that on which the bride's cart entered. In the cart are the bridegroom and his father and mother and best men. The mother is combing his locks.

The mother combs Khvétis's locks, moistening the comb in *kvas*.

At the end of the Tableau, Stravinsky

marks the measure in which

·The groom's train prepares for departure . . .

and the measures during which

The groom's train departs slowly, in their carts.

### Third Tableau

Enter the bride's cart (from the same side of the stage as in the First Tableau), all glittering with icons and mirrors. The characters (the same as in the First Tableau) are also dressed in sparkling clothes.

### Fourth Tableau

The backdrop is raised revealing a large room in a Russian *izba*. It is almost entirely filled by a table, around which a large number of people are seated. They eat and drink. A door is open at the back showing a large bed covered by an enormous eiderdown.

In the wedding parlor stands a table. On the table is a *karavay* [very large loaf of bread] with various wondrous decorations: the figure of a little man, a little bird, etc. This *karavay* is surrounded by other, smaller *karavays*, and by honey cakes, cookies, sweetmeats. The table is made of oak. The tablecloth is patterned [checkered?]. The dishes are made of wood. The mead is strong. The newlyweds eat the *karavay* first. The *karavay* signifies the marital union.

*Svadebka* ends with the following song, during which the *druzhka* and the *svaxa* [female matchmaker] lead the young couple to bed. When the *druzhka* and the *svaxa* have put them to bed and left them, the parents of Khvétis and Nastasia close the door, place four chairs in front of it, and sit on them. The act is over. The curtain falls slowly. The music continues throughout. At the very end a solo voice [tenor] sings, in a saccharine, or oily voice, drawing out the words:

"*Uzh i dushka, zhanushka Nastas'jushka,*
*Pozhivem my x toboju xoro-shenichka,*
*Shtoby ljudi nam zavdyvali.*"

### VI. The Text

### (W. H.)

After Russian fairy tales and the celebrated epic poems about such heroes as Ilyá Múromyets and Dobrýnya Nikítich, wedding songs are perhaps the largest and most interesting genre in Russian folklore. These songs, together with the wedding ritual itself, go back many centuries, and are extraordinarily poetic, rich in symbols and metaphors. The songs are not as well known in English as Russian fairy tales or epics, no doubt because of the lack of narrative in the wedding ritual; nor can many of the poetic and ritual expressions of the wedding ceremony be translated.

In his early period, Stravinsky found an almost exclusive source of inspiration in Russian folklore. *The Firebird*, *Petrushka*, *Renard*, the *Four Russian Peasant Songs*, the *Pribaoutki*, and *Histoire du Soldat* all derive from Russian folk material, while *The Rite of Spring* and *The Nightingale* have at least indirect connections with folklore, international as well as Russian. Stravinsky's work had many different sources: folk tales, puppet theater, and lyric songs. Still we may wonder that *Les Noces* is so far removed from being a narrative in the normal sense, and so close to pure ritual. Although ballet is close to certain kinds of ritual, *Les Noces* has no direct parallel in the history of music or ballet. Stravinsky was the first to see that the wedding songs and ritual could be transformed into a moving work for the stage.

The Russian peasant name for the wedding ceremony is *svádebnaya igrá*, or "wedding play," "play" in the sense of a dramatic spectacle in which each of the participants plays out a traditional part and in which the imagination, artistic performance, and vicarious participation by the guests are all important. Stravinsky must have been attracted to the theatrical quality of these "roles": his bride and groom are intensely human, yet they are not individuals, but symbols: they are caught up in something larger than themselves. No doubt this abstract quality suited Stravinsky's aesthetics, as well as the aesthetics of the period, which also witnessed cubism and the early phase of constructivism.

Stravinsky puts greater stress on the rhythmic cadence of words and syllables than he does on their sense and imagery. One thinks of *zaúm*, "trans-sense" language in the Russian poems of such contemporaries of Stravinsky as Khlébnikov or Kruchónykh, a language which at times comes close to nonsense. But it would be quite wrong, I believe, to limit the aesthetic importance of the language of *Les Noces* to its rhythmic impact.

Russian folk songs are strongly "tonic," with a fixed number of principal stresses to each line, and Stravinsky was highly conscious of the importance of this tonic principle. It is interesting that he chose, almost exclusively, folk songs with two principal stresses to the line, and avoided songs which have only a single stress or three stresses. Songs with single-stressed lines are relatively rare, while those with three principal stresses to the line tend to be narrative songs, often expanded to great length. Stravinsky preferred to use short lines from songs that do not tell a story. Often it was clearly the language, which is vigorous and expressive if not always beautiful, that attracted him. Moreover, lines with a double stress are doubtless more flexible; the triple stress requires a longer melodic line, which would tend to work against the percussive quality of this work.

By beginning after the marriage contract has been negotiated and the preliminary rituals are over and the main wedding ritual already underway –and by ending with the consummation–Stravinsky avoids a structure that is too schematic and ethnographic, as well as insufficiently dramatic. Though he generally remains faithful to the folk ceremony, he has not hesitated to change the conception of his work for dramatic reasons. For example, the Russian wedding ritual centers about the bride and her family, and largely ignores the bridegroom, no doubt because the wedding was a far greater emotional shock for the bride. The couple usually lived with the groom's family, often in another village. While the daily life of the husband hardly changed, that of the wife was totally disrupted, usually for the worse, since she was automatically subordinated in her new household to the authority of her mother-in-law and sisters-in-law.

Instead Stravinsky has given us a more harmonious and balanced drama, in which the roles of bride and groom are relatively equal. Thus, the second scene in which the bridegroom's blond locks are curled parallels the first in which the bride's hair is braided, though in the groom's case this rite is less symbolic and was less frequently practiced. Similarly, at the end of Part I, in Scene 3, the mothers of both bride and groom lament their desertion by their children. In the folk ceremony only the bride's desertion of her family was significant, since the groom after all remained at home. But the scene is psychologically sound: Stravinsky has deepened the lament, making it closer to human truth. □

175

### Lester Young's "Shoeshine Boy"
### Lawrence Gushee

This essay was originally entitled "What Kind of Oral Tradition Is Jazz?" and developed from the convergence of two interests of mine, jazz and medieval plain chant, for the latter of which recent work by Leo Treitler had opened new vistas of understanding. My consideration of a small sample of Lester Young's music was embedded in what now seems to me, and seemed at the time to the chairman of the study group, a rather artificial setting which purported to test the validity or applicability of the terms "oral composition" and "oral transmission"–as they had been construed by Albert Lord[1] in his work with Yugoslav epic singer-poets–to the music called jazz.

This attempt seemed worthwhile since it is immediately obvious that much of the musical expression and construction in the jazz idiom and style is "oral," in being carried on without the aid of musical notation. Furthermore, we have or can have a great deal of detailed evidence of various sorts for the cultural context and specific musical procedures of jazz, as contrasted with, say, Eskimo song or medieval plain chant.

Treitler, however, did not encourage my desire to discuss his patent dependence on Lord. In the course of the session it became clear to me why this was so, when he presented his historical-cultural models for musical transmission in which concrete circumstances of transmission and socially-defined function and value were made fundamental. From these models, as well as from some of the other papers, it emerged–although perhaps neither explicitly nor with the assent of all panelists–that "written" and "oral" *per se* were rather crude, if not misleading terms, each covering a variety of specific cultural or historical circumstances, and not very useful for a taxonomy of music, an analysis of poetic or "creative process," or an explanation of musical change.

My discussion of Lester Young's "Shoeshine Boy" seems in retrospect to recommend a versatility in analysis, not simply as an exercise in the exhaustion of possibilities, but in recognition that in music–perhaps especially with functionally differentiated or stratified ensembles (as in jazz bands)–different kinds of relationship operate over different time spans. It may be that within one and the same kind of music performers differ greatly in the emphasis or control of one kind of relationship, and in the way their memory functions on the various levels. And finally, I discover that my subject is chiefly oral composition, though the proximity in time of the two performances examined can be considered to involve a kind of transmission.

Some points to keep in mind in reading my remarks:
1) "Jazz" is used to denote style and practice of what is usually called "the Swing era," roughly the 1930s.
2) By the mid-1930s most professional jazz players could and did read music. Many had an acquaintance with harmony; some had studied standard instrumental etudes and methods (e.g., for trumpeters, Arban and Herbert L. Clarke).
3) Commercial recordings are made under special conditions, some of which run counter to oral compositional procedures.
4) The timing cycle which guides, stimulates and limits jazz solo playing is tangibly audible in the rhythm section.

\*

[1] Albert Lord, *The Singer of Tales* (New York, 1970).

151

Lester Young, nicknamed "Prez," as for "the President," was born in Mississippi in 1909 and died 50 years later in New York City. He came to national prominence with Count Basie's Orchestra, in which he played tenor saxophone between 1936 and 1940, and as accompanist to Billie Holiday in recordings of 1937 and 1938. Any history of jazz will name him as one of the two style leaders of saxophone playing between 1935 and 1945, along with his in some respects opposite number, Coleman Hawkins.

Young was first recorded commercially on October 9, 1936, in Chicago, with five other members of the Basie band, which was breaking in for national exposure at the Grand Terrace Ballroom on the South Side. Four tunes were recorded, "Shoe Shine Boy," "Lady Be Good," "Evenin'," and "Boogie Woogie," the last two with vocal by Jimmy Rushing. They were released on the Vocalion label a few months later under the name "Jones-Smith Inc." supposedly because the Basie band was under exclusive recording contract with Decca Records. The four performances have been reissued a number of times, and the first two named were well-known to players and serious listeners during the fifties and sixties.

It was not until four years ago or so that another take of "Shoe Shine Boy" came to light; it has since been reissued three times, twice in Europe and once in the United States. Two other performances of "Shoe Shine Boy" involving the same musicians along with the rest of Basie's band were recorded from this period, both from January, 1937. One is called "Roseland Shuffle," released by Decca; the other, "Shoe Shine Swing," recorded from a radio broadcast originating in the Hotel William Penn, Pittsburgh.

These four performances of "Shoe Shine Boy" all feature Lester Young and are the texts for this discussion. Transcriptions of most of Young's solo playing therein are included (Example 1).[2] The various versions will be lettered A–D according to the following key.

178

*Version A*

Chicago, 8/10/36

Jones-Smith Incorporated [Carl Smith, trumpet; Lester Young, tenor sax; Count Basie, piano; Walter Page, string bass; Jo Jones, drums.]

| mx C.1657–1 | *Shoe Shine Boy* | Vocalion 3441/Col CG 33502 (U.S.A.) |
| | | CBS 65384 (Europe) |
| | | Tax (Sweden) |

*Version B*

| mx C. 1657–2 | *Shoe Shine Boy* | unissued take / reissues as above |

*Version C*

Pittsburgh, 8/2/37

Count Basie and his Orchestra [Joe Keys, Carl Smith, Buck Clayton, trumpet; Dan Minor, George Hunt, trombone; Caughey Roberts, alto sax; Jack Washington, alto sax, baritone; Hershel Evans, tenor sax; Lester Young, tenor sax; Count Basie, piano; Walter Page, string bass; Claude Williams, guitar; Jo Jones, drums.]
(LP issue of a recording made from a radio broadcast)

| *Shoe Shine Swing* | Jazz Archives 16 |

[2] Peter Winkler has kindly granted me permission to use the transcription of version D prepared by him in conjunction with a paper read by him at the annual meeting of the AMS, Washington D.C., 1976.

*Version D*

New York, 21/1/37

Count Basie and his Orchestra [personnel as above]

mx 61545–A         *Roseland Shuffle*         Decca 1141/MCA 4050
                    (other issues as
                    *The Count & Lester*)

Specific locations within the versions are identified by the measure numbers of Example 1, along with the letter designating the version, e.g., B.14–15. Occasionally, eight-measure segments of the AABA song form will be called "A section" or "B section."

Example 1

180

154

181

155

## Preliminary Note on Jazz Analysis

There is no commonly accepted coherent method. The most thorough and consistent applications of analysis to jazz to date are those of Thomas Owens dealing with the playing of Charlie Parker, and of Gunther Schuller dealing with the playing of Afro-Americans during the 1920s. These represent, in my opinion, two distinct approaches, which I designate "formulaic" and "motivic," respectively. Two other approaches, called here "schematic" and "semiotic," are encountered, along with eclectic mixtures. The following table sums up my understanding of the characteristic features of the four approaches or types. Whether these types of analysis correspond to types of creation or perception is a question with no general answer. In the present instance I believe they do.

*TABLE I*

| Type of Analysis | Methods/Objectives/Content | Assumptions | Boundaries |
|---|---|---|---|
| MOTIVIC<br>Tirro[3]<br>Schuller[4] | Demonstration of organic relations, development, climactic (tension-release) structure. Logically-connected ideas. | Criteria of logic. Esthetic merit of the work. | The work itself |
| FORMULAIC<br>Owens[5] | Labelling of phrases according to the lexicon. Appropriate choice of compatible formulas, with relaxed logical requirements. | Learning and performance by rote or imitation. | The collective style |
| SCHEMATIC<br>Dauer[6]<br>Hodeir[7] | Generation of specific expression by transformation of fundamental structures (including a tune or chord progression as well as other patterns). | Separable levels of mental activity. | The process of forming |
| SEMIOTIC<br>(A great deal of the popular literature of jazz) | Meaning as given by the system of signs. Decoding of mythic structure. | The apparatus of general semiotics; or socio-political theory. | The culture |

## Attested Effects of "Shoe Shine Boy" A

The Jones-Smith Inc. recordings, along with those by the Count Basie Orchestra of 1937–38, have been much praised over the years as superb examples of a "classic" small-band swing style. Critics have perceived a rarely-achieved balance or equilibrium in the performance as a whole. But it is Lester Young's two solo choruses that have been heard as particularly coherent, flowing, and memorable.

[3] Frank Tirro, "Constructive Elements in Jazz Improvisation," *JAMS* XXVII (1974), pp. 285–305.
[4] Gunther Schuller, *Early Jazz: Its Roots and Musical Development* (New York, 1968); also "Sonny Rollins and the Challenge of Thematic Improvisation," *The Jazz Review* I (Nov. 1958), pp. 6–11, 21.
[5] Thomas Owens, *Charlie Parker: Techniques of Improvisation*, 2 vols., Ph.D. dissertation, University of California at Los Angeles, 1974.
[6] Alfons M. Dauer, "Improvisation: Zur Technik der spontanen Gestaltung im Jazz," *Jazzforschung/Jazz Research* I (1969), pp. 113–132.
[7] Andre Hodeir, *Jazz: Its Evolution and Essence*, trans. by David Noakes (New York, 1956).

Without pretending to have conducted an opinion poll, I am certain that this judgement applies to the 64 measures taken as a whole, rather than to each 32 measure chorus taken separately. This may be tested by reversing the order of the two choruses, either by manipulation of a tape or in the imagination. I recommend that this be done before one becomes too well acquainted with the actual order of events.

Although the welding of two choruses into a whole may seem a modest achievement by today's standards, it was not at all usual in 1936, with few players being given that much time on an approximately three-minute recording. Perhaps the thought is father of the deed: the drummer, Connie Kay, who worked with Lester Young off and on for a half-dozen years reported:

"He [Lester Young] had a funny, codelike way of talking . . . a chorus was one long and two choruses two longs . . ."[8]

### The Collective Structure of Jazz Performance

The discourse of "classic jazz" is carried out in four and eight measure phrases, choruses, and three-minute recordings, features which it shares with the U.S. popular song of the period. In jazz, these units of structure are not "deep," whether internal (in each player and fully explicable by him) or external (in the activity of the rhythm section). The listener's (or participant's) knowledge of such things is perhaps more tacit, with, in any event, strong reinforcement from dancing or knowing the words of a tune. In addition, the rhythm section is part of the performance and its behavior is articulated at various levels (pulse, harmonic rhythm, hierarchical punctuation of the larger units). Within this highly predictable binary structure there is much opportunity for briefly playing "against" the prevailing pulse, but not to the extent of muddling the major points of arrival or departure.

The jazz rhythm section is also noisy and resonant, with percussive time-keeping counteracted by cymbal shimmer, indistinct decay of the string bass, and the timbral liaison provided by guitar. Not only does such noise and resonance make for continuity, they may also be understood as "energizing" or giving a kind of meaning to single pitches which may be played by soloists (a concept more usually encountered in discussions of African musics).

These features combine to produce a merciful and supportive environment for the jazz soloist. It is difficult to become completely lost: at the rapid tempo of a "Shoe Shine Boy" there are points of reference passing by every four seconds or so. Errors are made, however, and in places that suggest the importance of eight-measure units in terms of memory encoding. In an AABA structure, a performer may forget the second A section (or play the bridge too soon, however you wish). Another related error is to play the wrong bridge, or to forget the correct one.

In this already strongly connected environment, a soloist may play "ideas" of quite incoherent character–as judged by the norms of written composition–in successive four-measure units, or sometimes, especially in the bridge, in successive two-measure units. They can be taken as surface detail floating on the rhythm section: thus Schuller's dictum that "the average improvisation is mostly a stringing together of unrelated ideas." Often such decisions as to incoherence do not take into account such features as timbral continuity or a characteristic personal timing with respect to the rhythm section. The piece is already so strongly connected in its rhythmic order that a time-span of four measures may be perceived as linked to a preceding one merely by virtue of a note-group, or even a single pitch, played in the equivalent metrical position. Pitch-centered or motivic analysis will often not take this sufficiently into account. Also, such connections, clearly as they may be *heard* in performance, lose much of their force when *viewed* in a transcription.

### Dramatization of the Collective Structure

In any popular song as well as in the harmonization which a jazz performance may follow, there are major and minor points of repetition and arrival in the timing cycle. Immediate repetition is relatively weak, but one which comes after significantly contrasting material on the same durational level is strong. The approach to measure 25 of a 32-measure chorus (repetition after contrast) is more portentous than to measure 9 (repetition). While such weighting factors may be given their full expression in the performance of a popular song (or even more, in an art song), and in the behavior of a jazz rhythm section, the situation is different for the jazz soloist. This is because practically all jazz

---

[8] Cited in Whitney Balliett, *Improvising* (New York, 1977), p. 188.

159

solo performance avoids literal or close to literal repetition of four and eight measure units. If encountered, such repetition is immediately labelled as "composition." If the strategic or weighty places of the timing cycle are to be recognized in the solo, some means other than literal repetition must be found.

There is another kind of weight in the solo enterprise. To play a solo is to step out of, emerge from the band, eventually to return. During whatever period of time that is given by prearrangement to the soloist, or that he can lay claim to, his goal is to demonstrate "chops" (technique), "soul" (expressivity), and "ideas" (originality, and to some degree, logic). While these need not be used separately to mark off one part of a solo from another, or used in the service of a rhetoric corresponding to the social and formal articulations of a solo, I believe that they may be, and *are* in the performances of "Shoe Shine Boy" by Lester Young.

*Formulas and Formulaic System*

The distinction between formulas–more or less literal motive or phrase repetitions–and formulaic system–a more generalized structural outline embracing many specific formulas–would seem to be more obvious to the student of music than to the student of literature. Music claims transformation and varied repetition as a fundamental forming process. Whether we can isolate levels of organization in music so neatly as in language (see Nowacki) is to me questionable. In any event, my ensuing discussion of formulas in these performances will deal with melody, then phrase and harmonic structure as reflected in melody. But according to my table above, these last two topics can be seen as instances of schematic, not formulaic analysis.

From attentive listening, but particularly from the paradigmatic transcription of versions A and B, certain phrases emerge as closely similar or identical. The one labelled γ (in Example 2, as others in this section) has a strongly accented *f sharp*, approached from below and left by eighth notes descending to the *g* below, then continued in a variety of ways, depending on the closeness of the cadence. With reference to the tune, the position of this peak tone is beat 3 of the first measure of the second half of the A section, and this is where we hear it in the performances, for the most part. But if it comes late, as in A.45 (due to the extension of the first four measure phrase) there is no time for the rest of the chain to follow. Here LY plays instead the second frequently-recurring formula (labelled δ), a descending Am7/D9 arpeggio, usually in the third measure of a four-measure section. The form δ' found in A.3–4, 11–12, and 36 is physically the same kind of gesture, but functions differently. Rather than a penultimate element of an eight-measure section, it is heard as transitional between the first and second four-measure sections.

Example 2

β

Repetition/oscillation

A.25

A.41

B.33

Related (?) prolongations

B.57

A.57

187

γ

G major 7th arpeggio with emphatic F♯

B.3

A.5                             extension          cadence

A.13

B.13

A.29

B.29

A.36

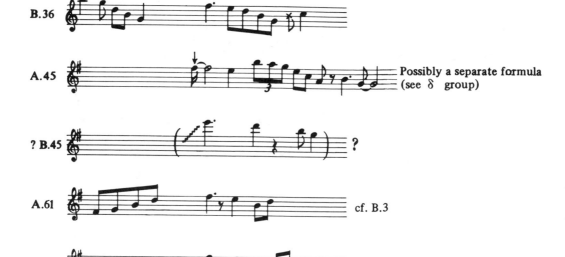

B.36

A.45  Possibly a separate formula (see δ group)

? B.45  ?

A.61  cf. B.3

B.61  cf. B.36

δ

Descending Am⁷/D arpeggio followed by G harmony

A.3

B.5  short suffix

A.11

A.29

A.35  can descend to F# in the chain of thirds, see below, A.62

C.39

A.46

C.47  cf. D.47

162

188

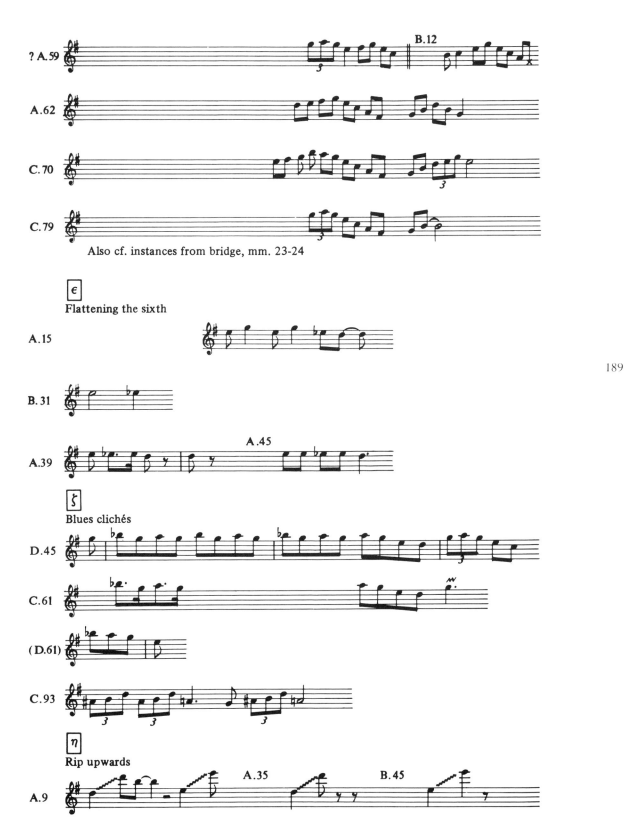

Also cf. instances from bridge, mm. 23-24

ϵ

Flattening the sixth

189

ζ

Blues clichés

η

Rip upwards

No less frequent, but far more variable in its appearances–and thus falling into the domain of a super-formula–is the initial phrase α, which I take to have the basic form (d,) e, d sharp, d in whole notes, also describable as a playing around with the fifth and sixth scale-degrees or with the fourth and little fingers of the right hand. It is a lengthy process, nearly filling a four-measure section.

Three other initial phrases can be grouped together as β, characterized by note repetition, and in two instances, oscillation across the octave break of the instrument. They share with α a considerable length and a static melodic and harmonic character.

Perhaps we should also make a group for a number of often quite short (two or three beats) cadential phrases. The most common of these are permutations of the tonic triad, usually not ending on the tonic. I am inclined to add the half-dozen five or six-note punctuating phrases (ε) using the descent e, e flat, d, which a motivically-inclined analyst might wish to describe as variants of α. From the formulaic point of view, as I understand it, this would be illusory, given the difference in time-span and function.

On the basis of LY's general style, one would also wish to label as formulas or characteristic gestures the three or four instances of a "rip" upwards to the palm keys (A.9 and 10; B.45).

The C and D versions do not, for the most part, employ these formulas. Indeed, if I am correct in ascribing a functional or quasi-syntactic role to them, it would be nonsense to use them in a dialogue performance. It is striking however, that the α formula is heard in a functionally ambiguous position in C.37 and D.61. Otherwise, in those performances we hear several occurrences of blues clichés, ζ, which although not formulaic in this very limited sample of LY's playing, are often used by him.

There is one major instance in which a formula that on first listening is easily assignable to one class must be cross-referenced to another. B.33–36, involving the repetition of the pitch e, thus a static element prolonging tonic harmony, as A.25–28 and A.41–44, is in fact dynamic, as shown by the successive lowering of pitch in my transcription. This is achieved not by lipping down but by the successive closing of tone-holes below the one which remains open to produce e'. To me at any rate, this makes a link to formula-group α. This level of hearing is in part permitted by the possibility of running the magnetic tape at half or quarter-speed, but it is something that saxophone players might well notice during a performance. Whether the unalerted layman would notice it–thus making it part of his perceived structure–is another question.

I doubt that such microscopic listening is required to study all jazz performance from the formulaic point of view. In the present instance, however, I believe it is, particularly because it relates to the boundary problem. For example, in A.5–8 we hear a well-formed phrase (a quotation from Louis Armstrong?) which might be parsed γ + infix + cadence, and completes the cadence on the first beat of m. 8. In B.13–15, the phrase ends early, leaving an awkward gap that might be called an elision of the clear degree-progression of A. Close listening to the recording seems to show an uncertainty of fingering at the critical point in version B, beat 3 of m. 14.

A related instance is A.4, in which I initially conceived the b' as the end of formula δ. This led me to consider the additional d' and b' of A.12 as a kind of additional flourish or as little "transitional" or residual tones. The discrepancy sent me back to the tape and relistening showed that d' and b' had been played there as well.

The things I have described so far constitute in my opinion a formulaic economy which we may see as the result of a considerable degree of digital memory as well as of an interest in working out in various manners certain degree-progressions (e.g., e, d sharp, d) or prolongations of tonic harmony. I do not think we need to think of LY as reaching more or less unconsciously, and under the pressure of time, into his bag of well-learned tricks. The one formula which might appear to function to give LY time to think of what to do next (δ) also serves as a formal element in an over-all repetition scheme, and its less frequent use in version B does not seem to entail any poverty of ideas. It seems clear that, as with Lord's singer-poet-instrumentalists, the order of events may be different in successive performances, but I think this is the case only within certain limits given by the general structure of the AABA song form: e.g., initial material or formulas can appear in measures 1, 9, or 25, but not in measures 5, 13 or 29.

*Phrasing and "Changes"*

Much solo jazz performance of the 20s and 30s can easily be regarded as melodic paraphrase. Even when this is not the case, one hears a solo quite frequently as following the phrasing of the melody.

Obviously this cannot be simply a matter of binary construction, which would hardly be enough to differentiate one tune from another, but must involve preservation of other features of the tune in a solo, such as the actual duration of phrases or the number of tones in them. There is some possibility for self-deception, however, when a listener knows the tune very well himself and "hears" it along with a performance. But I have no doubt that it is part of the perception for the musician jazz as listener.

Version A has been described in print as a relatively "straight" performance. I accept this judgement, but only with respect to the eight and four-measure articulations of the tune, and not with respect to the tune itself. The eight-measure units are very strongly marked terminally, as a rule by long silences, statements of tonic harmony, or both. The four-measure divisions are also articulated, but rather subtly, for instance by changes in direction or indefinite ("ghost") pitches, as in A and B.12. The shorter spans of one or two measures, analytically separable in the tune, do not generally appear to be observed, and a player would be unwise or unlikely to attempt to do so at this rapid a tempo. Also, melodic congruences at this level are not reflected in LY's performance. Anyone acquainted with jazz would be startled indeed to hear A.2 = A.4, etc.

If one regards the tune as consisting of four measures of one sort, followed by two markedly different two-measure phrases, then surely version A can be considered to be constructed in the same manner. Version B seems to be a different affair.

Of course, one salient feature of *Shoe Shine Boy* appears in all performances, namely the bridge or channel, with its contrastive character and sequential harmony. All versions reflect these features of the model with strongly similar renditions of the "underlying" chord progression. But it seems pretty clear that the playing of the bridge is something of a routine, with a fixed drum part accentuating LY's phrases.

Here is where we might hope to test Lord's "enjambement criterion," i.e. oral composition avoids such contradiction of construction in parallel verses.[9] I find it a tricky matter, inasmuch as the pick-up or anacrusis is generally prevalent. But I think it would be fair to say that the expected seams or joints are not disguised or blurred as a matter of course (as becomes true in later jazz). That makes all the more dramatic the places where we hear musical enjambement: at the end of the bridge (all versions, 23–24–25, B.55–56; between choruses, B.32–33). At least the first of these has obviously been worked out, but it is interesting to observe how the different forms of m. 24–involving a different position on the instrument–entail differences in m. 25 and subsequent ones.

Jazz performance is sometimes explained as based on harmonic progression. This is often meant in some fairly strict sense, i.e. jazz uses the pitches of the "vertical" harmonies as the primary constituents of "horizontal" phrases. An extreme example would be a solo consisting only of the arpeggiation of the changes. Approaches to such an extreme do exist, but are not generally admired, unless in some instances as *tours de force*. Generally the changes are not considered so much as a schematic feature greatly facilitating improvisation, but as a measure by which one may determine a player's originality, e.g. Bix Beiderbecke playing accented 9ths and 13ths, Charlie Parker playing on the tertial extensions upwards of seventh chords, and the like. It is my opinion that the changes are most important for the act of performance–as opposed to that of analysis–in their ability to orient a player in the 32-measure time cycle. Be that as it may, analysts of jazz are sometimes rather incautious in their assumptions about what the changes are, especially in deriving them from sheet music or a lead sheet or fake book, rather than from the rhythm section as actually recorded. In *Shoe Shine Boy*, for example, it is clear from listening to the various performances that the augmented V7 is much favored by Count Basie and his sidemen as well. Thus, a feature which might be considered a deviation from the sheet music harmony is normal with respect to the changes actually used.

All in all, the changes of *SSB* are, with the exception, once again, of the bridges, not prominently expressed in the melodies LY actually plays. For instance, the E7 of m. 1 etc. is neglected, the single exception being one of the most ear-catching measures of version B, m. 41, in which we note the suppression of the tonic chord in favor of an entire measure expressing E7 horizontally. It should be said that to reflect harmonies changing twice a second might well have seemed ludicrous to musician and listener alike in 1936. Although I certainly do not hear LY's performance as contradictory to the changes, neither do I hear it as in some sense following them. This is partly because V7 is only present

[9] Lord, *op. cit.*, p. 57f.

in considerably softened form, Am7 with normal or flat fifth, and the active *f sharp* is preempted as major seventh to the tonic. I would characterize the harmonic system underlying these solos in rather vague terms–or rather, vague from the standpoint of functional analysis, but concrete with reference to the instrument: one ascending gesture, a tonic major seventh arpeggio with possible extensions by a diatonic third, up or down; and its counterpoise, a descending chain of thirds outlining the supertonic minor seventh, but with extensions up or down also possible.

## Motives

Perhaps my questions so far might be considered as addressed to the how and the what of these performances. Be that as it may, I take the subsequent remarks to ask or answer, in part, why.

Should we relabel as "motives" the phrases or bundles of features I have designated formulas or expressions of an underlying scheme, the thrust of analysis shifts from the oral to the composed, from the performance as one possible arrangement among many to the performance as a unique creation, from the variations of a basic form, to the repetitions or transformations of a motive which make form. I don't believe such a shift to be profitable.

There are some features of version A which would recommend the shift and the relabelling, namely, the recurrences, both pleasing and surprising, of the initial rhythmic-melodic motive of m. 1 in m. 15, and of m. 25 ff. in m. 37. The esthetic effect depends on brevity and recognizability, placing condensations of the motives in a functionally different position.

The major objections, to my mind, to using this effect as a springboard to a general motivic, compositional analysis are first, that the many other instances of formulaic variation do not have the same dramatic effect and are not easily audible as repetitions; second, that in version B, the two most easily encoded, potentially motivic gestures (B.1: "descending scale"; B.41–42: "running the changes")–which are furthermore placed at strong points of the time cycle–are not reused.

There is no reason, though, to rule out intentional motivic work from the oral poetic of jazz, especially at slower tempos or in the longer time cycles of more recent jazz. It is simply that in this style, at such a tempo, the time-cycle's demands for change of any sort take precedence. In illustration of this constraint, I could mention the rather frequent judgement one makes that a pattern is ended too soon: the listener has the leisure to reflect that a process could have been continued to good effect. But the player, like Lord's epic singer, is always thinking ahead, and has perhaps already forgotten what he's playing while still doing it.

This line of speculation arises from the comparison of versions A and B. I believe that the former will be both heard and seen to be better balanced, more thrifty and more conjunct. But it may also be said that version A is more obvious, particularly from the schematic point of view. A.1–8 is a case in point. B.1–8 is more subtle; its balance is not so easy to represent in numbers or pitches, as the silences are part of a parallel rhythmic structure. It is parataxic or coordinate, rather than hierarchical.

Our first-level criteria of economy are also somewhat simpleminded or over-literal. It is immediately clear that A.33–35 is very like A.1–3 with respect to degree-progression. But B.33–36 (mentioned above), which might at first be judged to be an easy cliché, serving to heighten intensity and unconnected with the formulaic or motivic vocabulary of version B, can be heard as a form of the pervasive slowly-descending degree-progression.

If our model for LY's performances is that of oral composition the actual order of performance matters little. The comparative "straightness" of version A and the adventurousness of B may be understood either as a decision in the context of a recording session to take fewer chances, or a desire to play something a bit more challenging. But if the model is that of reflective composition, working towards a more socially comprehensible sequence of ideas, then B–A appears to be the necessary order.

What does historical investigation tell us? First, the recent U.S. Columbia reissue of these recordings is the first to give matrix numbers for the two takes. If these numbers reflect the order of recording and not some other bookkeeping or manufacturing procedure, then the order must be A–B. This does not agree with the recollection of John Hammond, the organizer of the session, who says that version B was the first take, and was marred by a messed-up run by Basie.

Careful listening supports the superiority of version A overall: in B the very end is messy, Jo Jones and Walter Page are uncertain in their breaks, and Tatti Smith breaks the flow of the concluding exchanges between the players. I am loath to believe that skilled players would do less well in such matters in successive performances. Unfortunately the only "run" which Basie plays less than perfectly is the whole-tone scale of version A, close to the end of his opening solo. Thus, external evidence is ambiguous, and internal evidence coercive only to the extent one accepts the principle stated two sentences above.

It may be that we must carefully distinguish immediately successive performances from those separated by an interval of time sufficient to diminish muscular memory. Also, conventionalization may be more prominent in the different circumstances.

The question of recording order is not without interest, but perhaps only a scenic tour that diverts us from asking whether behind the adventurous and variable detail of the two versions there lies an over-all shape–particularly one comprehensible or perceptible by the ordinary listener (a category which may include many musicians). I've already suggested above that there may be a kind of rhetorical plan, serving not only to give "meaning" to these performances, but to forge two choruses together. In fact, the plan I suggest could not practically unfold within the confines of one chorus.

I. The first move is a move out of the band or in juxtaposition to another soloist, or both. It must catch the attention, and in LY's case–who at this point in his career was not satisfied with rhetorical gestures alone–must be an intelligible musical idea. It will generally fill the first four measures.

The initial idea should not be too complicated. The place for tricky stuff, i.e. cute ideas or technical display, is later–but how much later? The obvious point in a two-chorus solo is at the beginning of the second chorus, though one might start after the first bridge. In any event,

II. Demonstration of mastery, "chops," technique identifiable with respect to the instrument, normal harmony or rhythmic construction. In LY's case this often involves polymetric or otherwise unbalanced phrasing rather than rapid playing.

A.33–34 is a particularly flamboyant saxophone gesture, hardly reproducible on another instrument. B.33–34, though not difficult, is a bit of cleverness depending on the construction of the instrument. A.41–44 is difficult because of leaping across the octave break, as well as being a greater upsetting of the meter than anything else so far heard; at the same position, B is not so technically difficult, but due to its special harmonic character and rapid quasi-sequence gives a sense of artistic pressure. In both A and B, the climax–if one be granted at all–is located here, five-eighths of the way along the 64 measures. (Friends of the golden section take note.)

III. Return to the band, "wrapping it up," an expressive peak reached by using common property, a riff, or a well-known lick.

The only possible place for this, within the 64 measure time frame, is in the last eight measures, particularly since the bridge is stereotyped. In any event, those sections of versions A and B are heard as closely related by pitch, duration and accent pattern. More important, they strike the ear as more naive and formulaic (in the communal frame) than anything else in these solos.

If the subjectivity of this last judgement be found disturbing, I suggest that the difference between these closing phrases and others can be stated without reference to a social infrastructure, and can be tested by consulting the equivalent of native speakers. (I can only offer myself as an immigrant.)

This three-part plan is not very complicated by itself, but is somewhat at odds with two choruses; three choruses would be ideal, but very rare in records of this time, except in blues, a very different undertaking. There is no reason why it should be complicated; after all, it only determines the course of musical events in a general way, and over relatively long durations. Perhaps it is in this respect not unlike the general thematic plan of an epic poet, or the sequence of movements in a concerto. Nor would I insist that Lester Young follows it always, for in playing two chorus solos he sometimes made each chorus in very much the same way (e.g. Count Basie's *12th Street Rag*, Decca). Nor does it preclude yet other plans, such as the single-minded dramatic "ride-out" of mounting intensity, much favored by trumpeters at this time.

Whether my characterization of these moves be found apt or not, I believe there is a *necessary* order in these performances which does not emerge from formula or schematic analysis, although not necessarily at every level (two, four, eight-measure) of temporal organization. One tool of verification is the commutation test at the various levels. I have done this in a rough-and-ready way (the making of unnoticeable splices is time-consuming) in real time and in my imagination, but knowing so well how the solos really go, I am hardly an ideal subject, particularly since my preference usually goes to the "true" order. This is not always the case, however: where my ear absolutely rejects exchange of the first and second eight-measure phrases of B, it will accept interchange of A.9–16 with B.9–16, even at the cost of the parallelism of B.4 and 15.

To recapitulate: I believe that one may perceive in versions A and B four different processes at work. In each of these processes or levels there are features which are collective or social and ones which are idiosyncratic. Some are more easily encoded–therefore memorable–or more easily imitated than others. They are all in some sense under the control of a performer at this level of mastery, but another player learning this piece, or Lester Young's style from this piece, can hardly be expected to (nor would he have been, in fact, expected to) remember or learn these bundles of features in the same way.[10]

I construe these processes according to the scheme of Table I in the following way:

1. Semiotic: Lester Young, like many players, thought of a solo as "telling a story." This story transcends the repetitive, hierarchical structure of the tune and its harmonization, and depends on the use of typologically different material.[11]

2. Schematic: He also affirmed the pop song structure of *Shoe Shine Boy* in differentiating measure four from measure eight cadences (*ouvert* and *clos*, if you will), in observing the conventional character of the channel or bridge, and so on. In a few cases, that structure is deliberately upset.

3. Formulaic: As a saxophone player, Young had his bag of propensities and tricks–call them conscious style or automatisms–such as false fingerings, rips upward to the palm keys, dramatic bombs in the extreme low register, chains of thirds. Beyond that, of course, he might use favorite motives having nothing to do with the saxophone *per se*.

4. Motivic: Young knew this tune as such–witness the prominent *f sharp*–and found a degree progression filling a four-measure segment which he used in various positions and shapes in versions A, B, and C. It may well not be specific to this tune.

In version C and D, a dialogue performance between piano and tenor saxophone, these levels can not work together or separately in the same way to produce a memorable esthetic effect. For example, if a story is to be told, it must be a different kind of story altogether.

I think it important to note that the other two performers with solos on *Shoe Shine Boy* A and B, Count Basie and Carl Smith pay little attention to the first and fourth processes detailed above. This does no injury to their work as good jazz or to their contribution to the excellent ensemble. It may, however, account for lesser "memorability," something I take to be easily perceptible. One can remember their brief two and four-measure phrases, but not necessarily in correct order, and sometimes transposing phrases from one version to the other.

It will perhaps seem a small accomplishment, if all I have done in these pages is to reaffirm the necessity of a sense of over-all structure or an image of the whole work, if that work is to be valued and remembered in detail by those who come after. (Without saying, to be sure, that this is a guarantee of survival.) More than that, I hope to have shown that oral composition, at least in the distinctly mixed oral-written tradition called jazz, in some of its expressions, proceeds along several tracks at once. I suppose that I have tried to show that in addition to the communal, highly conventional organizing schemata of jazz playing there are others which we must invoke or imagine in order to account for the extraordinary profundity or coherence of some jazz playing, wherever and whenever we may find it.

*Note to the transcriptions*

The transcriptions sound a major ninth lower than written; they make more sense to me–as a player of the instrument–in this form and eliminate the many ledger lines which would have to be used. I have left them in the form in which they were presented to the panel, including a great many faint diacritical marks indicating phrasing, articulation and accent. There is no need to review here the usual array of problems encountered in the transcription of highly individualistic performances, especially those

[10] According to Lee Konitz, Charlie Parker learned Young's performance of this piece (undoubtedly version A): " . . .Bird came noodling into the room and said, 'Hey, you ever heard this one?' and he played *Shoe Shine Swing* about twice as fast as the record." See L. Gottlieb, "Why So Sad, Pres?", *Jazz* 3 (Summer, 1959), p. 190.

[11] Richard Sudhalter and Philip Evans, *Bix, Man and Legend* (New Rochelle, N.Y., 1974), p. 192, report the following exchange between Wingy Manone and Louis Armstrong: "Hey, Pops, how do you play so many choruses the way you do?" . . . "Well, I tell you . . . the first chorus I plays the melody. The second chorus I plays the melody round the melody, and the third chorus I routines." Though one must doubt that this is a *verbatim* transcript of the conversation, it is descriptive of one of Armstrong's ways of dealing with multi-chorus solos.

which glory in playing *against* a consistent pulse. I think they will be found sufficiently reflective of the performance as it is considered here, although not for other conceivable discussions. Lester Young, it may be pointed out, suffers less in transcription than many another saxophonists of the time, particularly his section-mate, Hershel Evans.

The following special signs are used:

        *strong vibrato*

        "ghost" tone, almost inaudible

        a more definite, yet still indistinct pitch

        scooped pitch, usually beginning on the beat

        short "rip" upwards

        short fingered glissando before the beat

        indicates flattening or progressive flattening of pitch

        pitch or phrase earlier (or later) than notated

Many rhythmic subtleties of considerable importance to the "swing" style are audible at slow tape speed. For instance the very opening (A.1) which I represent ♪ ♩ ♪♩ is actually better represented ♩ ♪ ♪ ♪♩ Pairs of eighth notes are usually performed as triplets, although now and then they may be very close to equal, or very unequal.

I have not been entirely consistent in my indications of phrasing or articulation, partly because the transcriptions were made at different times, and intended to be suggestive of the over-all shape rather than completely descriptive. All triplets are *legato*, and most eighth notes also, even when not under a slur.

# EINFÜHRUNG IN DIE FORMEN-
# UND HARMONIENWELT BARTÓKS

*ERNŐ LENDVAI*

## DAS ACHSENSYSTEM

Im folgenden wollen wir das Bartóksche Tonsystem vom Gesichtspunkt der klassischen Harmonielehre, der Zwölftonmusik, der Akustik,
der historischen Entwicklung, ferner vom Gesichtspunkt der Proportionen
aus untersuchen. Stimmt das Ergebnis der Deduktionen in jedem Fall
überein, so ist das ein Beweis dafür, daß Bartók — bei der Schaffung seines
Materials — bis zu den Wurzeln der Musik, bis zu den elementarsten
Zusammenhängen vorgedrungen ist.

Vor allem versuchen wir, das Bartóksche Tonsystem in den Quinten-
zirkel einzufügen. Der Einfachheit halber betrachten wir das *c* als Tonika.
In diesem Falle erfüllt das *f* (als IV. Stufe) Subdominanten-, das *g* (als
V. Stufe) Dominanten-, das *a* (als Tonika-Parallele, VI. Stufe) Tonika-,
das *d* (als Subdominanten-Parallele, II. Stufe) Subdominanten-, das *e* (als
Dominanten-Parallele, III. Stufe) Dominanten-Funktion:

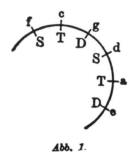

*Abb. 1.*

In diesen Beziehungen ist eine gewisse Regelmäßigkeit zu beobachten, und zwar wiederholen sich S-T-D in periodischen Abschnitten: S-T-D-S-T-D. Breiten wir diese Relationen auf den *ganzen Quintenzirkel* aus, so verfügen wir bereits über den Schlüssel zum Bartókschen Tonsystem:

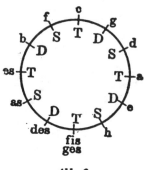

*Abb. 2.*

Isolieren wir die drei Funktionen voneinander und nennen wir sie einzeln — in Ermangelung eines passenderen Terminus technicus — Tonika-, Subdominanten- bzw. Dominanten-*Achse:*

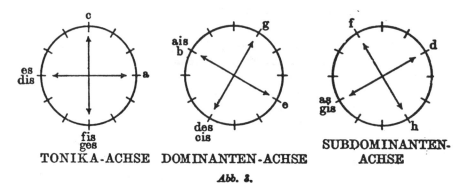

TONIKA-ACHSE    DOMINANTEN-ACHSE    SUBDOMINANTEN-ACHSE

*Abb. 3.*

Wichtig ist, die einzelnen Achsen nicht als verminderte Vierklänge zu betrachten, sondern als die Funktionsverwandtschaft von 4 verschiedenen, auf dem Grundriß des verminderten Vierklangs erscheinenden Tonalitäten, was am ehesten mit dem Dur-Moll-Verhältnis der klassischen Musik verglichen werden kann. (S. Abb. 4.)

Es kann aber beobachtet werden, daß die auf der Achse einander *gegenüberliegenden Seiten*, „Gegenpole", viel empfindlicher aufeinander reagieren als die benachbarten (z. B. *c* und *fis)*. Ein Pol kann immer mit

Abb. 4.

seinem Gegenpol vertauscht werden, ohne daß die Funktion eine Ver-
änderung erführe. Eine kadenziale Harmonienfolge: *E-A-D-G-C-F* ist im
Bartókschen System z. B. auch so vorstellbar: *E-A-As-Des-C-F*, wo das
vorige *D* und *G* vom Gegenpol *As* und *Des* vertreten wird. Das Pol-Gegen-
pol-Verhältnis ist das grundlegendste strukturelle und formative Prinzip
der Bartókschen Musik sowohl in den kleinen als auch in den großen Formen. Bereits *Herzog Blaubarts Burg* entwickelt sich in den spannungs-
erfüllten Beziehungen von Pol und Gegenpol: das Werk hebt sich aus dem
finsteren *fis*-Pol empor, kulminiert im strahlenden *C*-Dur-Akkord (Blaubarts Reich), schließlich versinkt es wieder in das nächtliche *fis*. Der Weg
der *Sonate für zwei Klaviere und Schlaginstrumente* führt aus der Tiefe in
die Höhe: aus dem *fis* zum *c*. Auf unserer Abb. 14 vertreten in den Takten
2—5 die Einsätze *fis—c* die Tonika, in den Takten 8—9 die Einsätze *g—des*
die Dominante, im 12. Takt die Einsätze *as—d* die Subdominante. Die
*H*-Dur Tonika des *Violinkonzerts* wird in der Durchführung vom *F*-Dur-
Gegenpol abgelöst. Der Satzbau der *Musik für Saiteninstrumente, Schlagzeug
und Celesta* ist wie folgt:

    I. Satz Anfang und Schluß: *a,*    formaler Mittelpunkt: *es* (56. T.)
   II. Satz Anfang und Schluß: *c,*    formaler Mittelpunkt: *fis* (263. T.)
 III. Satz Anfang und Schluß: *fis,*  formaler Mittelpunkt: *c* (46. T.)
 IV. Satz Anfang und Schluß: *a,*   formaler Mittelpunkt: *es* (83. T.)

Aus diesem Beispiel kann eine weitere Folgerung gezogen werden. Die vier
Sätze ruhen gemeinsam auf den vier Pfeilern der Tonika-Achse. Die Außen-
sätze stützen sich auf den *Hauptast* der Achse *(a-es)*, die Mittelsätze auf
ihren *Nebenast (c-fis)*. Jede Achse birgt also in sich selbst zwei Dimensionen,

eine doppelte Anziehung, je nachdem wir *Pol-Gegenpol* oder *Haupt- und Nebenast* einander gegenüberstellen:

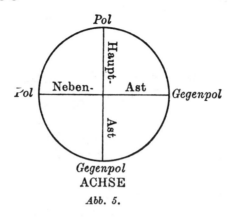

*Abb. 5.*

Der langsame Satz der *Sonate für zwei Klaviere und Schlaginstrumente* beruht auf der Subdominanten-Achse *h-d-f-as*. Die tonale Anordnung des Hauptthemas ist symmetrisch: Anfang und Schluß ruhen auf den Gegenpolen *h-f* bzw. auf dem Hauptast der Achse, der II. und der analoge IV. Halbsatz auf den Gegenpolen *d-as* bzw. auf dem Nebenast der Achse, im Mittelpunkt ist die Quint-Antwort *e:*

*Abb. 6.*

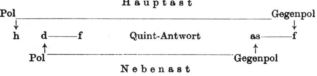

Ebenso schlingt sich die Melodie (s. Abb. 7), die den Kern des Mittelteils des Satzes bildet, um die Subdominanten-Achse: das Anfangs- und End-*gis* wird in der Mitte des Themas vom Gegenpol *d* abgelöst, im übrigen dreht sich jeder metrische und motivische Schwerpunkt um die Subdominanten-Achse *(gis-f-h-d)*.

*Abb. 7.*

Die zwei erwähnten Melodien spiegeln auch das Satzgerüst treu wider: die eine ist an den Ast *h-f* der Subdominanten-Achse, die andere an den Ast *gis-d* der Subdominanten-Achse gebunden.

Und sind wir gerade bei der *Sonate für zwei Klaviere,* so ist es der Mühe wert, einige charakteristische Punkte des I. Satzes näher zu betrachten. Z. B. die Takte 235—247 veranschaulichen von neuem die zweifache Dimension der Achse: einerseits finden wir die Gegenüberstellung des *gis*-Ostinatos und des *d*-Gegenpols, andererseits die Gegenüberstellung der Trichtergänge, die erst im Hauptast *d-gis,* dann im Nebenast *f-h* eingekeilt sind:

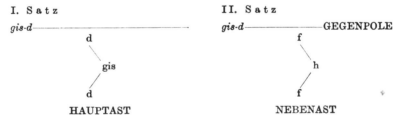

Die vier Glieder des Seitenthemas der Reprise bauen sich auf den vier Polen der Tonika-Achse auf, und zwar in der Weise, daß die Außen- bzw. Mittelglieder in der Pol-Gegenpol-Beziehung aufeinander reimen: *A-Fis-C-Es.* In ähnlich eindeutiger Weise stellt sich die Achsenstruktur der Coda dar (T. 417—431). Über der Begleitung im zerlegten Dur-Moll *es-ges-a-c* tritt das augmentierte Hauptthema polar in *a,* dann in *es,* schließlich in *a + es* auf, usw.

Eine mustergültige Achsenkonstruktion zeigt der Durchführungsteil des II. Satzes der *Musik*. Die Melodie schreitet in der Dursexten-Parallele; das begleitende Ostinato betont durchwegs die Tonalitäten *a* bezw. *es*.

202

Abb. 8.

Das Erscheinen der Pole *es-fis-a-c* wird auch immer durch den Schlag der großen Trommel (in unserer Skizze +) unterstrichen. Begleitung und Formgebung lassen gleicherweise erkennen, daß das Rückgrat der Struktur durch die Gegenpole *es-a* gebildet wird.

Als verwickelteres Beispiel erscheint das Seitenthema des *Violinkonzerts*, die bekannte „Reihe":

Abb. 9.

Obzwar die 12 Töne der Melodie die ganze Chromatik umfassen, bleiben wir über ihre Tonalität keinen Augenblick im Zweifel: in ihrer Achse stehen die Gegenpole *a-dis* (ihr Anfang, Halbierungspunkt, Schluß) bzw. die zerlegten *Fis-Dur-* und *C-Dur-Moll*-Gegenpole.

Das Gemeinsame der bisher vorgeführten Beispiele besteht darin, daß sich die Funktion innerhalb eines Teiles nicht ändert und der Vorgang immer im Kreise einer einzigen Achse verläuft. Wenn wir nun die Logik der funktionalen Anziehung, der Verbindung der Funktionen, ins Auge fassen, bietet sich uns Gelegenheit zu neuen interessanten Beobachtungen. Die einzelnen Funktionen (also Tonika, Subdominante bzw. Dominante) werden nämlich nicht von den Stufen I, IV bzw. V am kraftvollsten vertreten, sondern — die Tonalität *c* angenommen — die Subdominante von *as* und dessen Gegenpol, die Dominante von *e* und dessen Gegenpol. Damit sagten wir eigentlich nichts Neues, ist doch z. B. das in der *Dominante* befindliche Seitenthema der *C-Dur Sonate* (Waldstein) von Beethoven in *E*, der *subdominante* langsame Satz der *C-Moll Sonate* (Pathétique) in *As* verfaßt; die einzelnen Sätze der *I. Symphonie* von Brahms folgen einander in der Anordnung *C-E-As-C* im Sinne von Tonika-Dominante-Subdominante-Tonika etc. Trotz allem bietet die eben erfolgte Ableitung des Achsensystems keine befriedigende Erklärung dafür, warum Bartók eben diese Beziehungen der Verbindung I—IV—V—I *vorzieht*. An diesem Punkte erweist sich eine neuerliche Ableitung des Achsensystems als notwendig.

Wie bekannt, neigt die Zwölftonmusik sehr stark zu tonal indifferenten, intertonalen Relationen. Am geeignetsten hierfür scheinen die gleichstufig distanzierten Aufteilungen der Oktave (oder auch des Quintenzirkels). Teilen wir die Oktave in 12 gleiche Teile, so ergibt sich Chromatik, bei 6 gleichen Teilen eine Ganztonskala; teilen wir sie in 4 gleiche Teile, so erhalten wir einen verminderten Vierklang, bei 3 gleichen Teilen einen übermäßigen Dreiklang; schließlich erhalten wir bei der Teilung in 2 gleiche Teile einen Tritonus. Der Quinten- bzw. Quartenzirkel ist nichts weiter als eine andere Gruppierung der Chromatik. Aus obiger Aufzählung kann vorläufig der Tritonus ausgeschaltet werden, da er ein Bestandteil des verminderten Vierklangs ist (dieser kann nämlich aus zwei Tritonus gebildet werden), wir schalten auch die Ganztonskala aus, denn sie besitzt sehr begrenzte Möglichkeiten (zwei Ganztonskalen ergänzen einander zur Chromatik). Lediglich der Quinten-Quartenzirkel erstreckt sich auf die ganze Chromatik: dieser sei der Grundriß des Systems. Jede Art tonaler Ordnung setzt einen Mittelpunkt und dementsprechend Verhältnisse der Abhängigkeit bzw. der Unterordnung voraus. Wählen wir also ein Tonika-Zentrum, der Einfachheit halber wieder das *c*, stellen wir diesem „ministeriale" Töne bei, zur Rechten einen Ton mit positiver, zur Linken einen mit negativer Spannung, und schon haben wir das Gouvernement des Quintenzirkels vereinfacht. Die *gleichstufige Dreiteilung* des Quintenzirkels — *as-c-e* — paßt gerade, da wir das *e*, die große Oberterz der Tonika, ruhig als Dominante, das *as*, die große Unterterz der Tonika, als Subdominante verwenden können. Nun besteht noch die Frage, wie sich der Wirkungskreis der funktionalen Haupttöne *c*, *e*, *as* aufteilt. Verteilen wir die Zwölfton-Chromatik proportional auf die 3 funktionalen Haupttöne, so gehören zu den Funktionen eines jeden dieser Haupttöne je 4 Pole. Wenn man das Distanzprinzip fürderhin beibehält, bleibt nur eine einzige zweckentsprechende Möglichkeit übrig, die Pole derart zu verteilen, *daß sie den Quintzirkel gleichstufig vierteilen.* In diesem Fall erhalten wir verminderte Vierklänge. Dem Tonika-Hauptton *c* wird also der verminderte Vierklang *c-es-fis-a* angeführt, dem Dominanten-Hauptton *e* der verminderte Vierklang *e-g-b-cis* und dem Subdominanten-Hauptton *as* der verminderte Vierklang *as-h-d-f*. An Hand der gleichstufigen Aufteilung des Systems (Dreiteilung, dann Vierteilung) erhalten wir ein Tonsystem, das mit der obigen Abteilung des *Achsensystems* vollkommen übereinstimmt, lediglich durch Folgendes ergänzt:

Der Hauptton
$\begin{cases} \text{der tonalen Funktion ist: } c \text{ und sein Gegenpol: } \textit{fis} \\ \text{der dominanten Funktion ist: } e \text{ und sein Gegenpol: } b \\ \text{der subdominanten Funktion ist: } as \text{ und sein Gegenpol: } d \end{cases}$

Das System ist selbstverständlich transponierbar.[1]

Die Anordnung der Tonarten im *I. Rondo* ist folgende: Tonika *C*, Dominante *E*, Subdominante *As*, Tonika *C*. Der I. Satz des *Concerto für Orchester* wird durch das fünfmalige Erscheinen des Hauptthemas wie folgt gegliedert: *F* Tonika (Exposition), *Des* Subdominante (I. Hälfte der Durchführung), *A* Dominante (II. Hälfte der Durchführung), *F* Tonika (Reprise, Coda). Der I. Satz der *Sonate für zwei Klaviere* zeigt eine ähnliche Anordnung: *C* Tonika (Exposition), *E* Dominante (die ganze I. Hälfte der Durchführung), *Gis* Subdominante (die ganze II. Hälfte der Durchführung), *C* Tonika (Reprise). Am Anfang des *Violinkonzerts* wechselt die *H*-Dur-Tonika mit ihrer Dominante $A^7$, im Seitenthema der Reprise des II. Satzes der *Musik* die *C*-Dur-Tonika mit ihrer Dominante *B*-Moll; das Hauptthema der *Sonate für zwei Klaviere* wird über 14 Takte durch die Dominante *B* vorbereitet, was wiederum nur mit den oben angeführten Gesetzmäßigkeiten zu erklären ist.

---

[1] In der Zwölftonmusik ist dies — wenn man die drei Funktionen und das Distanzprinzip in Betracht zieht — das einzig mögliche tonale System.

*Titelblatt der Erstausgabe der „Vier Stücke" (1905)*

Abb. 10.

Besonders überzeugend ist das Hauptthema des II. Satzes der *Musik*, weil es den Kuppelbau und die Struktur Tonika-Tonika-Dominante-Tonika des ungarischen Volksliedes neuen Typs aufweist (s. Abb. 11). Die Tonika wird durch die Gegenpole *c-fis*, die Dominante durch die Gegenpole *e-b* (und nicht durch *g*) vertreten. Der zweite Tonika-Eintritt bringt die genaue „tonale Antwort" der *c-fis*-Achse (!), die Quarten *g-c* und *cis-fis* werden zu Quinten *c-g* und *fis-cis (ges-des)* umgedeutet. Eine ähnliche Verbindung Dominante-Tonika vollzieht sich in den Takten 171—178 des I. Satzes des *Divertimento:* den dominanten Gegenpolen *Es-A* entsprechen die Tonika-Gegenpole *H-F* usw.

Abb. 11.

Innerhalb des Achsensystems kann sich also eine Verbindung *Dominante-Tonika* — die Tonalität *c* vorausgesetzt — folgendermaßen gestalten: *G-C, E-C, B-C* und schließlich als vierte Möglichkeit: *Cis-C*, da ja im Achsensystem auch *Cis* Dominante von *C* ist. Die Lösung hält Bartók für Fälle bereit, wo eine unerwartete Wendung, eine Szenenveränderung eintritt. Die Erklärung dafür ist, daß nach *Cis* in der Kadenz *Fis* folgen müßte, dieses aber überraschenderweise mit dem *Gegenpol C* vertauscht wird: so löst sich der Vorgang, anstatt im erwarteten *Cis-Fis*, im Bartókschen „Trugschluß" mit der Wendung *Cis-C* auf. (Vgl. *Musik IV.* Satz, T. 73—74, 98—99, 113—114, 243—244.)

Die Theorie des Achsensystems wird auch von seiten der *Akustik* bestätigt. Voraussetzung für den Schritt von der Dominante zur Tonika ist die *Bewegung von einem Oberton zum Grundton.* Demnach hat das *c* nicht nur *g* als Dominante, sondern auch *e* und *b.* Und da die Beziehung T-D mit der Beziehung S-T und D-S übereinstimmt, erhält der Tonika-Hauptton *c* das *e* und *b* zur Dominante, die Dominante *e* oder *b* das *as* und *d* zur Subdominante und die Subdominante *as* oder *d* das *c* und *fis* zur Tonika. Ziehen wir dabei noch die Rolle des nächsten Obertons, der Quinte, in Betracht, so kann aus diesen Beziehungen das ganze Achsensystem abgeleitet werden.

Auf die Vergangenheit und Entwicklung des harmonischen Denkens zurückblickend, können wir behaupten, daß die Geburt des Achsensystems eine *historische Notwendigkeit* war und die logische Weiterentwicklung der europäischen Musik in gewissem Sinne die Krönung dieser Entwicklung bedeutet. Das funktionale Gefühl begann mit der Erkenntnis der Beziehungen I—IV—V—I (in der modalen Musik vorläufig nur in kadenzialer Form), Tonika *c* vorausgesetzt, also:

| Subdominante | Tonika | Dominante |
|---|---|---|
| *f* | *c* | *g* |

Die klassische Harmonielehre spricht bereits von Haupt- und Nebendreiklängen, insofern das *c* durch das parallele *a,* das *f* durch das parallele *d,* das *g* durch das parallele *e* vertreten werden können:

| Subdominante | Tonika | Dominante |
|---|---|---|
| *f* | *c* | *g* |
| *d* | *a* | *e* |

Die romantische Harmonielehre geht noch weiter, indem sie auch die oberen Parallelen in extremer Weise anwendet:[2]

| Subdominante | | Tonika | | Dominante | |
|---|---|---|---|---|---|
| *f* | | *c* | | *g* | |
| *d* | *as* | *a* | *es* | *e* | *b* |

Von hier ist nur noch ein Schritt zu tun, und das System wird zu einem geschlossenen Ganzen: die *Achse* erstreckt die Anwendung der Parallelen auf das ganze System; das Achsensystem ist die Erkenntnis dessen, daß *es* und *a* nicht nur *c* als gemeinsame Parallele besitzen (s. obiges Schema), sondern auch *fis (ges),* daß *as* und *d* nicht nur *f* als gemeinsame Parallele haben, sondern auch *h,* die gemeinsame Parallele von *e* und *b* nicht nur *g,* sondern auch *cis (des)* ist:

---

[2] Als Parallelen können nur Töne angesehen werden, auf die Dur- und Moll-Tonarten mit gleichem Vorzeichen aufgebaut werden können (z. B. C-dur und a-moll, c-moll und Es-dur).

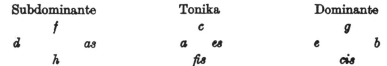

| Subdominante | | | Tonika | | | Dominante | |
| d | *as* | | *a* | *es* | | *e* | *b* |
| *h* | | | *fis* | | | *cis* | |

Das funktionale Prinzip behält bei all dem unverändert seine Geltung, nur wuchsen — dank dem Zwölfstufensystem — die Zahl der sich gegenüberstehenden Schichten und ihre Vielfältigkeit. Das harmonische System Bartóks ist also kein Neubeginnen, kein Neuansetzen, sondern *Zusammenfassung* und *Erfüllung*. Hier muß auch die Grenze gezogen werden zwischen dem Bartókschen Zwölfstufensystem und der Schönbergschen Zwölftonmusik. Schönberg löst die Tonalität auf und vernichtet sie, Bartók aber faßt die Prinzipien des harmonischen Denkens mit heroischer Kraftanspannung in eine bisher höchste, dem technischen Niveau unserer Zeit am vollkommensten entsprechende Synthese.

Bevor an eine neuerliche Ableitung des Achsensystems herangegangen wird, sollen noch einige Fragen der Bartókschen Form- und Proportionsbildung behandelt werden.


## DER GOLDENE SCHNITT

Die Fragen der Bartókschen Form- und Proportionsbildung stehen in enger Verbindung mit den Gesetzmäßigkeiten des *Goldenen Schnitts*. In der Musik Bartóks ist dies ein zumindest ebenso wichtiges Formelement, wie es der in 8—8 bzw. 4—4 Takten periodisierte Satzbau im Wiener Klassizismus war. Der Goldene Schnitt *(sectio aurea)* ist nichts anderes als die Teilung einer Distanz solcherweise, daß die Proportion zwischen der ganzen Distanz und dem größeren Schnitt geometrisch der Proportion zwischen dem größeren und dem kleineren Schnitt entspricht. (Oder: der größere Schnitt ist die geometrische mittlere Proportionale der ganzen Distanz und des kleineren Schnitts.) Die Rechnungen ergeben folgendes: Nehmen wir die ganze Distanz als Einheit an, so ist der Wert des größeren Schnitts gleich 0,618, der Wert des kleineren Schnitts gleich 0,382. Demnach kann der größere Schnitt jeder mittels Goldenen Schnitts geteilten Distanz durch das Produkt der die Distanz bezeichnenden Zahl und des Proportionsfaktors 0,618 ausgedrückt werden. Ähnlich wird der kleinere Schnitt durch das Produkt der die Distanz bezeichnenden Zahl und des Proportionsfaktors 0,382 ausgedrückt.

Als Beispiel diene der I. Satz der *Sonate für zwei Klaviere und Schlaginstrumente*. Der Satz enthält 443 Takte. Nach der obigen Formel ist sein

Goldener Schnitt 44.. ..al 0,618 = 274. Der 274. Takt fällt mit dem Schwerpunkt des Satzes, mit dem Eintritt der Reprise zusammen. Der I. Satz des *Divertimento* besteht aus 563 Triolen-Einheiten (der wechselnden Taktordnung wegen ist die Taktzahl nicht maßgebend). Der Goldene Schnitt von 563 (563 mal 0,618 = 348) deckt sich geometrisch wieder mit dem Eintritt der Reprise. Der I. Satz des *Contrasts-Trios* besteht aus 93 Takten, der Goldene Schnitt (93 mal 0,618) in der Mitte des 58. Taktes deutet die Reprise an. Im VI. Band des *Mikrokosmos* fällt der Goldene Schnitt der *Freien Variationen* mit dem *Molto più calmo* zusammen (denn: 82 mal 0,618 = 51), der Goldene Schnitt des *Märchens von der kleinen Fliege* deutet den Höhepunkt des Stückes, das zweifache *Sforzato* an (bei der Berechnung muß das 3/4 als anderthalb Takte gezählt werden), im Goldenen Schnitt der *Gebrochenen Klänge* steht die Reprise (denn: 80 mal 0,618 = 49) usw. Uns allen, die wir das *Allegro barbaro* am Klavier gespielt haben, verursachte seinerzeit das Rattern in *Fis-Moll*, das sich bald auf 8, bald auf 5 oder 3, ja auf 13 Takte erstreckt, besondere Schwierigkeiten. Nun, die Proportion 3 : 5 : 8 : 13 enthält die *einfachste*, durch ganze Zahlen ausdrückbare Reihe des Goldenen Schnitts *(Fibonaccische Zahlen)*. Bezeichnend für diese Reihe ist, daß jede Zahl der Summe der vorangehenden zwei Zahlen gleich ist — die Reihe kann also fortgesetzt werden: 2 : 3 : 5 : 8 : : 13 : 21 : 34 : 55 : 89 : ... und daß das Quadrat einer jeden Zahl dem Produkt der vorangehenden und der folgenden — plus oder minus 1 — gleich ist.

Vergleichen wir diese Zahlenreihe mit den Proportionen des Fugensatzes der *Musik*. Der Satz erreicht durch allmähliche Steigerung aus dem Pianissimo den Siedepunkt *(forte-fortissimo)* und fällt dann stufenweise in das *piano-pianissimo* zurück. Die 89 Takte des Satzes werden durch die Kulmination in 55 + 34taktige Glieder geteilt (vgl. obige Zahlenreihe; die 88 Takte der Partitur müssen wir nach dem Muster der Bülowschen Beethoven-Analysen um einen pausierten Takt ergänzen). Der Satz wird innerhalb dieser Einheiten, hinsichtlich des Kolorits und des dynamischen Aufbaus, durch Aufheben des Sordinos (im 34. Takt) bzw. durch neuerliche Vorschreibung desselben (im 69. Takt) gegliedert, und zwar der sich bis zur Kulmination erstreckende Teil im Verhältnis 34 + 21, der sich von der Kulmination entfernende Teil dagegen im Verhältnis 13 + 21. (Es ist auch kein Zufall, daß die Exposition im 21. Takt zu Ende ist und daß sich die 21 Schlußtakte des Satzes im Verhältnis 13 + 8 teilen.) Beachtenswert ist hier nicht nur, daß sich die Verhältnisse nach der obigen Zahlenreihe richten, sondern daß im ansteigenden Glied der *längere* Schnitt voraussteht (34 + 21), während im absteigenden Glied der *kürzere* Schnitt dem

210

längeren vorangeht (13 + 21), so daß die Knotenpunkte gegen die Kulmination gerichtet sind:

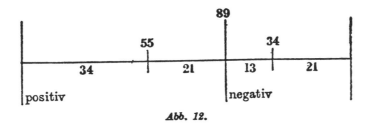

Abb. 12.

Benennen wir die eine Möglichkeit des Schnitts *positiv* (langer + kurzer Schnitt), die andere *negativ* (kurzer + langer Schnitt). Aus unseren Analysen ergibt sich eindeutig, daß der *positive* Schnitt mit einer Steigerung, mit einer Erhöhung der Dynamik oder einer Verdichtung des Stoffes, der *negative* Schnitt mit einer Senkung, einem Versiegen, einem Herabneigen Hand in Hand geht. Die Schnitte folgen immer genau dem formalen und tonalen Plan des Werkes. In unserem obigen Beispiel berühren sich positiver und negativer Schnitt wie die auf- und absteigende Linie einer einzigen Welle.

Auch die Proportionen des III. Satzes der *Musik* folgen der obigen Zahlenreihe (wenn wir einheitlich mit 4/4-Takten rechnen und den mitunter auftretenden 3/2-Takt als anderthalb Takte betrachten). Abb. 13 veranschaulicht den formalen und den übereinstimmenden geometrischen Aufbau.

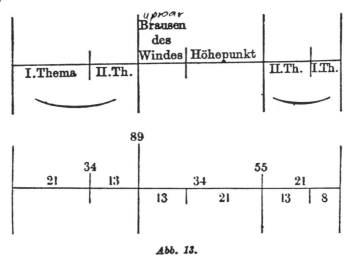

Abb. 13.

Im übrigen führt uns die obige Zahlenreihe später auf das Geheimnis des Intervallengebrauchs von Bartók.

Zu den schönsten Beispielen der Formbildung mittels Goldenen Schnitts gehören die 16 Einleitungstakte der *Sonate für zwei Klaviere* (Abb. 14; genauer: die Takte 2—17, da das organische Leben des Werkes erst hier beginnt).

Das erste Glied untersteht dem Wirkungskreis der Tonika-Gegenpole *fis-c* (T. 2—5), das zweite Glied dem Wirkungskreis der Dominanten-Gegenpole *des-g* (T. 8—9), das dritte Glied gehört zum Wirkungskreis der Subdominanten-Gegenpole *as-d* (vom 12. Takt an). Das dritte Glied ist thematisch die Umkehrung der beiden ersten:

$$\text{Thema} \begin{cases} \text{in der Grundlage (Tonika)} \\ \text{in der Grundlage (Dominante)} \\ \text{in der Umkehrung (Subdominante)} \end{cases}$$

Der wechselnden Taktordnung wegen müssen wir in Triolen-Einheiten (3/8) rechnen. Das volle Glied erstreckt sich auf 46 Triolen. Sein Goldener Schnitt ist also (46 mal 0,618) 28, und das deckt sich mit dem Umfang des bis zur Umkehrung des Themas verlaufenden Teiles („Hauptschnitt" von Abb. 14/b). Es kann beobachtet werden, daß der Goldene Schnitt immer die *wesentlichsten* formalen Wendepunkte berührt. Isolieren wir jetzt von der ganzen Form die Glieder der Grundlage (28 Einheiten). 28 mal 0,618 = 17,3, das Tonika-Glied ist eben hier zu Ende (beim Drittel der 18. Einheit). — Sowohl im Aufbau des Tonika- als auch des Dominanten-Gliedes entsteht durch den Beckenschlag ein scharfer Dualismus. Die Stelle der Beckenschläge wird in beiden Fällen durch den Goldenen Schnitt geometrisch bestimmt. Während aber die Tonika-Einheit durch *positiven* Schnitt gegliedert wird (17,3 mal 0,618 = 11), wird die Dominante durch *negativen* Schnitt gegliedert (denn das Dominanten-Glied besteht aus 10 Triolen, und der negative Schnitt von 10 ist 4); s. die *Becken*-Zeichen auf Abb. 14/b. So ergänzen sich positiver und negativer Schnitt spiegelig, der Berührungspunkt beider (Dominanten-Eintritt) trägt aber *positives* Vorzeichen. Man könnte auch sagen, daß durch die Verdichtung und Verdünnung der Knotenpunkte eine longitudinale Wellung entsteht und daß die Wellenspitzen sich im positiven Schnitt berühren. Wir finden das *negative* Ergänzungspaar dieses positiven Schnitts im Tamtam-Einsatz des „Umkehrungsgliedes", infolgedessen umschlingen sich positiver bzw. negativer Schnitt des Grund- und Umkehrungsgliedes wiederum spiegelig. Nicht nur der ganze Formbogen, auch die kleinsten Formzellen entsprechen restlos den strengsten geometrischen Anforderungen. Im *Dominantenglied* zählt z.

106

**B.** der sich bis zum Beckenschlag erstreckende Teil 11 Achteltöne, sein *positiver* Schnitt wird daher durch den infolge der Dehnung an Schwere gewinnenden *es*-Ton angezeigt (Proportion 7 : 4), im symmetrisch *negativen*

(*skizzenhafter Auszug, T. 2-17.*)

Abb. 14/a.

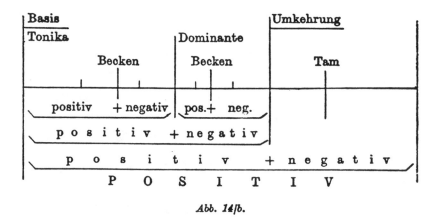

Schnitt des vom Beckenschlag fortschreitenden Teiles steht der kleine Trommelschlag. In ähnlicher Weise ist der *positive* Schnitt des bis zum Beckenschlag verlaufenden Teiles des *Tonika*-Gliedes der dritte Timpani-Einsatz in *cis* (der Form entsprechend), der symmetrische *negative* Schnitt des vom Beckenschlag fortschreitenden Teiles der Schlag der kleinen Trommel usw. Zusammenfassend: Positiver und negativer Schnitt vereinigen sich symmetrisch sowohl in den niederen als auch in den höheren Formteilen (s. Abb. 14/b). Aus diesen Verbindungen entsteht eine einzige große „potentiale" Form, in der sich die kleineren Teile schließlich im *positiven* Schnitt summieren: deshalb ist der Vorgang von einer kraftvollen dynamischen Steigerung begleitet.

Neben zahlreichen anderen Werken von Bartók zeugen alle Teile der *Sonate für zwei Klaviere* von ähnlicher Durchorganisiertheit. Geradezu unheimlich sind die Dimensionen des *ganzen* Werkes: der metrische Zeitwert der drei Sätze sind 6432 Achteltöne. Der Goldene Schnitt — 3975 Achtel — steht im Einklang mit der Struktur des Werkes (langsam-schnell + langsam-schnell) und fällt, bis auf die Achtel genau, auf die Grenzlinie zwischen I. und II. Satz.

## AKKORDIK UND INTERVALLENGEBRAUCH

### a) Chromatik

Die Untersuchung der Proportionen führt uns unmittelbar zu den Fragen der Anwendung der Intervalle. Vor allem müssen wir eine scharfe Grenze zwischen Bartókscher Chromatik und Diatonik ziehen. Die Chroma-

*Titelblatt der ungarischen Erstausgabe der „Drei Burlesken" (1912)*

tik Bartóks folgt den Gesetzen des Goldenen Schnitts *(GSch)*, genauer: der vorher besprochenen (Fibonaccischen) Zahlenreihe, von der wir sagten, daß sie die einfachsten, durch *ganze Zahlen* ausdrückbaren GSch-Zahlen in sich einschließe: 2, 3, 5, 8, 13, 21 etc. In Halbtonschritten gerechnet, bedeutet die Zahl 2 eine große Sekunde, die 3 eine kleine Terz, die 5 eine Quarte, die 8 eine kleine Sexte, die 13 eine übermäßige Oktave usw. Wir stellen uns dies vorläufig so vor, als ob sich das musikalische Gewebe ausschließlich aus 2er-, 3er-, 5er-, 8er- oder 13er-Zellen zusammenstellte und auch die Zellenspaltung gemäß den Proportionen der obigen Zahlenreihe vor sich ginge. Die 8 z. B. kann nur im Verhältnis 5 + 3 auseinanderfallen, eine Spaltungsmöglichkeit nach 4 + 4 oder 7 + 1 ist im System ausgeschlossen.

Im III. Satz des *Divertimento* ist die GSch-Zellenbildung gut merkbar. Im Laufe des Satzes erscheint das Hauptthema in sechs Variationen:

Abb. 15.

Auf Abb. 15 sind diese den Größenordnungen nach gruppiert, neben jeder Variation sind der Ambitus und die charakteristische Spaltung vermerkt.

Abb. 16 führt der Reihe nach die Themen der *Sonate für zwei Klaviere* vor:

*Abb. 16.*

Der Ambitus der einzelnen Melodien steigt der GSch-Ordnung gemäß an:

| | | |
|---|---|---|
| Leitmotiv | $3 + 5 =$ | 8 |
| Hauptthema | $5 + 8 =$ | 13 |
| Seitenthema | 13, | 21 |

Die Exposition desselben Satzes zeigt hinsichtlich *harmonischer* Struktur eine ähnliche Planmäßigkeit:

35. T.      41. T.      84. T.   95. T.      135. T.

*Abb. 17.*

Der Klangcharakter des Hauptthemas ist durch eine pentatonische Harmonie gegeben (Skizze „a", 35. Takt; erscheint auch in der Melodie: 37., 39. T.) und entspräche folgender Formel: $2 + 3 + 2$, d. i. große Sekunde +

112

+ kleine Terz + große Sekunde. Im Mittelteil des Hauptthemas ist durchgehend folgender Formelaufbau zu beobachten: 3 + 5 + 3, d. i. kleine Terz + Quarte + kleine Terz (Skizze „b", die Quarte *es-as* wird durch das *fis* weiter im Verhältnis 3 + 2 geteilt). An das Seitenthema knüpft sich eine Mixtur von Quarte und kleiner Sexte: 5 + 8 (Skizze „c"), schließlich geht durch das ganze Schlußthema eine Mixtur der kleinen Sexte: 8 (Skizze „d"). Wenn wir nun die obigen Formeln zu einer gemeinsamen zusammenfassen, finden wir eine schöne GSch-Beziehung:

| | |
|---|---|
| Hauptthema | 2—3—2 |
| Mittelteil des Hauptthemas | 3—5—3 |
| Seitenthema | 5—8 |
| Schlußthema | 8 |

Jede neue Harmonie steigt also um eine GSch-Stufe höher.

Interessant ist, daß in der Musik Bartóks trotz des häufigen Vorkommens der „*Mixturen*" solche von großen Terzen und großen Sexten kaum auftreten, weil sie in das auf obiger Zahlenreihe beruhende System nicht eingefügt werden können. Es ließe sich ebenso von einem Verbot dieser Mixturen sprechen wie in der klassischen Harmonielehre vom Verbot der Quinten- und Oktaven-Parallelen. Dagegen finden wir immer wieder Mixturen der kleinen Terz (3), der Quarte (5) und der kleinen Sexte (8), ja sogar der großen Sekunde (2). Besonders aufschlußreich ist in diesem Zusammenhang das Studium der Kompositionen aus den 30er Jahren (*Mikrokosmos!*). Die große Terz verfügt über keine erwähnenswerte melodienbildende Funktion. Natürlich, fast selbstverständlich ist dagegen die motivische Bedeutung der kleinen Terz (vgl. *Tanzsuite* II. Satz, *II. Streichquartett* II. Satz, *II. Klavierkonzert* III. Satz, *Der wunderbare Mandarin* usw.).

Daher kommt es, daß, wenn Bartók innerhalb eines chromatischen Satzes einen *Dreiklang* verwendet (z. B. im I. Satz der *Musik* oder der *Sonate für zwei Klaviere*), dieser über dem Grundton eine *Mollterz*, unter dem Grundton eine *Durterz* hat, so daß der Akkord auf die Proportion 8—5—3 gestimmt ist:

Abb. 18.

Aus der Synthese dieser zwei entstand der charakteristische Bartók-Akkord: wohl bekannt ist uns diese auf kleiner Terz-Quarte-kleiner Terz (3 + 5 + 3) aufgebaute, „dur-moll" klingende Gestalt:

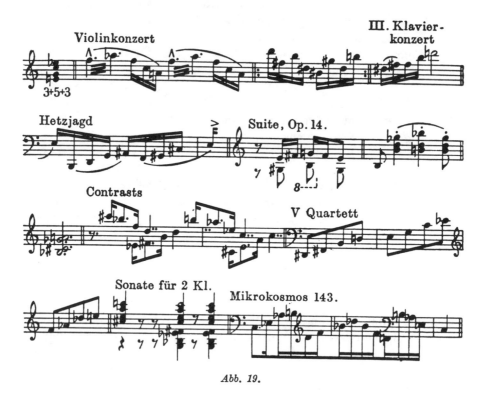

Abb. 19.

Dieser Durmoll-Klang wird häufig mit einer Septime ausgefüllt (z. B. der Akkord *e-g-c-es* mit dem *b*). Er kommt in einigen verwandt klingenden Gestalten vor, die wir, in Ermangelung einer entsprechenden Nomenklatur, mit einem zusammenfassenden Namen als Typ *a* bezeichnen werden. Die einzelnen Ausschnitte des *a*-Akkords nennen wir $\beta$, $\gamma$, bzw. $\delta$ (s. Abb. 20). Die vorige Gestalt ist also mit $\gamma$ identisch.

Der *a*-Typ kann leicht auf die Verhältnisse des *Achsensystems* zurückgeführt werden. Im *einfachsten* Fall ist zur Stützung der Tonalität die Quinte — als der nächste natürliche Oberton — am geeignetsten, z. B. zur Stützung der *c* Tonalität das *g*. In Anpassung an das System des GSch schreiben wir dies so wie zu Beginn von Abb. 21 nieder. Der Theorie des Achsensystems gemäß kann das *g* durch jeden anderen Ton der ent-

114

Abb. 20.

sprechenden Achse *(g-e-b-cis)* vertreten werden, ohne daß dadurch die
Tonalität *c* verändert würde; das *g* kann also durch *e*, *b*, ja sogar durch
*cis* ersetzt werden:

Abb. 21.

Zusammen ergeben die vier Möglichkeiten *β*. (Es muß bemerkt werden,
daß uns die drei ersten Möglichkeiten nichts Neues bedeuten, denn sie
stimmen mit dem Bestand der Dur-Septime überein.) — In Verbindung
mit dem *c* können auch andere ähnliche achsenartige Vertretungen durch-
geführt werden, ohne dadurch die Funktion zu verändern. An die Stelle
des *c* kann hier das die gleiche Achse vertretende *es*, *fis* oder *a* gesetzt
werden (Abb. 22. Die Gestalt *δ* ist die Summe der ersten drei Möglichkeiten
von Abb. 22.)

8*                                                                    115

Abb. 22.

Der Akkord α ist also nichts anderes als die achsenartige Anwendung der einfachen c-g-Beziehung. Vorbedingung ist bloß, daß sich der Klang immer aus *zwei Schichten* (Achsen) zusammensetze: aus der Tonika-Schicht und aus der sie deutenden Dominanten-Schicht. An Stelle des c tritt hier die Tonika-Achse, an Stelle des g die Dominanten-Achse:

Abb. 23.

Nach dem Muster der Schichtung des α-Akkords können noch umfangreichere α geschaffen werden.

Abb. 24.

Die Anwendung der α-Akkorde ist in der Musik Bartóks ebenso allgemein, wie es z. B. die Anwendung des Septimakkords im klassischen Stil gewesen ist.

Auf Abb. 25 haben wir das Tenorsolo der *Cantata Profana* analysiert (die 5 Anfangstakte beruhen auf dem später zu besprechenden Modell 1 : 3 *h-d-dis-fis-g-b*).

Daß der GSch eines der innersten Gesetze der Musik und nicht eine äußerliche Bindung darstellt, wird durch das vielleicht uralteste Tonsystem der Menschheit, durch die *Pentatonik*, die wir als die reinste musikalische Fassung des GSch-Gesetzes betrachten müssen, bewiesen. Die Pentatonik, besonders die *la*-Pentatonik, ruht nämlich auf einem Gerüst, das vor allem durch die Melodienschritte große Sekunde (2), kleine Terz (3) und Quarte (5) bestimmt werden kann (s. Abb. 26).

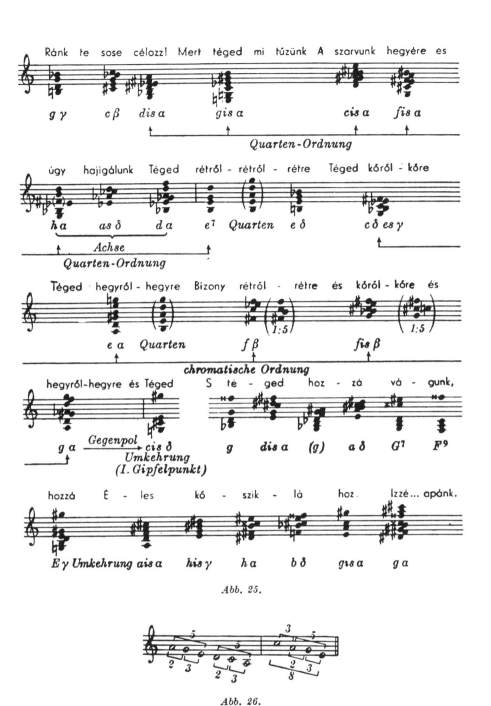

Abb. 25.

Abb. 26.

In dieser Weise also verwandelt sich die Pentatonik bei Bartók in einen α-Akkord:

*Abb. 27.*

Eine andere, häufig vorkommende Gruppe der Akkorde des GSch-Typs werden wir auf Grund ihres Aufbaus als *Modelle 1 : 5, 1 : 3* und *1 : 2* erwähnen. Die GSch-Beziehung zwischen den drei Formeln wird durch die Proportion 5—3—2 geschaffen. Für alle drei Modelle ist es charakteristisch, daß sie durch periodische Wiederholungen der Proportionen 1 : 5 bzw. 1 : 3 bzw. 1 : 2 entstehen, also

das Modell 1 : 5 abwechselnd aus kleinen Sekunden und Quarten, z. B. *c-cis-fis-g-c*...

das Modell 1 : 3 abwechselnd aus kleinen Sekunden und kleinen Terzen, z. B. *c-cis-e-f-gis-a-c*...

das Modell 1 : 2 abwechselnd aus kleinen und großen Sekunden, z. B. *c-cis-es-e-fis-g-a-b-c*...

Auf diese Weise wiederholt sich die Tonreihe in jeder Oktave, „findet sie sich selbst", d. h. bildet ein *geschlossenes* System:

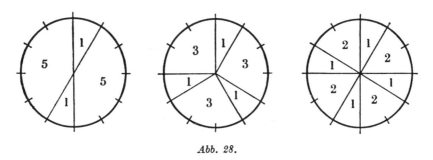

*Abb. 28.*

Unter den drei Modellen messen wir dem Modell 1 : 2 die größte Bedeutung bei. Es ist nämlich nichts anderes als die Skalengruppierung der auf Abb. 29 dargestellten *A c h s e: c-cis-es-e-fis-g-a-b* und kann als solche als

118

225

Abb. 28/a.

Abb. 28/b.

**MODELLE 1:2**

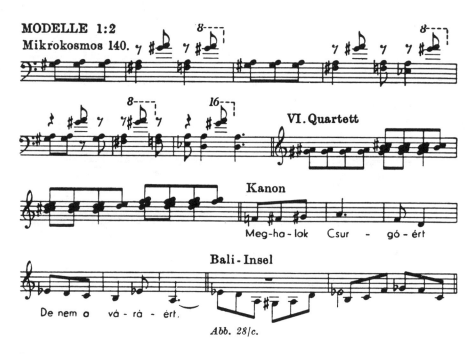

Abb. 28/c.

die „Tonika-Skala" der Bartókschen Chromatik angesehen werden. Mit ihrer Hilfe kann die Tonalität auch der kompliziertesten chromatischen Melodien gelöst werden. Hieraus ist sofort ersichtlich, daß zwischen dem Achsensystem, den *a*-Akkorden und den Modellen 1 : 2 und 1 : 5 ein organischer Zusammenhang besteht. Trennen wir die obere *(c-a-fis-es)* und die

Abb. 29.

untere Schicht *(b-g-e-cis)* der eben besprochenen Achse (s. Abb. 29) ab und bauen wir sie übereinander auf, so erhalten wir den *a*-Akkord (vgl. Abb. 23). Heben wir die Beziehungen Pol-Gegenpol der obigen Achse *(c-fis* bzw. *a-es)* hervor, so erhalten wir das Modell 1 : 5:

Abb. 30.

*Bartók im Jahre 1910*

Vereinen wir die Töne der obigen Achse, so erhalten wir das Modell 1 : 2: *c-cis-es-e-fis-g-a-b.* Diese Formeln bedeuten tonal immer ein und dasselbe. Den grundlegenden Charakter des Modells 1 : 2 unterstreicht noch der Umstand, daß es sowohl alle Möglichkeiten der Dur-, Moll- und der Septimen-Akkorde der Tonika *(C-Es-Fis-A)* enthält als auch die, die zum Typ *α, β, γ, δ* und Modell 1 : 5 gehören:

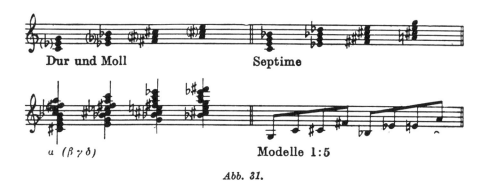

Abb. 31.

Ein frappantes Beispiel hierfür bietet uns das Reprisen-Hauptthema (III. Satz) des *Violinkonzerts.* Seine Tonreihe ist das Modell 1 : 2 *(e-f-g-as-b-h-cis-d)*, Takt 2—3 stützt sich auf die *cis-e-* und *g-* (Melodie und Begleitungsharmonie) Achse, der 7. Takt auf den *e-γ*-Akkord *(gis-h-e-g)*, die Melodie in den Takten 6—14 auf das Modell 1 : 5 *h-e-f-b:*

Abb. 32.

Ebenso ist das Seitenthema des II. Satzes der *Musik* eine „Achsenmelodie" *(C-Es-Fis-A)*, seine Tonreihe ist das Modell 1 : 2 *(c-cis-es-e-fis-g-a-b)*, das auch in der begleitenden Klavierstimme erklingt:

**123**

Abb. 33.

Im Zwölfstufensystem können drei verschiedene 1 : 2-Modelle aufgebaut werden: eines mit *Tonika*-Funktion *(c-cis-es-e-fis-g-a-b)*, eines mit *Dominanten*-Funktion *(cis-d-e-f-g-as-b-h)* und eines mit *Subdominanten*-Funktion *(d-es-f-fis-as-a-h-c)*. Jede weitere Gestalt stimmt mit irgendeiner der obigen überein.

Das *Achsen-Schema* von Abb. 29 läßt darüber hinaus noch einen wichtigen Zusammenhang erkennen (dies wäre eine neuerliche Ableitung des Achsensystems): *die Achse ist nichts weiter als das zum System gewordene Gesetz des GSch*, die einzige Möglichkeit, die Gesetze des GSch mit der für unser Tonsystem charakteristischen Zahl 12 in Übereinstimmung zu bringen. Die die Pole des Achsensystems abmessenden kleinen Terzen (3 + 3 + 3 + 3) und die die Pole unterstützenden Quarten (5, 5, 5, 5) beruhen auf den charakteristischen Schlüsselzahlen des GSch-Systems (was innerhalb der Achse zu weiteren GSch-Beziehungen führt, z. B. *g-a, e-fis* etc. große Sekunde, *c-e, a-cis* etc. kleine Sexte). Jetzt erhalten wir auch eine nähere Erklärung dafür, warum Bartók in seinem chromatischen System der subdominanten IV. Stufe gegenüber die *untere große Terz* (im Falle *c* das *as*) und der dominanten V. Stufe gegenüber die *obere große Terz* (im Falle *c* das *e*) bevorzugt. Das System des GSch duldet, wie wir wissen, keine große Terz. Da nun jede Achse ein in sich geschlossenes GSch-System bildet, führt der Funktionswechsel — das Transponieren des Systems um eine *große Terz* — zur völligen Auflösung der vorherigen Achse (= des GSch-Systems). Im Rahmen des GSch-Systems bedeutet die große Terz *entfernteste* Relationen, bei Funktionswechsel wird durch sie das GSch-System (die Achse) der vorherigen Funktion am radikalsten zunichte gemacht.

Wir müssen noch den dritten Typ der chromatischen Akkorde: die *gleichstufigen Klänge* erwähnen. Innerhalb des GSch-Systems sind folgende Gestalten gebräuchlich: die Ganzton-Skala, der verminderte Vierklang, der Quartakkord und der übermäßige Dreiklang; letzterer gehört aber nur in seiner auf kleinen Sexten aufgebauten Form (8 + 8 + 8) hierher. Isoliert kann keine dieser Gestalten als GSch-Formel angesehen werden, da der

230

124

GSch Relationen voraussetzt, die Gleichstufigkeit aber eine Möglichkeit der Relation von vornherein ausschließt. In ihrem Verhältnis *zueinander* und in ihrem Verhältnis zum *ganzen System* sind es trotzdem GSch-Formeln und werden als solche angewandt:

Ganzton-Skala:               2 + 2 + 2 + 2 + 2 + 2
Verminderter Vierklang:      3 + 3 + 3 + 3
Quartakkord:                 5 + 5 + 5 + 5...
Übermäßiger Dreiklang:       8 + 8 + 8

Unserem Tonsystem können zwei *Ganzton-Skalen* entnommen werden. Die eine ist die „geometrische Dominante", das ergänzende Modell der anderen und umgekehrt *(c-d-e-fis-as-b und cis-es-f-g-a-h)*:

Abb. 34.

125

Die Anwendung des *verminderten Vierklangs* entspricht vollends der Theorie des Achsensystems. Auffallend häufig ist die Harmonisierung und Themenbildung mit dem *Quartakkord* (als Beispiel könnte die *Tanzsuite* angeführt werden: Schluß des III. Satzes, V. Satz, Anfang des VI. Satzes). Im allgemeinen lassen die Quartakkorde zweierlei Kombinationen zu: nach dem 2 : 3-Prinzip der Pentatonik und nach dem Prinzip des Modells 1 : 5. Von zwei Quartakkorden, die nach dem 2 : 3-Prinzip der Pentatonik nebeneinandergestellt sind, ist immer derjenige der Tonika zugehörend, der um eine große Sekunde höher, bzw. um eine kleine Terz tiefer als der andere Quartakkord liegt, was auf die Schlußformel *do-so-la* der Volksmusik zurückzuführen ist:

Abb. 35.

Für die Assoziierung gemäß 1 : 5 bietet das Schlußthema des II. Satzes der *Musik* ein gutes Beispiel:

Abb. 36.

In ihrer Tonreihe vereinigen sich zwei Quartakkorde: *eses-g-c-f* und *as-des-ges-ces-fes*, deren Kern aber von 1 : 5-Modellen gebildet wird: *as-des-eses-g*, *des-ges-g-c* und *ges-ces-c-f*.

Die Anwendung der gleichstufigen Klänge und überhaupt der Akkorde des GSch-Typs fließt häufig ineinander. Abb. 37 führt das eine Ostinato der *Sonate für zwei Klaviere* vor:

Abb. 37.

Die 12 Töne des Ostinatos erschöpfen die ganze Chromatik. Die Oberstimme baut sich auf der Ganzton-Skala *a-h-des-es-f-g* auf, die Unterstimme

126

auf der diese ergänzenden Ganzton-Skala *fis-gis-b-c-d-e* (2 + 2 + 2 + 2 +
+ 2 + 2). Motivisch wird jede aus kleinen Sexten (8) gebildet, die Oberstimme aus den übermäßigen Dreiklängen *a-f-des* und *h-g-es*, die Unterstimme aus den übermäßigen Dreiklängen *fis-d-b* und *gis-e-c* (8 + 8 + 8).
Die beiden Stimmen verlaufen parallel in kleinen Terzen (3). Der Klang
des Ostinato wird durch das Modell 1 : 3 bzw. durch die Zerlegung der
Harmonie γ + γ charakterisiert:

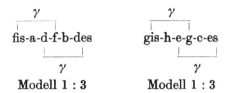

Alle Aufbauelemente sind also GSch-Formeln! Zwischen dem Anfangs- und
dem Schlußton des Ostinatos *(a-es* bzw. *fis-c)* besteht ein Verhältnis von
Pol-Gegenpol, d. h. ein Achsen-Verhältnis.

Ganz allgemein zusammenfassend kann gesagt werden, daß die Gesetzmäßigkeiten der Bartókschen Chromatik den tonartlichen Gesetzen des
GSch gehorchen.

### b) Diatonik

Dagegen ist die Bartóksche Diatonik nichts anderes als die *genaue
systematische Umkehrung* der Gesetze der Chromatik: der GSch-Regeln.

Die bezeichnendste Erscheinungsform der Diatonik bei Bartók ist die
*akustische* Tonreihe *(c-d-e-fis-g-a-b-c)* bzw. der *akustische* Akkord (C-Dur-
Septime mit *fis*), akustisch genannt, weil ihre Töne der *natürlichen Obertonreihe* entstammen:

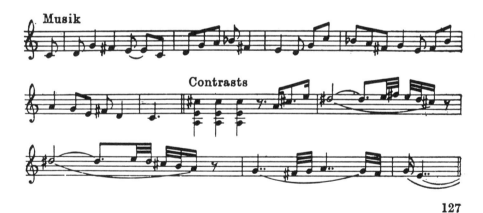

127

*Abb. 38.*

Abb. 39 veranschaulicht die systematische Verbindung der Chromatik und der Diatonik und ihren dialektischen Zusammenhang:

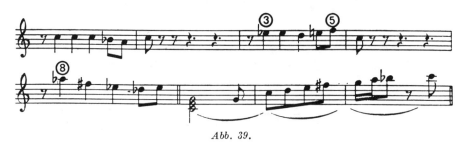

*Abb. 39.*

*Bartók mit seinem jüngeren Sohn (1927)*

Wir wollen die Hauptthemen des chromatischen I. Satzes und des diatonischen III. Satzes der *Sonate für zwei Klaviere* miteinander vergleichen. Das Hauptthema des I. Satzes ist aus *GSch*-Zellen gebildet, die Melodie wendet sich auf den Intervallen: kleine Terz-Quarte-kleine Sexte (3 — 5 — 8, *c-es-f-as*). Das Hauptthema des III. Satzes ist eine *akustische* Tonreihe. Stellen wir die beiden Tonreihen eng nebeneinander:

|  |  | 3 | 5 |  | 8 |  |  |
|---|---|---|---|---|---|---|---|
| GSch-Reihe | C | es | f |  | as |  |  |
| Akustische Tonreihe | C | d | e | fis | g | a | b |
|  |  | 2 | 4 | 6 | 7 | 9 | 10 |

so stellt es sich heraus, daß im akustischen System anstatt der kleinen Terz (3) eine große Terz, anstatt der Quarte (5) eine übermäßige Quarte, anstatt der kleinen Sexte (8) eine große Sexte fungieren. Die beiden Systeme ergänzen einander derart, daß die chromatische Skala in eine GSch-Reihe und eine akustische Tonreihe geteilt werden kann (das *cis* und das *h* verlangen als chromatische Intervalle eine chromatische Deutung). Die Harmonie, die unter der erwähnten akustischen Melodie erklingt (Abb. 39, *c-e-g*), ist in ihrer Wirkung vielleicht die größte Überraschung des Werkes. Sie baut sich auf den nächstliegenden natürlichen Obertonbeziehungen, auf der *Quinte* und der *großen Terz* auf und ist deshalb von so explosiver Wirkung, weil sie von der Bindung des GSch-Systems vollkommen befreit ist. Im chromatischen I. Satz erklingt der Dur-Dreiklang immer in GSch-Gestalt (s. Abb. 40, „a"). Die charakteristische Quarte (5) bzw. kleine Sexte (8) dieses GSch-Akkords wird mittels *Intervallumkehrung* zur Quinte bzw. großen Terz des akustischen Akkords konvertiert (s. Abb. 40, „b").

*Abb. 40.*

Schreiben wir nun diese beiden Formeln als Septimenakkord nieder:

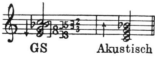

GS          Akustisch

*Abb. 41.*

Was im GSch-System auf den Grundton *c* bezogen, *von oben nach unten* gilt, gilt im akustischen System *von unten nach oben:* deshalb „Ober"-ton-Akkord. (Vielleicht steht die Tatsache, daß für unsere alten pentatonischen Melodien die abwärtsschreitende Linie charakteristisch ist, damit im Zusammenhang, daß die Pentatonik eine GSch-Reihe ist.)

Ein hierher gehörendes schönes Beispiel ist noch beiläufig zu erwähnen: Anfang und Schluß der *Cantata Profana:*

*Abb. 42.*

Die beiden Tonreihen bilden von Ton zu Ton ihr gegenseitiges Spiegelbild. Die eine ist eine GSch-Tonreihe, die andere eine akustische Tonreihe.

Wir haben also zwei Systeme ganz unabhängig voneinander behandelt: das GSch- und das akustische (chromatische und diatonische) System, und es hat sich schließlich herausgestellt, daß beide ein zusammenhängendes Ganzes bilden und die zwei Seiten, das Doppelgesicht ein und derselben Sache darstellen. Das eine System ist die Negierung des anderen, zugleich aber dessen ergänzendes Paar. Sie bedingen und schließen einander aus, bilden eine Einheit und einen Gegensatz.

In der Diatonik bezieht sich alles auf *einen* Ton, auf die natürliche Obertonreihe eines einzigen Grundtones. Die Chromatik hingegen muß immer in ihrem Verhältnis zum *ganzen System* untersucht werden, sie bedingt immer die virtuelle Gegenwärtigkeit des ganzen Systems, in ihr wird gleichsam die Kraftfeldveränderung des ganzen Tonsystems verwirklicht (es ist kein Zufall, daß wir die Formen der Chromatik immer im Quintenzirkel darstellen).

Daher kommt es, daß die Chromatik Bartóks in ständig *erweiternder-verengender* Bewegung ist, und das so sehr, daß dieses konzentrische Intervallwachstum bzw. Zusammenschrumpfen von der chromatischen Technik fast untrennbar ist. Die aus der *Sonate für zwei Klaviere* angeführten Themen (s. Abb. 16) sind z. B. in stetem Wachsen. Das Hauptthema erweitert sich von Takt zu Takt im Umfang einer kleinen Terz, einer Quarte, Sexte, Septime. Die diatonische Tonreihe des Seitenthemas breitet sich von Stufe zu Stufe aus: biegt in pentatonische Wendungen, dann in eine Quart- und Quint-Thematik ein und löst sich schließlich in Sextenbewegungen auf. Die sich verengenden „Trichter-Gänge" der Takte 239—247 wurden bereits im

Abschnitt über das Achsensystem erwähnt. Häufig ist die scherenartige Bewegung der Stimmen (z. B. in den Takten 256—263), die auf den erweiterten Stufen auftretende Sequenz (z. B. vom 208. Takt an) usw. In diesen Prozessen tritt ebenfalls eine Planmäßigkeit zutage, indem sich jeder Satzteil bis zum geometrischen Mittelpunkt des Stückes erweitert und vom Mittelpunkt an verengt. Dagegen sind im *diatonischen* III. Satz (und überhaupt in der diatonischen Setzart Bartóks) derartige Prozesse geradewegs *unvorstellbar*. Die Harmonien der Diatonik strahlen eine *Dauerhaftigkeit* aus. Der eine oder andere Akkord (z. B. die erwähnte *C*-Dur-Harmonie) zieht sich zumeist für längere Zeit in unveränderter Form durch den entsprechenden Teil hin.

Und da sich die Chromatik immer auf das *ganze* System bezieht, die Diatonik hingegen auf *einen* Ton, ist das eine ein *geschlossenes*, das andere ein *offenes* System (wir erwähnten, daß alle Formeln der Chromatik, im Gegensatz zum Obertonsystem, in einem „Kreis" darstellbar sind). Wie sehr diese Geschlossenheit bzw. Offenheit ein tiefes Geheimnis der Musik Bartóks ist, wird am greifbarsten durch die *Thematik* bewiesen: die Chromatik paart sich am natürlichsten mit der „*kreisförmigen*", die Diatonik hingegen mit der „*geraden*" Melodienlinie (mit Skalenmotivik):

Abb. 43.

Es wirkt fast wie ein dichterisches Symbol, daß die harmonischen Partialtöne im chromatischen System *unter* dem Grundton, im diatonischen System *über* dem Grundton auftreten. Interessant ist der Vergleich mit der Auffassung Riemanns, der den Ursprung des Moll-Dreiklangs in den *Unter*tönen, den Ursprung des Dur-Dreiklangs in den *Ober*tönen annimmt. Bei den Akkorden des GSch-Typs (a) gilt all dies umgekehrt: die Mollterz befindet sich über dem Grundton, die Durterz unter dem Grundton.

Auch das Verhältnis von *Konsonanz* und *Dissonanz* ist in der Chromatik bzw. in der Diatonik ein umgekehrtes. In der Chromatik steht das Ausmaß der Konsonanz im direkten Verhältnis zu den symmetrischen Teilungen; für sie ist der volle chromatische Klang der konsonanteste. Dagegen steht die Reinheit der diatonischen Konsonanz im direkten Verhältnis zu dem Zusammenklingen der Obertöne.

Die Diatonik besitzt einen *Grundton*, die Chromatik einen *Zentralton*. Im chromatischen System kann alles umgekehrt werden ohne jedwede Umdeutung des Zentraltons. Das Hauptthema in der Reprise des *Violinkonzerts* hat die Tonalität *H*, obwohl die *H*-Dur-Tonika durch die *Themenumkehrung* „auf dem Kopf" steht und unser Ohr, das nur zur Wahrnehmung von Oberton-Relationen eingerichtet ist, *e*-Moll empfindet (das Zentrum *h* ist auch durch Orgelpunkt hervorgehoben):

*Abb. 44.*

Gerade der Bartóksche „Spiegel" beweist, daß die Chromatik die Anforderungen des Obertonsystems nicht kennt, Begriffe wie „oben" oder „unten" verlieren für sie ganz ihre Bedeutung. Die hier unter dem Zentrum *h* erklingende Harmonie und mit ihr die Negierung des Obertonsystems wirkt, als ob die Gegenstände in der physikalischen Welt plötzlich ihren Schatten gegen das Licht wendeten.

Auch in mathematischer Hinsicht weisen die beiden Systeme einen eigenartigen Gegensatz auf. Die Schlüsselzahlen des Obertonsystems sind nämlich *ganze Zahlen*, die des GSch-Systems aber eine *irrationale Zahl* (0,618...; mathematisch ist die charakteristische Proportion 3 : 5 : 8 auch nur durch irrationale Zahlen ausdrückbar, z. B. 5 : 8,09061...).

Die Bartóksche Chromatik und Diatonik verhalten sich zueinander wie Dantes *Inferno* zum *Paradiso*. Die Diatonik Bartóks ist immer von Optimismus und Heiterkeit erfüllt, an seiner Chromatik haften jedoch dunkle, dämonische, irrationale Erlebnisse. Und darin erinnert er unwillkürlich an die chromatischen Versuche *Liszts* und *Mussorgskis*, in denen ausnahmslos die negative, dunkle Seite des Lebens erschlossen wird. Denken wir an die späten Klavierstücke von Liszt: an *Trübe Wolken, Unstern, Preludio funebre* und an die Todesmusik des *R. Wagner, Venezia*, an die gespenstischen *Trauergondeln*, an diese *vollkommen gleichstufigen* (!) Werke, oder an die Wahnsinnsszene aus *Boris Godunow*, wo Mussorgski ein reines „Achsensystem" anwendet und wo Intervall-Erweiterungen-Verengungen bereits die Bartóksche Technik antizipieren.

134

Eine besondere Bedeutung messen wir dem Umstand bei, daß die charakteristische Gestalt der Bartókschen „Chromatik" (GSch-System) die *Pentatonik,* die der Bartókschen „Diatonik" hingegen der *Oberton-Akkord* ist. Es scheint nämlich, daß sich in diesem Dualismus zwei der vielleicht ältesten Bestrebungen der Musik offenbaren. Die physiologische Anlage unseres Ohrs läßt auf primitiver Stufe am leichtesten die Melodienschritte der großen Sekunde, der kleinen Terz und der Quarte (2, 3, 5) wahrnehmen. Das beweist die Urschicht der Volksmusik: unsere ältesten Melodien beruhen auf der pentatonischen Tonreihe *la-so-mi-re* bzw. *re-do-la-so.* In diesen Melodienkulturen sind Dur-Empfinden und funktionale Anziehung noch unbekannt. Das *harmonische* Denken entsproß einem ganz anderen, einem gegensätzlichen Nährboden: dem Obertonsystem, das sich erst auf der Stufe der Instrumentalmusik vollends einbürgern konnte. Die Pentatonik ist in der Ableitung des *pythagoräischen* Tonsystems (Gruppierung von nächstliegenden Quinten) zu finden, die harmonische Musik aber in der Ableitung des *Obertonsystems.* — Ob es wohl zu gewagt wäre, vorauszusetzen, daß das GSch- (pentatonische) und das akustische (harmonische) System die beiden Ausgangspunkte und Wurzeln allen Musizierens waren? Wenn dem so ist, so hat Bartók die Musik an ihrer Wurzel erfaßt. Demnach ist das GSch-System eine Folge des *inneren* Hörens, das akustische System eine Folge des *äußeren* Gehörs. Das eine ist durch die Anlage des Ohrs, das andere durch die Berücksichtigung des physikalischen Zusammenklanges sanktioniert. Deshalb ist das erste glühender, ausdrucksvoller, das letztere aber leuchtender, strahlender.

Interessant ist, daß der Goldene Schnitt in der Natur nur in Verbindung mit *organischen* Stoffen vorkommt, während das akustische System diese Forderung nicht kennt und auch aus der Bewegung eines *anorganischen* Stoffes entstehen kann (z. B. einer metallenen Saite oder einer Luftsäule).

Aus den erwähnten Grundprinzipien erklärt sich jede weitere Form der Diatonik von selbst. Die grundlegenden Intervalle der Diatonik, die *Quinte* und die *große Terz,* werden von jenem *dur*-klingenden, auf Terzen aufgebauten Akkordtyp betont, dessen jede zweite Stufe in *Quinten* gereimt ist:

*Abb. 45.*

**135**

(Vgl. die Fanfarenstelle im I. Satz des *Violinkonzerts*, 233. Takt.) Daher stammt auch das bekannte „*Bartók-Namenszeichen*": *d-fis-a-cis*.

Da das akustische System nichts als die Umkehrung des GSch-Systems darstellt, kann durch *Vertauschen* der Schichten des *a*-Akkords (vgl. Abb. 23) ein „diatonischer" Akkord gebildet werden:

*Abb. 46.*

Durch den Austausch kommen nämlich die *große Terz* und die *Quinte* zur Geltung (die in der *a*-Harmonie von vornherein ausgeschlossen sind). Im Akkord hören wir jetzt auch schon unwillkürlich die großen Terzen *c-e, es-g, fis-b, a-cis* bzw. Quintenrelationen *c-g, es-b, fis-cis, a-e*. Es klingt paradox, aber in der Musik Bartóks ist der am meisten diatonische Akkord derjenige, der über dem Grundton eine *Dur*terz, unter dem Grundton eine *Moll*terz hat (*c*-Tonalität vorausgesetzt: *es-g-c-e*; z. B. im Schlußteil des *Violinkonzerts* bei den sordinierten Trompeteneinsätzen).

242

Und, um die Zusammenhänge vollends klarzustellen: die *a*-„Umkehrung" birgt auch den Kern des akustischen Akkords in sich:

akustischer
Akkord C

*Abb. 47.*

Ein häufiger Fall ist, daß zweideutig bald das *C*, bald das *Fis* im Grunde steht:

C⁷–Fis⁷ *oder* C⁹–Fis⁹
*Abb. 48.*

Diese Möglichkeit wird in der Achsen-Melodie des Hauptthemas des III. Satzes der *Musik* verwirklicht:

136

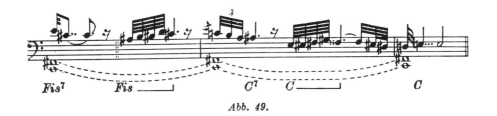

*Abb. 49.*

Wir  fassen  also  zusammen:

| *Die für das GSch-System bezeichnenden Typen* | *Die für das akustische System bezeichnenden Typen* |
|---|---|
| (Bartóksche Chromatik) . . . . . . . . . . | (Bartóksche Diatonik) |
| Pentatonik . . . . . . . . . . . . . . . . . . . | Oberton-Akkord bzw. Tonreihe |
| Akkord $\alpha$ ($\beta$, $\gamma$, $\delta$) . . . . . . . . . . . . . . | $\alpha$ „Umkehrung" |
| Modelle 1 : 2, 1 : 3, 1 : 5 . . . . . . . . . . | Dur-klingender Terzakkord mit Quintengerüst |
| Gleichstufige Gestalten : Ganzton-Skala, verminderter Vierklang, Quartakkord, übermäßiger Dreiklang (aus kleinen Sexten) | Quintakkord, Übermäßiger Dreiklang (aus großen Terzen) |

*

Sich dem materienschöpferischen Genius Bartóks zu nähern, bedeutet, die der Materie selbsttätig innewohnenden Möglichkeiten und natürlichen Anziehungskräfte zu erkennen.

244

*Bartók im Institut für Folklore in Bukarest (1934)*

# Ives and Mahler: Mutual Responses at the End of an Era

ROBERT P. MORGAN

Ralph Waldo Emerson once referred to himself as "an endless seeker with no Past at my back." In doing so, he adopted a perspective that has often supplied a framework for the characterization of American art and artists. According to this view, the most important examples of American art—its most characteristic and individual inventions—have been largely autonomous, independent of foreign influences. Relieved, above all, of the heavy burden of the European cultural tradition, our native artists have been free to develop in an atmosphere of almost limitless possibility for innovation and experimentation—without, as Emerson would have it, a Past at their back to hound them into submission and conformity.

Certainly this outlook has characterized much of the recent critical writing on Charles Ives that has appeared both here and abroad. Ives is commonly looked upon as a sort of innocent at home, a noble savage who, unencumbered by the strictures of inherited conventions, was able to create a radically new kind of music largely independent of the forces of European music history.

It is not my wish to belittle this viewpoint, which supplies a useful means for focusing upon, and thus emphasizing, certain characteristic aspects of Ives's music. Taken in isolation, however, it leads to a greatly oversimplified picture of the composer. Ives's music represents as much a confrontation with the larger Western musical tradition as with his own vernacular traditions; and it can be properly understood only by considering both of these dimensions. Thus a view of Ives outside the context of the European tradition, especially that of the eighteenth and nineteenth centuries, is as one-sided and intellectually impoverished as a view of Ives divorced from the context of his native America.

There are several ways one might go about revealing connections between Ives and the European past. One could show, for example, that Ives's work represents an extension of European conceptions of tonal and rhythmic structure, or indicate how earlier European composers anticipate techniques that reappear later—usually in a more intensified and exaggerated form—in Ives.

I have chosen a third possibility: that of comparing Ives to his European contemporary Gustav Mahler in order to indicate the extent to which these two composers shared common assumptions regarding the materials and techniques, as well as the underlying aesthetic, of musical composition. Mahler was a composer totally immersed in the European tradition—indeed, one sometimes feels that his music is almost overwhelmed by that tradition. And his similarities with Ives suggest that the apparent "idiosyncracies" of the latter were not simply those of a quirky composer working in isolation, but were rather a profound and articulate response to the critical situation in which the Western musical tradition found itself at the particular moment when both of these composers were active.

Although Mahler was some fourteen years older than Ives, and Ives lived some forty years after Mahler's death, the two were almost exact compositional contemporaries: their principal works were all conceived within a thirty-year period extending from 1888 to 1918. This period was, of course, one of extraordinary musical upheaval, characterized by an atmosphere of crisis brought on by the progressive deterioration of the pitch and rhythmic conventions of so-called "common practice" tonality. That Ives and Mahler should have reacted in certain similar respects to this crisis is a matter of considerable histor-

ical interest. It suggests that the obvious stylistic dissimilarities between their respective works may hide more fundamental underlying affinities, affinities which transcend both cultural and personal differences.

This raises an important point that should be clarified at the outset: the similarities between Ives and Mahler are almost never of a kind to make their music *sound* alike, at least in any significant sense. (One thinks, perhaps, of the last movement of Ives's Piano Trio, which has a slightly Mahlerian cast; but even here the similarities are minimal and superficial.) Rather, the correspondences pertain to their basic conceptions of what a musical composition is—how it relates to the surrounding world, the types of materials that are appropriate to it, and the way these materials are to be combined and organized. As Ives himself might have put it, the substance of their music is similar, while the manner—the specific form of its presentation—is altogether different. It is not, then, so much a matter of the musical surface as of the aesthetic interior.

The moment-to-moment succession of their music sounds very different, then; Mahler is as unmistakably Austrian as Ives is American. Yet both composers often cling to an historically regressive stage of the musical language of common practice tonality, a stage long since passed over by the currents of nineteenth-century evolutionary chromaticism. The chromatic saturation of the tonal field, so consistently evident in other advanced composers of the time, is often absent in Ives and Mahler, even in their later compositions. Clear examples are the largely diatonic opening sections of Ives's Fourth and Mahler's Ninth Symphonies. Moreover, the dominant retains its structural, key-defining role with surprising frequency—and not just in that elliptical, attenuated sense (as with Wagner) in which tonics are implied by their dominants but never explicitly stated. In both Ives and Mahler tonality in the strict, functional sense remains an active force. Moreover, it is by means of its very retention that its transformed historical meaning is reflected in their works in such a remarkably pointed way.

Tonal and diatonic conservatism forms part of a more general shared characteristic. This is the blatantly "popular," even "low-life" tone of much of their work, which lends it a complexion quite different from the "elevated" character of most eighteenth- and nineteenth-century art music.[1] Folk and popular elements are no longer neutralized, as in earlier composers, but appear undisguised—in their own clothing, as it were. The sense of intrusion from a foreign musical realm becomes an essential component of the compositional statement, and reflects a radically new conception of the nature and limits of serious musical language.

It is probably this matter of tone, more than anything else, that accounts for the aggressively negative reaction to both composers that persists even today in certain musical circles. The apparent ordinariness of the musical statements leads to charges of banality, and coupled with yet another shared attribute—the stigma of the part-time composer—fosters claims that neither was an artist of the first rank.

Significantly, Mahler, who was of course much more conscious of the weight of the European tradition, was himself beset by such doubts. It is well known that he was deeply troubled—and puzzled—by the intrusion of the commonplace in his work; and this seems to have been one of the reasons he felt a need to consult Sigmund Freud in the spring of 1910.[2] But Ives too had moments of self-doubt. One thinks particularly of his poignant remarks made after playing some of his works for an uncomprehending musician with whom he was acquainted: "I felt (but only temporarily) that perhaps there was something wrong with me . . . Are my ears on wrong? No one else seems to hear it the same way."[3]

Of course, in neither composer is the ultimate effect one of straightforward restatement, a point that again suggests an important correlation between the two. What is involved, I think, is a process of "defamiliarization," an idea that has been extensively developed in art and literature but less so, at least until more recently, in music.[4] It is grounded in the notion that as objects of perception become overly familiar, our experience of them takes on an habitual and automatic character. We no longer perceive the real object at all, but only its vague shadow or outline. Although the object is recognized, it is not truly seen or heard; it has becomes neutralized and thus deprived of its expressive potential. Only by removing what Coleridge called the "film of familiarity" can this potential be re-established.

This process, which depends upon both the use of recognizable, known musical objects and their placement in new and newly illuminating perspectives, is of the utmost importance for both Ives and Mahler. One of the most characteristic features of their music is the way it transforms the familiar, distancing it so as to rekindle its affective force. The quotations and the relative simplicity of large segments of the music are both part of this process, as is the revolutionary way in which the materials are integrated into the larger musical context.

A related charge is that both composers were incapable of inventing their own musical materials and thus had to borrow ideas from external sources. The use of quotation, closely connected with the previously discussed matter of tone, forms an essential aspect of their work. In Ives, of course, the hymn tunes, popular songs, and so on, are usually apparent and are clearly intended to be heard as quotations. In Mahler the matter is more complex,

---

[1]Cf. Theodor W. Adorno, *Mahler* (Frankfurt, 1960), p. 30ff.
[2]See Donald Mitchell, *Gustav Mahler. The Wunderhorn Years* (London, 1975), p. 73ff; also Ernest Jones, *Sigmund Freud* (London, 1955), II, 89.

[3]Charles E. Ives, *Memos*, ed. John Kirkpatrick (New York, 1972), p. 71.
[4]The classical statement is Victor Shklovsky's "Art as Technique" (1917), reprinted in English in *Russian Formalist Criticism: Four Essays*, trans. and ed. Lee T. Lemon and Marion J. Reis (Lincoln, 1965), pp. 3–24.

for his "quotations" are normally not so much literal borrowings as synthetic recreations of certain standard musical types. Literal quotations occasionally do occur: in the third movement of the First Symphony, where a minor-mode version of the song "Frère Jacques" provides the principal thematic material, or in the Scherzo of the Third Symphony, which incorporates a fragment of Liszt's *Rhapsodie espagnole*. But more commonly there is an artificial reconstruction of a specific compositional type—the march tunes in the first movement of the Third Symphony, the Alpine folk song in its third movement, the Bohemian music in the third movement of the First Symphony, or the bugle calls in the Fifth. Yet in effect—and this is the essential point—all of these passages are as clearly representative of the real thing as are Ives's literal borrowings.

What Ives and Mahler achieved in this regard represented a highly original reaction to the peculiarities of the musico-historical situation of their time. The hyperchromaticism and concomitant tonal decentralization of musical language at the turn of the twentieth century produced a radical neutralization of materials. The basic structural functions of the tonal system became more and more equivalent, tending to level out all musical statements and thus render them increasingly interchangeable. Every advanced composer of the period faced this problem. Strauss, for example, countered the tendency by developing an ever more exaggerated range of musical gestures, straining the already weakened substructure to its breaking point. This was of course consistent with the historical evolution of chromaticism and represented a development that would ultimately "progress" to the twelve-tone system.

Ives and Mahler approached the problem from an entirely different direction. As if realizing that Western music history, at least as it had been known, had reached the limits of its own history—had become, that is to say, incapable of continuing to generate a consistently progressive evolution—they fashioned a new type of music based on older and simpler models largely neglected by the main tradition. They thus set about renewing musical prototypes that, from the point of view of most of their contemporaries, seemed outmoded and historically regressive.

The twofold nature of the process required that the music be distinctly recognizable as a representative of its original source, and yet appear to be reactivated in a new context. The ways in which Ives and Mahler achieved this are essentially the same. Borrowed material is fragmented and juxtaposed against other kinds of music, combined simultaneously with different music, distorted through the appearance of unexpected intervals and through complex and ambiguous phrase relationships, or distanced by means of elaborate orchestrations that contradict the material's true heritage. But in each case the materials are transformed in such a way as to acquire new expressive life.

It is these procedures of "defamiliarization" that refute the charges of banality, charges which take into account the isolated event but ignore the larger context that supplies the materials with their expressive value and justifies their presence in the work of art. Through their context they are transfigured, and take on a new depth of meaning dependent upon the complex system of references in which they participate. Thus the almost shocking simplicity of the music in certain passages, a matter touched upon earlier, is normally limited to a single dimension of what is actually a multi-dimensional process. The straightforward diatonic character of the opening of Mahler's Ninth is belied by the way the music gradually forms itself out of bits and pieces of melodic and accompanimental figures, each of which by itself might be heard as a stock item drawn from the standard catalogue of nineteenth-century musical effects. Taken collectively, however, they produce a collage-like continuum of extraordinary subtlety and ambiguity. Similarly, the hymn tune that dominates the opening of Ives's Fourth, "Watchman, Tell Us of the Night," is transformed not only by its tonally obscure introduction, but by its remarkable scoring (especially telling is the faintly heard harp and violin ensemble), its harmonization (which occasionally—though only occasionally—injects a foreign, dissociative element), and through the deliberate truncation of its final cadential phrases.

It is sometimes said of both composers, and especially of Mahler, that their music sounds as if we have always known it. This touches upon an essential aspect of their work but leaves unmentioned the other, complementary side. What initially sounds familiar always ends up sounding very different from what we actually expected. The paradox implicit in this conjunction supplies the crucial point: what seems strange and extraordinary on one level does so only because, on another, it is so familiar and ordinary.

Perhaps even more characteristic than Ives and Mahler's use of quotation is their handling of form. A high degree of disjunction marks the music of both. The underlying continuity often appears to be cut off in mid-flight, rudely interrupted by the intrusion of heterogeneous elements. There are of course precedents for this kind of musical thinking—one thinks of late Beethoven or of Berlioz, where there is often an abrupt confrontation of radically contrasting musical units—but never before was this done with anything like the same frequency and exaggeration.

Formal disjunction can be understood as a necessary consequence of the reliance on foreign materials. Since the popular and folk elements are not "house-broken"—that is, not accommodated to the requirements of traditional symphonic structure (as they tended to be with the nationalist composers, for example)—it becomes necessary to "make room" for them in the musical structure. In Ives and Mahler this is often accomplished by a kind of *force majeure:* the structure is simply broken into, cut open to allow for the insertion of extraneous elements. As a result, forward motion is suspended, brought to a standstill so that a way can be cleared for the appearance of music drawn from another domain. Space is thus provided for elements that, quite literally, could "find no place" in earlier Western music.

This happens on various structural levels. On a small scale, Ives breaks into the highly dissonant, rhythmically driving music of the "Hawthorne" movement of the "Concord" Sonata to present a brief fragment of hymn music (which also pre-echoes the music of the "Alcott" movement), just as Mahler intersects the Trio of the third movement of his Seventh Symphony with occasional and sudden bursts of faster music. In both cases, it is as if a curtain is drawn open, giving view to a different and totally unexpected musical landscape. Or on a larger scale, an established, ongoing continuity will be rudely severed, or radically dissolved, to allow for the interpolation of entire sections of extraneous music—as in the Barn Dance episode of Ives's *Washington's Birthday*, or in the Posthorn episode from Mahler's Third Symphony. Despite the length of these sections and their apparent independence and self-sufficiency—or rather, perhaps, just because of these characteristics—they sound like isolated moments that have temporarily broken through from an altogether separate sphere of musical activity.

Such juxtaposed components can occur not only sequentially but also simultaneously. The band music in the finale of Mahler's Second Symphony first appears as a momentary interruption of the prevailing musical continuity; but later it recurs in simultaneous opposition with the latter, creating a multi-leveled structure made up of two independent but interconnected textural strands, each with its own rhythmic structure, tempo, instrumentation and general character. In this latter form it provides a striking parallel to those moments in Ives—*Putnam's Camp*, the second movement of the Fourth Symphony, or *Decoration Day*—where two independent "musics" collide in mutual and simultaneous confrontation.

The notion of combining or crosscutting between two different tempi is conspicuous in both composers. It appears in its most radical form in Ives, when he actually notates two independent rates of speed—as in the second and fourth movements of the Fourth Symphony, *Central Park in the Dark*, or *The Unanswered Question*, And there are many other passages in his music which give the effect of multiple tempi, even though everything is notated within a common metrical framework —as in the Scherzo *Over the Pavements*, where in the cadenza the wind instruments gradually accelerate against steady sixteenth-notes in the piano.

But Mahler too will disengage one strand of continuity from another by having it maintain an independent metric pulse. A common indication in the symphonies is that an instrument is to be played "without reference to the prevailing tempo." In the opening section of the first movement of the First Symphony, for example, the cuckoo call (once again a "borrowed" idea with an independent existence outside the work) continues at its previous pace after all the other instruments have taken up a new tempo. An even more striking example is the recapitulation in the opening movement of the Third. Here the reprise does not provide, as classical connotations of the term might suggest, a "resolution" for the development section. The latter is not resolved

at all, but is rather "dissolved"—gradually filtered out until it is finally represented by only a muffled snare drum figure in the distance. This figure is not completely extinguished at the return of the first principal section, but overlaps with the latter, persisting with its own tempo in conjunction with the other music. Only then does it gradually sink into complete inaudibility. (Indeed, in both composers the independent levels often seem to relinquish their hegemony only with the greatest reluctance.)

This passage from Mahler's Third recalls one of his most striking parallels with Ives: an interest in exploiting space in their musical conceptions. Mahler's snare drums sound distant, removed from the main locus of musical activity, not only because they are muffled; they are also placed off-stage, and are consequently perceived as occupying a different physical as well as musical territory. This is one of many such placements called for in his scores. As early as *Das Klagende Lied*, Mahler locates a wind band off-stage so that it can force itself upon the principal musical continuum from without. Later, when this band is heard simultaneously with the main orchestra, the distinct musical difference between the two combined layers is supported by an equally pronounced spatial one.

Several of Ives's scores—the Fourth Symphony, *The Unanswered Question*, the Second Orchestral Suite—call for a similar spatial separation of instrumental forces. The famous "Conductor's Note" to the second movement of his Fourth Symphony includes a lengthy discussion of the effect of hearing music from different directions and spatial distances, in the course of which Ives mentions the special quality of a horn heard at a distance across a lake. This passage vividly recalls the footnote to the finale of Mahler's Second Symphony, in which the composer states that he conceived of the off-stage music as the "isolated sounds of a barely audible music, carried on the wind." And in the same movement, just before the entrance of the chorus, Mahler concerns himself with the varying distances and specific directions from which four off-stage trumpets are heard. Here the music is conceived literally as moving in space, approaching and receding according to such indications as "from a great distance," "somewhat nearer and stronger," "much nearer and stronger," "again more distant," and "losing itself" into inaudibility.

The most significant point to be made about these similarities is that they are not simply isolated correspondences, which, though perhaps surprising in number, could be passed off as merely superficial or coincidental occurrences. On the contrary, they are conjoined with and subsumed under a more general conception that touches upon the nature of the musical composition itself. The tendency in Western music of the common practice period was to treat each composition as an autonomous whole, from which all elements foreign to the system of relationships defined within that whole were necessarily excluded. Emphasis was on internal consistency, with each contributing element justified by its role in a consistent and congruous structure. Extraneous material—material not actively participating in this process or, as

analysts of this music like to put it, not fulfilling a "structural function" essential to the working of the entire system—was thus rigorously barred.

In both Ives and Mahler there is a distinct shift away from this view of the work. The composition is opened up—made permeable, as it were, so as to be subject to outside influences. It becomes a more inclusionary whole, vulnerable to the ambiguities and contradictions of everyday experience, both musical and otherwise, and more truly reflective of the manifold conditions of human activity. Although the musical result may seem less consistent—and thus considerably more resistant to the kind of systematic analysis that we now seem to view as the only legitimate kind—it is both richer in possibilities and broader in perspective.

Quotations are perhaps the most forceful image of the work's surrender of its autonomy. One type of quotation that has not yet been mentioned, the self-quotation, is particularly suggestive in this regard. In both Ives and Mahler, the boundaries between compositions are often indistinct. Both are fond of quoting passages from their earlier works, and even entire movements may result from a reconstruction of previously used material. One thinks of those symphonic movements by Mahler, such as the first movement of the First Symphony or the third movement of the Second, that are to a considerable extent paraphrases of his earlier vocal compositions; or in a less literal sense, of the first movement of the Seventh, which can be viewed as an elaborate variation on the first movement of the Sixth.[5] In Ives the tendency is so developed that it frequently becomes difficult to say just where one work ends and another begins. Examples are the second movement of the Fourth Symphony, the "Hawthorne" movement of the "Concord" Sonata, and the

---

[5]The relationship of Mahler's symphonies to his earlier songs, as well as his use of material borrowed from other sources, is discussed in Monika Tibbe, *Lieder und Liedelemente in instrumentalen Symphoniesätzen Gustav Mahlers* (Munich, 1972).

piano fantasy *The Celestial Railroad*, all of which are closely interrelated with one another and share common material, or the last movement of the Fourth Violin Sonata, which incorporates the music of the song "Shall We Gather at the River" in its entirety.

There is, then, a pronounced "biographical" dimension in the music of both composers. One is almost inclined to see their individual compositions as parts of, and variants upon, a single aggregate work in progress which encompasses their entire output. The individual pieces provide their own particular comment on this aggregate work, and make their own unique contribution to it.

More generally, one notes a desire to accommodate the contradictory and variegated components of a complex reality quite different from that of the period in which common practice tonality flourished. Ives and Mahler no longer see the world as a neatly ordered entity, capable of being rendered into musical terms that are both consistent in content and syntactically logical. In this connection one recalls comments made by both composers on the effect of the simultaneous occurrence of two or more musical events, and on the importance of such multi-leveled textures for their own work. Ives's boyhood experience, reported by Henry and Sidney Cowell, of hearing a parade in Danbury in which a dissonant counterpoint was produced by two bands playing different pieces in different meters and keys, both at the same time, is widely known.[6] But it is perhaps worth quoting in full Mahler's extraordinarily Ivesian description of his own similar experiences, made in the presence of his friend Natalie Bauer-Lechner, who recalls:

Mahler told us at table that, on the woodland path at Klagenfurt with W. (who had come to settle his repertoire) he was much disturbed by a barrel-organ, whose noise seemed not to bother W. in the least. "But when a second one began to play, W. ex-

pressed horror at the caterwauling—which now, however, was beginning to amuse me. And when, into the bargain, a military band struck up in the distance, he covered up his ears, protesting vigorously—whereas I was listening with such delight that I wouldn't move from the spot."

When Rosé expressed surprise at this, Mahler said, "If you like my symphonies, you must like that too!"

The following Sunday, we were going on the same walk with Mahler. At the fête on the Kreuzberg, an even worse witches' sabbath was in progress. Not only were innumerable barrel-organs blaring out from merry-go-rounds, see-saws, shooting galleries and puppet shows, but a military band and a men's choral society had established themselves there as well. All these groups, in the same forest clearing, were creating an incredible musical pandemonium without paying the slightest attention to each other. Mahler exclaimed: "You hear? That's polyphony, and that's where I got it from! Even when I was quite a small child, in the woods at Iglau, this used to move me strangely, and impressed itself upon me. For it's all the same whether it resounds in a din like this or in a thousandfold bird song, in the howling of the storm, the lapping of the waves, or the crackling of the fire. Just so—from quite different directions—the themes must enter, and they must be just as different from each other in rhythm and melodic character. (Everything else is merely many-voiced writing, homophony is disguise.) The only difference is that the artist orders and unites them all into one concordant and harmonious whole."[7]

Excluding Ives himself, what other composer of the period could, or would, have said anything even remotely similar? Yet paradoxically, just because the similarity between Ives

[6]Henry and Sidney Cowell, *Charles Ives and his Music* (New York, 1969), pp. 144–45.

[7]Natalie Bauer-Lechner, *Erinnerungen an Gustav Mahler* (Leipzig, 1923), p. 147. This passage has been quoted and discussed in several recent books: Adorno, *Mahler*, p. 147ff; *Flawed Words and Stubborn Sounds: A Conversation with Elliott Carter*, by Allen Edwards (New York, 1971), p. 102fn; and Mitchell, *The Wunderhorn Years*, p. 339ff, from which the above translation is taken. Both Carter and Mitchell also touch upon, though briefly, similarities between Ives and Mahler. Mitchell feels that "one must not let the parallel, such as it is, carry one away" and attempts to draw a basic distinction between the two composers' attitudes toward their material:

It might have been, one guesses, that Mahler would have been intrigued by the acoustic experience from life that gave rise to, say, Ives's "Putnam's Camp" (the second of his *Three Places in New England*), but one does not need to guess at all that, had Mahler

and Mahler seems so personal, so intimately tied to the peculiar attributes of these two particular composers, one may hesitate to accord them more than coincidental value. That is, if the similarity does not embrace stylistic attributes generally characteristic of the period and thus equally attributable to other important composers of the time (and not just as isolated cases, but as essential features of an overall compositional approach), one may be inclined to see these correspondences as only idiosyncratic, and thus ultimately insignificant, "abnormalities."

I have tried to show, however, that the parallels between Ives and Mahler are comprehensible only when viewed within the context of the particular stage of Western music history during which both were active. So understood, the "abnormalities" take on a very different complexion. Moreover, their significance has become increasingly apparent in the light of more recent compositional trends. If the principal currents of musical evolution during the first half of this century tended to place Mahler and (especially) Ives outside the main stream, the compositional developments of the past quarter-century have forced them into its forefront. It would be difficult to name two composers who have had a more profound impact upon the dominant compositional attitudes of the present age.[8] And it is no accident, surely, that among all those composers who can now be considered "historical" figures, Ives and Mahler have enjoyed the greatest increase of interest in their music during the recent past.

When viewed within a wider context, the complex of interrelated techniques and attitudes common to Ives and Mahler can be seen to represent an articulate musical response to some of the most important intellectual and artistic ideas of the nineteenth century. Already at the turn of the century Novalis observed: "There must be poems that simply sound well and are full of beautiful words — but without sense and continuity — at most understandable as individual strophies — they must be like so many fragments of the most varied things." Coleridge spoke of a poetic imagination that "reveals itself in the balance and reconciliation of opposite and discordant qualities." Both Coleridge and Wordsworth were concerned with the idea of lifting the "film of familiarity." And later, in a modified form, this same concern reappears as an important component of the symbolist aesthetic. Finally, Hugo von Hofmannsthal, Ives and Mahler's contemporary, formulated the matter in terms that get very close to the spirit of their music. Commenting upon recent French poetry, he remarked:

The creative individual, surrounded by all too restricted forms of expression, as though by walls, casts himself into language itself and tries to find in it the drunkeness of inspiration, and through it opens up new entries into life in accordance with those senses of meaning which are freed from the control of conscious understanding. This is, and always was, the Latin approach to the unconscious: it occurs not in half-dreamy self-indulgence . . . but through an intense self-removal, in intoxication . . . through a simultaneous, confused piling up of objects, a violation of order.[9]

Nor is this line of thought restricted to literature: the manipulation of fragments so as to

---

actually written a piece out of that experience, it would have been purely musical considerations that would have governed its composition: the original acoustic event would, so to speak, have been musicalized, would have played a far less prominent role than the one alloted it by Ives (p. 170).

Although there is no question that Ives and Mahler transform what they have borrowed in very different ways, Mitchell's suggestion that Mahler's approach is governed more by "purely musical considerations," while Ives's is more "realistic" or "photographic," seems to me to miss the point completely. Ives's materials (in "Putnam's Camp," for example) are every bit as "musically" transformed—as "musicalized" (and thus as "unrealistic")—as are Mahler's. Mitchell, I suspect, has chosen the wrong word. Perhaps what he means is that Mahler's approach to his material is more "traditional," not more "musical."

[8] See my discussion of Ives in this connection in "Rewriting Music History: Second Thoughts on Ives and Varèse," *Musical Newsletter* 3 (1973), 3–12.

[9] Hugo von Hofmannsthal, *Gesammelte Werke, Prosa IV* (Frankfurt, 1966), pp. 489–90.

achieve a reconciliation of "opposite and discordant qualities" is one of the most characteristic features of nineteenth-century architecture, in which the structural surface often reveals an eclectic, though mediated, conglomeration of heterogeneous details drawn from a wide range of historical sources.

Further elaboration on these more general correspondences would take me too far afield.[10] I mention them, in any event, only to indicate that Ives and Mahler's procedures are in fact less peculiar than they may appear if considered solely within musical terms. They form close parallels with some of the main currents of nineteenth-century thought. Indeed, it is surprising that similar procedures were not more widely developed in nineteenth-century music. Of course they were not completely absent, as I have suggested. But only with Ives and Mahler do they begin to be extensively and consistently (one might even say "systematically") translated into musical terms, so that they assume a principal role in shaping the compositional statement and defining its aesthetic intent.

Finally, there is a well-known incident that, in light of these considerations, takes on particular interest. In 1911, when Mahler was in New York as conductor of the New York Philharmonic, he happened to see a score of Ives's Third Symphony in the office of his music copyist. Mahler was sufficiently interested to ask for a copy, which he took with him when he returned to Europe shortly before his death.[11] I like to think of this as more than just a pleasant anecdote; for it indicates that Mahler saw something in this extremely individual composition—which on the surface, at least, was worlds removed from all the music he knew and respected—that interested him and struck a responsive note. Ives was completely unknown, not only in Europe but in America; no other major composer of his time ever showed the slightest concern for his work. The similarities that have been pointed out above may help explain why it should have been Mahler, and Mahler alone, who was able to discern in his music something recognizable, something of interest and value.

255

[10]For a wide-ranging collection of essays on fragmentation as an historical phenomenon in the arts, see *Das Unvollendete als künstlerische Form*, ed. J. A. Schmoll gen. Eisenwerth (Bern and Munich, 1959).

[11]Ives, *Memos*, p. 121. For evidence that Mahler might have performed the symphony in Munich in 1910, see David Wooldridge, *From the Steeples and Mountains* (New York, 1974), pp. 150–51.

# Rewriting Music History
## Second Thoughts on Ives and Varèse

ROBERT P. MORGAN

# I

If there is one thing that Western man's recent obsession with historicism should have taught him, it is that each age writes its own history. Certainly in the area of music our view of the historical process seems to undergo more-or-less constant transformation: we are continually changing our minds about which composers are worth talking about, which are worth performing, and even which should be considered as central to the historical development of Western music. Indeed, even our conception of what constitutes the principal line of this development has not remained entirely stable.

Yet there persists a tendency to assume that music history represents a fixed, neatly compartmentalized area that provides us with a common ground of musical understanding. We rely upon it to supply an orderly framework for the great wealth of music to which we are now exposed almost daily (at least for those leading an active musical life). Moreover, we rely upon our conception of music history as a means for understanding the musical present. And since we tend to assume that the present is the child of the past—that its most significant features are realizations of prior implications—we tend to judge it in light of what we take those implications to be. Precisely for this reason, our view of the past holds such important consequences for our understanding of the musical present.

Given what appears to be the currently accepted view of the musical past, however, present-day music must inevitably seem little more than a strange aberration—a sort of musical freak cut off from all precedents. This view of new music may, of course, represent a reasonable account of the contemporary situation, but it raises the question as to whether a re-evaluation of our historical assumptions would not be in order. And since from the point of view of the present, the most important period in the historical chain is the immediate past, the music of the first half of the twentieth century would seem to be most urgently in need of a fresh consideration.

At this point we might usefully summarize what appears to be the present view of this period: stated somewhat roughly (but I think essentially accurately), it holds that music underwent a major crisis about 1910 as a result of the final disintegration of the tonal system. This led to a period of instability and experimentation in which the most important composers appeared to move in a no-man's land, groping for new compositional procedures through which to form a new stylistic basis for their music. (Significantly, almost all of the stylistic characteristics of this period have been described by musicologists in essentially negative terms, such as "atonal", "ametrical", and "non-melodic".) After some ten to fifteen years there was then a move toward stabilization: composers began to assume a more traditional approach, either by returning to a new kind of tonality or by establishing a new system (i.e., Schoenberg's twelve-tone system) designed to replace the tonal one, which was considered by these composers to have been exhausted. The most important figures who could be placed neatly into either one side or the other of this picture were Stravinsky, Schoenberg, Bartók, and Berg —and later—and as we shall see, by extension, Webern. (Some would add Prokofiev and Hindemith, both of whom are equally at home in this picture, to the list.)

This view solidified shortly after the Second World War. It thus appeared at a time that was ripe for a fresh appraisal of the music of the first half of the century, an appraisal where one could feel for the first time some sense of historical perspective. The war had made a convenient division which seemed to place the music written before 1940 or so emphatically in the past, and thereby suggested that the music of the 1950s belonged to a new era. There began to appear at this time a number of important books on twentieth-century music which developed the historical view just sketched and which placed the composers previously mentioned at the forefront of musical developments of the first half-century. Further, the music of the 1950s seemed to support this view: its most characteristic feature was a desire for ever greater control, epitomized by the development of total serialism, which appeared to represent a logical

3

continuation of the direction established by Schoenberg and the twelve-tone composers. It was the development of total serialism which resolved the question of Webern, who in his works written from the late 1920s until the end of his life had adopted a more rigorous, more completely structural approach to serialism than either of his Viennese colleagues, Schoenberg and Berg. This approach had the initial effect of placing Webern somewhat outside the mainstream, but with the increasing interest among composers in achieving tighter control over the compositional process, there was a corresponding tendency to include Webern among the most significan forerunners. Webern's acceptance, then, might be said to mark a first shift of emphasis in the prevailing picture of the musical past. But it was only that: a shift of emphasis rather than a complete realignment. For Webern's music embodied perhaps more profoundly than that of any of his contemporaries those qualities of formal logic and rationalism so characteristic of the whole neo-classical movement.

Yet today we seem to be at an historical impasse. The music of the past decade or so has brought about developments which, however confusing and contradictory in most regards, have in common the characteristic of seeming to run directly counter to this prevailing philosophy of twentieth-century music. And since this philosophy is still generally held by most of our historians (at least there is very little evidence to the contrary), it is scarcely surprising that recent music remains so totally incomprehensible to them.

This situation raises a real question as to how we should properly conceive of the musical past. It suggests that, rather than considering the present in terms of the past, we might find an answer by going in the reverse direction: a consideration of the musical past in terms of the present. This is not, of course, an altogether new way of thinking; it is undoubtedly the way many musicians (at least among non-historians) tend to think of the past in any case. But it does seem to me that historians have failed to keep abreast of today's rapidly changing musical environment and to evaluate the implications of that environment. Differently stated, I think we have reached a stage where music history needs to be rewritten in the light of recent musical developments—that the past needs to be brought more clearly in line with the musical present.

Rather than assume that recent musical developments are somehow outside of the mainstream of music history, perhaps we should ask whether this mainstream has not been mislocated, at least in regard to twentieth-century music. Was the first half of this century truly characterized by only a brief experimental, pluralistic,

and anti-traditional foray into the unknown, followed by a hurried retreat to the comforts of a more traditional and more stable compositional philosophy? Or was there a more prevailing experimental trend which did not lead to capitulation, as it were, but maintained itself consistently throughout the period?

I think such a current is clearly recognizable in the music of Charles Ives and Edgard Varèse. Significantly, both of these composers fall completely outside the accepted view of the period in question. Ives, for example, wrote all of his important works during the "experimental" period and the years immediately preceding it (roughly 1900-1920); then, for all intents, he stopped composing entirely. On the other hand, none of the music that Varèse wrote during the experimental period has survived, and he completed his first respresentative composition only in 1921, at the beginning of what is said to be the period of consolidation. Yet his music never reflected the concerns of either the tonal or the twelve-tone neo-classical schools. Varèse rather maintained a seemingly independent position for some fifteen years, when (rather like Ives) he suddenly stopped producing music completely, waiting some twenty years to bring out his next work. This appeared in the 1950s when the prevailing musical climate seemed somewhat more congenial to his ideas; but by that time Varèse had only some ten years left to live, and Ives, who died in 1952, was already a figure of the past.

It is instructive to examine the "official" position on these two composers. As both were clearly musicians of great originality, it has not been possible for historians of twentieth-century music simply to ignore them; yet since both fell so completely outside of the historical picture being presented, they have been treated as isolated figures outside the musical mainstream—peripheral composers who, though interesting, could be conveniently dismissed as "experimenters" of limited, local, or individual importance. Thus in William W. Austin's *Music in the 20th Century* (1966), which forms part of the Norton history of music series, certainly the most prestigious series of musico-historical works ever published in the United States (the Austin book received

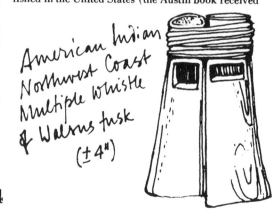
American Indian
Northwest Coast
Multiple whistle
& Walrus tusk
(± 4")

the Otto Kinkeldey Award of the American Musicological Society for the most distinguished work of musicological scholarship published in 1966 by an American), Ives is accorded only some four pages out of a total of over 700, while Varèse receives five. (Stravinsky, on the other hand, recives 61 pages, Schoenberg 56, and Webern 31, while Bartók and Prokofiev both have over 20.) Rather than list further statistics, let it suffice to say that comparable treatment is to be found in other volumes, ranging from such similarly synoptic treatments of the period as H. H. Stuckenschmidt's *Neue Musik* (1951), Karl H. Woerner's *Neue Musik in der Entscheidung* (1956), Claude Samuel's *Panorama de l'Art Musical Contemporain* (1962), and Juan Carlos Paz' *Introducción a la Música de Nuestro Tiempo* (1955), to such specialized studies as Theodor W. Adorno's *Philosophie der Neuen Musik* (1948), André Hodeir's *Since Debussy* (1961), and Donald Mitchell's *The Language of Modern Music* (1963).

Recent musical developments suggest, however, that it may well have been Ives and Varèse who represented the true center of twentieth-century music history, a view that this essay will attempt to defend. Obviously, this view is not intended to reflect negatively on the intrinsic quality of the music of those it "disposes". Rather, it suggests that from a specifically historical (as opposed to a purely aesthetic) point of view—history being that discipline which has always conceived itself with revealing connections within a temporal framework—these are the two composers who lead most directly to the musical present. Further, it suggests that, at least in the area of music history, a fundamental re-evaluation of Ives and Varèse and their importance in the full scope of twentieth-century music is long overdue.

I think it would be mistaken, however, to assume that the music historians erred in over-valuing the importance of the "tonal crisis" in the music of our century. Rather, it seems to me they have suffered from a failure to comprehend the true significance of that crisis. Conservatively oriented, they have preferred to view it in a wholly negative light, as something leading to "atonal" music—i.e., a music that could not be dealt with in positive terms. They have, as a result, primarily concerned themselves with locating musical developments which led out of this crisis and have failed to consider seriously the possibility of developments which might, in fact, have capitalized upon the loss of tonality. In so doing, they have consequently missed the essential point about both Ives and Varèse: namely, that both composers were able to establish styles which made a virtue of the new musical situation. Their music could not be conceived of as a negation of tonality, for though reflecting the tonal crisis as clearly as any atonal work, it remained tonal in essence; nor could the idea of re-establishing contact with the tradition be applied to their work, which at least in its non-traditional orientation, revealed a consistency notably lacking in, say, Schoenberg and Stravinsky.

What the loss of tonality, at least as a "system" (and as a system it was as lost to Ives and Varèse as it was to anyone else), opened up to these two composers was an entirely new way of thinking about musical material, and related to this, a new way of conceiving of the nature of musical continuity. Perhaps the most fundamental consequence of this loss resulted from the fact that the basic compositional material had been cut off from any intrinsic sense of mobility. The functional tonal system of the eighteenth and nineteenth centuries had placed the melodic content of a composition in a clear framework within which could be established directed musical motion toward clearly defined goals. Thus the melodic material associated with an "antecedent" phrase was no longer heard as simple raw material; it was heard as suggesting certain limited kinds of continuation. Put differently, it was given an explicit musical "meaning" —a context which determined the appropriate kind of continuation. The loss of this more-or-less-agreed-upon meaning clearly had a profound effect upon the way in which composers were able to approach their material, a point which will later be discussed in some detail in reference to specific works by Ives and Varèse. What is most important within the present context, however, is that, of the various "solutions" offered by different twentieth-century composers to the problem posed by the loss of tonality, those of Ives and Varèse have been most suggestive to composers of the past fifteen years or so.

From the present-day vantage point, the total serialism of the 1920s can be understood as a last phase of neo-classicism: the attempt to find a replacement for the tonal system in a new, analogous system carried to its logical (or as some would say, perhaps not without some justification, "absurd") conclusion. The compositional tendencies of the late 1950s and the 1960s, then, repre-

Pottery Whistles — Costa Rica
(± 3")
5

259

Bass Clarinet in C
(Italy – early 1913C)

sent a departure from what had been in essence a long attempt to establish a new "common practice". Thus although on the surface recent music seems in many respects more "traditional" (or at least, as some of our critics have been pointing out, more "approachable") than that of total serialism, when viewed in a somewhat larger context, it must be said to manifest a really quite "revolutionary" point of view. What has happened, I think, is that the true modern condition in music is being reflected for the first time with full clarity and on a really wide scale in the music of our own time.

It is ironic that the most systematic attempt to evolve such an approach, total serialism, should itself have been responsible for the realization that the search for a shared system of musical order was fruitless. As has frequently been pointed out, the actual music that resulted from such a completely controlled system more often than not sounded irrational and arbitrary—in fact, completely "out of control". Not surprisingly, this had the effect of suggesting to the serial composers themselves that *anything* could happen in their music, a realization which served to loosen up their compositional attitudes considerably. If it was impossible to establish any one common system giving meaningful, consistent results, there was no reason not to make use of entirely different kinds of music, even within a single piece. Certainly the most pervasive hallmark of the new music is its eclecticism: one finds aleatory, tonal, serial, and programmatic elements, for example, all coexisting (and apparently peacefully) in the same work. The problem of unity is no longer solved by a consistent adherence to one compositional approach or even one musical style, but by a consistent attitude towards the use of different approaches and styles. It is just this attitude, whose nature will, I hope, become clearer in the course of this article, that I think ultimately may be taken as representing the most fruitful response to the modern situation in music; and if I am right, it will place Ives and Varèse at the very center of the mainstream of twentieth-century music.

# II

It is certainly more than coincidence that everything about Charles Ives—the quality of his life as well as of his music—seems so completely outside the framework of the established picture of twentieth-century music. Although born in 1874 (and thus within the eleven-year span that produced all of the major composers of the period), Ives continued his principal compositional

activity to the first twenty years of the century, and nothing whatever (except for a few songs) was written during the period of consolidation. Moreover, he lived outside the established musical profession, deriving his livelihood from the insurance business, while preferring to treat his compositional activities as a more-or-less personal and private affair. It is hardly surprising, then, that most of his contemporaries considered him to be little more than a musical dabbler, and that his music received almost no performances during his lifetime. For this reason he was (and still is) frequently accused of dilettantism, a charge which would certainly hold within the framework of our traditional musical orientation. Viewed in the light of the special conditions of the time, however, his actions take on a somewhat different meaning. Musically considered, Ives chose to be a loner; it was not an unreasonable response to the existing musical conditions.

Ives' own attitude toward his compositions is equally symptomatic. He did not seem to think in terms of completed compositions, and his works consequently have a distinctly "provisional" quality about them. This is most noticeable in the many small, openly experimental pieces which were apparently never even intended for actual performance, but which Ives undertook as private confrontations with specific compositional problems. But it is also true of his biggest, most important works. Thus Ives himself said of the Second Piano Sonata (the *Concord*), that he thought of it as a kind of work in progress which he would have liked to change whenever he came back to it. (In his own words, "Everytime I play it, it seems unfinished".) Even the Fourth Symphony, perhaps Ives' greatest work (he himself referred to the last movement as the best thing he had done) was never put down in completely finished form, but had to be assembled from his manuscripts when it finally received its first complete performance some fifty years after its composition. From a traditional point of view, this appears to be unprofessional; yet again, I think this stems from a failure to appreciate the peculiarities of the modern situation, which seems to invite such an "open-ended" attitude, manifested by a reluctance to commit anything to final form.

Similarly, the accusation often encountered that Ives

260

lacked technical mastery appears to me unfounded. Ives, after all, was trained as a musican from his earliest childhood, receiving his first instruction from his father (who clearly had one of the more original musical minds of his time), and during his high school years he was active as an organist, an activity well suited for the acquisition of a broad musical education. Later Ives majored in music at Yale University, where he studied with Horatio Parker, certainly one of the foremost American composers of the later nineteenth century, and was exposed to what can presumably be taken to have been the best in academic musical instruction available in the United States at the time. He was apparently a perfectly adequate student at Yale, the only complaint being that he refused to be constricted by the limitations of the academic style. (That he, unlike so many of his gifted American contemporaries, chose not to carry on his studies in Europe is simply evidence of his feelings about the decadence of the European musical tradition.) In any case, Ives' supposed lack of technique can not be said to be a matter of his inability to master the tools of his trade; if anything, it was only a matter of his refusal to accept the relevance of these tools for his own artistic purposes, which had nothing whatever to do with a trade. I think there has been a real misunderstanding of Ives in this regard; and I am convinced that a close examination of his scores indicates that he knew precisely what he wanted and knew exactly how to go about realizing his intentions.

Looking over the music, one is amazed at the extent to which Ives anticipated compositional techniques that have occupied composers in recent years. There are, for example, several shorter pieces which experiment with serialism, notably the *Tone Roads No. 1* and *No. 3*, the *Chromatimelodtune*, and *From the Steeples and the Mountains* (all of which predate Schoenberg's earliest serial pieces). Yet significantly, there is in none of these pieces any systematic approach to serialism. In the two *Tone Roads*, for example, the series (there is more than one in each piece) are only one element among many making a contribution to the general pitch organization; and even within the serial voices there is no complete consistency as to the choice of pitches. The series is thus not thought of as the focus of a new musical system; it is simply one among several means of organization. What is even more advanced for the time, the serial idea is not confined to pitch alone, but also determines im-

portant rhythmic features in certain of these pieces. Thus in *From the Steeples and the Mountains* there is a rhythmic series in which one finds a gradual reduction of the durational values from half notes (eight sixteenths) to dotted eighths (three sixteenths), and then a retrograde of this so that ultimately the long values are reattained. (A similar passage also occurs in the coda of *Across the Pavements*.) But even in Ives' most tightly serial piece, the *Chromatimelodtune*, where the pitch series incorporates all twelve tones and is adhered to with uncharacteristic consistency, there is still a strong tonal orientation. (The pitch C, defined explicitly as a center in the three curious, quintessentially Ivesian cadential passages that punctuate important formal divisions in the piece, is also emphasized through the organization of the series itself: C almost always appears as the first or last note of the set, and further as the only repeated note in the six- and seven-note accompanimental chords which appear in pairs to form twelve-tone "aggregates".) Also notable, at least in the context of this somewhat rarified pitch structure, are the eight-measure phrase groups. Yet it is just this apparent inconsistency, both within the pitch structure itself—which is both tonal and twelve-tone—and between the treatment of pitch and rhythm, which to such a large extent accounts for the fascinating aural impression created by the work.

It is in the area of rhythm, however, that Ives can be most innovative and explorative. In *Over the Pavements*, for example, one finds an extraordinary wealth of cross-rhythms placed in juxtaposition to the prevailing (written) meter. At one point these give rise to a gradual acceleration of the beat, resulting in a "metrical modulation" quite similar in execution to many passages in the works of post-war composers (one thinks particularly of Elliott Carter, although the technique is by no means confined to one composer). (In regard to this piece, as well as to several others, the reader is referred to Gunther Schuller's excellent notes accompanying his recording on Columbia MS-7318 of some of Ives' short chamber works.) There are also several instances in Ives of the simultaneous coordination of two different tempos, such as in the second and last movements of the Fourth Symphony and in "Putnam's Camp", the second of the *Three Places in New England*.

It is useful to consider such rhythmic complications in relation to another "prophetic" feature in Ives' work: the textures. These are frequently of a truly staggering

261

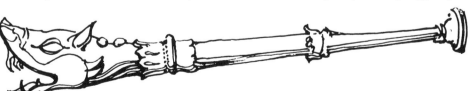

"RKANGLING"
Short trumpet
Tibet

7

complexity, characterized by the dissolution of all details in a total compositional complex in which one perceives only a generalized, overall effect, rather than the individual components. Such passages anticipate what is certainly one of the most characteristic developments in recent music: the emphasis on pure sound and texture, on the quality of the given musical event, at the expense of its relationship to others with which it is associated. (Examples are easy to find: i.e., Stockhausen's group compositions, Xenakis' sound masses and clouds, and the kind of cluster technique associated with Penderecki and Ligeti.) This is most obviously present in such large orchestral works as the Fourth Symphony, *Three Places in New England*, and *The Fourth of July*, where the saturation of the texture with individual elements creates a web of sound from which one is only occasionally able to grasp the specific. Ives had an unusual talent for creating interesting orchestral contexts for such passages. To take one of many possible examples, the beautiful "transcendental" music in the solo violins and harp which hovers over the last movement of the Fourth Symphony can rarely be heard as a distinct entity, yet it has a profound effect upon the general character of that movement. One of the most poignant aspects of the movement is the way this music occasionally is allowed to emerge from the blurred background to dominate briefly, only then to recede into obscurity once again. But there are also examples in works for smaller ensembles, such as the Second String Quartet. Even more remarkable is *From the Steeples and the Mountains*, where the notes associated with the accelerating rhythms in the orchestral bells (an instrument already by nature quite indistinct in regard to pitch) are completely absorbed into a mass of sound defined only in its most general outlines.

While on the subject of instrumentation, it is interesting that Ives at a very early date began to show a preference for "special" ensembles, i.e., groupings of instruments which do not conform to any of the standard ensembles (such as the string quartet and piano trio) inherited from the eighteenth and nineteenth centuries. As early as 1900 or so, for example, Ives became interested in the "theater orchestra" and wrote many compositions for what are in effect "pick-up" combinations: e.g., the several chamber music sets and the two *Tone Roads* pieces. Moreover, he also liked to choose combinations especially suited for the unique requirements of particular compositions, as in *From the Steeples and the Mountains* (scored for four sets of bells, trumpet, and trombone) and *The Unanswered Question* (for strings, four flutes, and trumpet).

A more general indication of the "modern" character

of Ives' musical thought can be found in his attitude toward the seriousness and exclusiveness of "classical" music. Ives was certainly no foe of the classics—there is much in both his music and in his prose writings which indicates that he had a firm knowledge of and real affection for the standard literature—but it is also apparent, again in both his music and words, that he objected to the rather sacrosanct aura which he felt surrounded much concert music. Thus he objected to what he considered the over-refined quality of the string quartet literature and remarked that he would like to write a piece which would make "those fiddlers get up and do something like men". (The result was the Second String Quartet.) Further, he repeatedly maintained that he saw no real distinction between different kinds of music—classical, popular, religious, secular, or whatever; and indeed, he did not hesitate to mix sources in composing his own works. Much of his music already evidences that element of self-mockery more commonly associated with Erik Satie, or in our own time with John Cage and his followers, and the kind of directness and unpretentiousness later found in the music of *Les Six*. This is most apparent in those incidences in which he incorporates well-known popular tunes, such as hymns, marches, or drinking songs, into his music, or where he chooses an instrumental combination with strong popular overtones, as in the theater orchestra pieces. But it also makes itself felt in other, apparently more "serious" compositions, as in his handling of the four players in the Second String Quartet, where the instruments are treated like proponents in a political argument.

But I have saved for last in this brief listing of precedents for later music, what is certainly the most striking anticipation of recent musical developments in Ives' work: namely, the quotation of known music. As I have already noted, these quotes include a wide range of material, encompassing, for example, the opening motive of Beethoven's Fifth Symphony, the hymn *Martyn* ("Jesus, lover of my soul"), and the patriotic song *The Red, White and Blue*—all of which, significantly, appear in the same work, the *Concord* Sonata. (Ives is also given to quoting his own earlier music.) This is con-

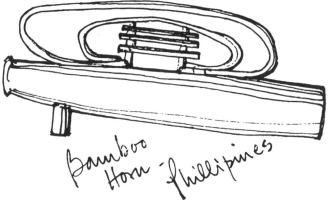

Bamboo Horn – Phillipines

sistent, of course, with Ives' attitude about the universality of music and the common roots of different kinds of music. But it does raise the question of why he chose specifically to *quote* such material, and why he particularly favored material that would be well-known to a wide range of listeners.

An answer to this question leads us back to problems associated with the collapse of the tonal system, for it seems to me that quotation represented a possible solution to these problems. To the question "What could form the substance, the basic musical material of a composition, after the underlying basis for the old kind of material—the tonal system—was no longer operational?" there could be only two radical (i.e., not neo-classical) solutions: either one could evolve a new kind of musical material altogether, or one could attempt to find radically new contexts for the old material. It is clearly the latter possibility which Ives explored. (It is no coincidence that this solution has reappeared—along with the other one, to be sure—in the past few years, when the aura of crisis has reasserted itself due to the questions raised by total serialism.) And it seems to me that in developing such contexts he was more successful than any other composer of his time in rethinking the asumptions of traditional musical material. Although Ives, through actual quotation, preserved more of the original character of this material than any of his important contemporaries, he managed to instill it with a completely new musical meaning. I do not think it is too much to say that, whereas the main thrust of compositional activity in the first half of the century was devoted to finding a way of reconciling new compositional "content" with traditional form, what Ives attempted was to develop a new kind of form for traditional musical content.

Any attempt to understand Ives' quotations must therefore deal with the question of their relationship to the total compositional intent. First, however, it is necessary to return to the question of Ives' technical competence, a question which needs further clarification before the true significance of his quotations can be properly understood. (It is sometimes said that the

quotations are themselves symptoms of Ives' inability to deal with purely compositional problems.) I have already discussed Ives' training with an eye toward showing that he had acquired a firm musical foundation. But there is also a portion of Ives' output which reveals a clear and sure handling of compositional procedures within the historical context of his time—thus countering the view that he existed in a sort of musical vacuum. I have in mind works such as the First Symphony and the two piano sonatas, which form strong links with the instrumental tradition of the nineteenth century. Thus the First Symphony, written when Ives was still a student at Yale, is a classic example of an academic, "school" exercise in traditional musical form. It is not, certainly, a work of profound intrinsic merit (although its many personal touches make it a fascinating study as a stage in the development of Ives' individual musical consciousness); yet considering the age of the composer, it reveals a remarkable sophistication, as well as an impressive technique in handling traditional compositional problems. But it is in the two piano sonatas that one can see the true fruits of this concern with large-scale formal organization. These are, of course, much later works (completed in 1909 and 1915 respectively) and are infinitely more original as personal expressions. Yet both works form clear extensions to the line of great instrumental compositions which leads from Beethoven through Liszt and Mahler. This is heard most immediately in the rich, idiomatic writing for the instrument, but it is also present in more subtle ways, such as in the overall formal construction, which is constantly expanding, built on wave upon wave of climactic motion. Thus the opening of the Second Sonata is obviously "dualistic" in conception, based on the opposition of two contrasting musical ideas (and thereby showing its debt to the sonata principle); but the whole texture of the piece is so continually developmental that the distinction between the contrasting elements is increasingly broken down during the course of the work. Also reminiscent of nineteenth-century inclinations is the frequent appearance in these works of a final, texturally rich climactic presentation of the basic melodic material in what Edward T. Cone, in writing about nineteenth-century music, has referred to as a thematic "apotheosis". One finds this, for example, in the first and last movements of both sonatas; and also in their slow movements there is what might be called a mirror image of this procedure: a marked simplification of the theme and its accompaniment, resulting in a kind of apotheosis "in reverse".

These pieces may appear to constitute exceptions to my point concerning Ives' break with the past. But I

Serpent in C
Italy—early 17thC

Bass Clarinet in C    Italy 20thC

think it is necessary to distinguish a "break" in this sense from a total rupture in which absolutely no factors are carried over into the new music. Certainly the latter is not the case with Ives, who remains in all his works unmistakably a part of the history of Western music. But what is important is the degree to which Ives is able to rethink traditional formal procedures for his own, new purposes.

An instructive example, both in this connection and in relation to the creation of new contexts for quoted material, is the slow, middle movement of the First Piano Sonata. This movement has been described as a theme and variation form constructed on "What a Friend We Have in Jesus". If this were literally true, I can well imagine that the results might be disastrous, or at best, an amusing parody in the manner of Ives' own very early (1891) *Variations on America for Organ*, written when the composer was only seventeen years old. But the truth of the matter is that this movement contains neither a theme nor a set of variations, at least in any normal sense. Although Ives does begin, after a very brief "introduction" (in quotes because it too maintains only the most tenuous relationship to classical models), with a passage derived from the tune in question, the latter is already fragmented, internally altered, and reharmonized almost beyond recognition ("almost", however, for the tune is incontrovertibly "there" in some sense), so much so as to raise a real question about whether there is a "statement" of the tune at all. In any case, Ives has certainly not taken the theme simply as given material and then proceeded to alter it through a set of variations. It is, as noted, varied to begin with, and then, throughout a highly rhapsodic, formally strikingly original movement of constantly developing structure, functions as a kind of periodic "reference point" for the total musical proceedings. Thus there is no trace of the kind of sectional layout indigenous to the variation form, nor does the theme (or its underlying structure), clothed in different guises and characters, appear as an ever-present central thread which determines the overall formal arrangement of the movement. Yet—and I think this is important—the movement unquestionably owes something to variation form. The "theme", for example, does play at least an analogous role to the variation theme in that it supplies the general framework of motivic and intervallic consistency which underlies the work. But its actual, recognizable appearances are of an entirely different order: it surfaces only occasionally, always in fragmentary form, creating a recurrent, though elusive, perspective for the myriad of events which swirl around it. (In this connection it resembles the orchestral work *The Housa-*

*tonic at Stockbridge*.) Further, it appears in its simplest form not at the beginning of the movement but near the end, in the reversed apotheosis mentioned earlier. The effect is thus one of gradual clarification, a procedure reminiscent of that used by Berg in *Lulu*, where in the variations on the *Lautenlied* the tune occurs in its "original" form *after* the variations. (But the more traditionally-oriented Berg is still dealing with a theme, not just a fragment, and with a series of fixed variations.)

I suspect that the main reason critics and analysts have been so prone to accuse Ives of technical incompetence is that they have been looking for the wrong kind of things in his music. It can scarcely be denied that, judged according to traditional criteria, Ives seems at times an awkward composer. The "naiveté" manifested by portions of even his best pieces—such as the Alcott movement of the *Concord* Sonata and the third, fugal movement of the Fourth Symphony, may understandably raise questions in a mind accustomed to looking for technical and emotional consistency in one work. Yet, in Ives, it is precisely the extreme contrasts created by these and similar movements that mark one of the essential aspects of the music. This is related to the point made earlier concerning Ives' interest in incorporating as many different kinds of "musics" into his own work as possible.

The fugal movement of the Fourth Symphony is interesting in this regard. First, it is undeniably different in both atmosphere and technique from the other three movements, which despite their own important differences have in common a degree of tension and complexity missing from the third (although the first movement might be said to stand as a kind of "buffer" between the second and fourth on the one hand and the third on the other). Further, it exhibits an internal inconsistency typical of Ives: namely, that a movement couched in the form of a traditional—in some respects an even rather academic—fugue (not even *that* kind of music is to be ruled out *a priori* from Ives' musical world) has as its subject the opening of Lowell Mason's *Missionary Hymn* ("From Greenland's Icy Mountains"). The essential point, typically Ivesian, is the movement's uneasy, though fascinating, balancing of form (or technical means) with content, in which this simple melody is subjected to the most rigorous contrapuntal devices, such as inversion, augmentation, and stretto.

But what is the "function" of this movement in the symphony as a whole? This question raises issues which are central not only to Ives' own work but to a great deal of more recent music. As the question is phrased (and I have purposely phrased it as an Ives critic would), it presupposes a particular kind of answer—one which would show that the movement reveals relationships, both technical and otherwise, to the symphony as a whole in some way analogous to those found in the great masterpieces of the eighteenth and nineteenth centuries. Yet it seems to me that Ives forces us to ask entirely different kinds of questions if we are to come to a closer understanding of his music. The main point to be grasped is that Ives' work should not be taken as presenting final solutions to musical problems in the way that, say, Beethoven's *Eroica* Symphony does; it presents only suggested, temporary, and provisional solutions. Further—and I think we are only now beginning to see this clearly—this is true not because Ives lacked the technical means to find completely consistent solutions to the musical problems which he confronted, but rather because he no longer believed that such unambiguous solutions continued to be artistically meaningful. It is just Ives' realization of this—indeed his finding a virtue in it—which makes his music so suggestive to the modern ear. I have already spoken of Ives' own conscious realization of this provisional, open-ended quality in his music. Significantly, this was something for which he never felt a need to apologize—which, indeed, he did not take to be "problematic" at all. This attitude is by no means unique to him. It is a strain running through all the arts in this century, and it is characteristic of some of the century's most focal works. (I need mention only Joyce's *Finnegans Wake*, which shares with Ives not only this open-ended quality but also its complex manipulation of extremely diverse materials.)

Returning to the Fourth Symphony: despite its pro-

visional quality, there is certainly a kind of logic embedded in the work. Indeed, if there were not at least some "sense of sense", I doubt that one could be so moved by it. But its logic is of a different order from the kind to which we are accustomed. This brings me back to Ives' use of quotation, which is closely tied to this question. There has been a realization in recent years that Ives is not just quoting "for the fun of it" (although I would maintain that this is certainly *one* important side of it), but that he orders his quote so as to establish certain structural relationships in his work. (See particularly the article "Charles Ives' Quotations: Manner or Substance", by Dennis Marshall in the Spring-Summer 1968 issue of *Perspectives of New Music*.) The Fourth Symphony is an excellent example of this, for it quotes from an astonishing variety of sources. (Those interested in specifics are referred to John Kirkpatrick's preface to the published score.) These vary widely, not only in genre (popular, folk, sacred, etc.), but also in character; and they make the piece appear, at least on casual hearing, to be little more than a musical hodgepodge or collage, a collection of artifacts drawn from the well of Ives' musical memory. Yet virtually all of these tunes share a structural association of considerable importance: they contain phrases which play on the relationship between the fifth and sixth degree of the diatonic major scale, a relationship which dominates each of the four movements of the symphony. Briefly, it must suffice here to point out that he "rewrites" the ending of the hymn "Watchman, Tell Us of the Night", which forms the nucleus of the first movement, so that it is not only "left hanging" at the close of the movement, but also serves to confirm this relationship (the way in which Ives manages to make equivocal the answer to the question framed by the opening lines of the hymn is itself a revealing study); that this interval and its derivatives play an important role in both the second and third movements; and that it completely dominates the coda of the last movement (like the first, ambiguous in its ending—or, one wants to say, its lack thereof), which is based on yet another tune, *Bethany*. Thus the work can be said to hang together in *some* sense, although to over-emphasize this fact by minimizing the importance of the violent contrasts is, I think, to misread, and even do an injustice, to the piece. For the contrasts—or let me just say it—the *contradictions* inherent in the composition are as important a part of it as are its logical connections. Thus although there is decidedly a kind of consistency in the work, it is nevertheless only a "kind of" consistency, and one which leaves open as many questions as it answers. It is as if Ives is saying: "Look, even these disparate musical elements have a relation-

"KYEN"
mouth Organ
Burma

Piccolo Fagottino
France 18thC

**11**

ship with one another". But it is nevertheless fundamental to the sense of the symphony that they are *disparate* elements.

As for the fugue itself, there is a further aspect to the movement which should be mentioned. This is the extraordinary fact that it was taken virtually intact from another, much earlier composition by Ives, the First String Quartet of 1896 (in which it serves as the opening movement). One could say, with some justification, that it has been borrowed from another musical world, relocated like an alien into a totally new and different context. Again, those traditionally-oriented may well wonder how this could possibly work. Surely there exists no comparable situation in all the masterpieces of the eighteenth and nineteenth centuries. It is as if Beethoven had inserted a movement from an early piano sonata into the Ninth Symphony, or Wagner a scene from *Das Liebesverbot* into *Tristan und Isolde*. Yet it *does* work, and I think for reasons similar to those I was getting at before. Although the few changes that Ives has made in transplanting the fugue tend to strengthen its connections with the rest of the symphony—such as the quote from *Antioch* ("Joy to the World") in the final cadential section, which brings out the inversion of the fifth-sixth relationship—it nevertheless appears to stand there essentially nude among the giants which surround it.

But it too has a place in Ives' musical world, and in our own musical world. It is thus both a part of the piece and not a part of it—or rather, *more* than a part of it. One has the feeling that Ives could, if he wished, find a place for almost *anything* in this symphony. It is, in that sense, an "all-encompassing" work, and as must be the case where inclusion rather than exclusion is the guideline, there are inevitable "inconsistencies". Ives is telling us that these *ought* to be there; they stand in his cluttered musical closet as faithful images of the modern cultural situation.

The quotations, too, can be viewed in the light of this inclusiveness. They seem to lend Ives' work an additional dimension, a dimension leading beyond the confines of any specific composition to the larger domain of our musical memories. Ives' preference for borrowed material that is well-known, laden with associations of both a musical and a purely personal nature, almost guarantees a "meaningful" response from the listener. Whether or not one likes Ives' music, it is difficult not to be strongly affected by it; for we hear him tampering, as it were, with our musical pasts, a fact which has the effect of drawing us almost as participants to the very core of his works. In this regard, there is undeniably inherent in Ives' choice of material a certain nostalgia for the past, a fact which undoubtedly enhances its appeal for many listeners. Yet this nostalgia is of a fundamentally different kind from that manifested by the neo-classical composers. With Ives there is no attempt to re-establish a sense of traditional order and coherence; if anything, he seems to be interested in disrupting those expectations of order evoked by his material. By placing the familiar in unfamiliar contexts, by dissociating it from its normal framework, Ives makes us acutely aware of the new conditions of twentieth-century life. Yet ultimately one experiences not so much a sense of regret for what has been lost as one of exhilaration in confrontation with the possibilities unleashed by a new world.

I would like to close this discussion of Ives by mentioning what is perhaps his most striking innovation, a procedure which can serve as a common link for the various stylistic factors that have been considered. I am referring to the simultaneous presentation of two or more seemingly independent events in one composite musical statement, creating layered textures that are frequently of extreme density. (Such passages can be taken to form a sub-group to the more general type of massed textural music discussed earlier.) Perhaps the most famous example is the second movement of the Fourth Symphony, where several different "musics" undergo independent, yet simultaneous lives throughout the course of the work—interacting with one another yet maintaining their own internal consistency (even to the extent of having their own tempos). Other well-known examples can be found in *The Unanswered Question* and *Three Places in New England*. On the one hand, these passages are simply extreme manifestations of Ives' "inclusiveness". Not only can two different kinds of music appear in the same piece, they may appear at the same time. In this way the totality becomes literally a fusion of its parts. More generally, such passages suggest a completely new way of organizing musical continuity, a way which is only now beginning to be explored in full.

Although I would again say that there is a structural sense to such passages (a close analysis could easily show that relationships exist among the various layers), their most striking feature is the fascinating ambiguity which stems from their textural multi-dimensionality. Quotations, new materials, and derivatives which belong somewhere in between all coexist in a shared universe in which each plays its own private role while at the same time influencing and being influenced by all others. There is no one perspective in such music; we are constantly being asked to consider the total picture from as many different points of view as possible. ⬜

*(This is the first part of a two-part article.)*

266

# Rewriting Music History
## Second Thoughts on Ives and Varèse (Part II)

ROBERT P. MORGAN

# I

Turning to Varèse after a consideration of Ives, one is struck first, certainly, by what appear to be fundamental differences between the two composers. The externals of Varèse's life, for example, clearly present a very different picture from those of Ives. Born in 1883, some ten years after Ives, his roots were European and cosmopolitan. Furthermore, Varèse was always a "professional" musician in the strict sense of the word; and, despite years of neglect as a composer, he was actively involved in the musical life of his time throughout the greater part of his career.

Yet there are certain aspects of Varèse's life that, in a curious way, recall Ives. His early training was not in music but in science, a fact which the composer felt to be of considerable importance in shaping his attitudes about composition—much as Ives always insisted upon the relevance of his business activities to his musical interests. Also, despite his European background and the fact that he had already attracted considerable attention as composer and conductor in both France and Germany, Varèse chose at the age of thirty-two to move to the United States, the "new world," where, with the exception of short visits to the continent, he remained for the rest of his life, marrying a U.S. citizen, and eventually took out citizenship himself. All of his principal compositions were written in this country and Varèse was thus, like Ives, in a very real sense an "American" composer working in an artistic milieu which, despite close ties with Europe, was nevertheless to a significant extent dissociated from the heartland of the Western musical heritage.

It is perhaps possible to overstress the coincidence of this geographical dislocation with a corresponding artistic one in Varèse's music. Yet it is difficult not to be impressed by the fact that the composer's first major representative work—which appeared relatively late in his career (he was almost forty)—was not undertaken until 1920, after he was firmly settled in the United

States. Significantly, Varèse chose to call the new work *Amériques*, a title which may be taken as symbolic of an attitude characterizing all the works written from this point: a determination to search for "new worlds" of musical sound and organization. At first glance, *Amériques* seems to occupy an unexceptional position in the history of twentieth-century music. Scored for a very large orchestra (the original called for some hundred and fifty instruments, but in the revised—and considerably shortened—version of 1929 this was reduced to one hundred and twenty-two), it is at times reminiscent of an earlier epoch-making large orchestral work, Stravinsky's *Sacre du Printemps*—particularly in those sections, such as the closing one, which feature highly repetitive motivic figures of an essentially rhythmic-percussive nature. But such surface similarities should not detract from the profound differences existing between the two works, or from the originality of Varèse's conception.

These differences are most clearly evident in the handling of the musical motive and its development, and more specifically in the relationship of the motive to the underlying metrical framework. In the Stravinsky, the playing off of motive against meter forms an essential aspect of the music: the motive, which, to begin with, carries very strong metrical implications, is consistently modified so as to affect the larger groupings of the basic pulse, and is thereby placed in a continuously varying metrical context. It is consequently important that the pulse be "present" (perceivable), and one of the most interesting facets of Stravinsky's score is the way it forces us to hear metrical groupings, while at the same time forcing a constant reinterpretation of what we take to be the basic pattern of these groupings. In most of *Amériques*, on the other hand, the sense of pulse is considerably more tenuous, and the larger metrical groupings, such as the measure, are less emphatically defined. Consequently, one is less inclined to "count out" the musical material, tending rather to perceive it as a total musical unit.

Also, there are important differences in the orchestration of the two works. Certainly the *Sacre* is one of

15

the most virtuosic orchestral conceptions in music, yet it owes much to the orchestral approach of the late nineteenth century. Specifically, it features the sort of orchestral dissolution of an underlying harmonic fabric in complex instrumental figurations that had become the hallmark of the post-Wagnerian orchestral style, a point which is well illustrated by the opening section of the work. Although the latter, with its characteristic use of the solo bassoon in its highest register, is undeniably a strikingly scored passage, the conception of the first section as a whole—consisting of a gradual expansion of the opening line through the addition of new instrumental layers, leading ultimately to a climax of considerable textural complexity—creates an orchestral (and also formal) framework stemming directly from such nineteenth-century models as the opening of *Das Rheingold*.

This passage is particularly instructive for our purposes, because the first section of *Amériques* seems in some respects so similar. Here too the opening is characterized by a solo woodwind in a "special" register (the low alto flute), but the method of extending this opening idea is quite different. There is no gradual building to a climax that serves to define the formal limits of the section; rather, the flute motive is presented and then repeated in an almost "neutral" manner —that is, it undergoes very little internal modification or development. It is, to be sure, occasionally interrupted by statements of different orchestral groups—a procedure which serves to indicate the overall orchestral scope of the work as well as to introduce the basic thematic material of the composition as a whole—but these are not arranged so as to lead to an "accumulation" of material in any traditional sense. Everything remains separated. What results is a kind of instrumental "field" —projected by the flute and articulated by the several orchestral interruptions—that remains essentially "flat" throughout the entire section.

Another notable aspect of *Amériques* is the importance of the percussion section. The use of percussion in orchestral music had, of course, already undergone considerable expansion by 1920. But whereas this had previously consisted mainly of the use of more and more percussion in an essentially traditional way, in *Amériques* the percussion writing takes on a fundamentally new meaning. Traditionally these instruments (and particularly those of indefinite pitch) had been used almost exclusively for purposes of "accent"—to help articulate features already inherent in the "real" voices of the composition, so that the sense, if not the character, of the music could survive without them. But with Varèse, even in this early work, the percussion begin to assume

an independent role: they establish a unique and essential component of the total compositional idea. Put differently, they no longer serve simply to "double" pitched parts, but delineate independent parts of their own. One notices this most clearly, of course, in those passages in *Amériques* where the percussion are heard alone (that they *are* heard alone is already an indication of a break with tradition); but the principle operates consistently throughout the entire composition.

Despite the many innovations in *Amériques*, however, in the series of works written over the following decade or so only the ideas implicit there reach full fruition. With one exception (the large orchestral piece *Arcana*, written in 1927), all of these compositions are scored for small instrumental combinations (two of them also involve the use of voice). This can be partially explained, perhaps, by the simple practicalities of musical life: it is considerably easier to get performances of pieces calling for small forces. But what is especially remarkable in these works is that not one is written for a standard instrumental combination; rather, each is scored for a special group determined by the requirements of the composition in question. No other major composer of this period so consistently avoided "normal" performance groups, a fact which reflects one of the most important assumptions of Varèse's approach: that the basic compositional idea is completely inseparable from those instruments which embody it. The choice of instruments has become as much a part of the essential concept of the piece as, for example, its motivic structure or its form.

But it is not only the uniqueness of the ensembles; the choice of specific instruments is also revealing. Most immediately striking is the absence of strings in all but two of these works (*Ecuatorial*, where a full string section is handled in a quite non-traditional manner, serving a basically accompanimental function; and in *Octandre*, where the only string instrument is a single contrabass). Certainly one reason for this exclusion was a purely negative one: the string section had by that time become so closely aligned with the intensely subjective, rhetorical style of late nineteenth- and early

268

**16**

twentieth-century romanticism that its avoidance assisted Varèse in establishing a new "emotional context" for his music. But more important, it seems to me, was the fact that the preferred brass and woodwinds, with their more precise attack characteristics and intonational qualities, were better suited to Varèse's specific intentions, which were principally concerned with short, sharply defined motivic fragments rather than with the long, sustained lines that characterized the preceding era and were so idiomatically suited to the string instruments.

In addition to this favoring of brass and woodwinds, there is an even more pronounced emphasis on the percussion section. I have already noted Varèse's use of percussion in reference to *Amériques*, but the tendency there becomes increasingly developed in the following chamber works. In all but one (*Octandre*, which uses no percussion at all), the percussion section is by far the richest in the ensemble in both number and variety; and in one instance, *Ionisation*, it actually accounts for the entire ensemble. In these works Varèse not only explored the new timbral possibilities opened up by the use of a radically expanded percussion section (significantly, the only part of the orchestra that failed to keep pace with the general expansion and enrichment that occured throughout the nineteenth and early twentieth centuries), but also extended the very "vocabulary" of percussion writing. By treating the percussion as equal components in the total ensemble, Varèse evolved what amounts to a completely new language for these instruments.

But, as I have already suggested, it is difficult to discuss Varèse's use of percussion—or for that matter, of any instruments—apart from the overall characteristics of his compositional approach. The chamber pieces written between 1921 and 1934 constitute an ideal basis for the extraction of the composer's general stylistic principles, and a consideration of some of the latter will be useful at this point. To begin with, almost every one of these works opens with a short, unaccompanied "motive" (the term, as we shall see, is not completely applicable) that presents the basic intervallic and rhythmic material of the piece. The most striking aspect of these motives is their highly repetitive structure—repetitive both in the way shorter, submotivic units occur over and over again (with slight alterations) to form the larger statement; and in the constant reappearance of one tone, which through its accented position relative to the others as well as its frequent repetition, tends to dominate, functioning not so much as a "tonal center" (which suggests too many parallels with traditional tonality), but as a kind of nucleus around

which the others are grouped. Most important, this basic melodic material is so unique in sound, so immediately identifiable as coming from Varèse and no other composer (I have discussed the fundamental differences from Stravinsky, the only other composer to use even superficially similar material) as to suggest at once that the means for its continuation and development will be (and indeed, must be) equally unique and unprecedented.

The problem of establishing musical continuity in the context of twentieth-century developments, already discussed in the first part of this article, bears closely on the general question of Varèse's stylistic procedures. I said earlier that what had been most characteristic of the opening material of pieces written in the eighteenth and nineteenth centuries (leaving aside such matters as slow introductions) was that it seemed to contain fairly explicit implications for its continuation. Thus we speak of "antecedent" phrases which are "answered"—and thus fulfilled—by "consequent" phrases. This characteristic is made possible, of course, by (among other things) the tonal system, which supplies a remarkably unambiguous framework for the establishment of musical motion toward *expected* goals. Moreover, it applies as much to the music of Wagner, where the material has become so loaded with possible implications for its continuation that the latter is always uncertain at best, as to Mozart's, where one has a much clearer idea of the specific kind of continuation that may follow. (The reader should understand that I am not suggesting that the listener knows *exactly* what to expect—frequently one's expectations are only very general in nature—or that he is "disappointed" if the kind of thing expected does not occur. Indeed, being "surprised" in this specific way—at hearing "Y" when "X" is expected—is a common response to this kind of music; but it is *only* because the music has this quality of evoking expectations that the ability to surprise is one of its most salient features.)

❧⊙❀⊙❧

As I have also indicated, one of the most pervasive (and most interesting) qualities of post-tonal music has been the attempt of almost all of the major composers to fashion musical material that despite its abnegation of the functional tonal system, *somehow*—usually through some sort of rhythmic and/or tonal analogy with earlier music—preserves this character of expected continuation. It is just this quality, however, which seems to me to be completely absent in Varèse's music (a point, incidentally, which distinguishes it sharply from that of Ives); his material seems to a large extent free of

**17**

any specific implications for its continuation. It is, as I noted in a somewhat different context, "neutral" in character. Thus, for example, the predominating tones—the tonal nuclei—never appear to "lean" toward other tones, but appear as "fixed" and "abstract" entities defined by an absolute value, rather than by their tendency to move toward their neighbors. Not surprisingly, such material has radically different characteristics from that of traditional music—and thus, I would argue. from the music of Varèse's contemporaries. The most general of these is that the material, since it is not suggestive of what is to follow, becomes more important in its *own* right, as an independent sonic event. One speaks frequently of the importance of "sound as such" in Varèse's music, a phrase that points clearly to his altered temporal orientation: the material's own inherent quality—and not its ultimate temporal "direction"—has become its essential attribute. Whether we are dealing with such unaccompanied melodic units as those which initiate most of these works, or with the larger, texturally more complex units that characterize later stages of the composition, the material is defined more by its overall character, its total sonic identity, than by individual details. Thus traditional concepts of melodic and harmonic combination and motivic development are less applicable here than such generalized features as instrumentation, density, volume, overall speed, registral distribution, etc. All of these work in conjunction to determine the total effect, what could be called the "timbre" of the material. And it is the latter which really matters, which accounts for the true substance of the musical idea in Varèse.

Clearly then, such material must be given a very strong profile, a shape that will lend it an unmistakable stamp and indicate its importance in the context of the work as a whole. Thus in Varèse one feels almost as if the material has been "projected" in time (to use one of his own terms), hurled out by virtue of its own intrinsic character, rather than because of any inherent tendency toward forward (temporal) motion. I wrote "in time," yet it is just this facet of Varèse's art which I think explains the frequent references one encounters to the "spatial" character of his work. It is precisely because we are forced to hear the musical assertions on their own terms, not in terms of their temporal implications for what is to follow, that we hear them "spatially," as being in some curious way "fixed in time." It is thus no coincidence that these ideas are frequently characterized more by some kind of registral (spatial) projection —for example, an *upward* (as opposed to forward) movement toward a high note—than by their specific "motivic" content.

One could go on, and the matter of "space" is one to

which I shall return. But the question to be considered now is: How is one to extend (i.e., compose with) musical material when no specific kind of extension is suggested ? (A history of recent compositional developments might well be written on the basis of this question.) Varèse's solution—recalling his predisposition, strengthened by his early technical training, to approach all phenomena in terms of their physical properties—is typically "corporeal." In listening to his compositions, one senses that the material is being handled like an *object*, a sort of basic building block which can be extended and developed by adding on other blocks. (It is suggestive in this regard, as well as in respect to the nature of the material itself, that Varèse referred to the units of his music as "sound *masses*.") The form of the piece, then, becomes the result of the relationships evolving out of the combination of these blocks, some of which are closely related, while others are more contrasting in nature.

❧❦❧

This represents a fundamentally new way of dealing with musical continuity (although here again, there are certain parallels with Stravinsky, particularly in the pre-neoclassical, "Russian" works), and one which has had an enormous influence on recent compositional conceptions. Although a consideration of the techniques Varèse evolved for combining these musical units leads us into a largely uncharted area, for which music theory is only just beginning to develop a vocabulary, it is nevertheless possible to give at least a general account of the principles involved. Certainly any discussion must take into consideration two basic types of combination: simultaneous combination, in which two units are superimposed upon one another (thus raising the question of the relationship of quasi-independent components in the total musical complex), and consecutive combination, in which one unit follows another (whereby the mode of progression from one to the next becomes crucial). Ultimately the two types are of course inseparable, for they work in close conjunction with one another in defining the overall sense of the music. It may be helpful, however, briefly to consider them independently.

The problem of dealing with simultaneous groupings led Varèse to the development of what can be termed a new kind of counterpoint, a "counterpoint of masses" rather than of individual lines. Since he was concerned with materials which, despite some degree of internal development, tended to maintain their overall, global characteristics, it was possible to "mix" them in such a way that they could maintain their own identity while at the same time contributing to the larger sonorous effect resulting from their combination. Any given mass, taken individually, can thus be said to define a "plane," and Varèse's "counterpoint" consists in a manipulation of several of these planes within the total, "three-dimensional space" of the composition as a whole. The planes are made to interact with one another in various combinations: they may appear separately, overlap, merge into new, "higher" identities drawn from the combination of two or more masses, etc. Varèse's own terms for these techniques are particularly instructive: he speaks of the "collision," "penetration," "repulsion," and "transmutation" of sound masses. The terminology is striking, not only for what it tells us about the composer's compositional procedures, but also for its clear indication of the need for a completely new vocabulary in dealing with this kind of music. This need is itself a most telling aspect of the Varèsian "situation."

As for the other type of combination, comprising those of a consecutive nature, here it is more difficult to make generalizations without reference to specific works. I have already spoken of the use of repetition, which is the most common technique for extending a musical unit. But I have also indicated that such repetition rarely occurs without some degree of variation. The questions of how much variation and of what kind are, however, closely tied to the individual formal features of a given composition. They are affected, above all, by the constantly changing relationship of one mass to the others. Furthermore, when one considers the relationship of two *different* masses that occur consecutively in the temporal continuum, the situation takes on increasing complexity. Matters of contrast and balance become paramount, as does the degree of association between "opposing" elements, which may itself undergo transformation during the course of a piece. What can be said, however, before we turn to a specific example, is that Varèse had an unerring sense for balancing the discrete units with which he worked, as well as a highly developed capacity for integrating these units into larger structures that allowed them both to unfold independently and to interact with one another, thereby acquiring new and deeper musical significance.

A detailed documentation of some of Varèse's techniques in a single work, *Intégrales*, has already been undertaken in a provocative article by the composer's former pupil Chou Wen-Chung, in the April, 1966 issue of *The Musical Quarterly*. Chou, however, is concerned almost exclusively with the pitch relationships of individual units with which the composer is working, indicating that the latter are all derived from transformations of a single cell, which serves as a basic source for all pitch events in the composition. Thus his article, al-

though it deals briefly with the connection between these transformations and such Varèsian concepts as "collision" and "penetration," seems to emphasize a close correspondence between Varèse's techniques and those of his contemporaries. (After all, what composer of this time was *not*, at least in some sense, dealing with transformations of some kind of basic pitch cell, twelve-tone or otherwise?) Thus the final effect is curiously (and I suspect unintentionally), to place Varèse squarely in the mainstream of the period. Nevertheless, the article, which confines itself mainly to the first section of *Intégrales*, provides a useful point of departure: and it will be helpful to take Chou's remarks as a base in considering some of the larger formal aspects of the same section. But only in these larger aspects does one see the relationship of the details of the pitch structure, which forms only one element of the total design, to the overall musical conception: and it is only in the latter that the innovative character of Varèse's music becomes apparent.

❧⊙❧⊙❧

Even in regard to the pitch structure, however, what is most striking in these opening twenty-nine measures is the almost total absence of harmonic motion.* Thus, at least in this area, the music seems completely "*non*-developmental." What, then, *is* developing? One factor, certainly, is the gradual increase of rhythmic activity over the course of the passage, although here this increase results more from the changing interrelationships of individual elements than from a developmental expansion of one basic musical event. Thus the opening idea, first stated in the E-flat clarinet, is brought into ever closer association with other components of the piece—specifically, with the two recurring chords, one of which is heard in the two piccolos and the B-flat clarinet (defining a sound mass or plane with a high registral distribution), and the other in the three muted trombones (defining a plane of low distribution). The single-line E-flat clarinet plane (later transferred to trumpet and oboe) is the only one of the three that develops at all in regard to pitch, and even here the pitches are always anchored to an ever-recurring B flat. This plane appears first completely alone (measures 1-3) and is then immediately repeated with rhythmic modifications and the

*Although the following discussion refers for convenience to measure numbers in the score, the musical points should be clear to record listeners. The recording on Nonesuch H-71269 is recommended. The score is published by Colfranc (Belwin-Mills): $6.

271

**19**

addition of percussion (measure 4). This second statement is terminated by the appearance of its own long, sustained final tone (here, as always, B flat) and the first appearance of the two sustained chordal units (mm. 5-6).

Not only have all the individual units been introduced at this point, but also the basic formal segment of the section has been defined: two statements of the clarinet plane leading to the two sustained chordal planes, which taken together provide a kind of "cadence" for the segment. The next segment (mm. 7-9) is simply an altered repetition of the first, modified so as to produce an acceleration of the time intervals between the two successive statements of the opening clarinet figure, and between these and the chordal units which terminate them. There follows (mm. 10-11) a further reduction of this segment, with the opening idea in the muted C trumpet and *immediately* followed (i.e., without being repeated) by the chords, leading to yet another statement, once again in the clarinet, now completely overlapping the single line with the chords (m. 11). This overlap results in a much less conclusive version of the segment, for the clarinet plane now continues to unfold after the entrance of the chords. It is this contracted, less stable version which then becomes the basis for subsequent development. Now, however, it is always preceded by an additional, "disconnected" (because it does not lead to the chords) statement of the opening idea, which—significantly—is always given to a different instrument (i.e., not the E-flat clarinet): first to the oboe (mm. 12-13) and later, in a longer, double statement, to the D trumpet (not muted), assisted briefly by the oboe (mm. 18-21). The E-flat clarinet/chordal segment itself continues to accelerate: it appears twice after the oboe statement of m.12 (mm. 14-15 and mm. 16-17), where it commands first 8½ beats and then 8 beats. After the long repeated trumpet statement that follows (mm.18-21), it again appears twice; but although the first statement (mm. 22-23) once more consists of 8 beats, the second (mm. 14-15) is cut short after only 2 beats (it is in fact literally "interrupted," with the result that the lower chordal plane never actually appears in its original form), leading immediately into the cadential material which closes the section. Thus it is as if the opening plane has branched out into two separate units, which, although still closely related (both continue to revolve around the same B flat), are differentiated by function and by instrumentation. One, in the original instrumentation, is still terminated by the chordal planes and continues to accelerate; the other, in the trumpet and oboe, is "isolated" and undergoes a process of retardation and relaxation.

It is, I think, the pull between these two opposing forces that makes the final cadence so convincing. The latter (mm. 25-29)—which, as mentioned, occurs after an interruption of the last statement of the E-flat clarinet/chordal group—consists of a tutti chord that is gradually built up out of a shifting of the previous pitch elements (discussed in some detail in Chou's article). New instruments are introduced: the previously unused French horn (muted), as well as the D and C trumpets (now both muted) and the oboe—heard before, but in a completely different context. A fresh chordal sonority is thereby established to delineate the end of the section, a chord which represents not only the goal of the accelerating group, but, in a more subtle way, the fulfillment of the retarding rhythmic motion of the earlier oboe and trumpet statements. Significantly, this chord marks the first point in the piece where the various components making up the first section undergo sufficient transformation to lose their individual identity and be absorbed into a single massed sonority. It also represents the loudest, densest, and registrally most extended event in the composition to this point. Moreover, each of the four major sections of the entire work ends with a similar sustained tutti chord (mm. 29, 78, 154, and 224). Thus, just as the overall shape of the first section mirrors that of the opening six measures (that is, both consist of linear activity that is "congealed" into a final vertical sonority), so the general shape of the succeeding sections mirrors that of the first.

Clearly, in such a totally static pitch structure as one finds in this opening section, the ear must focus primarily on non-pitch elements in order to follow the sense of the design. So far I have concentrated mainly on the rhythmic aspects of the section (although I have not discussed the rhythmic relationship of the two chordal planes, which—although always working in close association—nevertheless represent separate components that are developed in relation to one another, as well as to the clarinet plane). I have also mentioned the important role of register, both in defining the independence of the

272

**20**

individual elements and in helping to articulate the final cadence. Equally important is the organization of the dynamics. Varèse's indications are remarkable, both in their variety and precision; moreover, they not only create a fascinating pattern in themselves but also contribute to the formal design just outlined. They are consistently handled in such a way as to keep distinct the various planes of the section. This is especially important in the case of the two chordal units, which—since they are both sustained—could easily mix into one larger unit; indeed, it is only in the final tutti that these two planes are completely denied dynamic differentiation.

≈◎❦◎≈

There is one further non-pitch element to consider: the percussion. This large array, distributed among four players and consisting entirely of instruments of indefinite pitch, is in one sense completely independent of the pitched instruments—that is, it does not simply reinforce the pitched attacks but creates an accentual pattern entirely its own. Yet, if the percussion are considered in terms of their larger groupings, they also may be said to support the underlying formal process of the section. Their main timbral articulations (such as those at mm. 13-14 and at m. 18) coincide with the beginnings of important formal segments, and they assist in articulating the final cadence—in "reverse," by dropping out (to which extent they are also "consumed" by the tutti chord) for the first time since their appearance in the second measure. Thus they too form a plane which is, at least in detail, independent of the others, yet participates in shaping the overall pattern.

Before leaving *Intégrales*, I would like to mention an interesting development which, though perhaps inferrable from the overall structure, seems to run an almost contrary course. I am referring to the progress of the opening clarinet figure itself, which undergoes transformations quite different from those of traditional motivic treatment. Although it never recurs in exactly the same form, it is always similar enough to be easily identifiable, and it always turns around the same pitch. The motions on and around this pitch become consistently more elaborate, however, so that the figure, whose original statement consists of little more than one pitch, gradually gains in melodic definition. This process continues to a point approximately one-third through the section, the trumpet statements in the middle third (mm. 10-11 and 18-19) being the most elaborate; there is then a process of simplification in the final third, until just before the cadence at the end the figure has returned to a form very similar to that of the opening statement. This "circular" motion may seem to have

something in common with the retrograde motions favored by certain twelve-tone composers, but its formal meaning is quite different. To begin with, the "retrograde" is far from strict; and it applies only to the sequential arrangement of the component taken as a whole, and not to the internal structure of the component itself. Furthermore, it applies only to this figure, and not to the other planes. Finally, although it too helps to define the overall motion of the section, it is the only element which is circular, a point which adds yet another dimension to the formal meaning of the final cadence, which can thus be said to mark the completion of three distinct musical developments.

In this music there is no melody and accompaniment, or even a counterpoint of melodies, for the ear to follow. There is rather a continuous transformation of the total sound, ensuing from Varèse's "counterpoint of masses." This interaction of all the elements and, above all, the way it acts upon the pitch structure—bringing into motion something that in itself is "motionless"— is what lends the music its extraordinary vitality and accounts for the truly revolutionary character of Varèse's art. For if in tonal music the non-pitch elements may be said to serve an articulative function in a structure basically determined by its pitch relationships, in Varèse the pitch elements seem only to help clarify a structure that is essentially "non-pitched" in nature. We keep hearing the same pitches, yet they never sound the same. They are different, however, not because they themselves change or develop, but because the elements with which they are associated develop. To return to the spatial analogy, it is as if a set of "fixed" objects is constantly redefined and reinterpreted by the changing relationships of the objects to one another. These seem also to be transformed by changes in the surrounding "illumination," whereby the percussion plays a particularly important role, producing continuous variations in the light cast upon and reflected by the pitch events. It is, I think, no accident that one speaks so frequently of the "kaleidoscopic" effect of this music.

One should not close a discussion of the stylistic characteristics of Varèse's principal creative period without at least some mention of *Ionisation*. The fact that this work represented the first serious attempt in Western music to write a piece entirely for percussion instruments (and moreover, almost exclusively for non-pitched percussion: the few pitched instruments are confined to the final section) has set it apart as a special instance even among Varèse's own compositions. But it should be apparent that the techniques we have seen in *Intégrales* lend themselves so well to non-pitched as to pitched instruments. Pitch is only one of several impor-

**21**

tant components in the Varèsian "system," and as I have tried to indicate, there is much to suggest that it may not be so fundamental as others in determining the unique characteristics of his music. If I am right and these other values—such as timbre, register, and rhythm—can indeed be said to have taken over the main burden of the musical discourse, then there is no reason why a work for percussion alone should appear in any way "exceptional." In *Ionisation* it is not a question of Varèse's having "compensated" for the loss of pitch through the increased timbral variety offered by a greatly extended percussion ensemble: the compositional procedures to be found there correspond quite closely to those of his other works, at least in their general assumptions.

The question of music without pitch leads us finally to the area of electronic music, which unlike instrumental music. has no particular bias for fixed pitches. It is well-known that Varèse, who frequently complained of the "tyranny of the tempered scale," was interested in the possibilities of this new medium for his own music as early as the 1920s but was frustrated by the unavailability of adequate electronic instruments. As Varèse himself pointed out, the use of traditional instruments, even in the radically new combinations he favored during this period, seemed inconsistent with the altered syntax of his musical language. The contemporary state of electronics was, however, inadequate to allow for extensive application of the medium: and although Varèse did use two Ondes Martenot, an early electronic instrument, in *Ecuatorial* (composed in 1934). for the most part he had to make do with what was readily available—essentially, those instruments handed down from the past. This continued until about 1935, when Varèse stopped producing music. entering a period of silence which lasted almost twenty years. Certainly his dissatisfaction with existent instruments had a bearing on this; and there were apparently also problems of a personal nature. But a more inclusive explanation may simply be that the general cultural atmosphere of the period was not conducive to Varèse's musical philosophy: to write music consistent with the new conditions imposed upon the composer in the twentieth century. Amidst a general tendency to find ties with the past, Varèse was looking for access to the future. It was a sad phase in his life, and one in need of more complete biographical documentation. (One awaits impatiently the appearance of the second volume of his biography, *Varèse: A Looking Glass Diary*, written by his wife Louise. The first volume, published in 1972 by W. W. Norton is required reading for anyone interested in the composer, but covers only the years up until 1928.) We do know that he was not completely inactive: works were undertaken, but none was concluded.

It was only after the Second World War, when the general cultural picture began to appear somewhat more open, that Varèse ended his silence. One of the principal factors in his return was that more reliable electronic instruments were beginning to be built, and there was also greater general interest among composers, particularly those of the post-war generation, in exploring the possibilities of the medium. Significantly, the first work to appear—*Déserts*, completed in 1954—combined both instrumental and electronic elements, as if Varèse wished to demonstrate once and for all that there was no inherent contradiction between what he had previously done with old instruments and what could be done with the new. The next work, the *Poème Electronique* of 1958, was entirely electronic. But even here what one hears is basically a continuation of earlier concerns.

It is my own feeling that this composition, as well as the electronic portions of *Déserts*, does not rank with Varèse's best work. By this time the composer was almost seventy, and his most innovative years were behind him. It would be too much to expect that at this stage in his life he would be able to familiarize himself with the new techniques of electronic sound and produce music of the quality of the earlier masterpieces (although, by comparison with other electronic efforts from this early period, these works are immediately striking for their considerable interest and vitality).

As for the final works, several were underway in the 1960s. but all remained unfinished at the time of Varèse's death in 1965. Two of these were close enough to completion to be put into performable state by Chou Wen-Chung. Entitled *Nocturnal* and *Nuit*, they are both vocal compositions of unusual beauty and intensity. But they tell us nothing essentially new about their composer: as their titles seem to suggest, the main work had been accomplished.

# II

In a brief essay of Kafka's forerunners, Jorge Luis Borges remarks that "every writer *creates* his precursors" (his italics). Borges, who has just finished pointing out some common themes in works of such diverse writers as Zeno, Han Yu, Kierkegaard, Browning, Leon Bloy, and Lord Dunsany, notes that although all the writings in question have in common their resemblance to Kafka, their resemblance to each other is not nearly so apparent. In fact, before having read Kafka, he suggests, one could not have seen any close relationship among them at all. As he goes on to note: "His

[Kafka's] work modifies our conception of the past, as it will modify the future."

I think a similar situation exists in respect to Ives and Varèse: only after having heard the music of the past twenty years or so can we see clearly the strong connections that exist between them. Perhaps some of these have become apparent during the course of the present article, but I would like to summarize by making a few general observations about their similarities.

In writing about Varèse, I had occasion to mention the "spatial" aspect of his music. Of the many attributes of his style which lend it this quality, the most prominent is perhaps the essentially static pitch structure, which seems to suspend the music in time—and thus to locate it in space. In Ives too, we frequently encounter such passages. The song *Incantation*, for example, reveals virtually no pitch development throughout; and there are sections of longer works—such as the second theme of the first movement of the First Piano Sonata, or the opening of the last movement—which are similarly "immobile." In these instances the music depends upon other factors, such as its rhythmic structure or the sheer interest of its sound, to sustain it. This shift of focus, I suspect, led both composers to explore the possibilities of a "layered" approach to writing music. As we have seen in the works of both, several seemingly independent components are used simultaneously to create textures of uncommon density. The result is a music which seems to be made up of heterogeneous mixtures. It is "multidimensional" music—and, more importantly, each of the dimensions is accorded more-or-less equal weight in the total musical balance. Thus in Ives, as well as in Varèse, there are many passages where the texture cannot be broken down into a main part and a subordinate one: everything coexists on an equal footing.

In this regard, it is interesting to read Ives' comments on the inception of his *Universe Symphony*, an orchestral work of considerable scope which the composer worked on for several years but never completed:

"When we were in Keene Valley, on the plateau ...I started something that I'd had in mind for some time...trying out a parallel way of listening to music, suggested by looking at a view (1) with the eyes toward the sky or tops of the trees, taking in the earth or foreground subjectively—that is, not focussing the eye on it—(2) then looking at the earth and land, and seeing the sky and the top of the foreground subjectively. In other words, giving a musical piece in two parts, but played at the same time—the lower parts (the basses, cellos, tubas, trombones, bassoons, etc.) working out something representing the earth and listening to that primarily—and then the upper parts (strings, upper woodwinds, piano, bells, etc.) reflecting the skies and the Heavens—and that this piece be played twice, first when the listener focusses his ears on the lower or earth music, and the next time on the upper or Heaven music."

Ives' description is typically subjective and personal, yet the musical conception which lies behind it is very close to Varèse. Indeed, the following remarks made by Varèse could almost be taken as a free translation of those by Ives, converted into the (for Varèse more comfortable) language of physical science:

"In order to make myself better understood—for the eye is quicker and more disciplined that the ear—let us transfer this conception into the visual sphere and consider the changing projection of a geometrical figure onto a plane surface, with both geometrical figure and plane surface, moving in space, but each at its own changing and varying aspects of lateral movement and rotation. The form of the projection at any given instant is determined by the relative orientation of the figures and the surface at that instant. But by allowing both figure and surface to have their own movements, one is able to represent with that projection an apparently unpredictable image of a high degree of complexity; moreover, these qualities can be increased subsequently by permitting the form of the geometrical figure to vary as well as its speeds..."

There are further specific parallels that might be mentioned, such as the fact that both composers experimented with extensions of the twelve-tone tempered scale. There is even a reference made by Ives to a passage in *The Fourth of July*, in which he says that "the rhythms are used in a kind of chemical order"—reminding us of Varèse's quotation of Paracelsus, the Swiss chemist and alchemist, as an epigraph to *Arcana*. But ultimately their most basic correspondence lies in the nature of their radical responses to the dilemma brought

*(continued on page 28 )*

275

**23**

(**Morgan on Varèse.** *Continued from page 23*)

on by the collapse of tonality. Rather than trying to repair the break, they both accepted the conditions of working within a fundamentally different framework of musical orientation. Their individual responses were, of course, completely different. Ives developed new contexts for material which he borrowed from the past, whether through actual quotation or through the invention of similar kinds of material. Varèse chose to invent a new kind of material altogether, creating formal contexts especially designed for its development. Ives' approach can be said to be "subjective"—an attempt to play with the listener's expectations through the manipulation of musical material that is loaded with connotations; Varèse's approach, conversely, is "objective"—an attempt to build structures out of "abstract" material that is devoid of specific musical implications. But both represent fundamentally new ways of looking at the problem of establishing continuity and coherence in the context of the twentieth-century musical situation. This sets them apart from the other major composers of the period, and indicates their analogous position—each a sort of mirror image of the other in post-tonal music.

Finally, a word about the quality of Ives' and Varèse's work. Even if I am right about their central historical position in the first half of the century, the question of the music's intrinsic value remains open. Is it really on the same level as that of, say, Schoenberg and Stravinsky? Any answer must be of course partly subjective. Granting this, it nevertheless appears to me that the question must be approached quite differently in the case of the two composers. With Ives we are dealing, in a sense, with an almost "limitless" composer—one willing to take on virtually any compositional problem. We have seen this both in the variety of his compositions and in what I have called the "inclusive" nature of individual works. Obviously with such a composer there will be some degree of unevenness in the quality of his work, and I do not deny that there are many minor pieces by Ives which are of little musical interest. With Varèse, on the other hand, we are dealing with a "limited" composer—one who wrote very few works and whose compositions were all conceived from an essentially unified point of view. In this sense Varèse is rather like Webern: he is a very "even" composer, but also a somewhat restricted one. Furthermore, the music of both Ives and Varèse seems to lack that quality of almost "Beethovenian" struggle which is so marked, for example, in Schoenberg's music. As I have noted elsewhere, one of the most interesting and moving aspects of the latter's twelve-tone works is the intense effort one hears in the attempt to reconcile a new pitch structure with the basic assumptions of a traditional rhythmic and formal approach. This particular kind of tension, so characteristic of our century, is largely absent from the music of both Ives and Varèse.

But I am purposely going to leave the question unanswered. Music history is not, after all, a popularity contest or a system of musical ratings. What really matters is that Ives and Varèse initiated an important line in twentieth-century musical developments. and one which, at the present time at least, seems to be in the ascendancy. That alone would be sufficient reason to grant them our serious consideration and respect. But I hope I have also offered evidence that their music is able to stand on the strength of inherent quality and interest.

# The Secret Programme of the Lyric Suite—1

## George Perle

Shortly after the sudden death, on 27 November 1968, of the International Alban Berg Society's founding vice-president, Hans Ferdinand Redlich, I visited his widow in Manchester to offer my condolences and to give her what assistance I could in ordering and classifying that portion of his library and papers concerned with his Berg studies. Because Mrs Redlich did not wish her husband's research materials on Berg to remain unused, she donated his notes and documents to the society in accordance with his hope that the society 'would in time establish and maintain a collection of basic source materials for research on the life and work of Alban Berg' (letter from Erika Redlich to George Perle, 3 February 1969).

Among the materials donated by Mrs Redlich were certain letters relating to her husband's work on his book, *Alban Berg: Versuch einer Würdigung* ('Attempt at an Evaluation', 1957). Familiarity with this correspondence turned out to be essential to a 'Versuch einer Würdigung' of Redlich's contributions as a Berg scholar, as I wrote in an obituary of him: 'The difficulties of undertaking such a task so soon after the years of Nazism, war, and reaction that had rung the curtain down on Berg's music immediately after the composer's death can only be appreciated by one who has had an opportunity to study Dr Redlich's relevant notes and correspondence'.

In an appendix to his book Redlich provided a chronological index to Berg's compositions, arrangements and writings. Each work was listed with its supposed date of composition, the supposed location of the manuscript, a list of editions and dates of publication, and information about the supposed first performance. The cautionary adjective is used advisedly, and indeed Redlich himself was far from regarding his catalogue as definitive. It was only a preliminary attempt, and there was very little to build on—even less than Redlich himself suspected at the time—in the collating of basic data from antecedent studies. But a beginning had to be made, and 20 years after the death of his subject was none too soon. Today, a further 20 years after the publication of his book, Redlich's descriptive catalogue of the works of Alban Berg has still not been supplanted; errors that he himself had discovered very soon after the book's appearance continue to be repeated and reprinted.

Obviously, the primary references in such a catalogue will be to the original manuscripts themselves. Here one is repeatedly dismayed and frustrated by the word *verschollen*, 'missing'. The complete catalogue, inclusive of juvenilia and student works, comprises only 20 entries. For six of these,

*A shorter version of this article appeared earlier this year in the newsletter of the International Alban Berg Society.*

the manuscript is 'missing'. And three of these 'missing' manuscripts, the Piano Sonata op.1, the Four Songs op.2 and the Quartet op.3, belong to the composer's recognized output. The number of missing manuscripts is excessively large, considering that Berg would not have got beyond op.12 had he continued to use opus numbers after *Wozzeck* (op.7).

It is reasonable to suppose that a delay of a few years in the publication of his book might have allowed Redlich to produce a catalogue with fewer 'missing' manuscripts, but his correspondence shows that such a delay would in fact have had the opposite result. An additional manuscript would have been transferred to the category of *verschollen*, and that of no less a work than the *Lyric Suite*. In Redlich's catalogue the autograph of the *Lyric Suite* is stated to be in the possession of the heirs of Alexander von Zemlinsky. There is no indication of how they may have acquired it, but it is logical to suppose that Berg left or gave the manuscript to Zemlinsky, since the work is dedicated to him and one of its most memorable themes is a quotation from Zemlinsky's own *Lyric Symphony*. Redlich's statement was based on information provided by Helene Berg and relayed to him by Universal Edition on 24 November 1953.

In autumn 1960 Helmuth Hoever of the Strauss String Quartet wrote to Redlich from Germany regarding certain points of disagreement with Redlich's analysis of the *Lyric Suite*. The ensuing correspondence led to a discussion of apparent errors in the published version and the desirability of obtaining a photocopy of the manuscript for comparison. On 28 August 1961 Hoever wrote to Redlich that his efforts to learn the address of the Zemlinsky heirs had been unsuccessful. The next month Redlich was in New York for the 8th Congress of the International Musicological Society. On his return he informed Universal Edition that while he was in the USA he had learnt that the Zemlinsky heirs had never been in possession of the manuscript; he suggested that Mrs Berg be asked to ascertain whether in fact it might not be in her own possession. Further correspondence between Redlich and Hoever and between Redlich and Universal Edition describes Redlich's search for the manuscript on the basis of his telephone conversations with Mrs Zemlinsky and with a sister of Franz Werfel, referred to in the letters as 'Frau Hanna Werfel-Robettin'. There are contradictions and misunderstandings, and a number of letters referred to in the correspondence are missing.

On the basis of information recently acquired I can eliminate the discrepancies in Redlich's letters to Hoever and Universal Edition. The manuscript of the *Lyric Suite* was never in the possession of Zemlinsky or his heirs. Alban Berg himself gave it to Frau Hanna Fuchs-Robettin, née Werfel. After

Berg's death, Alma Mahler Werfel prevailed upon her sister-in-law to cede the manuscript to Helene Berg, and dispatched her close friend, the Catholic priest Johannes Hollinsteiner, to act as intermediary in the transfer of the manuscript.

A letter from Universal Edition to Redlich, dated 31 January 1962, reports receipt of a letter from Mrs Zemlinsky stating that neither she nor her husband had ever owned the manuscript of the *Lyric Suite*. Both the publisher and Mrs Berg were alarmed to learn that the manuscript was missing, and solicited Redlich's further assistance in tracing its whereabouts. The last letter relative to this matter, dated 13 November 1962, reports no progress in locating the manuscript.

I had first written to Dr Redlich in 1959, in connection with my work on *Lulu*, but correspondence on a regular basis began only after my trip to Vienna in August 1963 to examine the third-act materials. We met for the first time at the Edinburgh Festival in summer 1966 and saw much of each other during the following ten months, when I was living in London. We discussed many problems of Berg research in addition to our main concern, the continuing suppression of the third act of *Lulu*. I do not recall that Dr Redlich ever referred to the *Lyric Suite*, as he surely would have done had the manuscript still been missing. Thus when the above-mentioned correspondence came to my attention after Redlich's death, I assumed that the search for the manuscript had later been successful, and that it had been safely deposited in Vienna; this assumption was confirmed in *Schoenberg, Berg, Webern: the String Quartets: a Documentary Study*, edited by Ursula von Rauchhaupt and published in 1971 in connection with the LaSalle Quartet's recordings.

On 9 August 1976 Douglass M. Green informed me of his discovery that the complete text of Stefan George's translation of Baudelaire's *De profundis clamavi*, in a cryptic shorthand form, was 'written into the sketch of the finale of the *Lyric Suite*'. For anyone who knows Berg's masterpiece, Dr Green's discovery is astounding in its immediate implications for the meaning of the work as a whole. I find the following remarks on serial and other musical relations among the different movements in an essay (unpublished) that I wrote about six years ago:

Though only one movement, the fourth, is literally programmatic, these musical cross-references are not—no more than they are in *Wozzeck*—simply a means of assuring the musical unity of the whole. They are *Leitmotive* and *Leitsektionen*, like the musical cross-references in *Wozzeck* and later in *Lulu*. The six movements are six acts in what Adorno called a 'latent opera', a wholly subjective psychological drama.

We have suddenly been given a text for the last act of this 'latent opera'. And a whole new level of meaning now hangs on the *Tristan* quotation when the latter, with all its attendant associations, is seen as a setting of the line from George's translation of the Baudelaire poem: 'Nicht einmal Bach und Baum noch Feld noch Herde'. By implication there has always been a verbal reference at the two statements of the Zemlinsky theme in the Adagio, which in Zemlinsky's song cycle is a setting for the words 'Du bist mein Eigen, mein Eigen'. But if the sixth movement as well as the fourth has an explicit programme, what about the other movements and the work as a whole? Themes and even whole passages of the Adagio are initially presented in the two preceding movements, the Andante amoroso and the Allegro misterioso, without substantive change. And the Adagio is similarly connected with the movement that follows. I quote from my essay:

> One of the most striking instances of the leit-motivic character of the musical cross-references occurs at bars 356–70 of the following movement, a hallucinatory recollection of the 12-note melody that prefaces a second statement of the quotation from Zemlinsky in the Adagio (bars 45ff).

Ex. 1

So langsam rollt sich ab der Zeit - en Spin - del.

In the finale, the last line of the text (ex.1) is preceded by an interlude in which bars 5–6 and 38–9 of the first movement are quoted. Thus every movement is involved, through extensive musical quotations, in the two movements that contain explicit verbal references.

Are there such references in the other movements as well? Berg had kept the text of the finale, and the very fact that there was in fact a text, a secret. I quote from Professor Green's letter of August 9:

> The following people have told me they knew nothing of any poem in connection with the finale, much less a Baudelaire poem: Helene Berg, Willi Reich, Fritz Heinrich Klein, Rudolf Kolisch, Felix Galimir, Adrienne Galimir Krasner (the last three, as you know, rehearsed the *Lyric Suite* with Berg). Although Berg wrote out nine pages about the *Lyric Suite* for Kolisch, he says nothing about the poem, though he does refer to the finale as 'liedförmig' [having a song form], then crosses this out and substitutes 'durchwegs Cantabile' [cantabile throughout].

The composer would have been equally secretive about explicit programmatic and textural elements in the other movements. But the fact that he might have been, and probably was, keeping secret something important about the *Lyric Suite* has long been sensed by everyone really familiar with the score. Like anyone who commits a perfect crime, Berg was proud of his accomplishment and wanted us to know about it. The newly discovered text for the finale is the first clue we have had to the actual nature of the 'crime', the secret programme of the *Lyric Suite*. The text must be part of this programme, but what the programme is we still do not know. The previously known numerological clues in the score had merely pointed to the possible presence of a secret programme. I quote my essay again:

> In the *Lyric Suite* every one of the numerous changes of tempo is governed by . . . one or the other of two sets of proportional relations, each metronome mark being a multiple of either 23 or 50. It is the interrelating of tempos throughout a composition that is of musical significance—

not the private number symbolism that motivated the composer's selection of these two integers rather than others and that led him to choose multiples of the same integers for the number of bars in each movement.[1]

In the context of the present discussion it is precisely that private number symbolism that interests us. Berg's obsession with the number 23 as having some special and personal significance in his life is well known. The date of completion that he gives for a number of works is the 23rd of the month, but a composer has certain options in selecting the date that he chooses to give as marking the completion of a composition, since this may refer to the short score, a rough or fair copy of the full score, or various revisions of one or another 'completed' version. Only in the *Lyric Suite* does Berg's supposedly fateful number play a consistent role in the work itself. It would seem that the other consistent numerical elements in the work must also have had a symbolic meaning for him. It can hardly have been through chance or any inherent musical necessity that the number of bars in each section of the Presto delirando came to be a multiple of 10 (50, 70, 90, 110, 120, 20) and the number of bars in the entire movement (460) a multiple of both 23 and 10. We know the significance of 23 for Berg; but what is the meaning of 10? The Baudelaire poem only heightens the mystery of the *Lyric Suite*. It establishes that there is, indeed, a mystery. If in all these years we have not known the text of the finale, nor even that there was a text, what may we still not know about the remaining movements, and about the work as a whole?

Shortly after receiving Professor Green's news I was introduced to Alexander Zemlinsky's widow by my good friend and colleague, Jacques-Louis Monod. Through Mrs Zemlinsky I was finally able to clarify the confused and contradictory history of the manuscript in the Redlich correspondence. I also learnt that there might exist a score of the *Lyric Suite* in which the composer himself had inserted programmatic annotations.

I had by this time identified Hanna Fuchs-Robettin as the 'Mopinka' of Berg's *Letters to his Wife*. The original German edition of those letters, published four years before the Redlich correspondence came into my hands, contains no editorial notes, no footnotes, no commentary, no index. The reader must deduce for himself that 'Almschi' is Alma Mahler and that 'Gucki' is her daughter Anna, who is not to be confused with Berg's sister-in-law Anna, who is called 'Antschi'. It had not occurred to me to look there for references to the 'Hanna Werfel-Robettin' mentioned in Redlich's letters. Moreover, in the inconsistent accounts Redlich gave of Mrs Fuchs-Robettin's ownership at one time of the autograph of the *Lyric Suite*, there was no suggestion of a special relationship between her and the composer. (So far was I from any understanding of the implications of that relationship that I had overlooked Redlich's passing refer-

[1] In the third movement, the tempo at the beginning and conclusion of the Trio estatico can only be measured in terms of minims, not crochets. The composer nevertheless preferred to represent the tempo metronomically as crochet = 150, and to show the half-bar at MM 75 in parentheses as an equivalent.

ence, in a letter to Hoever, to a detail that Mrs Fuchs-Robettin had mentioned in her conversation on the telephone with him—that she possessed a 'printed pocket score with (allegedly very significant) notations in Berg's own handwriting'. He expected that she would send him a photocopy, but when it was not forthcoming he did not pursue the matter. Relative to the object of his immediate research, the location of the manuscript itself, the pocket score did not seem important, and he did not mention it again.) By the time I was led to a second perusal of the correspondence I had read the footnoted and indexed English translations by Bernard Grun (1971) of Berg's *Letters to his Wife* and could recall the following lines from memory:

It goes against the grain, really, to have to 'reassure' you about me and Mopinka. Perhaps I'll just say that faithfulness is one of my main qualities (I'm sure I must have been a dog in a previous incarnation, and perhaps shall be in a later one, but anyhow, to start from the beginning, may I die of distemper if I ever sin against faithfulness!). Faithfulness towards you, and also towards myself, music, Schoenberg (and *he* makes this really hard for one).

Berg was writing this letter while he was on the way to Berlin for rehearsals of the first *Wozzeck* production, and was about to interrupt his journey with an overnight stay in Prague with the Fuchs family. He had spent a few days as their house guest six months earlier, in May 1925, when he had gone to Prague to attend the third ISCM festival, where Zemlinsky had conducted the Three Excerpts from *Wozzeck*. Berg's introduction to the Fuchs family would undoubtedly have come through Alma Mahler, Mrs Fuchs-Robettin's sister-in-law and Helene Berg's closest friend. A footnote in the English edition of the letters identifies Herbert Fuchs-Robettin as a 'Prague industrialist and

musical enthusiast, married to Franz Werfel's sister (Mopinka)'. Berg was quite overwhelmed with 'the matter-of-course luxury of this life'. He was charmed by the children:

At eight a knock on the door, and in burst the two children, who won't be satisfied unless they can at last see the 'famous' composer. A seven-year-old boy [and] a girl of 3½. Very sweet, I found them most refreshing.

Writing from his room during his second stay with the Fuchs family, 11 November 1925, he again spoke of the 'friendliness and warm-heartedness' of the family, the magnificent food, 'and a superb wine! Herbert and I drank a whole bottle'. He explained why he was 'making so much of this. Not because it's so terrific here (my thoughts are already in Berlin), but to stop you worrying about Mopinka's charms!'.

Mrs Zemlinsky told me that she had never seen the annotated score of the *Lyric Suite*, but had been told of its existence by the woman for whom Berg had prepared this score, Mrs Fuchs-Robettin. She was certain that on Mrs Fuchs-Robettin's death in 1964 it would have passed into the hands of her daughter, Dorothea. When, three seemingly endless weeks later, I managed to locate her, Dorothea Robetin (as she spells the name) informed me that she did in fact own a miniature score of the *Lyric Suite* containing copious annotations by the composer. She knew that it was an important and valuable document, but had never shown it to anyone, since no-one had ever asked to see it. She seemed very pleased to receive my inquiry and was happy to show me the score and to elucidate certain references among the composer's annotations that would otherwise have been incomprehensible.

# The Secret Programme of the Lyric Suite—2

## George Perle

The annotated miniature score of the *Lyric Suite* comprises, inclusive of the frontispiece, title-page, preface and dedication, 90 pages. Of these, only eight are without handwritten annotations by Berg, and these eight pages are comprehended within the context of the programme by explicit references (the composer's underlinings in the printed prefatory notes by Erwin Stein), by obvious musical connections with annotated pages, or even through signs in adjacent pages. This copy of the first edition, printed in 1927, has been well cared for and still looks fresh and new. The annotations have been inserted with extraordinary attention to graphic details. The handwriting is often extremely small, but always clear and legible, in marked contrast to Berg's everyday hand. Three different coloured inks are used, each having a different function in the programmatic analysis: chiefly red, occasionally blue and, in the second movement only, green as well. The annotations are calligraphic in their elegance and neatness. Indeed, an understanding of the programme often depends on purely graphic aspects of the handwritten insertions. (In the following description of the score, these insertions are understood to be in red unless otherwise specified.)

Beneath his photograph and covering his printed name Berg has written 'Alban'. At the head of the title-page there is a dedication, 'Für meine Hanna'. The fifth and sixth sentences of Stein's preface ('Die Entwicklung . . . Verzweiflung') are marked by a marginal bracket. Further down the page, in the sentence, 'Die anderen bewegten Sätze aber, der dritte und fünfte, haben Scherzocharakter und Scherzoform', the words 'Scherzocharakter und' are blacked out in pencil and illegible. Other portions of the preface that are emphasized through marginal brackets or underlining refer to the increasing contrasts in the character and tempos of successive movements and to the interrelation of different movements through thematic and other cross-references. The concluding sentence of Stein's preface points out that in the last movement the 'seemingly restrictive system of 12-note composition has allowed the composer the freedom to quote the opening bars of *Tristan*'. Berg underlines 'Die Freiheit gelassen hat' and draws an arrow from this phrase to the following insertion in the blank space that follows the preface:

Sie hat mir, meine Hanna, auch noch andere Freiheiten gelassen! Z. Bsp. die, in dieser Musik immer wieder unsere Buchstaben, H, F und A, B hineinzugeheimnissen; jeden Satz und Satzteil in Beziehung zu unseren Zahlen 10 und 23 zu bringen.

Ich habe dies und vieles andere Beziehungsvolle für Dich (für die allein - - - trotz umstehender offizieller Widmung - - - ja jede Note dieses Werks geschrieben ist) in diese Partitur hineingeschrieben.

Möge sie so ein kleines Denkmal sein einer grossen Liebe.[2]

On the page facing the first page of music the composer has written:

Dieser erste Satz, dessen fast belanglose Stimmung die folgende Tragödie nicht ahnen lässt, streift immerwährend die Tonarten *H* und *F dur*. Auch das Hauptthema (die dem ganzen Quartett zugrundeliegende 12-Tonreihe) wird von deinen Buchstaben F-H umschlossen.[3]

The initial statement of the note-row is the first violin, bars 2–4, and its recapitulation in the viola and cello, bars 42–4, are marked 'Hauptthema' and the boundary pitches of the row are labelled and connected by a broken line:

$$\text{F}--------------\text{H}$$

Throughout the movement Berg indicates what he interprets as suggestions of the 'Tonarten H und F'. Everything is inserted in red ink except at the first and last chords of the movement. Below the bass note of the first chord and above the soprano note of the last the composer has indicated their respective pitches, 'F' and 'H', in blue, with a diagonal arrow directed upwards to the right following 'F' and, again, immediately preceding 'H'. We are thus asked to imagine that the score is laid out in a single system encompassed by 'F' and 'H' (ex.2).

**Ex. 2**

The number of the last bar of the movement, **69**, is circled, and above it Berg has written '3 x 23 Takte'.

The most elaborately annotated movement is the second. It is preceded by the following 'dedication':

Dir und Deinen Kindern ist dieses 'Rondo' gewidmet: eine musikalische Form, in der die

[2] 'It has also, my Hanna, allowed me other freedoms! For example, that of secretly inserting our initials, H.F. and A.B., into this music, and of relating every movement and every section of every movement to our numbers, 10 and 23. I have written these, and much that has other meanings, into this score for you (for whom, and only for whom - - - in spite of the official dedication on the following page - - - every note of this work was written). May it be a small monument to a great love.'
[3] 'This first movement, whose almost inconsequential mood gives no hint of the tragedy to follow, continually touches upon the keys of H [i.e. B] and F major. The principal theme (the basic 12-note row of the whole quartet) is likewise enclosed by your initials, F-H.'

Themen, (namentlich Deines) . . . den lieblichen Kreis schliessend . . . immer wiederkehren.[4]

Each page is framed by a line in red, blue or green, with feathered end and arrowhead to show its direction and continuation. The red lines, interrupted for the insertion of an elaborately drawn 'Du' in the same colour, embrace the statements of the principal subject. At bars 16ff blue replaces red, for the theme of Hanna's seven-year-old son 'Munzo'. The character of the new theme is indicated in an insertion after the tempo marking: 'nicht ohne Absicht: mit einem leisen czechischen Einschlag' ('not unintentionally, with a gentle Czech touch')—Miss Robetin explained that her brother was going to a Czech elementary school at the time, and therefore spoke Czech more fluently than German. At bars 35ff the solid line is broken. The bridge to the return of the principal theme is simultaneously shown in the same way, beginning with the upbeat to bar 36 in the second violin and becoming a solid line at bar 41: 'zu Dir zurückkehrend – – – – – und – – – wieder – – – ganz Du' ('returning to you – – – – and – – – again – – – wholly you'). At bars 56ff the red line that marks the principal subject is supplanted by a green line for the theme of 'Dodo', the child's nickname of Dorothea herself, spelt out in the repeated-C figure, 'do do', in the viola. At bars 73–9 the same figure returns with the lower octave added. The composer's handwritten insertions are completed by the printed instructions in the score: 'Do do— drohend, aber es ist nicht ernst zu nehmen – – – – – – – poco f – – – dimin. – – – – – – – In Gegenteil: dolciss. – – – – – p' ('threatening, but it is not to be taken seriously – – – – on the contrary: dolciss.').

Bars 81–142 are simultaneously recapitulation and development. The first violin's *teneramente* at bar 81 is underlined in red. The red line that embraces the principal subject from the first violin at bar 81 to the cello at bar 94 is marked 'wieder Du' ('again, you') at its inception. A blue line at bars 94–104 marks the return of 'Munzo'. At bars 101–5 we have the following annotation: 'Munzo – – – – – – Dazu gesellt sich gleichsam spielend Dodo' ('Munzo – – – – joining him in play, Dodo'). Munzo's blue is replaced by Dodo's green only at her name. The repeated-C figures in the viola in bars 106 and 108 are labelled 'do do'. In the cello at bars 110ff we have 'wieder Munzo', in the two violins at 113ff 'wieder Dodo', and in the viola entry at bar 114 terminating on the downbeat of bar 118: 'dazu Dein Thema – – –' ('thereto, your theme'). In bars 118–30 the development of the two subordinate subjects is marked by repeated insertions of 'Munzo' and 'Dodo', in their respective colours, blue and green. Two vertical parallel lines in blue and green in the right margin of page 23 terminate in arrow-heads. Between them, reading vertically upwards the composer has inserted: 'Aus dem Spiel wird Ernst – – –' ('The game gets serious – – –'). When the viola's repeated-C figure returns at the climax of the development section, bars 129–32, Berg's insert above that figure is no longer merely an identification of the repeated syllable-name of the

pitch. Where we formerly had 'do do', we now have 'Do-do!'. And at bar 131, with the entrance of the first violin, 'Da trittst Du dazwischen' ('Now you step between'). Bars 131–43, the concluding bars of the recapitulation-development, are encompassed by marginal lines in red, blue and green. The themes of Munzo and Dodo retire at bar 143. The coda, bars 143–50, is Hanna's. 'Du' above the first violin part at bar 143 identifies her theme, and a red line curves around the top of the final page of the movement and, growing ever thicker, down the right margin, to terminate with a horizontal stroke at a level with the first line of the cello staff. Beneath that staff there is a last reference, in green of course, to the younger child, with her name marking the two pizzicato notes on the open C-string: 'wie aus der Ferne: "Do-do" ' ('as from a distance: "Do-do" '). At the last bar of the first movement, Berg had called attention to the presence of his number, 23, as a factor of 69. There are 150 bars in the second movement, and the composer calls attention to the fact that this is a multiple, '15 × 10 Takte', of Hanna's number.

The third movement is prefaced only by a date, '20.5.25', doubly underlined in red. The 'misterioso' in the tempo marking is incorporated into an inscription: 'Allegro misterioso, denn noch war alles geheimnis – – – uns selbst geheimnis – – – –' ('Allegro misterioso, for everything was still a mystery – – – a mystery to us – – –'). The four notes B, F, A and B♭ whose pitch names in German coincide with the initials of Hanna Fuchs and Alban Berg, form a cell that is embedded in the note-row of the third movement. The basic set-forms that are employed in the movement each unfold another permutation of the same cell. The composer had called attention to an anticipation of this cell at two points in the preceding movement (ex.3). Each statement of the

Ex. 3

cell in the third movement is marked by the pitch names of its four notes or by an 'etc' for recurrent statements of the same permutation of the cell. The *poco meno p* passage in the second violin and viola is annotated 'wie ein geflüster' ('like a whisper') at bars 34f and 'wieder wie geflüstert' ('again, as though whispered') at bars 37f. The expository statement of the *misterioso*, comprising '3 × 23 Takte', is followed by the Trio estatico, 'plötzlich ausbrechend' ('suddenly bursting out'), on the upbeat to bar 70. Here, and at bar 84, the basic cell occurs independently of the note-row (ex.4).

Ex. 4

[4]'To you and your children, I have dedicated this "Rondo" – – – a musical form in which the themes (specifically, your theme) enclosing the charming circle, continually recur.'

282

The programmatic implication of the fact that the mutes are not removed for the Trio, even though the dynamic level called for is *ff*, is suggested in an annotation: 'Trio estatico (sempre f possibile: aber verhalten, gleichsam noch mit Dämpfer)' ('but repressed, still with mutes'). Attention is called to the quotation at bars 77–8: 'Vgl. Dein Thema im Takt 13–14 des II. Satzes! Aber welche Form hat es indessen angenommen' ('Compare your theme at bar 13–14 of the second movement! But what shape it has meanwhile assumed'). The first violin part in bar 89 happens to unfold the same series of pitches, except for the lack of the concluding G, as Marie's Cradle Song in *Wozzeck*, Act I scene iii, at its concluding words, 'Lauter kühle Wein muss es sein'. These words are inserted in parentheses above the staff. They are probably a reference, veiled to be sure, and the only one in the work, to Herbert Fuchs-Robettin. Dorothea Robetin told me that her father had one of the most famous wine cellars in Prague, and we have already seen how impressed Berg was with the wine served by his host. With the conclusion of the Trio we arrive at bar 92, '4 x 23', of the movement. The recapitulation of the *misterioso* is marked 'plötzlich wieder wie ein geflüster – – –'. The programmatic meaning of the fact that the *misterioso* returns in the retrograde is implied in the annotation at the beginning of the recapitulation, 'Vergessen Sie es – – –!' ('Forget it – – – !'). The complete movement comprises 138 bars, '6 x 23 Takte'.

The fourth movement is prefaced: 'Tags darauf' ('the next day'). Except for the underlining of 'appassionato' at the head of the movement, there are no more insertions until bar 24. However, Berg had already implicitly referred to this section of the Adagio by underlining, in Stein's preface (its wording was adjusted in subsequent editions), the phrase 'das Trio des 3. ist gleichzeitig Exposition des 4' ('the Trio of the 3rd is simultaneously exposition of the 4th'). In fact almost the whole of the Trio estatico of the preceding movement is incorporated at bars 12–13, 22–3 and 34–9 of the Adagio. Apart from these direct quotations, the Adagio derives its first theme from the Trio estatico, bars 74–5.

At bars 24ff the viola and first violin, respectively representing 'ich und Du', are in quasi-canonic imitation. The quotation that begins on the fourth quaver beat of bar 30 in the first violin is identified: 'Immer Du (vgl. Dein Thema aus. d. 2. Satz)'. The citation from Zemlinsky's *Lyric Symphony* is underlaid with its original text, and the speaker in the present instance is identified: 'Ich: "Du bist mein eigen, mein eigen!" '. The basic cell at bar 44 is identified by its pitch names, H, F, A and B. Both words and music of the Zemlinsky phrase are quoted again at bars 46ff in the second violin: 'Nun sagt es auch Du: "Du bist mein eigen, mein eigen – – –" '. The inscriptions at bars 51–2 incorporate the printed dynamic markings: 'u. noch einmal cresc. sempre cresc. – – – – – bis – – – –', and lead into the reiterated statements of the basic cell, its pitches always identified by the letter names, at the climax of the passage. The last verbal annotation begins at bars 57–8: 'pesante e riten. und verebbend – – – – – ins' ('fading – – – into'), and is completed above the first violin part at bars 59ff: ' – – ganz Vergeistigte, Seelenvolle, überirdische – – – – – ' ( – – – the wholly ethereal, spiritual, transcendental – – – '). H, F, A, and B are marked in bar 59, and B, A, H and F in the two violins at the last three quaver beats of bar 62 up to the downbeat of bar 63. The number of bars in the movement is again a multiple of Berg's personal number: '3 x 23 Takte'.

A continuous text is inserted into the fifth movement, incorporating the printed headings in the score. I have added bar numbers (in parentheses) to show correspondences between verbal text and score.

Dieses Presto delirando kann nur verstehen, wer eine Ahnung hat von den Schrecken und Qualen, die nun folgten. – – Von den Schrecken der Tage (15) mit ihren jagenden Pulsen, %(19) (51)% von dem qualvollen Tenebroso der Nächte, mit ihrem kaum schlaf zu nennenden Dahin Dämmern – – – – (70) (121) Und wieder Tag mit seinem wahnsinnig (124) gehetztem Herzschlag (127) (201) Als möchte sich das Herz beruhigen – – – – – (210) (211) di nuovo tenebroso mit ihren, die qualvolle Unruhe kaum verhaltenen schweren Athem zügen (230) – – – (231) (262) als ob sich für Augenblicke der süsse Trost eines wirklichen (274) – – – – alles vergessenden Schlummers über Einem senkte (283) – – – – – – – – – – – – (306) Aber schon meldet sich (311) das Herz (312) [crescendo sign] (320) und wieder (321) Tag und (324) – – – – – (330) so – – fort – – – – – – – – – (369) ohne (370) Stillstand (371) – – – – – – – – – – – – – – – – – – – (409) dieses (410) Delirium (411) – – – – – – (445) ohne (446) Ende (447) – – – – – – – – (460)[5]

The text given above is incomplete in the sense that its physical layout on the page is itself part of that text. The very way in which the first 23 words, in red ink and in a small neat hand, run from the printed heading of the movement, straggle gently upwards above the page number, around it, and down the outside edge of the page to the lower right margin, where the final stroke of 'Tage' is elongated into a line running along the lower edge of the page to the left and around the cello staff, where the words 'mit ihren jagenden Pulsen' slope diagonally upward to the right to reflect the successive entrances of the 'Herzschlag' motif in each of the four instruments . . . these graphic components add another dimension that could be represented fully only in a facsimile edition of the annotated score. I have noted the crescendo sign (a hairpin in the original) that connects bars 312 to bar 320, but not the brackets that mark the 'Herzschlag' motif at bars 133, 142, 145, 147, 183, 189, 201 etc, nor the redrawing that dramatizes the diagonally placed wedge crescendo sign at bars 329–36, nor the carefully ruled arrow that continues the annotation which begins above bar 356, 'Vgl. IV. Satz Takt

---

5 'This Presto delirando can be understood only by one who has a foreboding of the horrors and pains which now follow. – – – Of the horrors of the days with their racing pulses, % % of the painful Tenebroso of the nights, with their darkening drift into what can hardly be called sleep – – – – – And again day with its insanely rapid heartbeat As though the heart would rest itself – – – – – di nuovo tenebroso with its heavy breaths which barely conceal the painful unrest – – – as though for moments the sweet comfort of a true, all-forgetful slumber sank over one – – – – But already the heart makes itself felt *crescendo* and again day and – – – – – so – – forth – – – – without ceasing – – – – this delirium – – – –without end.'

45/46', and carries it through bar 370, nor much else besides. I called attention earlier to the fact that each section of the movement adds another multiple of 10 to the number of bars that have passed. This too is shown in the inserts: 5 x 10, 12 x 10, 21 x 10, 32 x 10, and finally 2 x 23 x 10.

The last movement is prefaced by the title of the text, 'De profundis clamavi', and the name of its author and of the translator. The boundary pitches of the initial statement of the note-row in the cello and its inversion at the second violin's entry are marked, 'F' and 'H'. Attention is called to the footnote in which the cellist is instructed to lower the tuning of his C-string to B natural, by the box that is carefully drawn around H, Hanna's initial. At bars 26–7, from the A and F at the fourth and fifth quaver beats of the cello to the B and H of the viola and second violin at the beginning of bar 27, the *Tristan* motif is encircled in blue and identified beneath the staff in the same colour: 'Anfang – – – u.– – – Ende des Tristanmotifs'.

The setting of the text is shown in ex.5. It is impossible to mistake Berg's intention in the layout of the text. The stem, flag and beam of each note of the 'vocal' part are carefully redrawn in red ink. Except at bar 31, each note of the vocal part dupli-

cates one or another string part. There are no indications of octave transpositions to accommodate a realistic vocal range, except at the doubling of the cello's E♭ and E in bar 31. As Professor Green has pointed out, such octave transpositions are in fact indicated in the sketch of the finale.[6] My own belief is that the composer would not have been opposed to a vocal performance of the finale, but only under conditions that he could not possibly have allowed, nor (perhaps) even imagined—only as part of the disclosure of the secret programme of the whole work.

Two additional annotations in the finale remain to be pointed out: the circled final bar number and the insert above it, '2 x 23 Takte', and the words, in blue, that follow the final notes, *morendo*, of the movement: 'ersterbend in Liebe, Sehnsucht und Trauer – – –' ('dying away in love, yearning, and grief – – –'). But the absence of an expected annotation can speak as eloquently and coherently as its presence. I quote once more from my essay on the *Lyric Suite*: 'In the last seven bars there are ten overlapping set statements, with no set-form repeated, but none of these incorporates the basic cell at its primary pitch-level' – – – the pitch-level that

[6]International Alban Berg Society *Newsletter*, no. 5

284

Ex. 5

To you, you sole dear one, my cry rises
Out of the deepest abyss in which my heart has fallen.
There the landscape is dead, the air like lead
And in the dark, curse and terror well up.

Six moons without warmth stands the sun.
During [the other] six darkness lies over the earth.
Even the polar land is not so barren—
Not even brook and tree, nor field nor flock.

But no terror born of brain approaches
The cold horror of this icy star
And of this night, a gigantic Chaos!

I envy the lot of the most common animal
Which can plunge into the dizziness of a senseless sleep . . .
So slowly does the spindle of time unwind!

(translation by Douglass M. Green; reprinted from the International Alban Berg Society *Newsletter*)

will give us the initials of Hanna Fuchs and Alban Berg. The ten overlapping set statements, of course, give us Hanna's number; we have already noted that the composer calls attention to the implicit presence of his own number 23 on the last page of the score. 'The final dissolution of identity in death is thus represented through a musical metaphor in these last bars of the Largo desolato.' A last statement of the basic cell at its primary pitch-level occurs in the first violin at the return to Tempo II in bars 34–5. Only here does Berg fail to identify the pitch names of the cell, B, A, F and H. The omission in itself adds another level of meaning to the text of the accompanying 'vocal' line. The loss of awareness 'in stumpfen Schlafes Schwindel' already prefigures 'the final dissolution of identity in death'.

Another omission is more difficult to explain. Berg chose to draw Hanna's attention 'to our numbers, 10 and 23', by showing these numbers as factors of the numbers of bars comprised in each movement and in sections of movements. Why did he fail to make any reference whatever to the metronomic numbers, which are likewise multiples of 10 and 23? Having said so much in his annotations, did he wish to leave something still unsaid? Did he hope that some day the cryptic clues to the presence of a mystery that he had placed in the public's version of the score would be understood? and did he look upon those clues that were hidden in the metronomic numbers as something of a special nature, to be shared with his brothers in art rather than with Hanna?[7]

[7]Both attitudes, or either, are consistent with the secret musical metaphors of *Wozzeck* and *Lulu*; see my articles, 'Symbol and Representation in the Music of *Wozzeck*', *Music Review*, xxxii (1971), 281, and 'Die Reihe als Symbol in Bergs *Lulu*', *Osterreichische Musikzeitschrift*, xxii (1967), 589.

# The Secret Programme of the Lyric Suite—3

## George Perle

Berg's annotated miniature score of the *Lyric Suite* is a unique document in the history of music. Imagine that Berlioz had kept the programme of the *Symphonie fantastique* a secret from everyone except Harriet Smithson; that in addition to the unmistakable suggestions of a programme, whatever it might be, in the musical character of the work, there were coded references to the composer's secret in purely notational or numerical details of the score; that a full understanding of this secret programme involved, aside from musical and verbal elements, purely graphic elements in the one copy of the score that Berlioz had prepared for Miss Smithson, and only for her; and that, but for this one copy, Harriet Smithson and her role in the evolution of the work and in the composer's life would have remained unknown.

What of Berg's preparatory study for the first movement of the *Lyric Suite*, the 12-note version of *Schliesse mir die Augen beide*? In a letter to Webern dated 12 October 1925 Berg mentions his 'first attempt at strict 12-note serial composition', a new setting of the same poem by Theodor Storm that he had already provided with a tonal setting in 1907.[8] The two songs are published together in *Die Musik* of February 1930 with a dedication to Emil Hertzka, founder of Universal Edition, in recognition of the 25th anniversary of the firm and as an illustration of musical evolution in those 25 years, 'from the C major triad' of the first song to the 'Mutterakkord', the symmetrical all-interval series of the second. In the same letter in which Berg told Webern of the song—'I too sent a (love-) song whose words have no connection with the (Hertzka) anniversary, or rather two songs on the same poem, a very old one and a brand new one'— he reported that he was working on a projected 'suite for string quartet', to consist of 'six rather short movements of a lyrical rather than symphonic character'.

Though I know of no annotated copy of the second Storm song, it too appears to be secretly dedicated to Hanna, in spite of an official dedication to someone else. The number of bars is twice Hanna's number. The principal set-form of the first movement of the quartet and of the song is the same—a prime set bounded by the pitches F and H (B). The vocal part is entirely limited to this set-form. At bar 11, in the piano part, an inverted set bounded by Ab and D is introduced, but this is cyclically permuted to begin on F and end on B. The close of the first half of the song is marked by a 12-note simultaneity derived from the prime set, the close of the second half by a 12-note simultaneity derived from the inverted set. The outermost pitches of each chord are F and B.

The second Storm song, as his 'first attempt at strict 12-note serial composition?' marked a new

beginning for Berg in the development of his musical language. In spring 1907 he had offered the same verses to Helene, and 58 years later she chose them for the opening lines of the *Letters to his Wife*:

> Schliesse mir die Augen beide
> Mit den lieben Händen zu;
> Geht doch alles, was ich leide,
> Unter Deiner Hand zur Ruh.
> Und wie leise sich der Schmerz
> Well' und Welle schlafen legt,
> Wie der letzte Schlag sich regt,
> Füllest Du mein ganzes Herz.

Characteristically, the composer who was to assign a role to himself in his own opera, *Lulu*, with its symmetries and doublings and musico-dramatic recapitulations, chose to mark a new beginning in his emotional life by writing a new love-song to the same text, on an entirely new level of technical complexity and maturity.

Until now we have had only 'authorized' biographies of Berg's life, or biographies entirely dependent on authorized sources. The publisher of the most recent of these was even pleased to announce that his book was issued with 'Mrs Berg's approval'. But the unauthorized biographer should not fail to recognize the limits of even so self-revelatory a document as the annotated copy of the *Lyric Suite* score. It is not for nothing that in *Lulu* Berg

[8]Redlich erroneously assigns the song to the year 1900. The year given by Reich, 1907, is correct.

809

transformed Wedekind's Alwa from a writer into a composer—the composer of *Wozzeck* and the *Lyric Suite*, as he tells us in a musical reference to the former and verbal reference to the latter. Simultaneously inside the drama as a participant, and outside the drama as its author, Alwa, as he himself says in the play, is 'a martyr to his profession'. Berg's need and capacity for such a role should already have been evident to the sensitive reader of the *Letters to his Wife*. Kept apart from the woman he was determined to marry by the implacable opposition of her (presumably adoptive) father,[9] the 24-year-old Berg facetiously describes himself as a 'writer' whose daily letters to her are

> chapters of a vast novel entitled HELENE AND ALBAN: the story of a Great Love. We might collect 70 or 80 letters, put them in order, and make them into quite a nice book—a present for your old man? It could even convert him!

To the end of his life, the letters he wrote daily to Helene when they were separated continued to read like chapters in the same hypothetical novel. They are the letters of a perpetual adolescent, the letters of one who cannot free himself, who does not wish to free himself, from the painfully acute sensitivity, the intense selfconsciousness, the anxiety and perfectionism of youth.

*

In the light of the annotated score of the *Lyric Suite* some of Berg's *Letters to his Wife* acquire a biographical relevance they did not have before. The letters from Prague during his first visit with the Fuchs family are dated 15-19 May 1925. The date that stands at the head of the Allegro misterioso is 20 May 1925. 18 months before this Helene was staying at a sanatorium, where in place of the medical treatment she had expected, she found herself subjected to the ministrations of a psychoanalyst, who, according to Helene's letter to her husband, informed her that she was unhappily married. Berg was furious.

> Don't go to any more 'sessions'. Tell the doctor I've forbidden it, and say that if there had been any question of psychoanalytic treatment, we should have gone to Dr Freud or Dr Adler, both of whom we have known very well for many years . . . It takes two to make a marriage unhappy. For me it's a happy one.

Influenced, perhaps, by the negative views of Karl Kraus, he had more to say on the subject of psychoanalysis in his next letter: 'these ideas of unfulfilled desires and obscenities about "glands" and similar pseudo-science, invented by the "prostate": the brain of a psychoanalyst'.

For 41 years after her husband's death, Helene Berg continued to play the role that he had assigned to her in the 'vast novel' of his adolescence. This role took priority over every other consideration. 'For 28 years I lived in the Paradise of his love', she wrote, in a prefatory note to the *Letters*. 'His death was a catastrophe I only had the strength to survive because our souls were long ago joined together in a union beyond space and time, a union through all eternity.'

[9] Helene Berg is supposed to have been the natural daughter of the Emperor Franz Josef.

A few days before my departure to visit Dorothea Robetin, the Österreichische Nationalbibliothek replied as follows to my inquiry as to the status of the Berg manuscripts that Redlich had described as 'missing': 'Op.1 is still not on record, nor op.2 . . . It has been a well-known fact for many years that Mrs Zemlinsky returned the *Lyric Suite* to Mrs Berg, who subsequently gave it to the library . . . Op.3 is also in our collection'. A few days after my return I received a letter from Mrs Zemlinsky confirming the statements that she had made in 1961-2 to Dr Redlich and Universal Edition: 'The manuscript of Alban Berg's *Lyric Suite* was never in my husband's possession, nor in mine'.

*

Dorothea Robetin has in her possession 14 letters from Alban Berg to her mother, covering the span of years that still remained to him between the composition of the *Lyric Suite* and his death on 24 December 1935. They speak in unchanging terms of a passionate but unfulfilled love. Hanna's brother, Franz Werfel, and her sister-in-law, Alma, served as Berg's emissaries to Hanna, delivering his letters in person on their occasional visits to Prague. The première of *Wozzeck* in Berlin a few weeks after his second stay with the Fuchs-Robettin family had made Berg a famous man, and appearances that had been maintained within the circle of his friends, acquaintances, and colleagues had now to be maintained before the world. In a most moving and poignant letter to Hanna, dated October 1931, the composer himself passes judgment on the picture of his domestic and personal life that has been preserved from that day to this:

> . . . Not a day passes, not half a day, not a night, when I do not think of you, not a week, when I am not suddenly flooded by yearning, which submerges all my thoughts and feelings and wishes in an ardour which is not weaker by a breath than that of May 1925 – – only still shadowed by a grief which since that time rules me more and more, and which, for a long time now, has made me into a double, or better said, a play-acting person. For you must know: everything that you may hear of me, and perhaps even read about me, pertains, insofar as it is not completely false – – as, for example, this, which I read today by chance in a Zurich programme: 'A completely happy domesticity, with which his wife has surrounded him, allows him to create without disturbance' – – pertains to what is only peripheral. But it pertains only to a person who constitutes only a completely exterior layer of myself, to a part of me which in the course of recent years has separated itself (ah, how painfully separated) from my real existence, and has formed a detached being, the one I seem to my surroundings and to the world. In the frame of *this* life everything takes place that a normal life brings with it: vexation and joy, ill-humour and gaiety, interest and indifference, business and pleasure, art and nature – – – But believe me, Hanna (and now I can finally address you properly: *one and only eternal love*), all this pertains only to this *exterior* person, the one I have been forced to present myself as to my fellow human beings and whom you (thank God) have never known, and who (only in order to characterize him in *some* way) might for a time be fulfilled with the joys of motor-

ing, but could never be able to compose *Lulu*. That I am, however, doing this may be proof to you that the other person (and now I can speak again in the first person), that *I* still exist! When I work and take hold of your pen, at that moment *I* am here, and am also with you, as I am with myself when I am with you in thought . . . .

Public pretensions to an idyllic domestic life are hardly uncommon, but the extent of Berg's collaboration in the fabrication and perpetuation of the myth of a perfect marriage was extraordinary. An authentic biography of the man would have to explain this. Obviously, he remained strongly attached to his wife, even though the nature of that attachment had changed. 'Faithfulness' was, in fact, one of his 'main qualities'. He could hardly have contemplated a physical separation without considering what effect this would have had upon Helene. Ought we not to inquire into her mind and character, as well as his, in trying to understand his behaviour? For 41 years after his death she persisted in the tragic role of a recently bereaved widow. It is surprising that no-one should have seen—in Freud's own Vienna—anything suspect in her obsessive clinging to this role and to its special privileges. May not the endearments that continued to pervade the *Letters to his Wife* have been expressions of solicitude, rather than of love? May they not also have been expressions of fear of what her jealousy could lead to? We have already seen what it could lead to, in the story of the manuscript of the *Lyric Suite*: her invention of a fictional account of the history of the manuscript in order to prevent discovery of its one-time ownership by Hanna Fuchs-Robettin; her pretence, after her fictional account was disputed by Redlich, that the manuscript was missing when in fact it was in her very own possession; her eventual reinstatement of the original fiction with a new twist to explain how the manuscript had come into her own hands. Helene's younger brother, Franz Joseph, was a schizophrenic whose care was a source of concern for Berg and his wife throughout their married life. Is it not also possible that Berg may have believed that he had reason to be apprehensive about Helene's mental health?

There remains another question: to what extent are the *Letters to his Wife* altogether reliable as a record of Berg's own words? It would be well to recall the curious circumstances that surrounded the publication of the original German edition in 1965. The editor, Dr Franz Willnauer, worked from typed copies of the letters, prepared under Mrs Berg's direction. He was permitted neither to check their authenticity by comparing them with the autographs nor to determine the scope and significance of passages and letters that Mrs Berg chose not to release for publication. Differences between Mrs Berg and Dr Willnauer led her to ban not only his introductory note on the editorial procedures followed but also his notes to the letters and his 40-page commentary. The German edition omits Dr Willnauer's name altogether, contain no editorial notes, no footnotes, no commentary, no index, and was released for distribution by the publishers only after a number of passages had been inked out by hand, at Mrs Berg's insistence. In an article in *Forum* (October 1965) Dr Willnauer wrote:

No deposition can be made as to the fidelity of the published letters to the originals, nor as to the scope and significance of the material withheld by Helene Berg. In spite of this, it can be assumed that [Mrs Berg] herself would have had the greatest interest in the documentary character of this edition and that she would therefore have been concerned for optimum authenticity in preparing the transcriptions.

We know now that Mrs Berg would have had priorities other than 'optimum authenticity' in publishing her husband's letters. The critical reader will recognize these other priorities in a number of statements which appear in Mrs Berg's last will and testament.[10] A list of mementos includes 'Berg's golden fountain pen (a gift from Franz Werfel, with which he wrote his opera *Lulu* and the violin concerto)'. This misrepresentation is probably not a deliberate one, for it is unlikely that Mrs Berg would have known that Werfel was acting only as his sister's agent in presenting Berg with this gift. The same cannot be said of Mrs Berg's well-known explanation, repeated here once again, for her refusal to permit the completion of the full score of the third act of *Lulu*: 'Nachdem Arnold Schoenberg, Anton Webern und Alexander Zemlinsky nach Einsicht in das Manuskript erklärten, dass sie es nicht fertigmachen können, war mir die Ansicht dieser 3 nächsten Freunde Albans für meinen Entschluss, das Manuskript nicht freizugeben, bestimmend' ('Once Arnold Schoenberg, Anton Webern and Alexander Zemlinsky had examined the manuscript and declared they could not complete it, the opinion of Alban's 3 closest friends confirmed my decision not to release the manuscript'). Mrs Berg's supposed recollections, which first saw the light of day only after all three composers were dead, remain to this day the only source for the reported opinions of Schoenberg, Webern and Zemlinsky as to the feasibility of a completion of the scoring. Another phrase in the will gives cause for the gravest concern. A list of manuscripts in the custody of the Österreichische Nationalbibliothek refers to three folders containing, respectively, certain manuscripts of Acts 1, 2 and 3. The content of each folder is described. Here is the complete reference to Act 3: 'Mappe 3 (3. Akt) 76 Bl. + 2 grosse Partiturblätter + 2 Bl. Notizen + 4 Partiturblätter (Schluss der Oper) gingen in der Universal Edition verloren, sind dort unauffindbar!' ('Folder 3 (Act 3) 76 pp. + 2 large pages of full score + 2 pp. of notes + 4 pages of full score (end of the opera) were lost at Universal Edition and cannot be found there!'). The possible implications of this statement are alarming indeed, especially in the context of the injunctions that introduce Mrs Berg's assertions as to the views of Schoenberg, Webern, and Zemlinsky: 'Der 3. Akt von "Lulu" darf von niemandem eingesehen werden! Ebenso darf die Photokopie bei der Universal-Edition auch nicht eingesehen werden' ('Nobody is allowed to examine Act 3 of "Lulu"! Neither may the Universal Edition photocopy be examined').

There is a circularity in all this that is much like the recapitulative design of the third act of *Lulu*.[11]

[10] extensive excerpts from the will have been published in the *Österreichische Musikzeitschrift*, xxxii/4 (1977).
[11] see my article 'Lulu: the Formal Design', *Journal of the American Musicological Society*, xvii (1964), 179

288

Berg's first stay with the Fuchs-Robettin family was in connection with the performance in Prague of the Three Excerpts from *Wozzeck*; his second was occasioned by his journey to Berlin for the rehearsals of the first *Wozzeck* production. In an article on *Wozzeck* written ten years before I had ever heard of Hanna Fuchs-Robettin I showed how the notes B(=H) and F serve as a compound tone centre 'in the context of both the largest and the smallest dimensions of the work'.[12] It is unlikely that Berg would have failed to notice what to him would have seemed a prophetic coincidence, the identity of these notes with Hanna's initials. Though the Berlin première of *Wozzeck* brought Berg instant fame, whereas the author of the drama died in obscurity, there is a curious, though fortunately limited, correspondence in their posthumous fates. When Georg Büchner died in 1837, at the age of 23, he left only the preliminary drafts and sketches of what was to become the libretto of Berg's masterpiece. Had it not been for Karl Emil Franzos, the Galician-Jewish novelist who deciphered the faded and almost illegible manuscripts 38 years after Büchner's death, neither the drama nor its author would be known to us today. A portion of Georg Büchner's legacy, possibly including the lost play, *Pietro Aretino*, and a final fair copy of *Wozzeck*, had passed into the hands of the author's fiancée at the time of his death. Surviving her lover by 43 years, Minna Jaegle remained devoted to his memory. She never married, and loyally guarded the papers in her possession from the one man, Franzos, who was concerned to rescue them for posterity. Franzos's importunities were definitively rejected in the following letter:

> In your esteemed letter of 17 February [1877] you say that I have a moral duty to assist the edition of Georg Büchner's works by making available such papers of his as are in my possession. To this I have the honour to reply to you that I feel no moral duty whatever to make the said papers public. Some of them concern only me personally. Others are incomplete abstracts and notes. The memory of Georg Büchner is so dear to me that I cannot wish to expose anything of his that is unfinished to review by literary critics. Having been prevented by serious illness from replying to you sooner, I have had to postpone it until today. I would be obliged to you, esteemed sir, if you would permit this explanation to suffice for the future.

Whatever writings of Büchner's Minna Jaegle may still have possessed had vanished without a trace by the time of her death three years later.

[12]'The Musical Language of *Wozzeck*', *Music Forum*, i (1967), 210-18

289

✱

*Addendum*

When the foregoing article was published in the year following Mrs. Berg's death, there still seemed to be every good reason for my apprehension regarding the fate of *Lulu*, Act III. Erwin Stein's vocal score of Act III, whose forthcoming publication was first announced in 1936, was finally published a year after my article appeared, in an edition by the Viennese composer Friedrich Cerha, who had, with the permission of the publisher, secretly completed the orchestration while the widow was still alive. The Alban Berg Stiftung, founded by Mrs. Berg and bound by the provisions of her will to enforce the continued suppression of the third act, only terminated its legal action against the publisher in 1980, a year after the premiere of the complete opera in Paris on February 24, 1979.

# Strategics of Variation in the Second Movement of Bartók's Violin Concerto 1937—1938

by

László Somfai

We have reasonable ground to assume that in his Violin Concerto Bartók considered the middle variation movement, composed in a new style and a particular manner, to be of the greatest importance. We know it from Zoltán Székely, who commissioned the work that Bartók originally intended to write a one-movement composition for him.[1] Around 1936—1938 the first and third movements, with their principles built on common themes, and displaying inversions of themes in the recapitulations within the individual movements, represented the well-skilled multimovement central model in Bartók's formal realm. From a structural point of view a new piece counted more like a variant within this model. There are compositional proofs to bear out that Bartók was practically seeking for a way out from the self-imposed symmetrical 5-section form ("bridge form", "arch form" or "palindromic form", arranged into 5 or 3 movements)[2] which by that time he felt to be oppressive as a procedure which could easily become a routine. The main document for this lies in the extraordinarily individual 4-movement model of the

---

[1] Verbal communication of Zoltán Székely. With regard to the fact that the one-movement *Concertstück*-like piece could hardly have been the first movement, see data and hypotheses under footnote 3.

[2] The term *bridge form* has come into usage in the Hungarian Bartók analyses (E. Lendvai, József Ujfalussy, etc.). In the short analytical texts on his own works, Bartók himself generally used the term *symmetrical form*, or described the five-section structure arranged around a nucleus movement, as a such. E.g. on the Piano Concerto No. 2: " . . . the entire work shows symmetrical form [ . . . ] A similar construction was used in my String Quartets Nos. 4 and 5 also." (English translation of the French orig.: *Béla Bartók Essays*. Selected and Edited by Benjamin Suchoff. Faber 1976, 423.) In his preface to the pocket score of the 4th quartet he also defined the symmetrical form (*Bartók Essays*, 412), and he demonstrated it with a graphical arrangement in his analysis on the 5th quartet (*Bartók Essays*, 414). Bartók used the term bridge form — retaining the German expression also in the English translation — in his preface to the pocket score of Music for Strings, Percussion and Celesta, in connection with the symmetrical form of the 3rd movement: „ . . . 'Brückenform', (Rondo) A, B, C, B, A" (*Bartók Essays*, 416).

Music for Strings, Percussion, and Celesta written in 1936. But the plan
of the Violin Concerto also emerged during the summer of 1936 (even
though the date at the end of the score reads: *Budapest, 1937 aug.—1938
dec. 31.),*[3] which ousted the bridge form to the external crust of the structure, and placed something new in the centre, which perhaps has not yet
been properly appreciated.

[3] Here one has to account for two compositional plans which in the summer of
1936 were probably still independent from one another: the commissioning of the
*Violin Concerto,* first mentioned in Zoltán Székely's letter of August 10. 1936, and
the orchestral piece which Bartók began upon the commission of the *Musikdirektion
Baden Baden* and for which he made a provisional promise in a letter of July 14,
1936, that would have been *eine Reihe kürzerer Stücke.* To understand the excerpt
from Székely's letter, published here for the first time, it has to be known that in
1935 Bartók's Dutch concert manager, Madame Kossar, tried to induce Bartók to
write a piano trio, and in January 1936 she repeatedly urged the writing of at least
a one-movement trio piece. Székely's Hungarian letter of August 10, 1936 refers to
this: "... Ez a trió dolog úgylátom egészen dugába dőlt. Kár! Volna kedved
hasonló alapon egy hegedű versenyt írni? Én nagyon szeretném. [ ... ] Nekem nagy
örömet okoznál ha beleegyeznél, mert már régi titkos vágyam egy Bartók koncert."
(I think this trio business has completely failed. A pity! Would you be inclined to
write, on a similar basis, a violin concerto? I would like it very much. [ ... ] You
would give me great pleasure should you agree, because a Bartók concerto has been
an old secret wish of mine.) Bartók immediately took up the idea as indicated by
the fact that he soon asked his publisher, the Vienna Universal Edition to send him
some scores recently issued by them (in a letter dated September 26, the firm apolo-
gized for posting the scores of the Berg, Weill and Szymanowski concertos only
then). — As regards the other case, it has been György Kroó's study that called
attention to it (*Unrealized Plans and Ideas for Projects by Bartók* = Studia Musicologica XII, 1970, 17—18; here I quote the letters in their original German text).
Accordingly, in addition to the four-movement work, Music for Strings, Percussion
and Celesta, being written upon a commission from Paul Sacher in Basle, he also
worked on another symphonic series: "*Auch ein anderes Orchesterstück plane ich
(normale 2-fache Besetzung; eine Reihe kürzerer Stücke)*" (July 24, 1936). Bartók
referred to it even in a letter of September 1, discussing the future form of publication: "*... das andere Orchesterwerk bezüglich [ ... ] zu dem die Skizzen teilweise
ebenfalls schon vorliegen [ ... ]*". In this form the work was never completed, Kroó,
however, has very correctly pointed out: "But in all probability the drafts of 1936
for an 'other orchestral work' were amalgamated into the Violin Concerto finished
in 1938" (Kroó op.cit. 18). — The question now is into which section of the Violin
Concerto were these symphonic drafts amalgamated? Hardly into the first movement, since Bartók drafted its principal theme and the twelve-tone contrast theme
only in the summer of 1937 (see Bartók's letter mentioned under note 7), together
with the themes of the Sonata for Two Pianos and Percussion. The third movement
(in its thematic material a variation of the first) was written last, as it has been long
known by Bartók research. This leaves the second movement, with its orchestra
of a »normale 2-fache Besetzung*", most of the variations in which could be composed
also without the solo violin. And if we take a look at the sections of an expressedly
solo violin conception (variation I following the theme; the *Più mosso* variation
III; and perhaps even the *Comodo* variation VI), we will see that, stepping out from
the logically accomplished circle of minor thirds, these solo sections show alien
tonalities, or tonal repeats: G *(G)*! E *(B)*! D flat B flat *(B flat)*! G; for greater detail
see chapter II and Ex. 14. It is most probable that these solo sections, two of them
marked *poco rubato,* were included in the score in the course of the transformation
of the series originally meant as short symphonic pieces, into a violin concerto
movement. This hypothesis can however be justified or rejected only by an analysis
of the sketches preserved in New York, which for the time being are unaccessible.

Especially the Hungarian Bartók analyses of the last three decades have comprehensively demonstrated the fact which Bartók himself kept emphasizing in his articles and interviews — namely that with him the bent for variation, the transformation of themes stemmed partly from the nature of his own musicianship, and partly from his thorough studies of the folk music of various peoples.[4] But while variation was present on all possible scales of form — ranging from the variational correspondence between the movements to the variative development of the shortest motives — the form "Theme and Variations" in conformity with European tradition, is decidedly rare in Bartók's works. Its appearance is for the most part of secondary significance, usually with an educational aim, or didactically regular in form.[5] The second movement of the Violin Concerto stands pre-eminent among them, if only for its length equalling an individual composition, and for its conceptual significance. Two further characteristics lend added eminence to the movement: On the one hand, the number of components involved in variation and the complexity of their interrelationship provide a veritable encyclopedical character and, indeed, a conceptual-aesthetic definition of Bartók's interpretation of the variation, in the same way as a "Goldberg" or "Diabelli" variation throws light on its composer. On the other hand, the movement points to some compositional principles which around 1936—38 were really new for Bartók, and which (in spite of the undeniably classical, indeed "romantic" harmonic character of the whole piece) can be also brought in line with the development of serial composition after World War II.

The following examination has been stimulated by certain external motifs; some of them negative, such as e.g. the trend of Bartók research initiated by analysts under the influence of serial composition, with their irritatingly erroneous starting points, and arriving only at partial results; or like analyses which make a fetish of the basic recognitions and terminology of E. Lendvai, and by this gradually blocking the way to further research; and also positive ones, such as the recently published Harvard lectures of Bartók in which the composer scanned his own style, and which on certain points may beneficially correct the stiffening conception

[4] See, among others, D. Dille's interview with Bartók, in French: *Sirène*, Bruxelles, mars 1937.
[5] Of the youthful works *Változatok* [Theme with Twelve Variations] for piano, with its romantic conception (413 bars; Dille-Nr. 64) is yet really traditional. The number of piano variations written on folksongs is rather small, the most important of them, already marked as variations being: For Children III. 5 (=II. 5); Fifteen Hungarian Peasant Songs, No 6 *Ballade (tema con variazioni)*; Mikrokosmos IV. 112 Variations on a Folk Tune. VI. 140 written on his own theme, already in its title indicates Free Variations.

11*

of Bartók analysis. The inner demand that has most strongly motivated my research, however, arises from my firm conviction that in trying to understand Bartók's own compositional logic, we still take very little notice (or only on a most elemental grade) of those direct and indirect compositional impulses he gained in the course of classifying and analyzing the folk music of various peoples for various purposes and with different methods, and which kept fermenting in him. During the course of my examination 1 will occasionally touch upon some available manuscript documents of the genesis of the movement, which will serve as important and authentic partial data on Bartók's compositional logic, through the interpretation of his intended corrections and improvements. At certain points I intend to link some phenomena of the movement with the theoretical statements in Bartók's essays and lectures. Despite all this, the following analysis is merely a posterior reconstruction of what is believed Bartók's compositional logic. It is not at all sure that the phenomena emphasized here were the important recognitions for Bartók as well, or whether he brought forth these structures in a deliberate manner. Furthermore, it is absolutely certain that some of the concepts and terms applied here are typically post-war ones which were never used by Bartók.

After an introductory presentation of the Theme (I) the analysis will be restricted mainly to the examination of four factors of the numerous variation phenomena, in each case calling attention to the intended global structure emerging from the consecutive variations. These factors are as follows:

(II) the variation of tonal structure (including melodic modification of the theme);

(III) the variation of phrase structure (including modification of meter and rhythm);

(IV) the variation of instrumental groups (including modification of timbre);

(V) the variation of register formations (including density of tone-space, modification and motion of tone-bands).

## I. *The Theme*

The theme was conceived in Bartók as a *melodic theme,*[6] as borne out by his first sketch which he noted down not even on music-paper but a

---

[6] The only harmonic idea (A minor chord in bar 5), in a characteristic manner, is not employed in the exposition of the theme, but it is present in the recapitulation (bar 122).

small hand-lined sheet.[7] Disregarding the slurs, the violin melody already here appears in a nearly final perfection (Ex. 1). The corrections Bartók made on his first thought right in the sketch, partly indicate his hesitation with regard to the continuation of the first phrase (bar 2; incidentally both here and in bar 3 the final form was to bring constructive novelties), and partly resulted in a more organic variation of the rhythm (bars 3—4).[8]

Ex.1

295

Two things evolve from the formulation of the theme as a melody. One that the melody, shaped of breath-long phrases in a *Lied*-type compass with an almost vocal simplicity — similarly to an unaccompanied folksong — formulates its own shape and articulation independent of its accompaniment. The other speciality is that this melody — irrespective of the chordal accompaniment created around it subsequently — manifests itself in scale, tonal and interval structures suitable for further variations.

With regard to the first consideration, the *form* of the theme, similarly to several instrumental Bartók themes of a *Lied* form, the structure of a *Periode* (as a German and Austrian classical tradition) and the

[7] The original is in the possession of Tossy Spivakovsky (who has presented a photocopy to the Budapest Bartók Archives). The following is an excerpt from the letter Bartók enclosed with the sketches: "Dear Mr. Spivakovsky, finally I found those first sketches to the violin concerto I mentioned to you, so I am sending them closed. They are hurriedly written just as they came to my mind: the 1st theme of the I. and II. movement, and various, tentative forms of the 2nd theme of the I. movement [ . . . ]" (Bartók went on to mention that the sketches written for the first movement of the Violin Concerto, and those on the back side of the sheet, belonging to the Sonata for Two Pianos, naturally did not belong together, but they could not be separated.)

[8] It is perhaps a simple slip of the pen that with the two last notes of bar 4 Bartók originally started a new bar. The omission of note *b* at the end of bar 7 is justified partly by the introduction of a rhythmically new variant, and partly by the intention to clarify tonal relationships, i.e. the descent of the D-C-B terraces would be disturbed by the premature exposition of tone *b*.

folksong-like stanza structure built of lines (on the inspiration mainly
of the most general 4-line stanza of Hungarian, Slovak, etc. folk music)
here too, are present simultaneously. The 8-bar solo violin theme —
which in the final score is to be supplemented by the *tutti* recapitulation
of bars 7—8 — is of a symmetrical quadruplet structure of one- and
double-bar phrases, since $8 = 4 + 4$, and within this $4 = 2 + 2$, and
finally $2 = 1 + 1$. (On a smaller scale the key-number is 3; the 9/8 bar is
divided into 3 motives, and one motive into 3 quavers; the smallest
rhythmic length, the semiquaver is reached again by halving.) If we inter-
pret the 8-bar melody (Ex. 2) as what is known a *große Periode*, bars 4
and 8 end, in the traditional manner, with an imperfect and perfect
cadence, respectively. A half *Periode* (4 bars) however, can also be interpreted — in its form, size, and the function of the parts — as a 4-line
folksong-like stanza, mainly because the first, second and third lines are
strictly separated by "breath pauses". (The cohesion of lines 3 and 4, and
the recapitulation of the third and fourth lines at the end of the stanza,
form almost typical Hungarian folk music features.)

296

Ex. 2

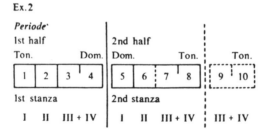

As for their musical contents, of course, these so-called stanzas are
not folksong-like in a direct manner. For example, this kind of tonal
discrepancy between beginning and end of a stanza does not point to
folksong. The motivic content of the first or second four lines (here: bars)
each, and their melodic contour ranging throughout the register, are not
folksong-like either — if only in the generality of the first and second
lines being of related material, and the third line introducing the highest
register. The manner in which Bartók creates an intricate relationship
already between the first and second bars of the melody (the essentially
identical rhythm is coupled with an almost exact retrograde motion),
or the way in which he further varies this second bar in bars 5 and 6, by
the joint use of repetition, transposition and inversion, is even less folksong-like, and at the same time not really characteristic of the classical *Periode* structure either (Ex. 3).

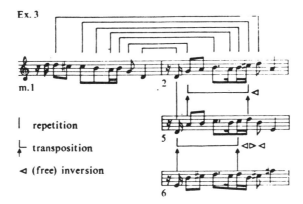

Another significant aim of Bartók is to link the phrases, markedly divided by pauses, by striking motivic spans: the first two notes of the joining new phrase are the retrograde of the last two notes of the previous one (incidentally with a diminution of rhythmic values: ♪♩/♪♪). Where there are no pauses (bars 3—4, 6—7 and 7—8), this link is not present either, and where Bartók brings forth the main articulation (bars 4—5) he restricts himself to a correspondence of one note each (Ex. 4).

The significant motivic intervals used for articulation point to the question of tonal, modal and interval characteristics arising from the formulation of the theme as a melody. This violin melody may be remembered as a simple tune, almost of an idyllic folksong tone, but indeed it constitutes one of the most elaborate Bartók themes. Its composition strictly determines the chain of variations built out of it, just like a late Webern 12-tone set defines the strategy of the given composition. Let us remind the reader of the composer's argumentations in his Harvard lectures (1943)[9] to shed light on the fact that Bartók was very much concerned with the various scales he analyzed and classified in the folk music of different peoples, with the modal scales just as much as with other scale formations unknown is Western art music. Modelled on them,

[9] The most important excerpts were issued by John Vinton (*Bartók on His Own Music*, JAMS XIX, 1966. 232—243). The full text is included in Benjamin Suchoff's volume (*Bartók Essays*, 354—392).

but naturally in a much more complex manner, he himself consciously composed in bimodal or polymodal[10] structures. He also proved it with examples that e.g. *As a result of superposing a Lydian and Phrygian pentachord with a common fundamental tone, we get a diatonic pentachord filled out with all the possible flat and sharp degrees. These seemingly chromatic degrees, however, are totally different in their function from the altered chord degrees of the chromatic styles of the previous periods [ . . . ] In our polymodal chromaticism [ . . . ] the flat and sharp tones are not altered degrees at all; they are diatonic ingredients of a diatonic modal scale.*[11] He deduced in a similar manner the *triad with a double third: one minor, the other major*[12] (which he incidentally also encountered in Rumanian folk music performance) that constitutes a marked chord of his music. [Hereinafter it will be referred as the *"alpha" formula*, borrowing the Greek letter from E. Lendvai's widely known terminology].[13] It also becomes clear from Bartók's Harvard lectures that in his own music he made a deliberate use of the principle of polymodal construction both in the successive and simultaneous performance of tones. And, what is of special significance in examining the theme of the Violin Concerto, in another context Bartók referred to the very fast changes in the succession of different modalities: *In our works, as well as in other contemporary works, various methods and principles cross each other. For instance, you cannot expect to find among our works one in which the upper part continuously uses a certain mode and the lower part continuously uses another mode. So if we say our art music is polymodal, this means that polymodality or bimodality appears in longer or shorter portions of our work, sometimes only in single bars. So, changes may succeed from bar to bar, or even from beat to beat in a bar.*[14]

Next let us survey the tonal events of the 8 bars of the theme, neglecting the rhythm, minor tone repetitions, and naturally the whole accompaniment which was to be composed to it later. Above the staff (Ex. 5) the modes are indicated which, in the token of Bartók's folkmusicological essays, can safely be termed as such; at the same time the

---

[10] *Bartók Essays*, 363ff.
[11] *Bartók Essays*, 367.
[12] *Bartók Essays*, 368—369.
[13] In the most widely known English language survey of Ernő Lendvai's terminology, developed since 1948 (*Béla Bartók. An Analysis of this Music.* Kahn & Averill 1971, 40ff) he writes about type alpha, introducing its different sections (section beta, gamma, delta, epsilon). In the present study we use the term alpha formula in the broadest sense, ranging from the major-minor type chord to the scale phenomena within the frames of a diminished octave, since they all have common roots.
[14] *Bartók Essays*, 370.

unambiguous central tone (tonal centre) of the given section is noted under the staff. Sections requiring more exhaustive interpretation are marked by one to four asterisks.

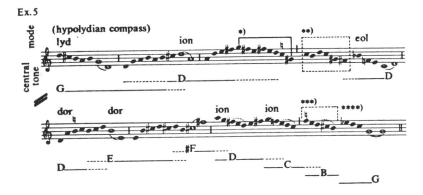

Ex. 5

Bartók clearly distinguishes at least 4, but rather 5 modes (lydian, ionian, aeolian, dorian and in the end phrygian; see about the last below). At the same time, for longer or shorter sections a tonal centre built on 5 or 6 different tones becomes fixed. It should be added that the various modes or tonal centres turn from one solid form into the other by dissolving, and thus there are three different "grades": coherent tonal (modal) section; bimodal transition; and loosened modal chromatic section. It is obvious that Bartók deliberately composed from numerous principles typical of monophonic melodic styles; such a juxtaposition is to be found, for example, in the plagal *vs.* authentic compass at the beginning of the two halves of the melody (bar 1: hypolydian; bar 5: dorian).

Before explaining the sections marked by asteriks, certain basic terms have to be clarified. We are indebted to Lajos Bárdos for the excellent recognition and practical term of the concept of *heptatonia secunda* and *tertia*.[15] Bárdos pointed out that in addition to the common diatonic system, in which the tones and semitones take up the position $2-1-3-1$ (i.e. a $1+1+1/2+1+1+1+1/2$-tone set, or its modes that may be started from any tone), and which thus presents the first, most natural heptatony (let us call it *heptatonia prima*!), there are two further heptatonic systems, heptatonia secunda and heptatonia tertia, offering the same number of modes and transposition possibilities (Ex. 6). To distinguish

[15] Its first detailed explanation, L. Bárdos: *Heptatonia secunda* = Magyar Zene 1962, III/6, 583 ff.

between these three basic systems, in the present study I use the symbols I. 7°, II. 7° and III. 7° (First Seven-Degree [system], etc.). III. 7° is relatively rare, but certain modes of II. 7° are most frequent in folk music (e.g. in Rumanian) and in Bartók's works. Suffice it to mention the mode which is also known as the *acoustic scale* (e.g. g-a-b-c sharp-d-e-f-g).[16] As regards Bartók's style, and more concretely the second movement of the Violin Concerto, it deserves attention that by creating a full scale of the most characteristic segment of heptatonia secunda the *1 : 2 model-scale* is arrived at,[17] from which the major-minor *alpha formula* may also develop. At the same time the III. 7° includes the possibility of deviation towards the *whole-tone scale*, since only one of its tones has to be skipped and omitted (Ex. 6).

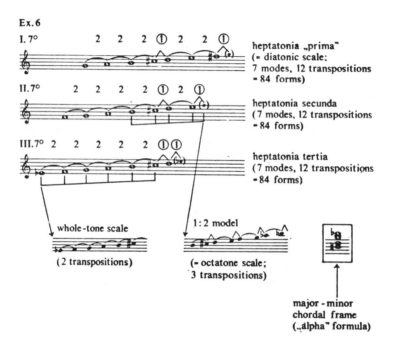

---

[16] *Bartók Essays*, 363, Bartók's example refers to three scales as "some others absolutely unknown from modal music", and they also include a g-a-b flat-c-d flat-e flat-f scale, which, although incomplete, is one of the modes of heptatonia secunda. Bartók does not give it any name, only draws attention to the fact that it is not diatonic.

[17] E. Lendvai's denomination; it is so appropriate that its use is more practical than either the term "octatone scale" which has spread in Princeton University circles, or Messiaen's "second mode of limited transpositions".

In accordance with Bartók's logic it is natural that in the melody of the Violin Concerto (see again Ex. 5) the more traditional introductory sections of a diatonic general impression, formed from the modes of I. 7°, should be followed by less simple formations of a virtually chromatic effect, concentrated around the "dissonant" penultimate sections:

    \* alpha formula (structurally its tonal centre could be E, but due to the antecedents, here we are more inclined to accept D);

    \*\* 1:2 model segment: d-c-b-[a]-g sharp-f sharp;

    \*\*\* 1:2 model segment.

We may already here advance that the modes of II. 7°, and to a less extent those of III. 7° assume significance in the course of the variations.

The cadence of bar 8, marked by \*\*\*\* in Ex. 5 is of such an incomplete tonal system that it may be identified with more than one mode; e.g. hypo-aeolian or phrygian (even though the melody lacks precisely B flat and A flat). The chordal accompaniment in any case supports the G phrygian mode. This constitutes a typical instance of Bartók's polymodal "strategy" (Ex. 7): the beginning and end of the theme are lydian and phrygian with identical tonal centres, representing the strongest possible contrast (they would complement each other into a twelve-tone field, having only the prime and the fifth in common), while at the same time the imperfect cadence and the beginning of the second half with two fresh modes, present the most harmonic bimodal relationship (D aeolian and dorian).

Ex. 7

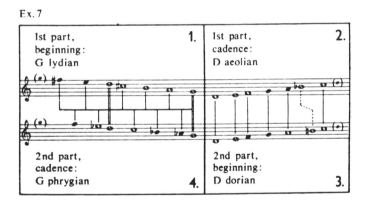

A different depiction of the tonal events of these first 8 bars (Ex. 8) offers a survey of the fact that in addition to the fast sequence of events of the modes and tonal centres embodied in the various sections, the ex-

302

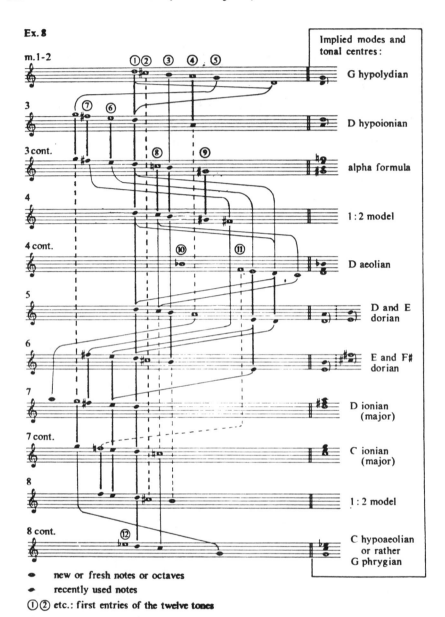

Ex. 8

- new or fresh notes or octaves
- recently used notes
①② etc.: first entries of the twelve tones

ploitation of the 12 pitches is not naively "folksong-like" either. The number and manner in which the 12 tones placed in the 19 different concrete pitch positions are assigned a role reveal veritable compositional tactics. They are by far not of equal rank, only the D opening the melody is present in all the sections, otherwise a still unused tone, or one used relatively farther back is determinant in the shaping of each new modal-tonal surface.

It is not by chance that up till the very last bar Bartók had fresh melodic tones in reserve, and that the tones appearing as ⑩ ⑪ and ⑫ respectively, are precisely the determinative tones of the modes of the imperfect and perfect cadences. In this polymodal melodic style, instead of a deliberate or instinctive equalization of the 12 tones, the aim is rather to create a constructive equilibrum, in which the extremes are: *common tones* (frequently applied, and of a decreasing information value), and *distinct tones* (rarely heard, and bringing turns at important points). Some of the characteristics include the great amplitudes in the frequency ratio (max. 1 : 17, see Ex. 9) of the altogether 82 notes of the 8-bar melody (9+9+13+11; 9+9+12+10); the only medium frequency of the appearance of tone G that represents the basic tonality; and the very choice of the frequent resp. non-recurring tones in this tonal system.

303

Ex. 9

Finally, for a better understanding of the variations, the interval characteristics of the melody of the theme may form the subject of special observation. To study this in accordance with Bartók's logic, who analyzed and compared thousands of folksongs, one should equally consider the *successive intervals* on the one hand, and the fictitious *"out-line intervals"* on the other, that serve to accentuate, and provide a framework for the various connected melodic phrases (melodic lines, motives, etc.). In this melody, for example, all the 12 intervals not greater than one octave may be ascertained (Ex. 10), but only half of them appear as successive intervals (in the first half of the melody the 5-semiton [perfect fourth], in the second half the 7-semiton [perfect fifth] being significant of them), while the other six are present as the outline intervals of the individual melodic sections, with the lydian fourth (6), the octave (12) and the diminished octave, serving as the framework of the alpha formula (11), being especially characteristic.

**Ex. 10**

$\frac{1}{2}$ **tones**

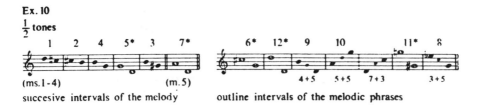

succesive intervals of the melody     outline intervals of the melodic phrases

*Chordal accompaniment.* The "accompaniment" surrounding the exposition of the melodic theme resembles the mature Bartókian technique of folksong arrangements. This is primarily evident in the fact that the harmonies clearly originate from the characteristic features of the melody, and refer back to them, that is, similar characteristics are present in a horizontal and vertical elaboration, correlating with each other. From a harmonic point of view the accompaniment of the violin theme is simple in sections where, through its modal and tonal characteristic, the melody itself is simple too, and wherever the melody becomes more complex, the accompaniment also becomes richer and more dissonant, through similar means. Bar 1, setting the tonality already before the opening of the theme, for example, lays down the D major tonality, by equally starting from D downwards, and foreshadowing the melodic contour to be heard immediately afterwards (Ex. 11a). The chordal realm then first lays down the lydian character (Ex. 11b). The melodic alpha formula and 1 : 2 model of the two following bars are given an exact correlation in the bass passage of the cello (Ex. 11c).

**Ex. 11**

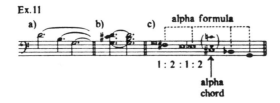

The melodic modulation taking place in the melody of bars 6—7 (from D-dorian to E-dorian and from E-dorian to F sharp-dorian) finds a respond, in a logical manner, in the simultaneous bitonality between the melody and the harmonic accompaniment. The instance of the two last bars of the theme, also repeated in the *tutti*, is especially interesting, providing as it does a veritable key to Bartók's conception of harmonic

contrasts. The theoretical basis of the first harmonization lies in the successive polymodality within the melody, with the extension of the relevant
alterations to the polyphonic fabric. A strongly linear 4-part writing ensues (Ex. 12a), in which two, or indeed, more simultaneous modes logically shape their own parts, and they are linked to the leading melody
mainly by negation, i.e. by the immediate alteration of its mode. Here
acoustically dissonant chords, e.g. diminished triads (bar 8, I, II), augmented triad (bar 9, I) occur on beats, whereas the "acoustic" dominant
seventh originates almost accidentally, on the weakest up-beat. — Another
characteristic of the same two bars of the melody lies in the periodic
procession of pedal-tones of the melodic wave-line (a-g-f-e flat), and the
chain of fourths and fifths embedded in the melody. This is expressed
with an elemental simplicity in the chain of dominant sevenths in the
*tutti* recapitulation (Ex. 12b), perhaps deliberately reminiscent of Zoltán
Kodály, constituting a total contrast after the two previous chromatic
bars (not only in its tonal structure but metrically as well, since the basic
rhythm of three times 3/8 = 9/8 is counterpointed here by the 2/4 cycle
of the accompaniment.)

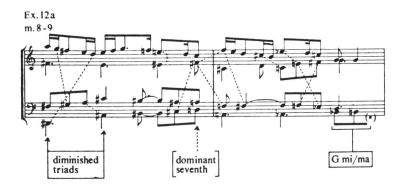

Ex. 12a
m. 8-9

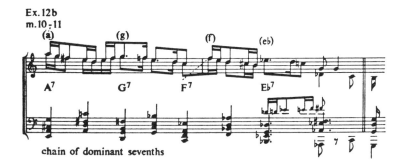

Ex. 12b
m. 10-11

This bass passage of the *tutti* bars, interchanging fourth and fifth intervals, as a motivically independent element of the logical harmonic projection of the melody, is in the following variations assigned a role in the variation of the melody itself, too.

## II. *The Variation of Tonal Structure*

In the course of the theme, its six variations and its recapitulation[18] — that is the metamorphosis of the theme taking place in eight sections during the movement — the opening of the melody at the beginning of the various sections forecasts with the sensitivity of a barometer the changes in the tonal structure. As it is summed up in the comprehensive table (Ex. 13), apart from the recapitulation there are no two variations opening with the same mode and scale characteristics. One might even say that in contrast to the classical types of the Theme and Variations, here it is not the tonal, harmonic and thematic substance which is constant (and in comparison to which the figuration, the character and many other features undergo variation), but it is above all the tonal structure itself that forms the subject of variation. This variation, however, is not simply a traditional "variation" bearing the token of a search for variety, but a logical, disciplined and methodical "modification". Here Bartók's strategy is based on a few axiomatic principles which can be theoretically formulated as the following:

(1) Of the modes of the heptatonia prima, the exposition of the lydian, emphasizing the critical "tense" augmented fourth, makes it logical to further stretch the central chain of major seconds, that is, to arrive at the heptatonia secunda (var. II), and indeed, in way of its further development, at the heptatonia tertia (e.g. var. VI), as in one direction the final point (see Ex. 13).

(2) At the same time the presence of the heptatonia secunda not only involves the further expansion of the chain of major seconds, but also implies, as the accomplishment of the other characteristic section, that the 1 : 2 model assumes independence. (Var. III after var. II).

---

[18] For brevity's sake, this study will use the following obvious terms in referring to the formal sections of the score divided by double lines but given no serial numbers of variations:

| | |
|---|---|
| THEME, bars 1—11 | VAR. IV, bars 58—82 |
| VARIATION I, 12—22 | VAR. V, 83—104 |
| VAR. II, 23—42 | VAR. VI, 105—117 |
| VAR. III, 43—57 | RECAPITULATION, 118—127 |

Ex. 13

Characteristic beginnings of the theme

307

(3) The scale characteristics which in the theme are isolated far from each other, attract one another, and by cumulating at the beginning of the melody, gradually add "dissonance" to it. (Theme: the alpha formula is still at a distance of 2 bars; var. I: the first phrase is joined by an alpha formula, creating a dissonant cadence, as it were; var. II: advancing even further, the alpha formula gets inserted into the first bar of the theme, before the cadence.)

Gradual and directional modification plus contrast principle, as two driving forces of the change of tonal structure, interestingly coincide with the basic tonality plan of the individual variations (Ex. 14).

Ex. 14

According to this there are three types of relationship between the tonal centres of two adjacent sections:

(1) identical tonal centres (TH + I; V + VI);

(2) the achievement of related centres by circling round the axis of minor thirds in a descending direction (I + II; IV + V; VI + REC);

(3) an unexpected relationship that stands out dissonantly from the chain (II // III; III // IV).

The relationship between the neighbouring sections with identical tonal centres may be compared to the *double* principle of Baroque music, naturally achieved by Bartókian means. After the above mentioned overwhelmingly diatonic character of the Theme variation I is determined by melodic chromaticism.[19] In the case of variations V and VI the chromatic crowdedness arising from the complementary structure of the 1 : 2 models is counterbalanced by the spaced scales of II. 7°, and even III. 7°. Systematically they supplement each other in Bartók's music in the same way as the *minore* supplements the *maggiore*, or the version embellished with chromatic ornamentations supplements the simple melodic form in Bach. In the modification of tonal structure the real contrast appear exactly at the dissonant links of the basic tonality chain. After

[19] Bartók described his own chromatic style in great detail, and concretely used the expression "this kind of melodic chromaticism" (*Bartók Essays*, 380, NB the music example selected by the editor of the *Essays* from the 2nd movement of the String Quartet No. 4 is the most unfortunate possible illustration, since it serves mostly as an example precisely of traditional chromaticism).

*Studia Musicologica Academiae Scientiarum Hungaricae 19, 1977*

variation II, abounding in acoustic scales, the chromaticism of variation III, having the effect of a free twelve-tone chromatic style, brings a profound contrast (even though this chromaticism constitutes the jointing of two 1 : 2 model scales). And after this variation the "Hungarian notturno" opening of variation IV, with pentatonic trichord phrases in the bass (driving the 1 : 2 model back into the ornamentation) once again presents a tremendous contrast.

However, looking now beyond the bars characteristically determining the beginning of the various variations, the development process of the tonal structure is, of course, much more complicated than indicated in Ex. 13. By way of example, let us point to variation II. *Un poco più tranquillo* which, with the two-note invocation of the horn, and the acoustic scale passages rolled on the harp, conveys an exceptionally lovely "landscape", related somewhere to the wild forest of the Cantata profana. Here, despite the above analyzed crowdedness of the events in the headphrase (the exposed appearance of II. 7°, the embedding of the alpha formula in the middle of the first phrase), the complexity becomes essentially resolved after one phrase. Incidentally, in this variation the violin theme consists of 3 and not 4 phrases each, and during the first three phrases the fourth structure gradually assumes the leading role (Ex. 15). While in the original theme the first stanza was taken by a sequence of events that may be characterized by the labels simple →simple →complex→cadence, with relation to the tonal system the three phrases of the same section here can be symbolized rather as a chain of complex → simpler→simplest — and it hardly needs any analysis to see what decisive consequences this complete remodelling involves.

309

Ex. 15

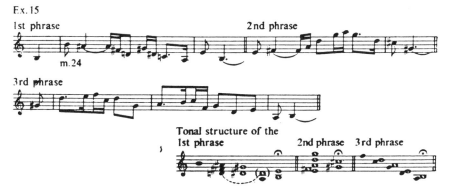

The tonal modification of the violin theme in the second half of variation II shows a no less strikingly marked deviation from the corresponding section of the original theme (Ex. 16). The dorian sections beginning with perfect fifth steps are here replaced by a tritone opening of the 4th and 5th phrases. Compared to each other, the two phrases are characterized by the extension of these intervals, without exactly corresponding with some known scale.[20] Finally, the 6th, closing phrase places all the characteristics of the original 2 closing bars of the theme (polymodality, terrace descent, fourth-fifth intervals) into a new relationship, amidst a chromatic descent in which the major-minor chords and the fourth chord keep periodically interchanging at descending grades.

**Ex. 16**

The modification of the last phrase of the original theme in each variation is incidentally just as significant and purposeful with Bartók as that of the opening motive. Already the first variation raises the separation of the fourth-fifth intervals (Ex. 17a) and that of an alpha formula (Ex. 17b), and their isolation for further development. In variation II, as

[20] Although the 4th phrase — in a tempered scale with enharmonic notation — is conceivable also in a 1 : 2 model, let us note Bartók's correct notation for the string instrument: below b, above b flat and c flat (that is, diminished octave and diminished ninth). And the 5th phrase can go into the system of heptatonia secunda only if we disregard the notes g sharp-d.

we have seen (Ex. 16), Bartók periodically interchanged these two phenomena in a vertical condensation. At the same place in variation III the solo violin plays solely alpha formulae at the descending terraces of an axis of minor thirds, in fortissimo double-stops (Ex. 18). Variation IV,

Ex. 18

m.54-55 etc.

in which Bartók remodelled the full second half of the theme from a *Lied*-style articulation into a continuous contrapuntal texture, includes at this place a section expanding in the number of parts, and turning from contrary motion to parallel motion (see Ex. 19; for simplicity's sake we have omitted the gradually disappearing contrary motion from the music example). The "moderator" of the section is a completely original 24-note scale, which employs all three of the diatonic systems (I. 7°, II. 7°, III. 7°), in such a manner that before the firm establishment of the various tonal sensations (because the beginning e.g. seems to set E flat major) it immediately modifies the scale. A special word should be added here about the fact — since so far one has not even surmised this phenomenon to exist in Bartók — that Bartók, by asserting his polymodal principles, in certain moments reached the *negation of tonal identity of octaves* (in this scale, for example, precisely in the case of the most significant, opening tone, there is a chain of non-octave periodization: e flat$^2$ . . . e$^1$ . . . d sharp$_1$ . . . d$_2$!)

311

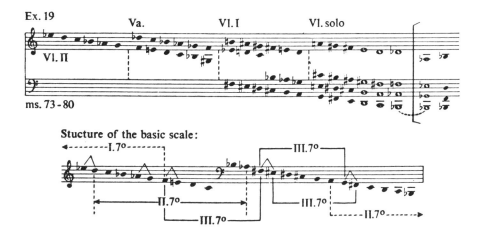

Ex. 19

Va.   VI. I   VI. solo

VI. II

ms. 73 - 80

Stucture of the basic scale:

I.7°   III.7°

II.7°   III.7°

III.7°   II.7°

Similarly original scales may be found at the corresponding place of
variation VI (bars 113—115): different combinations of the traditional
1 : 1 chromaticism and the typically Bartókian 1 : 2 set are to be found
here, such as for example 1 : 1 : 2, 1 : 1 : 1 : 2 etc.

All the phenomena pointed out so far still show a purposeful *planning*
and seem to be individual compositional *decisions* of a structural value.
Here I end this chapter of my analysis, because a more detailed *description*
of what can be found in the score would threaten with listing examples of
the vocabulary of Bartók's harmony, which has already been done in the
analyses of E. Lendvai and others — instead of outlining the individual
strategy of an individual composition.

### III. *The Variation of Phrase Structure*

The almost provokingly simple, song-like phrase structure of the
theme is the starting point of a variation process which — regarding its
principles, dimensions and high quality — may be considered unparalleled
even among the great 20th century variation movements of Schoenberg,
Webern and Stravinsky. Naturally this is not simply a question of varying
"phrase structure". It is the form itself, the formal characteristics of the
various sections of the movement which are essential here, since the
phrase variation is not restricted to its own scale, but is carried out in a
functional manner, in the interest of remodelling higher units. Nevertheless, the examination is more faithful to Bartók's spirit if it does not start
out from the *interpretation* of large scale formal functions which in the
final analysis can be only verbally surmised and circumscribed, but from
the systematic *description* of a quasi-monophonic music. It is as if we had
to define folksong stanzas and melodic variants analytically.

First of all let us recall the theme constituting bars 2—11 of the score,
the actual structure of the phrases of the melody, and let us emphasize,
as significant phenomena, the following:

— although the first and second halves of the theme are both of a
length of 4 bars, but according to its motivic content the music shows
the following structure: $a^1 + a^2 + b$ and $c^1 + c^2 + d$ respectively,
each of 3 phrases, where $b$ and $d$ are of double bars;

— the originally 8-bar theme is supplemented at the beginning and
the end by accessory elements, affixed to it already at its first appearance; of which the introduction bar $(i)$ is of secondary significance, while the recapitulation of the $d$ phrase in a variation form
(in different harmonization, with different rhythmic accent, dy-

312

namics and instrumentation) is of truly primary importance, because it lends — not in its motives but in its tonal mass! — a sort of *Stollen-Stollen-Abgesang Barform* impression to the whole exposition of the theme.

Now, the mere presence of the rigidly quadruple kernel of the theme and the two structural "irregularities" pointed to above, foreshadow some natural endeavours in Bartók's workshop, a strategy which was to be applied by all means:

(1) The simple ratios (1, 2, 4, 8) of the quadruple theme, as a position of stability, had to be followed by more asymmetrical proportions in general; furthermore, a differentiation in the length of the corresponding phrases was to be expected both in the case of the neighbouring phrases, and in relation to phrases of similar positions from the first and second halves of the melody, and indeed, even in comparing the two halves of the theme to each other.

(2) The "four-line" stanza proportions as the most static situation, stemming from the three-motive composition of the lines, had to be followed

313

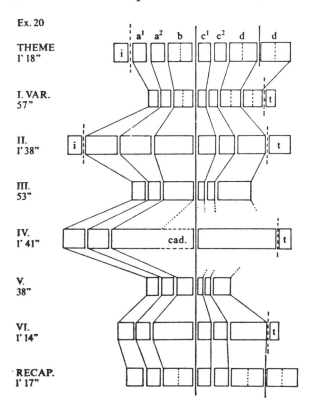

by a structure which would "divide into three parts" based on a phrase structure of equal or approximately equal rank, according to the motives $a^1$-$a^2$-$b$ and $c^1$-$c^2$-$d$.

(3) It was to be expected that the two halves of the theme would be flanked by extensions $(i = $ introductory, $t = $ transitory bar[s]); it was also to be expected that the extensions might also be embedded, with an "interlude" character, between the various phrases; and finally, that the existence, omission and character of the *Abgesang*-like climax resp. shift in style become the subject of further variations.

The realization of (1) and (2) of these strategies is demonstrated in Ex. 20 and Ex. 21. Ex. 20, taking into consideration Bartók's durata data, proportionately projects the rough surfaces of the eight consecutive sections of the movement: one can trace through the modifications of proportions, the 4 or 3-section divisions, the $i$ and $t$ extensions, and the presence or lack of the repeated $d$ *(Abgesang)* phrase. Ex. 21 merely serves to indicate the exact numerical length of the phrases, thus rendering them comparable (in cases where the bar constitutes the unit, in bars, in case of changing metres, in eighth- or fourth-notes offering themselves as common denominators).

314

Ex. 21

| | | (intr.) | $a^1$ | $a^2$ | b | $c^1$ | $c^2$ | d | d | (trans.) |
|---|---|---|---|---|---|---|---|---|---|---|
| THEME | bar | (1) | 1 | 1 | 2 | 1 | 1 | 2 | 2 | |
| I. VAR. | bar | | 1 | 1 | 2 | $1^{21)}$ | 1 | 2 | 2 | (1) |
| II. | ♪ | (9) | 20 | 20 | 26 | 12 | 12 | 19 | | (15) |
| III. | ♪ | | 15 | 15 | 35 | 9 | 9 | 36 | | |
| IV. | ♩ | | 10 | 10 | 24+4 | ⊢——43——⊣ | | | | (6) |
| V. | ♪ | | 27 | 30 | 42 | 15 | 15 | 42 | | |
| VI. | ♩ | | 6 | 6 | 18 | 6 | 6 | 16 | | (4) |
| RECAP. | bar | | 1 | 1 | 2 | 1 | 1 | 2 | 2 | |

The collation of the two diagrams and Bartók's score, naturally shows countless phenomena which may be designated as being of structural significance. In my appraisal the really important ones seem to be the following:

*Variation I*, indeed, is a *double*. It preserves the 9/8 metre,[21] the phrase structure and the proportions of the theme, although the role of $i$ is replaced by that of $t$ (which is made necessary by the modulation).

[21] Although bar 16 is in 12/8 time, it is nothing else but the '-caesura written out between the two halves of the melody.

With *variation II* the homogeneous metre disappears, the rigid repeat of the *d* phrase is omitted, *b* is diminishing compared to $a^1$ and $a^2$, and thus the first half of the theme assumes approx. ternary form (20 : 20 : 26; this tendency becomes weaker in the second half of the theme). In another context, $c^1$-$c^2$ is diminishing as compared to $a^1$-$a^2$, and the second part is altogether shorter. Or more exactly, it is more concise, because the interlude motives between the melodic phrases of the violin solo, which are exposed by the harp, and then by the harp and celesta (one assuming an individual rhythmic profile through the rolling semi-quaver triplets, the other through the even semiquaver or quaver scales) are here omitted.

*Variation III* maintains the diminishing tendency between the first and second halves of the theme, but the 3rd phrases within the two halves becomes more and more pointedly lengthened at the expense of the 1st and 2nd phrases (15 + 15 < 35, 9 + 9 ≪ 36; the two halves: 65 > 54, but within this 35 < 36). The proportions of the whole variation are placed, in the final analysis, in a new light by the new texture starting in bar 54 which is of a strong *Abgesang* effect.

*Variation IV* represents the extreme point of removal from the original *Lied* structure. Here the first and second halves are of such differing characters, motives and texture that Bartók even accentuates this by the tempo as well as by the strongest caesura of the whole movement (at the end of the first half the pulsation of the rhythm comes to a stand-still, the violin plays a short solo cadence, and the "measurability" of the length of the phrases is suspended). The whole conception of the second half is extreme, essentially — through the elaborated imitation — terminating the divisions into phrases, and the tracable character of the original $c^1$-$c^2$-$d$ motives.[22]

*Variation V* opens the road back towards more regular forms and phrasing. The proportions of variation III are repeated, as it were (while the technique of the interlude motives embedded between the phrases recalls variation II), with the difference that here in the first half the gradual increase is accentuated (27 : 30 : 42), while *b* and *d* this time are exactly identical (42 = 42).

In *variation VI* the proportion of the phrases continues to acquire an "angular character", since motives *a* and *c* are already of 6 quarter notes each, and the two halves of the theme are nearly identical in length.

[22] Theoretically it may of course be demonstrated that $c^1$=bar 69 from the vl.solo entry; $c^2$=bar 72 vl.solo; *d*=approx. bar 73 from the scale texture beginning in vl. II.

In the *Recapitulation* — apart from the lack of bar *i* — the original phrase structure becomes restored, the proportions once again are quadruple, *d* is again repeated, even if this time not as a tutti with an *Abgesang* effect, but in way of a lyrical coda.

Surveying this process and seeing it on the scale of the movement form, the *deviation—re-approach* model of Theme < variation IV > Recapitulation, as a compositional design, is most consistently realized with regard to the variation of the length of the phrases. There is, however, another point of departure — no less authentic from the point of view of Bartók's variation logic — for the interpretation of the phrase structure: the examination of the *metrical schemes* employed in the movement. A mere catalogue of the elements — lifted from the laws of Bartók's rhythmic realm as a whole — would not lead us far, since it represents no kind of entirety, and the point chosen for departure (the 9/8 metre) is unique rather than typical in Bartók. It is more worth while to study the general metric character of the variations, drawing from the supposition that with Bartók stable metres create a more static situation, while combined metres a more dynamic one in unfolding the length of the phrases, and indeed, within this, in that of the motivic lengths too. Because, who is familiar with his ethnomusicological rhythm analyses and systematizations, must presume that for Bartók as a composer it was not only the spontaneously arising ("inspired") motives that marked out their combined or stable metres, but sometimes it was the other way round: a previously decided metrical scheme defined the rhythm and phrase structure of the thematic material to be formulated. From this point of view there are three levels, three intensity-grades of the quiet or restless development of the length of phrases in the movement (Ex. 22):

Ex. 22

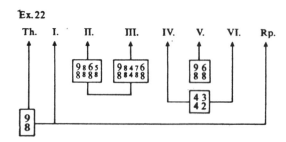

(1) The 9/8 static basic layer:[23] represented by the Theme, its *double* variation I and the Recapitulation.

[23] We have already spoken of bar 16 in 12/8 time as agogic 9/8.

(2) Interchanging 9/8 and 6/8 as the main metric schemes, coloured with further contracted bars (9/8 > 8/8, 7/8; 6/8 > 5/8) and different divisions of a bar:[24] represented by the block of variations II—III, however, with a great tempo and character contrast in comparison to each other.

(3) A ternary symmetrical block out of variations IV—V—VI, with a fast movement (var. V) in the middle, in duple and triple time, both compound (9/8, 6/8), while the two slower sections preceding and following it consist of triple and quadruple time, both simple (3/2, 4/4).[25]

Ex. 23

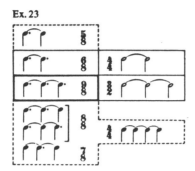

Now it already becomes worth while to register the metric schemes thus employed dramaturgically in the movement, in a systematic manner (Ex. 23). The kernel of the stock of metres is formed by triple and duple time, both compound and simple (rather similar to the *tempus perfectum* and *tempus imperfectum*, both with *prolatio maior* as well as *prolatio minor*) — and this also constitutes the centuries old basic stock of European art music, in this context almost Renaissance rather than Viennese classical. In Bartók's rhythmic semiology the 9/8 starting metre is not at all a folk music type. At the same time the rest of the bars surrounding the four central metres — according to Bartók's rhythmic logic — essentially constitute their *diminution* (actually this is how they appear one after the other, at the *contracted repeat* of a complete form). This practice of diminution and rhythmic modification, on the other hand, became consciously implanted in Bartók's music, as a result of his experiences drawn from peasant music.[26] There is at least one conclusion worth drawing

---

[24] Bars 48—49 are in 8/8 and 4/4 time, respectively, because they are of subdivisions 3+3+2 and 2+2+2+2.

[25] Bar 68 in variation IV, owing to the solo cadenza, is essentially a bar with a fermata; in the transitional section at the end of the variation (79—82) the types of metre characteristic of the variation undergo diminution, giving rise to 3/4, 2/4.

[26] *Bartók Essays,* 391—392.

from this, namely that in a movement, which presents variations of a theme that in all other respects is so much of a *Lied* type, and indeed, shows expressedly folksong-features, Bartók links the original form of the theme with a non-folk musical metre and rhythm, and when, in the course of the variations, the theme becomes increasingly complex and individual, he evokes the metric and rhythmic styles also to be found in folk music.

In conclusion, to focus the analysis from the metric scheme to a catalogue of the employed rhythmic values, the question of the *shortest rhythmic value* of each section (variation) deserves attention, followed by a second question: whether this movement includes any "ornamental

**Ex. 24**

embellishment" at all. The bulk of the movement simply does not contain any uncontrolled, short rhythmic values emerging for the sake of ornamentation, anything of the kind which would correspond with the inclination for embellishment and overabundance in instrumental folk music performance. The semiquaver as the shortest value, remains thematic throughout the Theme, variations I and III, and the Recapitulation. In variation V the harp glissando (noted in small type or as semiquaver sextola) is actually negligible. In variation II the sixteenth triplet passage is not ornamental either, but thematically independent (forming the countersubject of the harp). Disregarding the two cadential sixteenth triplets of bar 56, ornamental embellishments actually appear only in those two sections (variations IV and VI, see Ex. 24) where the shortest value of the thematic rhythm is longer than in the other sections of the movement,[27] that is, where the ornamental embellishment is clearly of a structural determination representing a way of rhythmic variation.

[27] It is worth registering that the 1/4 : 1/32 proportion of var. IV exactly corresponds with the 1/8 : 1/64 note rhythmic difference of principal note —shortest ornament in var. VI, so that this, too, affiliates the two variations.

To avoid any possible misunderstanding, mainly in the interest of readers of non-Hungarian musical mother tongue, while speaking about rhythmic styles let us add that the two different *poco rubato* variations in the movement (I, III) do not intend to refer to any concrete folk music rubato, any parlando-rubato style that was known to Bartók. It was naturally in the wake of the repeatedly recurring folk music inspiration that the parlando-like performance itself assumed countless forms and stylistic variants in his music. But these two rubatos — one of a sighing-choking tone, the other with its loud declamation and crying — represent individual intonations stemming from a high level stylization. Fortunately we know fairly exactly the extent and shade of the poco rubato Bartók had in mind, since the world première performed by Zoltán Székely, whom he coached and who came to know thoroughly his intentions, is perfectly authentic in this regard too, and it is accessible for study.[28]

## IV. *The Variation of Instrumental Groups*

319

The evaluation of the instrumentation for a traditional symphonic orchestra forms one of the delicate spheres of the examination of Bartók's music. Up to his Concerto for Orchestra, a kind of ponderosity — interchanging with scintillating ideas — was undoubtedly present in Bartók (in *tutti* sections of a traditional full orchestra; in heavy doubling; in the somewhat clumsy treatment of certain instruments etc). It is equally obvious that he instinctively composed more originally for strings or a combination of strings and percussion. Now, however, let us restrict the analysis to our subject, and let us start by stating that Bartók's scoring shows a well perceptible side-line development in the sequence of major scores in which he methodically dealt with *timbre* by dividing his orchestra into instrumental blocks, isolated and contrasting each other, and finally uniting in a *tutti*. In this respect the Piano Concertos Nos 1 and 2 assume special significance through the elaboration of the isolated treatment of the winds and strings, the contraposition of the piano and one of the groups, the principle of a reduced orchestra in the middle movement, the confrontation of the exposition and recapitulation with the help of their instrumentation or the performing manner of identical groups of instru-

[28] The world première of the concert at the Amsterdam Concertgebow on March 23, 1939 (conducted by W. Mengelberg) was recorded on a lacquer disc by Hilversum Radio; the Budapest Hungaroton company released it as an LP in 1971 (LPX 11573).

ments, etc. The first and third movements of the Violin Concerto do not even necessarily represent a step forward after the piano concertos. The situation, however, is different with the second movement. As regards its instrumentation it constitutes one of Bartók's best works, and not only because of its faultless perfection, but mainly because the principles it embodies are already virtually un-Bartók-like in foreshadowing the purposefulness, the permutations and the graphic ideas of the serial composers.

Naturally, the Theme and Variations form in itself would explain this profusion of colours, *timbre* combinations and the grades and shades of density and relaxation of texture. But perhaps it was just the other way round: Bartók wanted to write a symphonic work of a variation form amongst others just because he intended to try out new possibilities, splendid sound and timbre combinations, and a new system of their relationships.[29]

What makes the instrumental ensemble of the second movement worthy of attention lies by no means in the fact that it is more restricted than those of the Ist and IIIrd movements (the lack of the English horn, the double bassoon, the trumpets, the trombones and certain percussion), but in the combination of the instruments employed. Similarly to some particularly exquisite Stravinsky or Webern scores, here Bartók too, uses only a single *tutti* position: two bars at the end of the introduction of the theme, in a manner that recalls Kodály. The 12 winds, all the parts of the string section, as well as the harp and the timpani (surrounding the soloist as chief *Klangfarben* instruments in way of a "continuo" as it were) are all playing here, even if not throughout. (On the other hand, the celesta, the triangle and the side drum remain silent.) The other 125 bars include only different segments, one may safely say, colour-spectra of this *tutti*.

[29] It is of no minor interest what details Bartók referred to in two relevant letters after Spivakovsky's performance in October 1943: „ . . . I wanted to hear the performance of my violinconcerto which I yet never heard from orchestra. The performance was really excellent: soloist, conductor, orchestra were first rate (and the composer too!), the orchestration proved to have no mistakes" (to Wilhelmine Creel on December 17, 1945, in English). "The thing I was most pleased with was that there is nothing wrong with the orchestration. Nothing has to be altered in it. And yet, precisely an orchestral 'accompaniment' to the violin is a most delicate thing" (to Joseph Szigeti on January 30, 1944, in Hungarian). It is unlikely that Bartók would have been concerned only about whether the violin solo came into full display. If he had been anxious he must have been concerned for the concept of the violin concerto, because the orchestral section was too independent, of a much too symphonic texture.

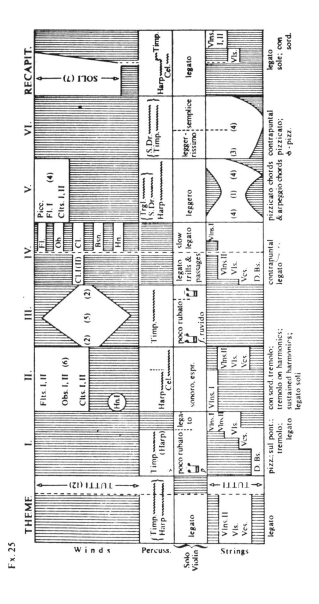

Fx. 25

321

Let us try with the help of a diagram (Ex. 25) to survey the pattern of the instrumental formations of the score of the 8-section movement, because in this way the contrasts and correspondences, the formations suggesting almost a graphical provenience, become more conspicuous. Some of the contrasts — mainly the rests for complete groups of instruments — become immediately evident, calling attention to certain symmetrical correspondences:

Winds suspended: Theme till the *tutti;* variations I and VI;
Strings suspended: first half of the Recapitulation and var. III;
Percussion etc. suspended: var IV;
Solo violin suspended: Tutti of the Theme.

Closer study of the score will establish that all the formations within the groups of instruments and all the variations are unique in this movement, they are not exactly repeated anywhere. Some of the characteristics are listed below.

*Woods.* Significant soloistic positions: horn at the beginning of var. II, Bartók's "nature" invocation motive; clarinet (later bass clarinet) in the first half of var. IV with dotted rhythm, as a symbol of the "Hungarian" *Lento* intonation. There are five kinds of ensemble formation, sharply differing both in the number of parts and the character of the texture. Var. II: a chordal sextet with two Flts, Obs, Clts each. Var. V: a quartet of Picc, Fl and 2 Clts with virtuoso passages. Var. III: A bell-shaped *cresc.—decresc.* texture between bars 43—53, with a minimum of 2, and a maximum of 5 woods playing simultaneously; the ff-dim-pp progression of bars 54—57 is joined by another textural decrescendo with 5—3—2—1 woods. Var. IV, second half: imitation of a player each of the five woods as a counterpoint of the strings. Recapitulation: accompanying texture with little motion, generally with 3 parts each, employing 7 solo instruments.

*Percussion and harp.* Each appearance of all the instruments in various combinations represents a new style of performance or technique, except the naturally strongly accentuated correspondence between the first and last 2 notes of the timpani part. The timpani itself, for example, vary five idioms (traditional cadential figure on 2 drums in piano, tritone cadential figures on 2 drums with continuous pedal tuning in pianissimo,

[20] We may primarily think of the interpretations of Stefi Geyer, Jelly Arányi, Adila Arányi (Mrs. Fachiri), Imre Waldbauer, Joseph Szigeti, Zoltán Székely, Ede Zathureczky and André Gertler, with whom Bartók played music in a really intensive manner.

pedal tremolo, etc.). The harp presents even more kinds of performing styles, altogether ten of them. As regards combination, the echo imitation of the *col legno* timpani and the side drum in bars 105ff is particularly original, in the way they continue to echo the so-called Bartók pizzicato of the strings, slapped on the finger-board, and its reverberation in the solo violin's *ricochet* staccato-repetitions.

*Tutti Strings.* In all the seven sections of the movement where strings were given a role, they are present with ensembles of differing formations, as regards the number of actively playing parts, the nature of terraced or gradual entries and exits. Here the deliberate variation of the performing style is even more obvious, and it is not even the great diversity of legatos, pizzicatos, tremolos, flageolets, etc., and the large number of isolable string timbres which is most striking, but partly the originality of certain transformations and discolourations within the variation (e.g. var. I), and partly those constructive correspondences which — even by the means of technical idioms — support with this parameter a higher structural aspect (e.g. the correspondence of the contrapuntal legato and the contrapuntal pizzicato between variations IV and VI). It is not by chance that the string player is reminded of the concentration of certain micromovements of Webern when, e.g. in variation II, the 2nd violinists or the cellists bow only a single important note, or the viola players perform a single motive.

*Solo Violin.* It has been left to the end, because it is self-evident that in the eight sections of the movement, or — if we add the stylistic shifts of an *Abgesang* effect at the end of certain variations — even in more sections, Bartók provides his soloist with about a dozen independent, brilliant performing styles of modern violin playing. The discussion of these would call for a professional violinist, if after reading the score a description is necessary at all. Nevertheless, there are two historical questions worth raising at this point. First, whether this solo part may be considered as the special style of a whole range of illustrious Hubay pupils,[30] as the *idiomatic* formulation of a composer well aware of their capabilities, also gauged in the performance of Bartók works — in other words, as a representative part revealing the merits of this school, and to be performed according to the natural interpretation of the exponents of this school? I would say yes, even though this style, this consensus should be considered not so much as a stimulus for Bartók's invention as rather a performing condition which considerably facilitates the authentic performance. Undoubtedly a young violinist now discovering the score, may study, as a supplementary document, the above mentioned recording of Zoltán Székely's world première, because it contains a great many absolutely authentic hints with regard to the true sense of certain instructions and conventions in interpretation, as well as the extent they should be adhered to in keeping with Bartók's taste.

The mentioning of Székely's name leads to the second question: whether we may consider this solo part, presenting a profusion of different performing manners, as one which, at least in some details, was tailor-made to fit the commissioner of the concerto. We have to leave the material part of the answer to Zoltán Székely. In way of a contribution to the fact that in similar cases it can always be documented that Bartók, at the stage of the final arrangement always listened to, and indeed, asked for, the opinion of some great violinists on technical issues relevant to the instrument[31] we may refer to two interesting aspects of the particella.[32] The first is of a "structural" nature: in the penultimate stage of the drafting of variation VI the leggerissimo figuration of the solo violin was still missing, and the soloist also was supposed to play some more simple, pizzicato material (Ex. 26a).[33] Is the final figuration an original compositional idea, or one that came to Bartók's mind while remembering the famous bowing and fast staccatos of the Hubay school? The second interesting feature may easily be considered a matter of performing detail, since it merely regards the slurs of the introduction of the theme. And yet it is of significance because, as compared to Bartók's conception as seen in the particella, the "corrected" version decided upon after the joint rehearsals in Paris (Ex. 26/b) might mean that Bartók thought this to be the proper form of scoring the exact performing style he heard from Székely during the rehearsal, and considered to be the ideal one. But an explanation for what exactly this style implies is provided by the document of the record of the world première performed by Székely.

[31] Let us refer to Bartók's correspondence with Menuhin with regard to the Solo Sonata, to the role of the Waldbauers before the finalization of Quartets Nos. 3 and 4, and the relevant letters of R. Kolisch, J. Szigeti and others to Bartók (several of these have been published by D. Dille in *Documenta Bartókiana* Heft 3, Budapest 1968).

[32] The version called *particella* is a *Lichtdruck* (Bartók, based on earlier sketches, wrote it on *Lichtpaus* paper and multiplied in a few copies, as most of his late manuscripts), with MS additions. This copy was used during the rehearsals with Zoltán Székely, and Bartók noted down in it the changes in two different coloured pencils, and by way of preparing the orchestration, he completed it with relevant detailed notes. It is preserved in the Budapest Bartók Archives, (BAB 4091/a); the second movement on pages 15 – 21 of the manuscript.

[33] The last lines on page 19 of the particella show this earlier form of the first 2 bars of the variation (for the vl. solo line see Ex. 26a), still without any dynamic and other instructions. On page 20 of the particella, i. e. in the new version, Bartók already marked the pizzicato in the lines of the orchestral accompaniment.

Ex. 26a

Ex. 26b
Particella:

Final sore:

Part.:

etc.

Score:

The art of instrumentation naturally is of much wider scope than planning out the variation of the instrumental blocks, the composition of the groups of instruments and the choice of the idiom of performance. It is precisely at this point that true artistic, intuitive activity begins. Yet, the present essay cannot undertake to analyze this, as its aim does not lie in reviewing the various marvellous solutions in Bartók's instrumentation, and it does not intend to draw up the typology of his instrumentation (this again would fall under the category of idiom and personal style which has to be examined in conjunction with many other scores). It only presents the supposedly most deliberate plan and strategy which become apparent in the operation with tone colours and in the motion of sound masses; a unique speciality which in such a highly developed form is peerless in Bartók's symphonic oeuvre.

Here the survey of the variations of tone *colour* should by all means be separated from the somewhat independent examination of the pitch *register* employed by Bartók, and in relation with this, the question of tonal *density* within the fulled up tone-bands.

## V. *The Variation of Register Formations*

At a number of points in the movement — for example at the beginning of new variations, at the end of variations, or at their linking points — certain characteristic register-positions, narrowing tone-bands, and curving tone-bands will attract attention even at first hearing. These make it obvious that at the time of writing this movement Bartók was more than usually occupied with ideas suggestive of Varèse, as regards the filling in of sound space and the moving of masses of sound. Such conspicuous moments suggesting a purposeful concept occur for example, at the end of Var. I at the encounter of the bands of descending and ascending string motions; after the horn invocation of var. II, in the position and parallel filling in of the 2nd and 3rd high octave bands in relation to the melody of the solo violin transferred to the bass; at the end of Var. V, in the upward curve of the complete moving tone-band, etc.

In addition to these two-dimensional phenomena in the score of the movement (which elicit a graphic association of horizontal surfaces or bands), there are other, equally striking features associating with mass relations. (Contrasts of density and transparency, even and uneven mass distributions, homogeneous mass, or mass made up of heterogeneous material, etc.) For example, listening to variation V — with the colour accompaniment of "noises" surrounding the violin part above and below — let us keep in mind that while in the case of a master of Schoenberg's type even in the most complex moments of part writing the individual tones are really "of equal rank" and "related only with one another" both horizontally and vertically in a homogeneous medium, Bartók in certain sections of this movement is in command of a musical space of nearly the same character as that of an electronic composer. Within this space filled in with sound, the various tones of completely differing origin are not authentically commensurable with the pitch component any more. The thematic parts composed of discrete tones are surrounded by other tonal events that cannot be appreciated in their pitch, but are perceivable in colour value, dynamics or the direction of motion.

As is generally known, Bartók's manifestations regarded his own music show no trace of such explications, and it would be really unfounded to give a tendentious ultra-progressive interpretation to the main aspirations of Bartók's music as a whole. Nevertheless, the features that may be registered in the second movement of the Violin Concerto — which in many other respects was composed with special care — do factually confirm that here, perhaps to a greater extent than in his works of a more avant-garde tone and external features, Bartók forged far ahead, and reached certain abstractions in the problem of filling in music space.

Bartók undoubtedly fills in the tonal space with a consideration for twelve-tone system, and octave-identity in general. It is equally indubitable that not all the "clever" register positions suggesting purposefulness are cunning innovations. If in the Recapitulation the violin mel-

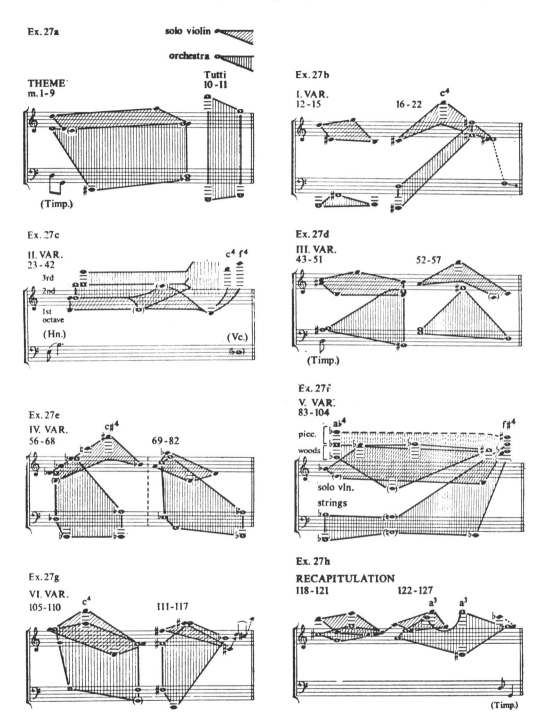

327

ody returns one octave higher, drawing along the whole accompaniment into the high octave, this in itself shows nothing novel, being, as it is, an old finesse of the classical and Romantic violin concerto. If in the course of the variation the composer employs the solo instrument, treble by nature, sometimes as the middle part, or in extreme cases, even as the bass (var. II), this in itself does not count yet as progression. But when even in the printed score Bartók had the word *sic* written in at the last note of the harp's left hand in the 35th bar (meaning that the note *b* was no printing error), this serves as a document for the fact that even at the cost of distorting the motive, the transgression of the solo violin's *b* as an absolute band limit, must be prevented!

The following diagrams (Ex. 27a—h), taking all the eight sections of the movement in turn, should be compared with the score by keeping in mind that — due to the pattern of depiction — perhaps even the self-evident and traditional exploitation of the registers may show here an "interesting" design. Proper care should also be taken not to consider the surfaces based on the extreme tones of the parts of the solo instrument and those of the orchestra as tone bands filled in with some kind of even density. And finally, no one should believe these designs either to a be composer's plan (since Bartók never sketched such outlines), or an exact depiction of events, because they only wish to survey the main tendencies, the decisive directions of shifts.

Notes to the exploitation of registers in the various sections of the movement.

*Theme.* Two traditional registers: reminiscent of the contrast between the *concertino* and *concerto grosso*. Here the broader register traditionally implies a proportionately greater part density and higher dynamic level.

*Variation I.* Two purposeful formations: (a) the band exploited during the introduction of the Theme (Vl. II, Va, Vlc.) is left empty, and (b) the high and low bands are approaching and encountering each other. The variation is also determined by the gradual modulation of tone colours, which, synchronized with the register approach, gradually leads from the unbridgeable colour contrast of treble and bass, through mixed colours of bars 16—17 *(sul pont.* Vlc. tremolo; *arco* D. Bs., etc.), to the homogeneous string *legato.*

*Variation II.* The opening strictly marks the function of the three octave bands: *1st octave* (b-b¹) is the octave of the melodic development of the theme on the solo violin (in bars 25—29 the Cl. reinforces the long notes of the violin); *2nd octave* (b-¹b²) is the register of the chordal accompaniment (woods) and the thematic counterpoint (harp); *3rd octave* (b²-b³), according to the logic of the complete reversion of the texture, is the quasi-bass (violin *con sord.* tremolo)! This at first rigid band arrangement becomes gradually loosened, allowing also for interesting register transpositions (e.g. bars 34—35—36 on the woods), yet Bartók does not violate the "rules" set by himself — as indicated also by the instruction *sic* in bar 35.

*Variation III.* The register plan is determined by the solo violin part. The dense and rough texture of the woodwind accompaniment, virtually verging on ugliness, also follows from the tonal density characteristic of the double stops on the violin.

*Variation IV.* Two isolated register formations, both of them traditional. As against the first section, thickened by two- and three-part octave doubling (filled in with sparse motion below, and with dense motion above), the second is of a homogeneous, contrapuntal texture with even mass distribution.

*Variation V.* Similarly to variation II, it shows a strict register scheme, with the thematic violin part in the middle; a plucked chordal accompaniment below (string-pizz. and harp arpeggio); and an interlude of motivic, or rather colour value above (4 woods, harp). The colour and noise materials moving in the low and high registers are linked together, as it were, by the rhythmic action of the two unpitched percussions (triangle, S. Dr.), belonging to both regions. The section also include several register formations which suggest "graphic" two-dimensional elements, as e.g. a "pyramid" (bar 84); a steep upward line followed by a slow descent (bars 88—89, 90—92, woods); the contraction of the register and part number of the string pizzicatos, and then their re-expansion (the narrowest point being at bar 90, already played only by Vlc); the narrowing and upward swing of the registers of all the instruments at the end of the variation (bars 101—104).

*Variation VI.* Two separated register formation, with a leading part rising from the thin pizzicato texture in both sections in a different style. In the last bars the upward motion of the pizzicatos and the descent of the legato part pierce through each other, and the *d-c sharp* motive, repeated one octave higher, virtually climbs out from this position (bar 117, with this the solo violin has regained its treble position). This repeat of the motive one octave higher can logically be repeated even higher: and here, in the high register, the recapitulation begins.

*Recapulation.* Contrary to the exposition of the theme, the launching of the register on a forced orbit is preceptible already in the first 4 bars, with a tendency to shrink it towards one point (one tone), a point where motion really stops. It is certainly also purposeful that in the last bars

Bartók recalls in retrograde motion certain memorable episodes of register, timbre or motives: bar 125, harp and celesta = var. II; bars 126—127, adherent string registers = var. I; end of bar 127, timpani = beginning of the movement.


## Conclusion

We started from the assumption that the second movement of the Violin Concerto constitutes one of Bartók's notable endeavours to break through the concept of symmetric bridge-form. It is justified therefore to collate the formative tendencies we came to recognize in the course of the examination of the various parameters of variation. Are the same strategies, tactics of development, main articulations and main climaxes being formulated on all levels? Has a new form "model" emerged in place of the bridge form?

The answer is an unequivocal no. We were able to isolate several plans, some of them contradictory. A sequence of "modulating" events, — uniformly deviating from, and then re-approaching the starting-point, with variation IV in the centre, — can clearly be ascertained (see phrase structure, Ex. 20). There is a four-section structure present, too, unfolding on three different levels (see metrical schemes, Ex. 22). A continuous and systematic deviation — disrupted by variations III and IV as an inner contrast enclave — is discernible (see tonal structure, Ex. 13). Even the faint outlines of the bridge (arch) symmetry may be traced by pairing the various tone colour blocks of instrumentation — the strings, woods and combined groups (see the correspondence between I and VI resp. II and V; contrast of III and IV resp. Theme and Recap., Ex. 25). In the movement of the register formations variations III and V mark a basically new articulation which is not organically joined with the antecedents (Ex. 27).

And finally the factor of *tempo*, that has been given little attention so far, should not be left out of consideration either, since the great contrasts in the movement, the definite types of the various characters, are to no small extent determined by the tempo. The tempo structure, especially if by tempo we mean the speed of the real rhythmic denominators of the thematic movement and not just the metronome numbers of the score, constitutes of two layers: there are two fast variations, numbers III and V (MM 113—112), flanked by slow variations (MM 30—38). Of course, these two variations are only formally identical in speed: in variation III it is only the solo that moves against a virtually standing chordal background, *poco rubato, ruvido;* variation V, on the other hand, is a real fast *Allegro scherzando.*

Ex. 28.

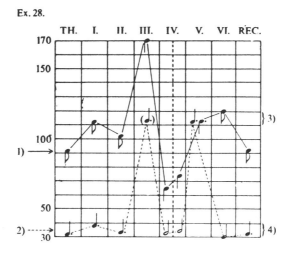

1) Metronome indications of the score.
2) Actual speed of the movement.
3) „Fast" variations around MM 113-112.
4) „Slow" variations around MM 30-38

Taking everything into account: this eight-section form shows no unambiguous inner articulation or structure, either according to the halving principle (8 = 4 + 4; 4 = 2 + 2 etc), or according to what is known as the golden section ratios (8 = 5 + 3 or 3 + 5) — because it is more complex. Its high-grade complexity can be seen by a bird's-eye view of the character and function of the individual sections, and their correlations perceptible even aurally (Ex. 29). This is reinforced by the tonal plan as well: the TH and I, as an introductory "*Air & Double*", as well as V and VI, as "*Scherzo & Double*", are really in pairs. There are three further important correspondences: variations I and III, as two sorts of *rubato solo* variations; II and (the first half of) IV, as two typical slow Bartók *nocturnos,* one rather a nature picture, the other of a Hungarian tone; as well as the (second half of) IV and VI, as emphytically *contrapuntal* sections, with two kinds of texture — each of these three pairs are "Theme and Double"-like. Actually, variation IV — by and large at the critical point, to the delight of those attesting major significance to the golden section — really has various meanings, and several functions, constituting really a section split into two halves. Bartók had every reason not to mark the score formally: variations I, II, etc., but to indicate the beginning of new sections only by one or two tempo instructions (and naturally by double bar lines and durata data marking the real limits).

Ex. 29

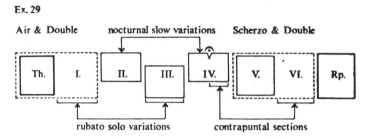

It is a beautiful and complex movement form; one might go on and on analyzing the characters it incorporates, and all the further formal correspondences. Nevertheless — and I hope the present analysis has borne this out — Bartók's great innovation did not lie in a *precompositional* invention of some new architecture, a block form other than, and contrary to the bridge symmetry and its subsequent arrangement. No; the pre-compositional idea was the creation of such a lengthy theme (and not a relatively simple motivic formation suitable for the inversion forms inherent in the bridge form!) which allowed for the development of a work in variation form, systematic and encyclopedic in its nature, though essentially differing from all the classical and contemporary models of "variation" known so far, — because of employing the specific Bartókian practices and consistency with regard to varying tonal and phrase structures. In the course of realizing this primary, precompositional plan, Bartók — perhaps as a secondary thought — also set into motion plans and methods (such as combinations of instrumental groups and tone colours, or the variation of registers and tonal densities), by which he foreshadowed some developments of the post-serial scenary long after World War II.

And the fact that all this lies concealed in this intimately lyrical, almost romantically soft movement does not alter these facts in the least — it may, at most, shed light on Bartók's innovations emerging at once in a classical-harmonic manner.

# 1/XII/99: Tonal Relations in Schoenberg's *Verklärte Nacht*

RICHARD SWIFT

December 1899, emotionally if not legally the end of the old century, was the month in which two compositions were completed that would point the direction for much of the dawning century's music: Claude Debussy's *Nocturnes*, almost ten years in the process of composition, and Arnold Schoenberg's *Verklärte Nacht*, composed during that autumn of 1899. Each of these compositions has been said to be indebted to Wagner, the headiest musical force of the nineteenth century: *Nocturnes* to *Parsifal*, *Verklärte Nacht* to *Tristan und Isolde*. Even as received opinions go, this falls far short of the mark; it serves here as a reminder of the muffled critical attitudes typically applied to much turn-of-the-century music. With its subtle, luminous and subversive evasions of conventional late nineteenth-century tonal and structural processes, *Nocturnes*—especially *Nuages* and *Sirènes*—would seem to be the more drastic of the two works. In *Verklärte Nacht*, however, nineteenth-century compositional practice is confronted, embraced, and resolved: transformed by its twenty-five-year-old autodidact composer with an astonishing power and virtuosity of compositional thinking. And yet, despite its popularity in the concert hall—a fact often regretted by Schoenberg—the compositional ordering of the internal relations of *Verklärte Nacht* has remained almost uncharted territory.[1] While clinging to the bounds and

---

[1]Exceptions include Andrew Porter's youthful essay with its comments on relations among motive contours, Arnold Whittall's discussion of relations among the early chamber music of Schoenberg, and Philip Friedheim's unpublished study of Schoenberg's early music which pioneered in acknowledging the sonata structure of *Verklärte Nacht*. Andrew Porter, "Modern German Chamber Music," in *Chamber Music*, ed. Alec Robertson (Harmondsworth, 1957); Arnold Whittall, *Schoenberg Chamber Music* (London, 1972); Philip Friedheim, *Tonality and Structure in the Early Works of Schoenberg* (Ph.D. dissertation, New York University, 1963).

expectations of triadic tonality and tonal structure, it suggests, through its paradoxical combination of rigor and ambiguity, the air of other planets that would await its composer, as well as the art and craft of music, in the awakening twentieth century.

Schoenberg's obeisance to the nineteenth century's treasured notion of "program music" in *Verklärte Nacht*, and later in *Pelleas und Melisande*, is far more subtle than that of most of his predecessors or contemporaries. The symphonic poems of Liszt and his epigones are often makeshift affairs, the texts an effort to plaster over the seams of the music with literary vinegar-and-brown-paper. Often texts purporting to have some connection with the music were added later. Naturally enough, composers of such program music offered other, rather nobler, reasons for their reliance upon texts or upon literary and historical references: the "new music" of the mid-century had believed such programs were enough to guarantee its novelty, its estrangement from the "classical" past, its adherence to imagined "precepts" of Berlioz, Schumann, and the Beethoven of the *Pastoral* Symphony. For many composers, though, programmatic texts remained an easy means of assembling otherwise unrelated musical materials. Tchaikovsky, at work on *Romeo and Juliet* in 1869, received this advice from Balakirev: "Determine your plan. Do not worry about the actual musical ideas."[2] Such a cold-blooded dismissal of the musical generation of a composition would have repelled Schoenberg; for his sextet, he chose a poem with internal structural relations that could be correlated with purely musical processes. The music is not a meandering fantasy or loose improvisation illustrating an anterior verbal plan, but a determined manifestation of the tonal principles of sonata structure. If the music does suggest the action of the poem and its psychological motion, it does so because the structural processes of both the poem and the music, considered abstractly, are similar. Egon Wellesz, in his

book on Schoenberg,[3] tried to make point-to-point identifications between the poem and the music in the approved nineteenth-century fashion, and Schoenberg himself, despite his fixed disavowal of such equivalences, wrote program notes as late as 1950 that attempt a similar set of connections.[4] Much earlier, in a 1912 essay in *Die Blaue Reiter*, he had stated unequivocally his opposition to program music of the common variety: "The assumption that a piece of music must summon up images of one sort or another . . . is as widespread as only the false and banal can be."[5]

As he transcended program music in *Verklärte Nacht*, so Schoenberg also transformed many compositional techniques of the immediate past. The music of the sextet does not slavishly imitate models, but it does owe much to the music of Brahms and Wagner, "to which a flavor of Liszt, Bruckner, and perhaps also Hugo Wolf was added."[6] Having confronted and having mastered those techniques—including modes of thematic construction and combination, of development and extension ("Brahms's technique of developing variation"[7])—the youthful composer achieved an intensely personal style. Gone were the times of blind partisanship for either Brahms or Wagner, for "what in 1883 seemed an impassable gulf was in 1897 no longer a problem."[8] The stylistic and technical accomplishments of those masters could now be blended without hesitation, for there was no longer any incongruity in their propinquity. Later, in "Brahms the Progressive," Schoenberg analyzed types of thematic construction to be found in Brahms's music. Many

[2]M. D. Calvacoressi and Gerald Abraham, *Masters of Russian Music* (New York, 1936).

[3]Egon Wellesz, *Arnold Schoenberg* (London, 1925).
[4]Arnold Schoenberg, notes for *Verklärte Nacht*, 26 August 1950, in the booklet for "The Music of Arnold Schoenberg," vol. 2, Columbia Records M2S 694. Schoenberg wrote that the music "does not illustrate any action or drama, but is restricted to portray nature and to express human feelings. It seems that, due to this attitude, my composition has gained qualities which can also satisfy if one does not know what it illustrates, or, in other words, it offers the possibility to be appreciated as 'pure' music."
[5]Arnold Schoenberg, *Style and Idea*, 2nd edn., ed. Leonard Stein (London, 1975), p. 141.
[6]Ibid., p. 80.    [7]Ibid.    [8]Ibid., p. 399.

334

4

of these—such as model and sequence, incomplete sequence, the extension and expansion of thematic contours by diminution or augmentation of temporal patterns—are similar to the essential thematic unfoldings, continuations and developments of *Verklärte Nacht*.

To cite a specific case, the melody in example 1 unfolds downward-leaping fourths that expand to fifths and sixths in a sequence (mm. 259–61) whose half measure is a diminution of m. 255. The climax of the melody (mm. 262–64) combines upward fourths and downward fifths in a rhythmic structure that includes both the previous eighth-note pattern and an irregular diminution of m. 256. The final descending scale in even eighths smooths out the linear and rhythmic angularities of the melody (ex. 1):

Example 1

Schoenberg was to dub *Grundgestalt*, or basic shape, that rationalization of the materials of music made to create relational connections at every level, to make richly congruent compositional contexts. Hierarchical reduction as a critical tool was deduced from this fundamental and universal aspect of compositional thinking; in the twentieth century, reduction becomes a primary mode of apprehending works of art (in music, from Schenker onward) and, in an extended interpretation, a mode of comprehending the relations of human nature in the world (from Husserl onward). When applied to the music of *Verklärte Nacht*, reduction reveals the inter-

relationships of one diatonic scale segment *(ut-re-mi-fa)* nested in the perfect fourth. The profound effects of this scale segment in shaping the musical structure and its textures can be traced both in relations among strands of primary and subsidiary motivic material and in large-scale tonal relations, while local tonal connections unfold a network of parallel intervallic relations.

To have begun by emphasizing the purely musical aspects of *Verklärte Nacht* is not to minimize the importance to Schoenberg of the poetry of Richard Dehmel. "At the end of the 19th century, the foremost representatives of the 'Zeitgeist' in poetry were Detlev von Liliencron, Hugo von Hofmannsthal, and Richard Dehmel."[9] Between 1897 and 1907, according to Jan Maegaard's brilliant reconstruction of the chronology of Schoenberg's music,[10] Schoenberg completed or sketched fourteen settings of Dehmel's poems, in addition to sketching two uncompleted orchestral works and composing the sextet. Three of these settings were completed shortly before or during the composition of *Verklärte Nacht: Warnung*, op. 3, no. 3; *Erwartung*, op. 2, no. 1; and *Erhebung*, op. 2, no. 3. In 1912, Schoenberg replied to a letter from Dehmel, who had expressed the pleasure given him by a recent performance of the sextet:

Your poems had a decisive influence on my development as a composer. They were what first made me try to find a new tone in the lyrical mood. Or rather, I found it even without looking, simply by reflecting in music what your poems stirred up in me. People who know my music can bear witness to the fact that my first attempts to compose settings for your poems contain more of what subsequently developed in my work than there is in many a much later composition.[11]

The estimate of the importance of Schoenberg's Dehmel settings in the development of his style

---

[9] Schoenberg, notes for *Verklärte Nacht*, Columbia Records, op. cit.
[10] Jan Maegaard, *Studien zur Entwicklung des dodekaphonen Satzes bei Arnold Schoenberg* (Copenhagen, 1972).
[11] Arnold Schoenberg, *Letters*, ed. Erwin Stein (London, 1964), p. 35.

contained in the last sentence quoted above has not been surpassed by later critics. Richly worked-out contrapuntal textures and a dense allusiveness of pitch and interval relations make the settings of the Dehmel poems in opera 2, 3 and 6 far superior to the settings of other texts in the same collections, admirable as these may be on their own terms.

Despite the present low ebb of his literary reputation, Dehmel's poems enjoyed considerable vogue in pre-World War I Germany and Austria. Their mildly erotic tone combined with striking post-Baudelairean and post-Nietzschean sensuousness of imagery and language to give an impression of sexual candor so typical of *Jugendstil*. The poem that serves as point of departure for Schoenberg's sextet was published with the title *Verklärte Nacht* in the first edition of Dehmel's collection *Weib und Welt* (1896), and later was incorporated into his verse novel *Zwei Menschen* (1903).[12] Although the novel postdates the composition of the sextet, it exhibits a pre-compositional planning that must have appealed to the composer. It consists of three parts, each containing thirty-six poems *(Vorgänge)* of thirty-six lines each. A twelve-line *Eingang* precedes each part; there is an eight-line *Leitlied* at the beginning, and a four-line *Ausgang* at the end of the novel. Allusions and resonances among words and themes abound among the poems in the three parts of the novel. For example, the first poem in each part has beginning and ending lines that echo back and forth, like a transformed refrain:

I.1 Zwei Menschen gehn durch kahlen, kalten Hain.
. . . . . . . . . .
Zwei Menschen gehn durch hohe, helle Nacht.

II.1 Zwei Menschen reiten durch maihellen Hain
. . . . . . . . . .
Zwei Menschen reiten in die Welt.

III.1 Zwei Menschen gehn durch nebelnassen Hain
. . . . . . . . . .
Zwei Menschen stehn, als sei ein Schwur gefallen.

Similar constructional ingenuities are shared by the other poems in the novel; they are typical of Dehmel's poetry.

The *Verklärte Nacht* poem, printed in the score of the string orchestra arrangement, has irregular line groupings—six lines for the opening description of the physical scene, twelve lines for the woman's confession, four more lines of description, eleven lines for the man's avowal, and a final three lines affirming their union—and a rhyme scheme which illuminates line structure with pairs of rhymes at the beginning of each division, intricately unfolding rhymes for the woman's speech, and tightly enfolding rhymes for the man's. The "double" exposition of the poem, with direct speech of the woman and the man, must have provided an impetus for Schoenberg's novel structure—a pair of sonatas with contrasting, although closely related, motivic materials and tonal relationships. It must also have suggested the combining and blending of motives from the first sonata with those in the second. The great, if simple, shift of mode from predominantly minor in the first sonata to predominantly major in the second serves to emphasize the relative rhythmic and melodic incompleteness of the first and the relative rhythmic and melodic completeness of the second. The development of these contrasts is resolved in the tonal serenity of the coda.

Although usually described as being in five sections, *Verklärte Nacht* consists of the two intimately related sonata movements, the first of which has a truncated—if not to say impacted—recapitulation of first group materials only. The two sonata structures are preceded by an Introduction, and they are linked by a Transition in which the materials of the Introduction return in a tonal area made important in the Introduction ($\flat$vi) and are provided with a new cadence. Sonata II has a normal recapitulation. (References are to the sextet; measure numbers are the same in the string orchestra arrangement.)

---

[12]*Verklärte Nacht* appeared on p. 61 of the 1896 edition of *Weib und Welt*; it was removed from later editions after *Zwei Menschen* was published serially in *Die Insel*, 1900–01 and in book form, 1903. I am indebted to Barbara and Roland Hoermann (who are not responsible for opinions expressed here) for discussions of Dehmel's poetry and the *fin de siècle* German literary world; also to Dorothy Swift for her usual invaluable help and advice.

| | | |
|---|---|---|
| Introduction (1–28) | i (D minor) | |
| | | |
| Sonata I | | |
| Exposition | | |
| First Group, Part I (29–49) | i | |
| Part II (50–62) | ♭vi | |
| Bridge (63–104) | | |
| Second Group (105–132) | II | |
| Development | | |
| Part I (132–168) | | |
| Part II (169–180) | | |
| "Recapitulation" (shortened) | | |
| First Group (181–187) | i | |
| | | |
| Transition (188–228) | ♭vi | |
| | | |
| Sonata II | | |
| Exposition | | |
| First Group (229–244) | I | |
| Bridge (244–48) | V of iii | |
| Second Group (249–277) | III | |
| Codetta (278–294) | III of V—♭III of V | |
| Development | | |
| Part I (294–319) | ♭III—V | |
| Part II (320–340) | III of V—V | |
| Recapitulation | | |
| First Group (341–363) | I | |
| Bridge (363–369) | | |
| Second Group (370–390) | I—(♭III–i–iv)—I | |
| Coda (391–end) | I | |

Reduction of Tonal Plan:
First Sonata    Second Sonata
i – II – (i–♭vi) – I – III – (iv) – I

"The very essence of romance is uncertainty," Algernon remarks in *The Importance of Being Earnest*—a principle those composers commonly called Romantic were quick to discover. Algernon would have been the first to recognize the pleasures of uncertainty in the tonal ambiguity of the first movement of Schumann's *Fantasy,* or in the tensions of the open structure of the first song of *Dichterliebe;* he might have been slower to perceive the clouded whole-step progression from the beginning to the end of *Tristan.* For Schoenberg in the sextet, the shaping of rhythms, motive contours, and local tonal relationships are contingent upon uncertainty and its capacity for ambiguity. In *Verklärte Nacht,* the first of his one-movement sonata compositions—*Pelleas und Melisande,* the First Quartet, and the First Chamber Symphony are prominent among its

successors—Schoenberg was to transcend by such means the tonal principles of sonata exemplified by the neo-classicism of Brahms, Bruckner, and Strauss.

In its simplest form, the global tonal scaffolding of *Verklärte Nacht* can be reduced to: i–II–(i)–III–iv–I, or *ut–re–mi–fa.* This scale segment permeates the fundamental linear and vertical progressions of the entire sextet. It is the primary element of the Introduction, whose falling scale motive ranges over the "tonic hexachord" (the sixth to first scale degrees), initiating a contour that is at once incomplete—its many repetitions arouse anticipation for completion of the scale pattern—and static. At m. 13, completion seems near, for the motive moves to the "dominant hexachord" (third downward to fifth scale degrees); but the shift involves a conflict over the raised and lowered forms of the sixth and seventh scale degrees, a conflict that serves to extend the sense of scalar, as well as motivic, incompleteness. Rhythmic fragmentation, arising from the amassing of one-measure units, creates a temporal breathlessness that will not be dispelled fully until the broader and rhythmically more stable expanses of Sonata II are reached.

While it is in the nature of introductions to expose weakly shaped contours and immediately unresolved harmonic contexts, the motives and progressions that occur in Sonata I itself are scarcely more complete, giving rise to the uncertainty that is so prominent a part of the character of this music. The first group sentence begins with a continuation of the one-measure unit inherited from the Introduction, and the sentence motive is repeated rather than transposed. The bass line is formed from an inversion of the chief Introduction motive; its ascending diatonic scale pattern in—at first—one-measure units serves to emphasize the ambiguous nature of the sentence itself. The cadence of the first group (end of m. 57–m. 62) presents the whole step in the melody with thirds in the opposing bass; the whole step is then used as the basis for the sequence of augmented chords and chromatic motives that concludes the exposition, a sequence proceeding by whole steps in each of the voices (mm. 128–31).

The most remote tonal relations, the most complicated chromatic inflections, the lengthiest of delays in resolving non-chord tones in the sextet are rooted firmly in the plainness of diatonic reduction. Certainly the passage that begins the development of Sonata I (mm. 135–52) is the furthest removed from an encompassing triadic tonal area of any in *Verklärte Nacht*. In "How One Becomes Lonely," Schoenberg compared this passage with a similar passage in the Fourth Quartet as an instance of "more violent expression."[13] In the sextet, its expressive role is clear because its structural function as the commencement of the development—the area of a sonata in which wide-ranging tonal movement is expected—is clear. The section consists of a complex segment of music that is repeated a whole step higher. Each of the elements of the segment functions within the framework of a diatonic scale segment. First, there occurs a linear contour that creates the effect of appoggiatura-resolution by half step—a Neapolitan-derived scale-degree relation—to the members of the C♯-minor triad. When the last member (E in this spelling) is reached, the other voices have changed so that the meaning of the final resolution (mm. 135–36) becomes ambiguous. This process is followed immediately by a descending contour incorporating an augmented triad within its pattern and harmonized by minor and diminished triads. The second element consists of an expanded version of the motive of the second part of the first group, here heard in conjunction with an expanded version of the appoggiatura-resolution pattern (mm. 137–40). The final element consists of a shortened version of the motive from the beginning of the first group with a chromatic scale anticipation, its model and sequence moving by whole step in all voices (mm. 141–43). The normalizing characteristics of the diatonic scale segments, voice-leading expectations, whole-step relations, and patterns of motive expansion and reduction contrive to nest this section into the music that precedes and follows. Tonally re-

mote as this section must have seemed at its first performance, it fits smoothly into the compositional processes of the music; the dissonance treatment employed is far more rigorously and exactly controlled than in many another less tonally vagrant section of the music.

At the center of *Verklärte Nacht* (m. 188ff), there occurs the section—the Transition—that rounds off Sonata I and at the same time links the two sonatas together. Again, the whole step and diatonic scale segment provide the essential tonal scheme. The music returns to the downward scale motive from the Introduction, a return prepared for by a long, almost unaccompanied, passage. This thirteen-measure passage (mm. 188–200) conveys *in petto* the subtlety, strength, and originality of Schoenberg's manner of evolving melodic contours and contrapuntal voices, demonstrating anew the essentially diatonic nature of the musical elements, however transmuted by chromatic inflection (ex. 2):

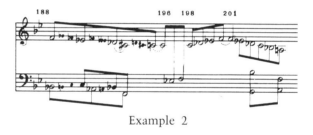

Example 2

The downward motion of the recitative-like melodic line and its bass contains the *ur*-motive of a diatonic scale segment forming a perfect fourth (two whole steps and a half step). The passage may be considered a paradigm of those fundamental elements, a compositional reduction that reveals a capacious potential for transformation and connection. The upper and lower neighbor tones and passing tones that are introduced into the downward melodic motion focus upon its diatonic basis. The bass, too, projects the same image as it moves by whole step and by leap through the fourth. As the whole motive emerges in its usual contour (m. 201ff), it

---

[13]*Style and Idea*, pp. 30–33.

338

8

shocks by commencing its descent on the "wrong" scale degree: not on the sixth, as in the Introduction, but on the fourth scale degree, descending to the seventh. This is as disruptive of the sense of tonal location as are the chromatic chords within which the melody is placed, a diminished chord moving to an augmented triad. This shuddering and constantly iterated music is eventually heard in a sequence that finally reaches the tranquillity of the subdominant of ♭vi. That pitch, E♭, reaches back to the beginning of the motive in m. 201, rounding off the passage with a return to that contextually important fourth scale degree.

The whole step continues to play a major role in Sonata II, combining with the fourth and the thirds implicit in both foreground and background of the thematic material to produce the consoling—because intervallically explicit —climactic melody that concludes the development section, a melody that will be heard briefly at the onset of the coda (ex. 3):

Example 3

As the outline of major tonal areas of *Verklärte Nacht* (page 7) demonstrates, there is an astonishing absence of emphasis upon the dominant as a large-scale tonal area. This evasion of the dominant is reflected in local harmonic progressions as well, especially in Sonata I, although there are many dominant-substitute progressions, both in tonic and other chord areas, whose function is to modify their respective tonal areas indirectly, deceptively and ambiguously. Even when a dominant function is implied by a pedal—as in mm. 100–04, where the dominant of II is in the bass—the harmonic meaning of the pedal is blurred by nondominant pitches. In this instance, the domi-

nant of the dominant appears over the dominant pedal; the pitches of that chord establish a connection with the second group material by becoming the main pitches of its first melodic contour, this time over a tonic pedal (mm. 105–07). The tension produced by these large-scale suspensions, for so they are treated contextually, is tightened by irregular temporal resolutions; often, when a resolution takes place, the note of resolution has become part of a new and uncertain harmonic context, to assume a meaning different from the one anticipated. It is through such means that restless motion and melodic incompleteness are achieved in Sonata I.

In structural positions where powerful dominant areas might be expected—such as the end of an exposition, the beginning or end of a development section—Sonata I again evades the issue. The sequence of augmented triads that ends the exposition has nothing directly to do with the dominant, although the need for resolution may suggest a typical function of the dominant. It leads to a cadence on a chord which serves as a substitute for the dominant of ♭III, and the lowest note (E) of that dominant-substitute chord becomes the initiator of the development section. This unsupported, ferociously sustained pitch refers in several directions: back to the II area of the second group, to the dominant, and to the extremely ambiguous ♭III that follows. The preparation for the recapitulation of Sonata I takes place on the dominant-substitute of the dominant. While this is scarcely an unusual procedure in itself, its significance here lies in its oblique evasion of the dominant.

In Sonata II, relations among large-scale progressions, melodic contours, local harmony, and rhythmic movement are manifestly more complete and more strongly shaped than in Sonata I, a set of circumstances that is confirmed by the more normative use of dominant area relations. The broad, succinctly presented first-group sentence, with its cloud of motives from Sonata I, cadences on iii. In the bridge, the dominant of iii is prolonged and, with a shift to the major mode, the second group begins its long, firmly structured melody. The codetta, on the dominant of III (written enharmonically as D♭), presents a new melodic contour that moves downward over the triad and whose second phrase begins with a form of the downward scale motive in diminution. Although the codetta concludes with a tonicization of ♭III—through the dominant of the dominant—the development section pivots about two powerful dominant statements. The first part of the development section cadences emphatically on the dominant (mm. 316–19), with a deceptive movement from that cadence into a new tonal area (V of III). At the end of the second part of the development (mm. 332–40), the harmony is violently wrenched from the dominant of the III area to the dominant itself in order to prepare for the recapitulation in a normal tonal manner.

The dominant, then, plays a secondary part in the unfolding of major tonal areas of the sextet. There are several other tonal areas whose importance is greater in shaping the large-scale tonal functions. The Introduction first hints at and later emphasizes strongly two chords destined to assume crucial roles in subsequent and subsidiary events in the two sonatas: ♭vi/♭VI and ♭III. The latter sometimes appears in its function as the dominant of the former; it sometimes exists as a tonal area by itself. The progression that links the two parts of the first group (mm. 41–49) moves through the dominant of ♭III, which quickly turns toward the dominant of ♭vi in mm. 46–49. Schoenberg was

inordinantly proud of this progression, referring to the passage several times in his writings, notably in *Harmonielehre* where he was intent upon explaining the theoretical status of the famous ninth chord with the ninth (marked "X") in the bass (ex. 4):

Example 4

In "Criteria for the Evaluation of Music," he explained that because of this "*one* single uncatalogued dissonance," *Verklärte Nacht* was rejected for performance by a Viennese concert group.[14] But this progression has a grander function in the sextet than as a source for a particular chord-construction and usage, or even as a local linking passage, for it returns at two crucial structural points. First, it is the harmonic scaffolding for the recapitulation of the first group sentence (mm. 181–87), and is in part responsible for the ambiguity and uncertainty of that return (ex. 5):

Example 5

_____
[14]Ibid., pp. 131–32.

Second, this "uncatalogued dissonance" returns in the first part of the coda as part of a succession of important motives from the composition, this time beginning on the raised third scale degree to reflect the modal shift of Sonata II (ex. 6):

Example 6

The ♭vi chord, touched upon in the Introduction, emerges as the tonal area of the second part of the first group of Sonata I; it is prepared for linearly by the F♯ (=G♭) of mm. 46–49, a lowered sixth scale degree in ♭vi, which functions here as the Neapolitan of the dominant of ♭vi, a common Brucknerian relationship. The other extensive ♭vi area of Sonata I occurs in the Transition, discussed above. Its role in Sonata II is limited to minor appearances.

These third relations among tonal areas, such as i–♭vi or i–♭III or I–III, are extended to other compositional levels, particularly as intervals of transposition for sequence segments. In Sonata I, the minor third is often the basis for sequences—for example, the large-scale repetition of mm. 75–82 rising a minor third higher in mm. 83–90, or the series of sequences in the development section from m. 153 with each segment rising a minor third. The ambiguity of tonal direction that results from the linear diminished triads is especially potent in its intensification of the weak and uncertain motivic contours and harmonic progressions in Sonata I. The major third appears somewhat less prominently in such circumstances; but when it occurs, the resulting linearly and vertically stated augmented triads have a powerful effect on harmonic and melodic stability. A compelling summary of linear and vertical third relations occurs at the conclusion of the development section, Sonata I, m. 169ff, where augmented, major, minor and diminished triads are systematically exhibited both as melodic contours and as chords in the preparation for the dominant of the dominant.

In Sonata II, ♭III continues in its strong modifying support of the primary tonal areas. The development section begins (mm. 294ff) in the area of ♭III. In its function of the dominant of ♭vi, it is the point of arrival of the sequence arising from the end of the melody of example 3 at the beginning of m. 322, as well as the moment in which the first of the tonal abruptions occurs as the development is pulled toward the dominant. It functions in the second group of the recapitulation as part of a larger progression toward the minor subdominant (mm. 376–78), where it is heard for a final time in the sextet as a member of the global scale degree motion D–E–F–G.

The half-step relationship that has the most far-reaching consequences in *Verklärte Nacht* is that of the Neapolitan. It is encountered frequently as a modification of local linear and vertical contexts, as in the linkage between two tonal areas in mm. 46–49. In this passage, discussed above, the F♯(=G♭) assumes the function of the Neapolitan of V of ♭vi; and it later takes on the function of ♭vi of ♭vi. This resultant complex of meanings is an essential characteristic of the oblique and ambiguous tonal movement of Sonata I, encouraged by linear and vertical Neapolitan relations. By analogy, the chromatic inflection of linear elements reflects and prolongs the action of the Neapolitan relation. The Neapolitan serves as an intensification of the ii–V–iv progression in m. 34ff. Yet another instance of Neapolitan linkage, whose dramatic intensity is in part owed to those previously encountered Neapolitan relations, occurs between the Transition and Sonata II. The

Transition cadences upon the minor subdominant of ♭vi with only the B♭ remaining from the subdominant triad. The B♭, in a manner analogous to that of mm. 46–49, leads to the major tonic as the Neapolitan of the fifth scale degree, as ♭vi of I, and as a foreshadowing of the A♯ of the III region, the tonal area of the second group.

The Neapolitan also has a major function in the tonal wrenching toward the dominant that takes place near the end of the development section of Sonata II (mm. 332–36). The sequences of the preceding section halt abruptly, leaving the melody and its subsidiary contrapuntal lines stuck for some time in the same place, ♭ii, before they plunge with equal abruptness to the dominant in preparation for the recapitulation.

II has functioned, more or less conventionally, as a substitute for IV in earlier phases of the music, but from the beginning of this recapitulation, it comes to the fore as an independent entity to isolate the subdominant area in preparation for the iv–♭II–I cadence which concludes the sextet. The brief detail of the major-minor subdominant triads in the first group exposition (ex. 7):

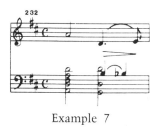

Example 7

is expanded in the recapitulation both through repetition (mm. 342, 349, 351, and 355) and through the cadence on the subdominant (mm. 358–61) that is an element in a large-scale progression: I–ii–V–IV–V (mm. 353–63). This expanded statement of subdominant function continues with equal force in the return of the second group, where, as the minor subdominant, it becomes an element in that progression toward ♭III discussed above, as well as the immediate goal of the progression of which ♭III is itself an element (mm. 375–80). The articulation of the subdominant area at this, the penultimate stage of the composition, is an affirmation of those stable and stabilizing properties of diatonic tonality. It is generally in such a position, near the end of a tonal composition, that the subdominant (or its substitute, II) is given strong functional emphasis; Schenker's analytical reduction of tonal function on the model of a complete cadence pattern—I–IV– (or II–) V–I—is rooted in the observation of this phenomenon in tonal music. Schoenberg was not blindly obeying some unwritten canon, for in *Verklärte Nacht* the structural emphasis upon the subdominant links back to the II area of Sonata I, and forward, in combination with ♭II, to the coda's concluding cadence, incorporating in its references those Neapolitan relations that function so compellingly throughout the sextet. The sustained emphasis upon the tonic from the beginning of the recapitulation of Sonata II to the end at once rights the intensely dramatic tonic imbalance of much of the preceding music, and at the same time provides a stable context in which the combined subdominant-Neapolitan cadence may make its full effect.

In this discussion of tonal functions in *Verklärte Nacht*, much has been said about the correlation between motive generation and the explicit global tonal relations of the music, particularly as an aspect of the unfolding of the diatonic intervals from the perfect fourth. The ingenuity and fluency with which linear contours represent compositional prolongations of those intervals is nowhere more clearly discernible than at the beginning of the coda (m. 391ff), where the succession of motives from earlier stages of the sextet succinctly displays that framework for motive and tonal generation (ex. 8):

Example 8

Schoenberg was justly proud of the speed and facility with which he composed the sextet, even permitting his memory to compress the actual composition time to a dramatic three weeks.[15] The sense of compression and rigor of composition conveyed by Schoenberg's exaggerated statement is matched in its intensity by the music, with its controlled contrapuntal density of motive combinations flourishing as prolongations of the basic tonal materials. Schoenberg, in the same essay, cites the passage that occurs at the beginning of the development of Sonata I (mm. 161–68), where a motive is presented in its original and inverted forms both in succession and, finally, in combination, as an instance of contrapuntal ingenuity that cost him some effort to accomplish.[16] It is precisely such a passage—and there are many others that are comparable, including the recapitulation, Sonata I (ex. 5), and the return of the second group, Sonata II—where textures display functional connections in layer upon layer of voices, that further confirms the sense of compression in the sextet. Similarly, compression is conveyed by the spatial placement of melodic lines conceived as a mingling of several voices in several registers. One such melodic contour, existing within a network of timbres and registers, occurs at the beginning of the second part of the first group, Sonata I (ex. 9):

343

Example 9

The upper voice, presented in octaves, is both a counterpoint to and an answering variation and amplification of the cello line. Such modes of extending and proliferating melodic contours from a single line into wider zones of instrumental space mark off other structural areas of the music—as in the second group of Sonata II—and share in non-imitative contrapuntal textures—as in the bridge of Sonata I, m. 69ff. Through such melodic configurations, Schoenberg was able to widen the forms motives may take and to deepen the connections among them with their engendering elements.

In Schoenberg's later version for string orchestra (1917, revised 1943), there are no substantive changes from the music of the original sextet. This version, with its bold and luxurious sonorities, is more familiar to the concert-goer than is the leaner, more intimate sextet version, for concerts by string sextets are rarities. There are many added or expanded indications of nuances, clarifications of tempo markings (all instructions are given in Italian instead of the German of the original), metronome markings (absent from the sextet), and occasional revisions of notation. Among the latter, there is a written-out late instance of the triplet interpretation of duple notation that occurs in the sextet (ex. 10):

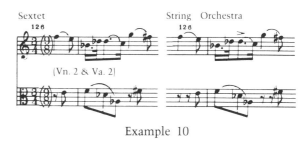

Example 10

[15]"Heart and Brain in Music," ibid., pp. 55–56. See Maegaard, op. cit., for details of the chronology of *Verklärte Nacht*.

[16]*Style and Idea*, pp. 55–56. The example given by Schoenberg is incorrect, presenting only those measures in which the two motive forms appear in succession (mm. 161–62), not in combination—an error future editors may wish to correct.

Among the many subtle shifts of string sonorities and masses with which Schoenberg contrived to articulate the musical structure in this new medium, the passage from m. 161—with the motive in both its original and inverted forms—is notable for its clarity and delicacy, made possible by the use of eleven solo strings and divided second violins to articulate primary and secondary contrapuntal voices. The textural clarity is aided by octave doubling and by the contrasts in sonority provided by muted solo instruments while the second violins remain unmuted.

Schoenberg often heard the plaintive remark about *Verklärte Nacht,* "If only he had continued to compose in this style," to which he replied: "I have not discontinued composing in the same style and in the same way as at the very beginning. The difference is only that I do it better now than before; it is more concentrated, more mature."[17] That vocation for composition, to which the sextet is a burning witness, radically transformed musical thinking in the new century by creating a music whose every layer and corner is permeated by concentrated relations and connections—enmeshing all, as Henry James wrote, in "the wonder of the consciousness of everything."

344

---

[17]Ibid., p. 30ff.